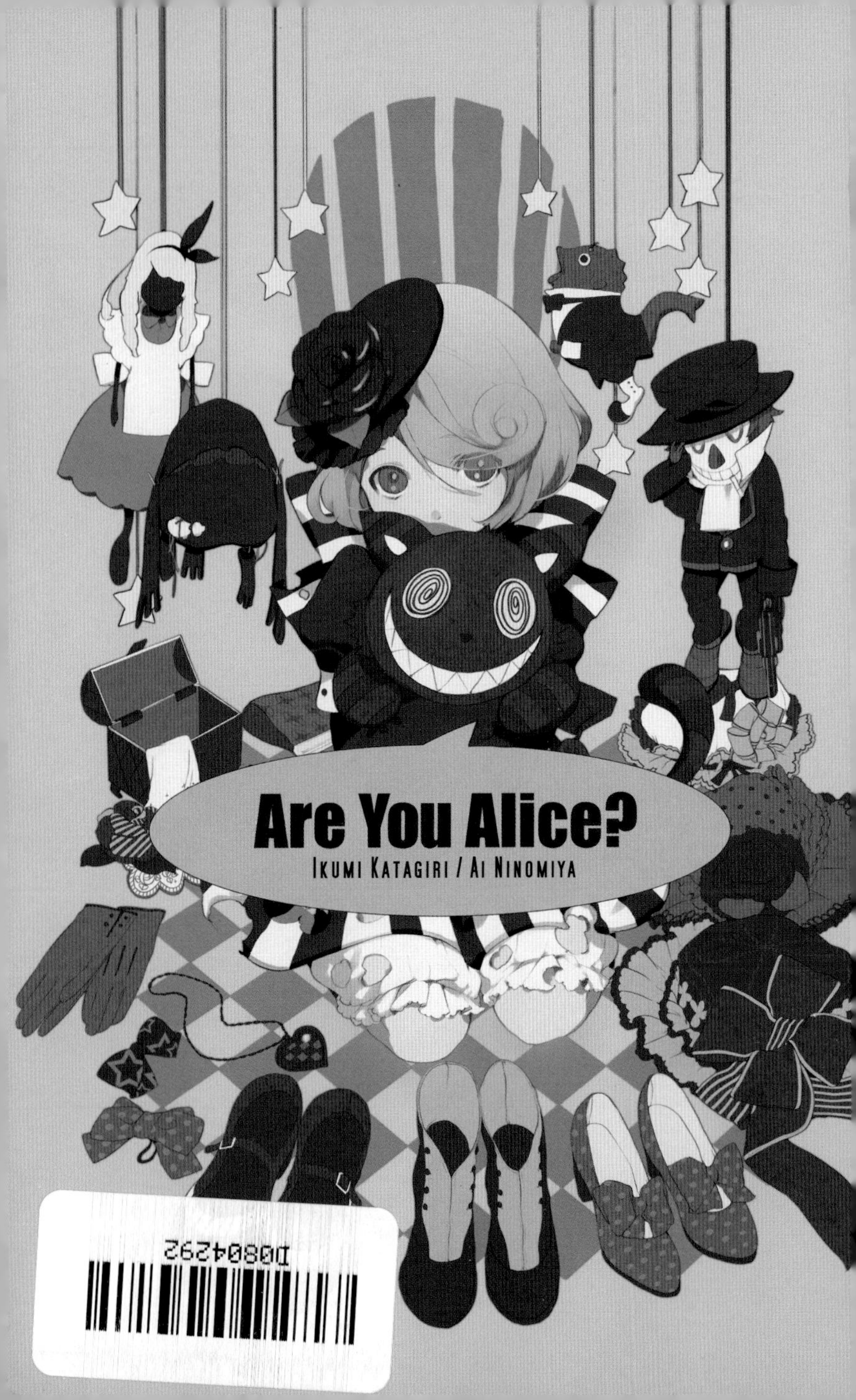
Are You Alice?
Ikumi Katagiri / Ai Ninomiya

DRINK ME

Are You Alice?
2
CONTENTS!

Chapter : 6
Scrape Bottom, 3

Chapter : 7
Advice from a Caterpillar, 47

Chapter : 8
BAD END, 77

Chapter : 9
Bubblegum Music, 109

Chapter : 10
Let's Cut the Crap, 137

Chapter : 11
BlackLady, 163

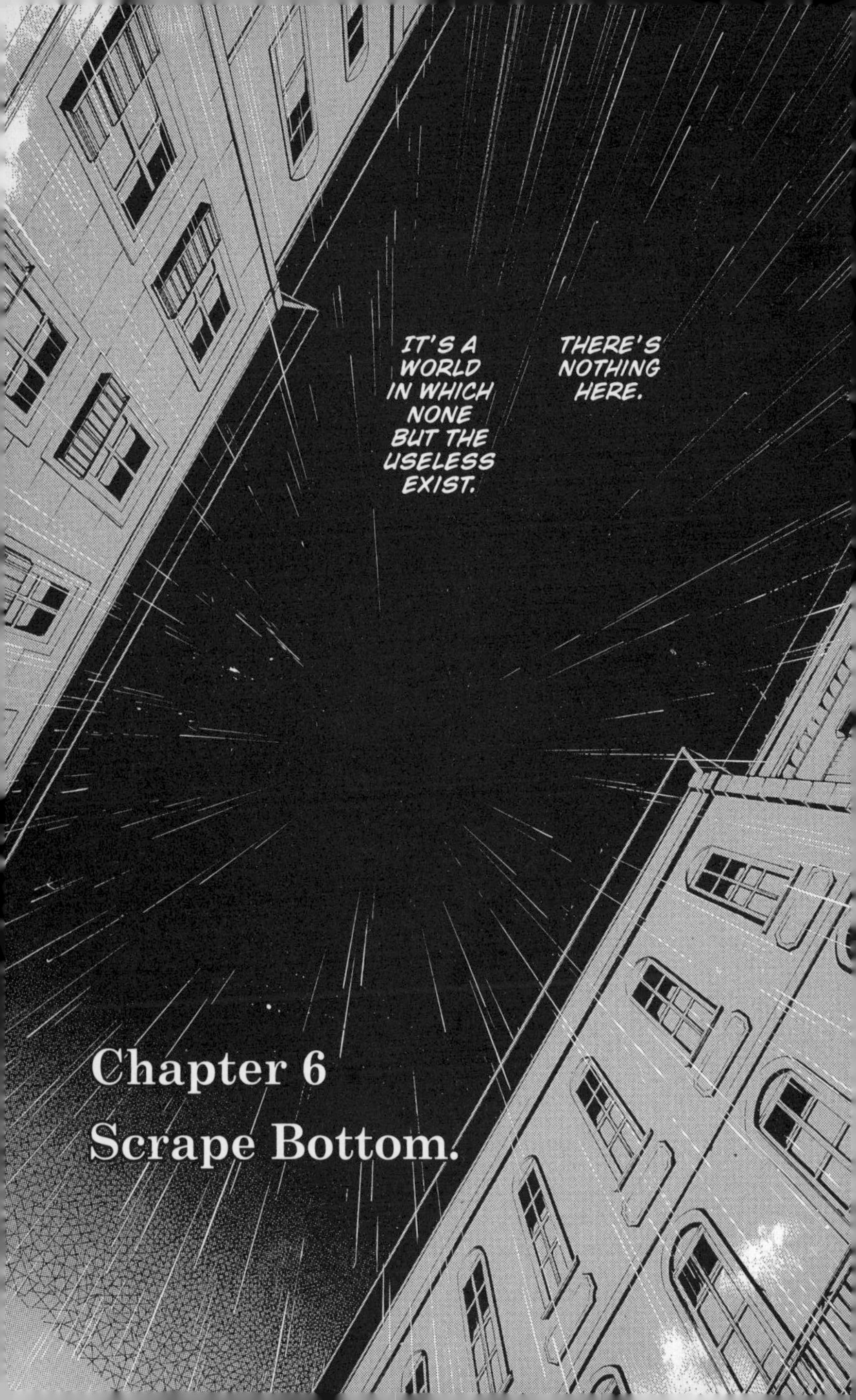
THERE'S NOTHING HERE.
IT'S A WORLD IN WHICH NONE BUT THE USELESS EXIST.
Chapter 6
Scrape Bottom.

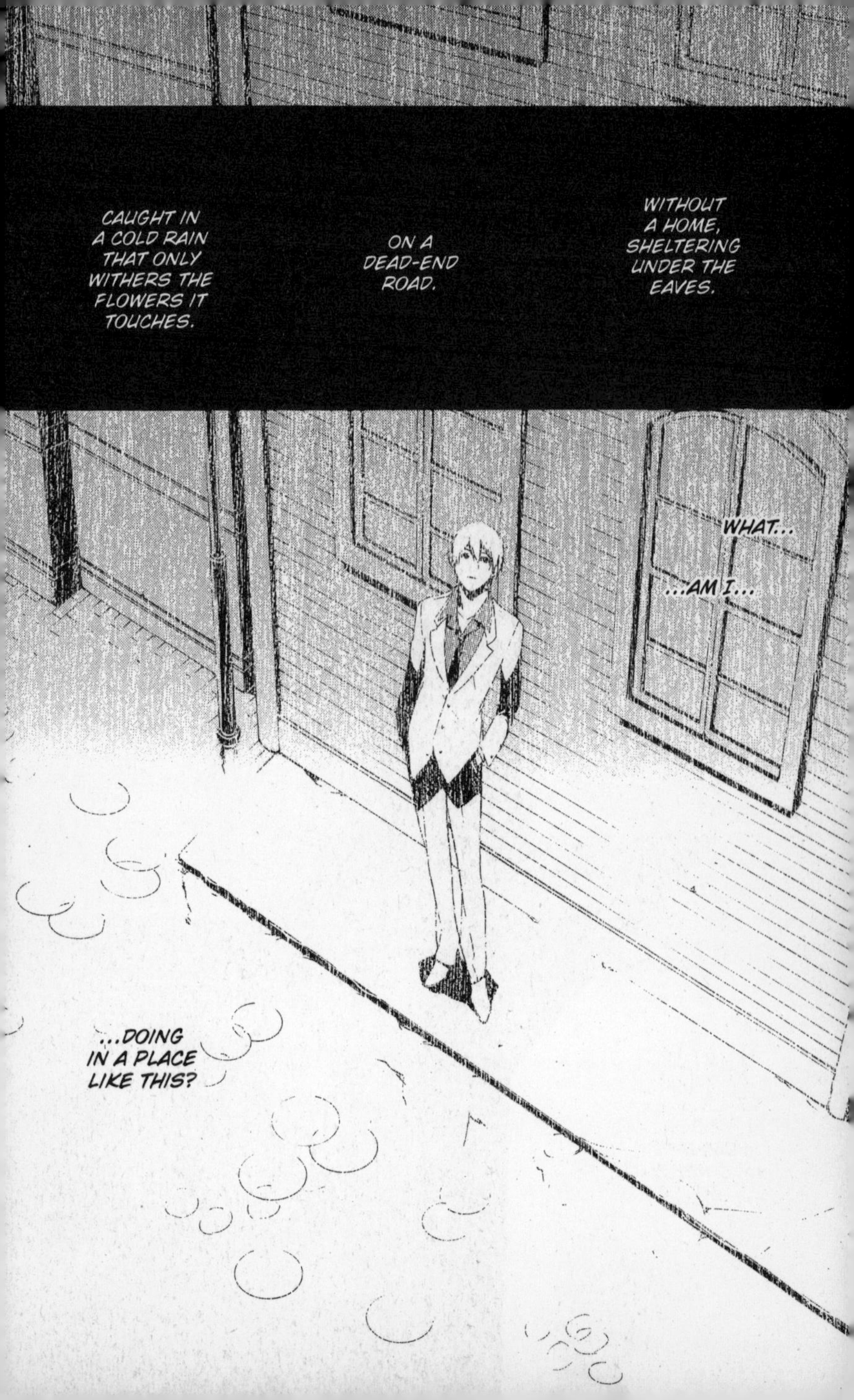
WITHOUT A HOME, SHELTERING UNDER THE EAVES.
ON A DEAD-END ROAD.
CAUGHT IN A COLD RAIN THAT ONLY WITHERS THE FLOWERS IT TOUCHES.
WHAT...
...AM I...
...DOING IN A PLACE LIKE THIS?

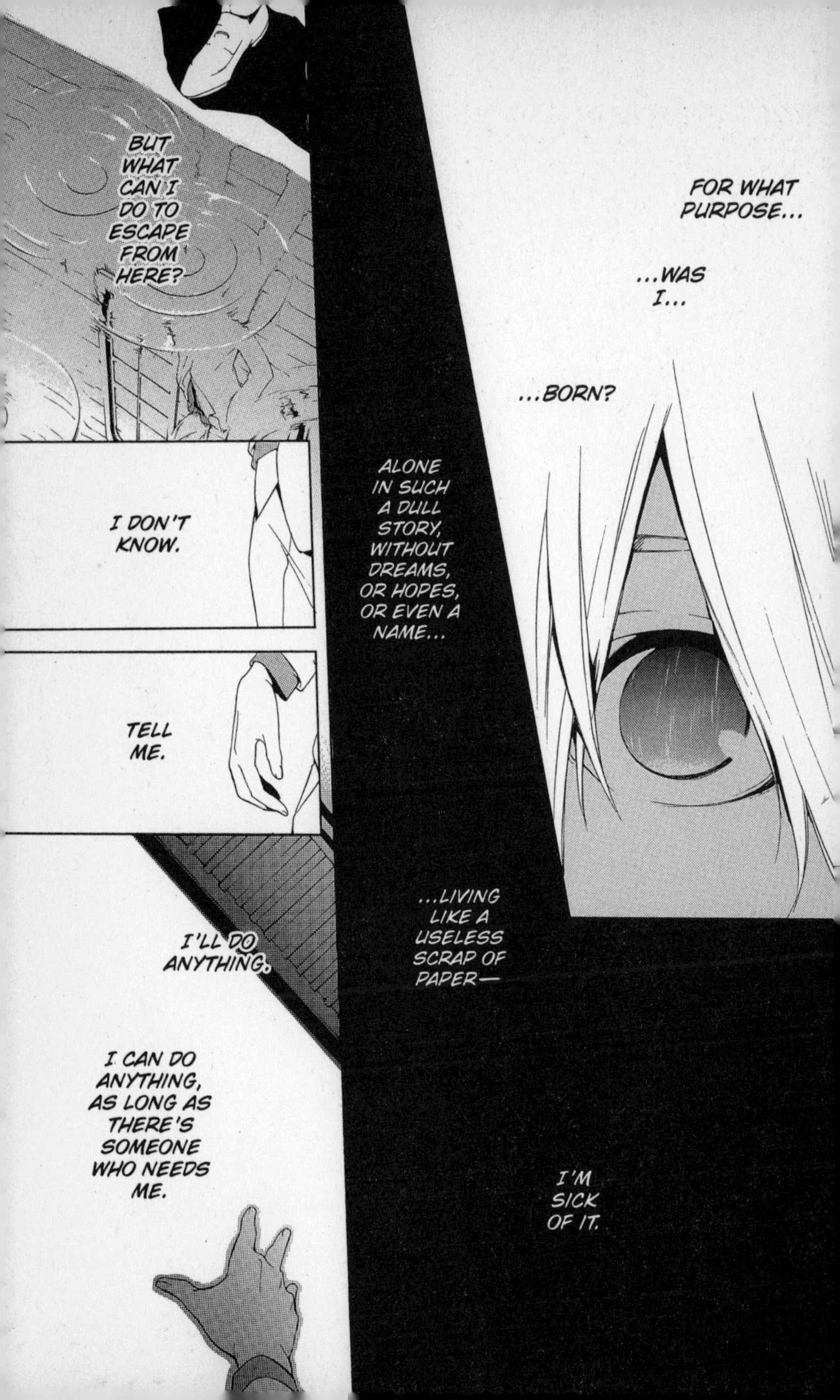

FOR WHAT PURPOSE...
...WAS I...
...BORN?
ALONE IN SUCH A DULL STORY, WITHOUT DREAMS, OR HOPES, OR EVEN A NAME...
...LIVING LIKE A USELESS SCRAP OF PAPER—
I'M SICK OF IT.
BUT WHAT CAN I DO TO ESCAPE FROM HERE?
I DON'T KNOW.
TELL ME.
I'LL DO ANYTHING.
I CAN DO ANYTHING, AS LONG AS THERE'S SOMEONE WHO NEEDS ME.

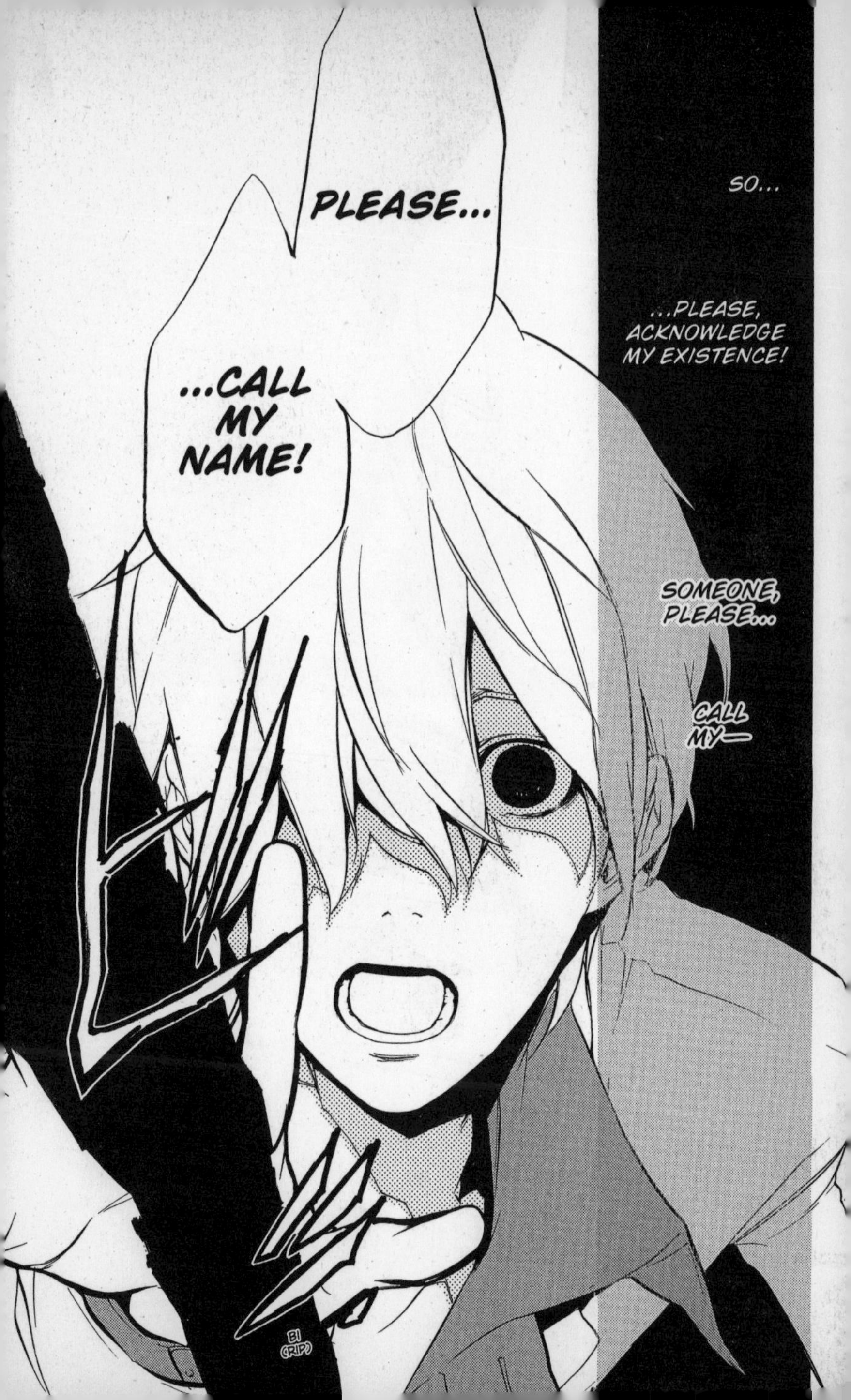
SO...
...PLEASE, ACKNOWLEDGE MY EXISTENCE!
SOMEONE, PLEASE...
CALL MY—
PLEASE...
...CALL MY NAME!
BI (RIP)

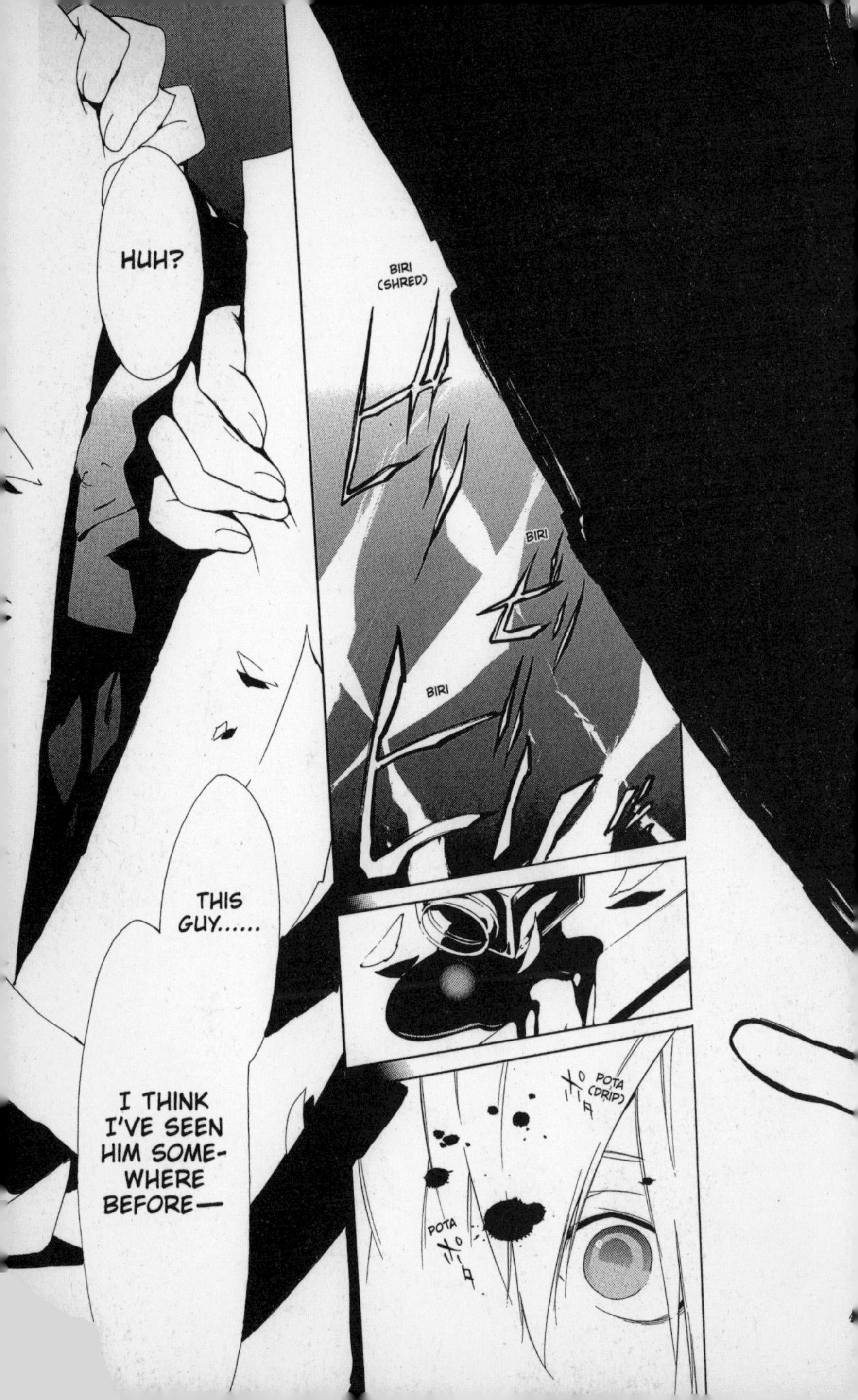
BIRI (SHRED)
BIRI
BIRI
POTA (DRIP)
POTA
HUH?
THIS GUY......
I THINK I'VE SEEN HIM SOME-WHERE BEFORE—

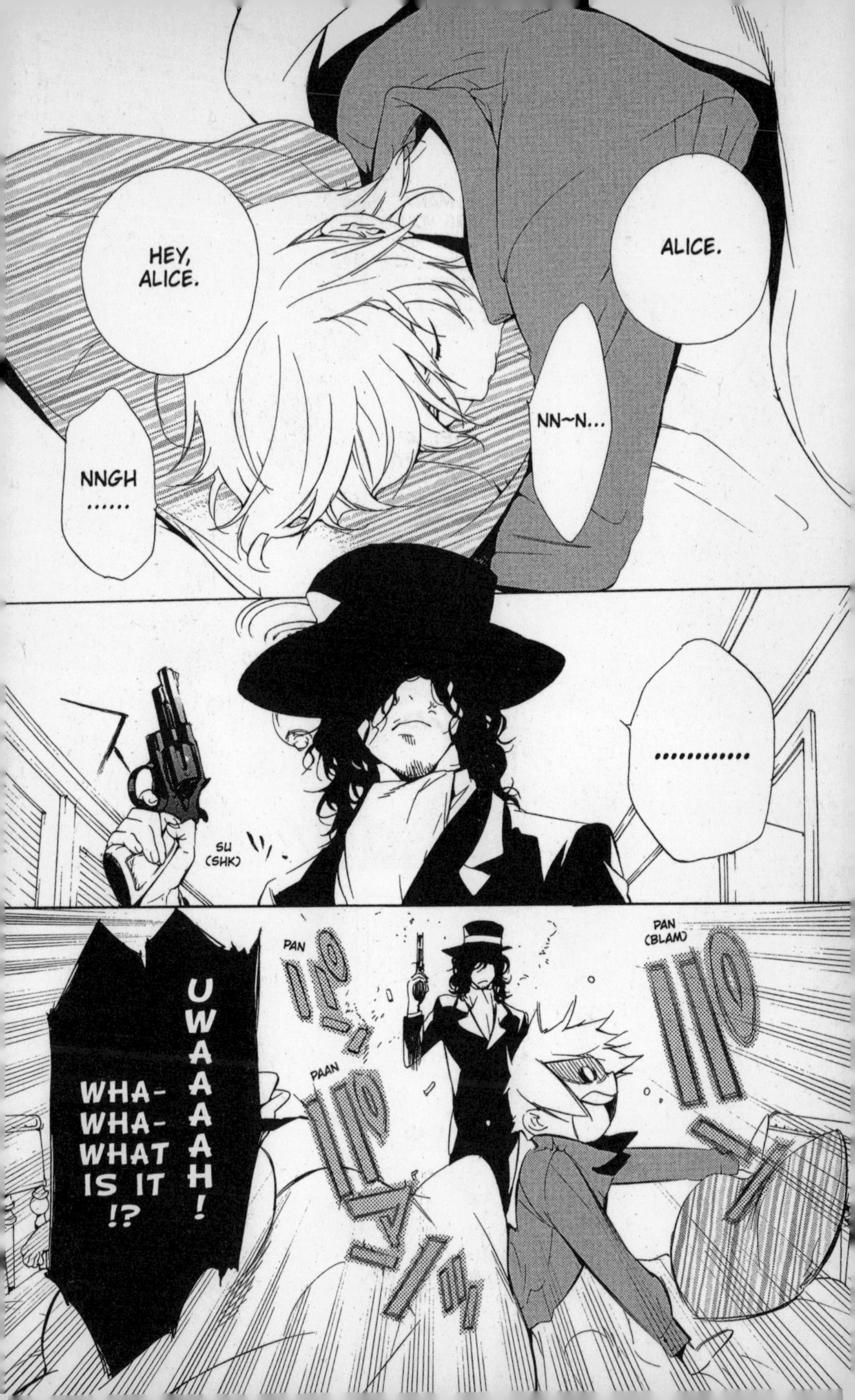
ALICE.
NN~N...
HEY, ALICE.
NNGH ......
....
SU (SHK)
PAN (BLAM)
PAN
PAAN
UWAAAAAAH!
WHA-WHA-WHAT IS IT !?

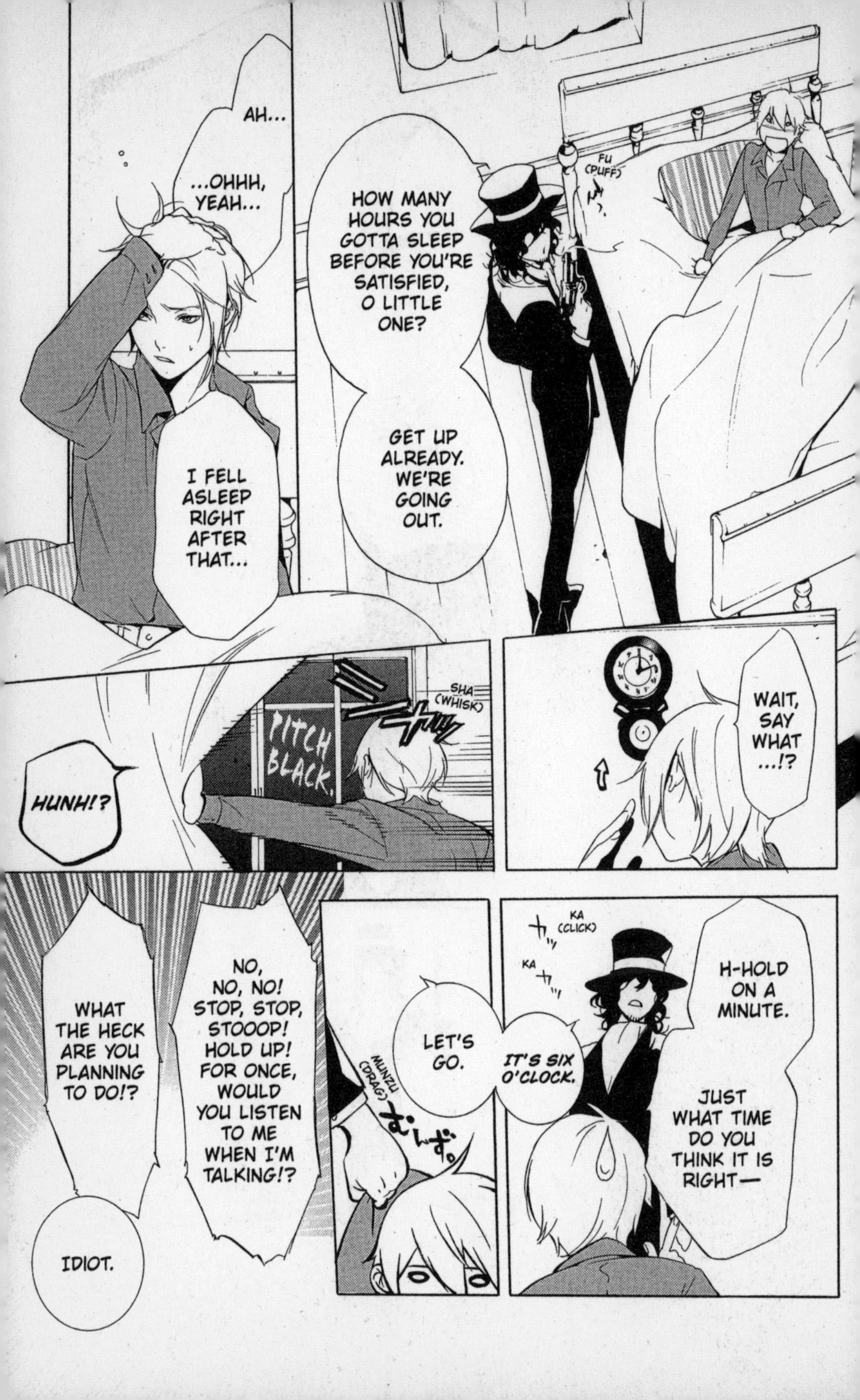
FU (PUFF)
HOW MANY HOURS YOU GOTTA SLEEP BEFORE YOU'RE SATISFIED, O LITTLE ONE?
GET UP ALREADY. WE'RE GOING OUT.
AH...
...OHHH, YEAH...
I FELL ASLEEP RIGHT AFTER THAT...
WAIT, SAY WHAT ...!?
SHA (WHISK)
PITCH BLACK.
HUNH!?
KA (CLICK)
KA
H-HOLD ON A MINUTE.
JUST WHAT TIME DO YOU THINK IT IS RIGHT—
IT'S SIX O'CLOCK.
LET'S GO.
MUNZU (DRAG)
NO, NO, NO! STOP, STOP, STOOOP! HOLD UP! FOR ONCE, WOULD YOU LISTEN TO ME WHEN I'M TALKING!?
WHAT THE HECK ARE YOU PLANNING TO DO!?
IDIOT.

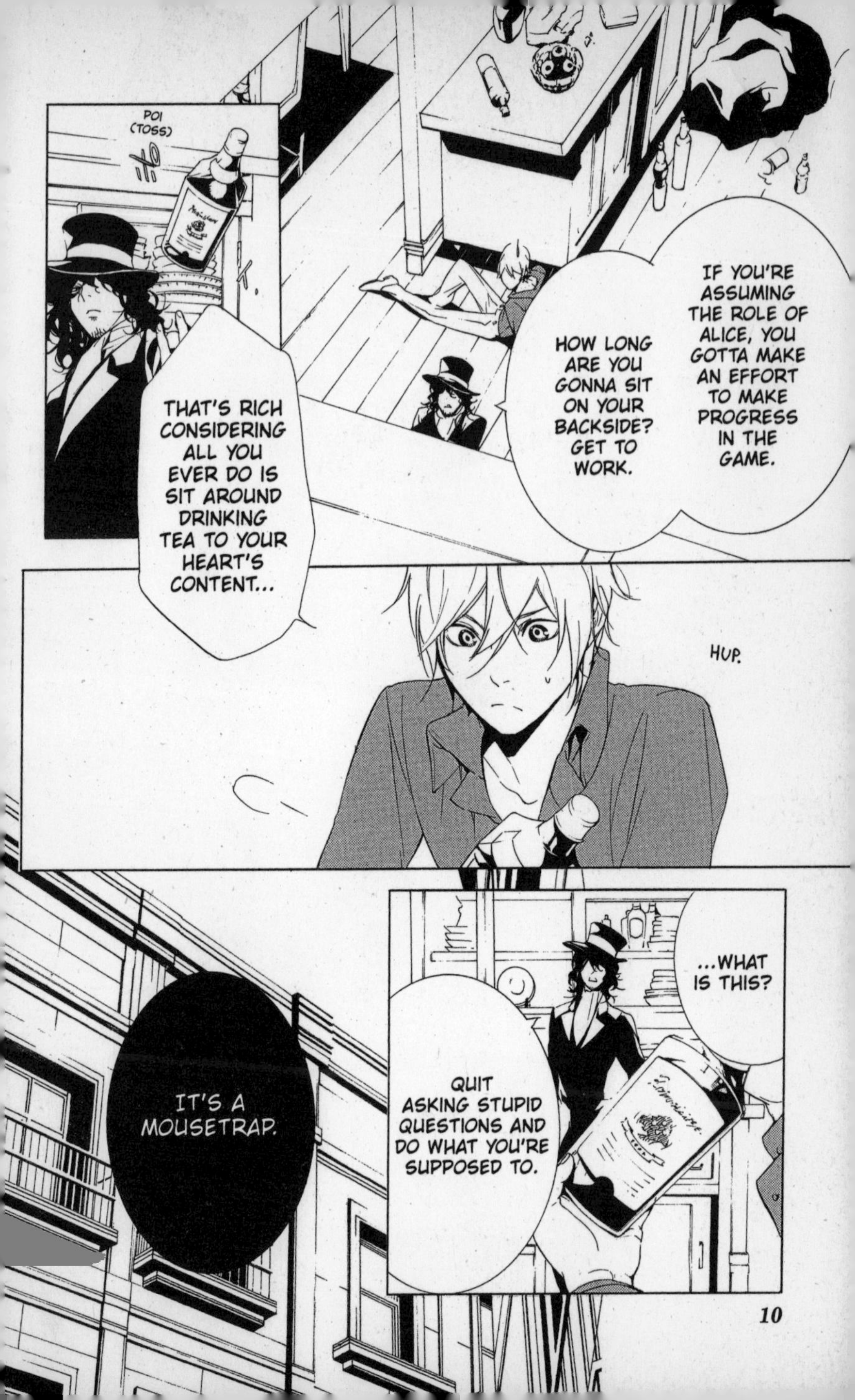
IF YOU'RE ASSUMING THE ROLE OF ALICE, YOU GOTTA MAKE AN EFFORT TO MAKE PROGRESS IN THE GAME.
HOW LONG ARE YOU GONNA SIT ON YOUR BACKSIDE? GET TO WORK.
POI (TOSS)
THAT'S RICH CONSIDERING ALL YOU EVER DO IS SIT AROUND DRINKING TEA TO YOUR HEART'S CONTENT...
HUP.
...WHAT IS THIS?
QUIT ASKING STUPID QUESTIONS AND DO WHAT YOU'RE SUPPOSED TO.
IT'S A MOUSETRAP.

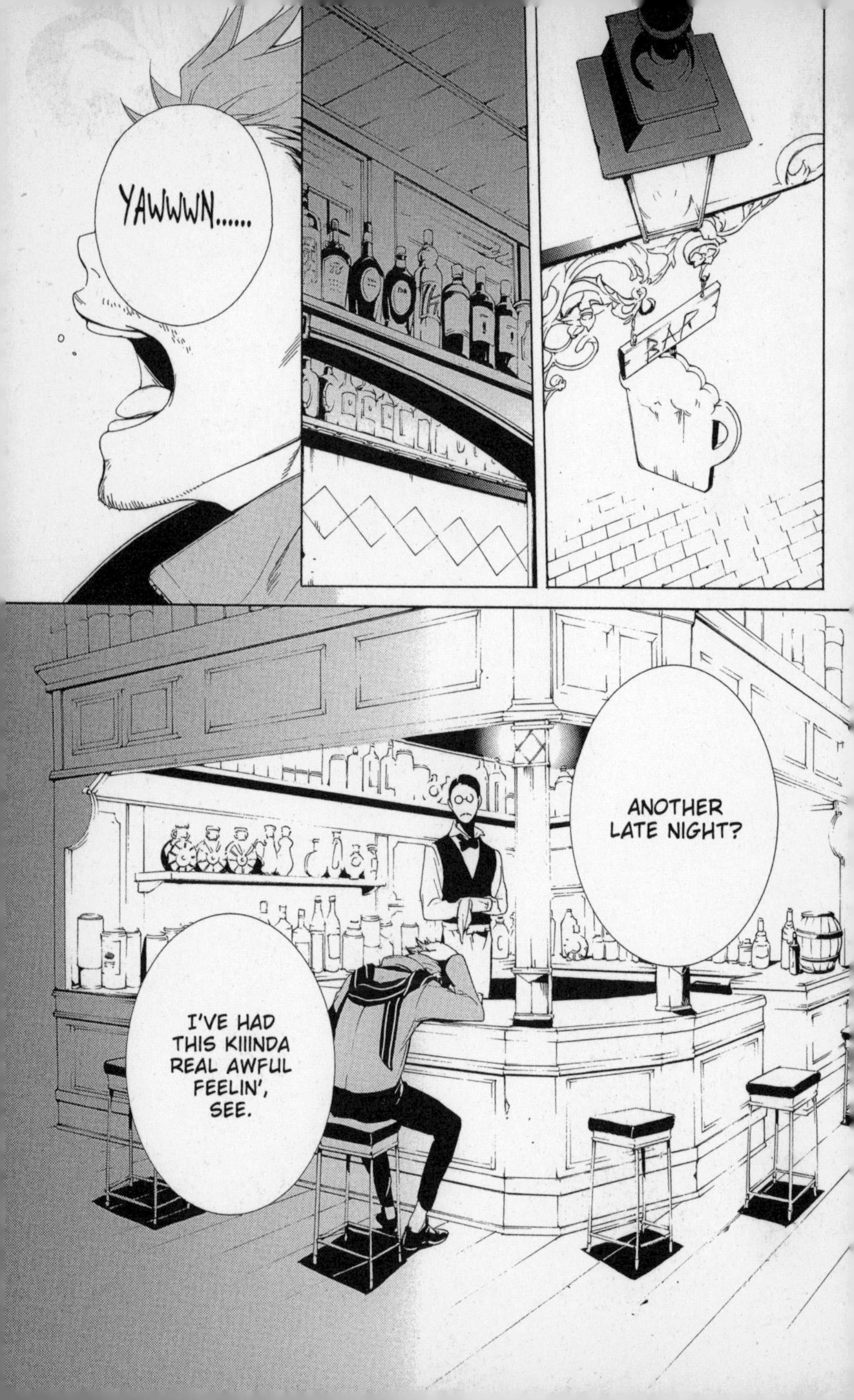
YAWWWN......
ANOTHER LATE NIGHT?
I'VE HAD THIS KIIINDA REAL AWFUL FEELIN', SEE.

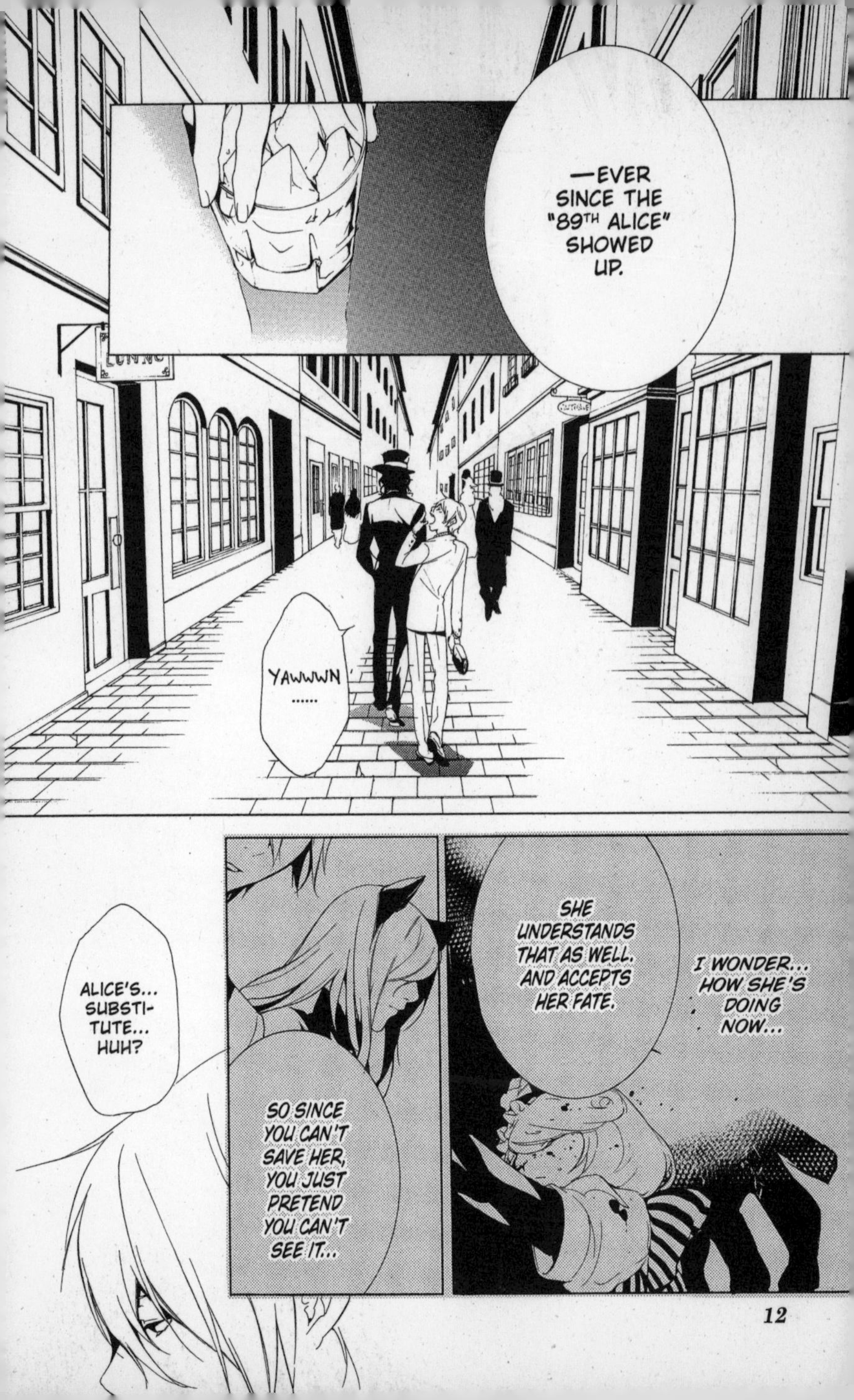
—EVER SINCE THE "89TH ALICE" SHOWED UP.
YAWWWN ......
SHE UNDERSTANDS THAT AS WELL. AND ACCEPTS HER FATE.
I WONDER... HOW SHE'S DOING NOW...
SO SINCE YOU CAN'T SAVE HER, YOU JUST PRETEND YOU CAN'T SEE IT...
ALICE'S... SUBSTI-TUTE... HUH?

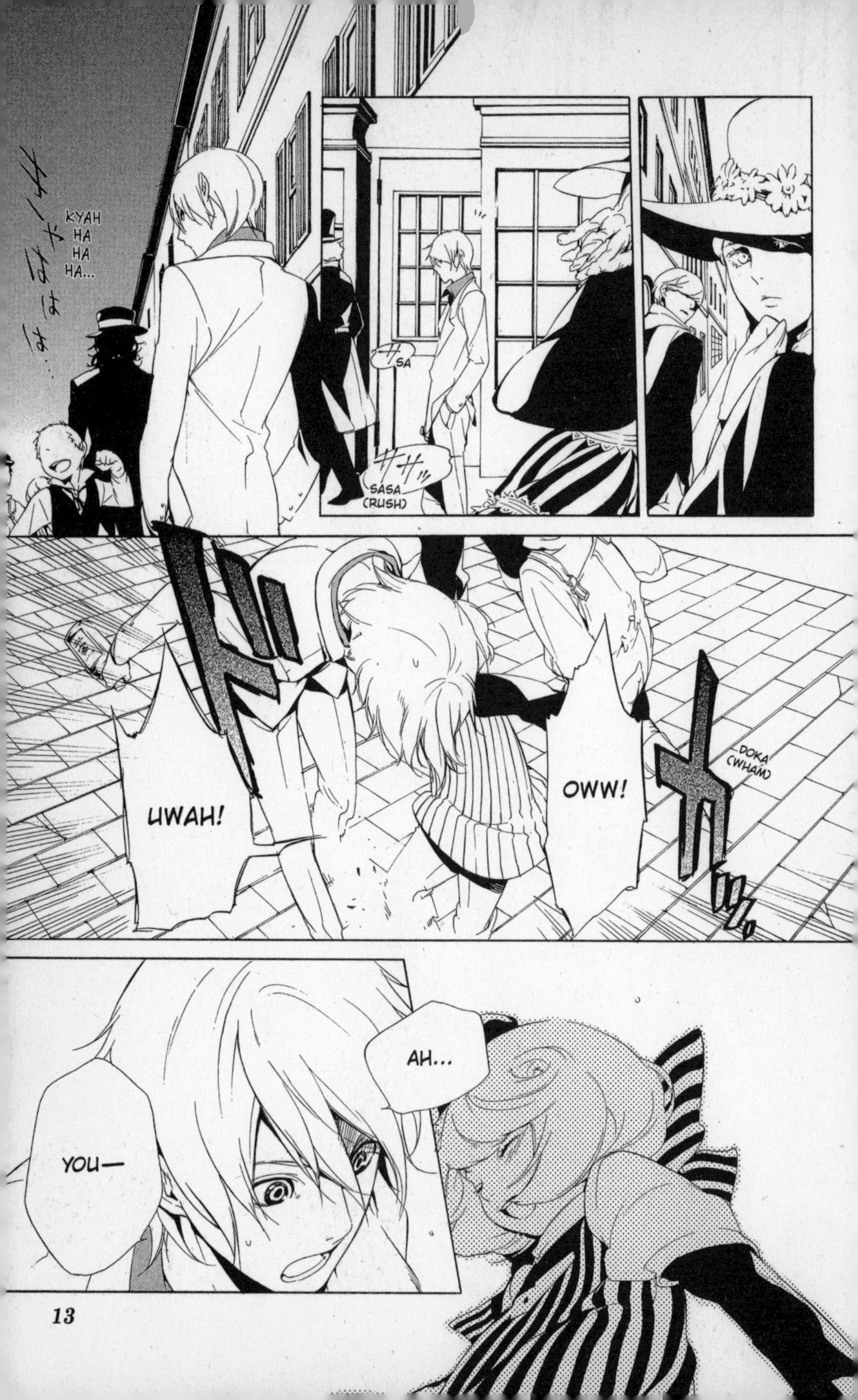
SA
SASA (RUSH)
KYAH HA HA HA...
DOKA (WHAM)
OWW!
UWAH!
AH...
YOU—

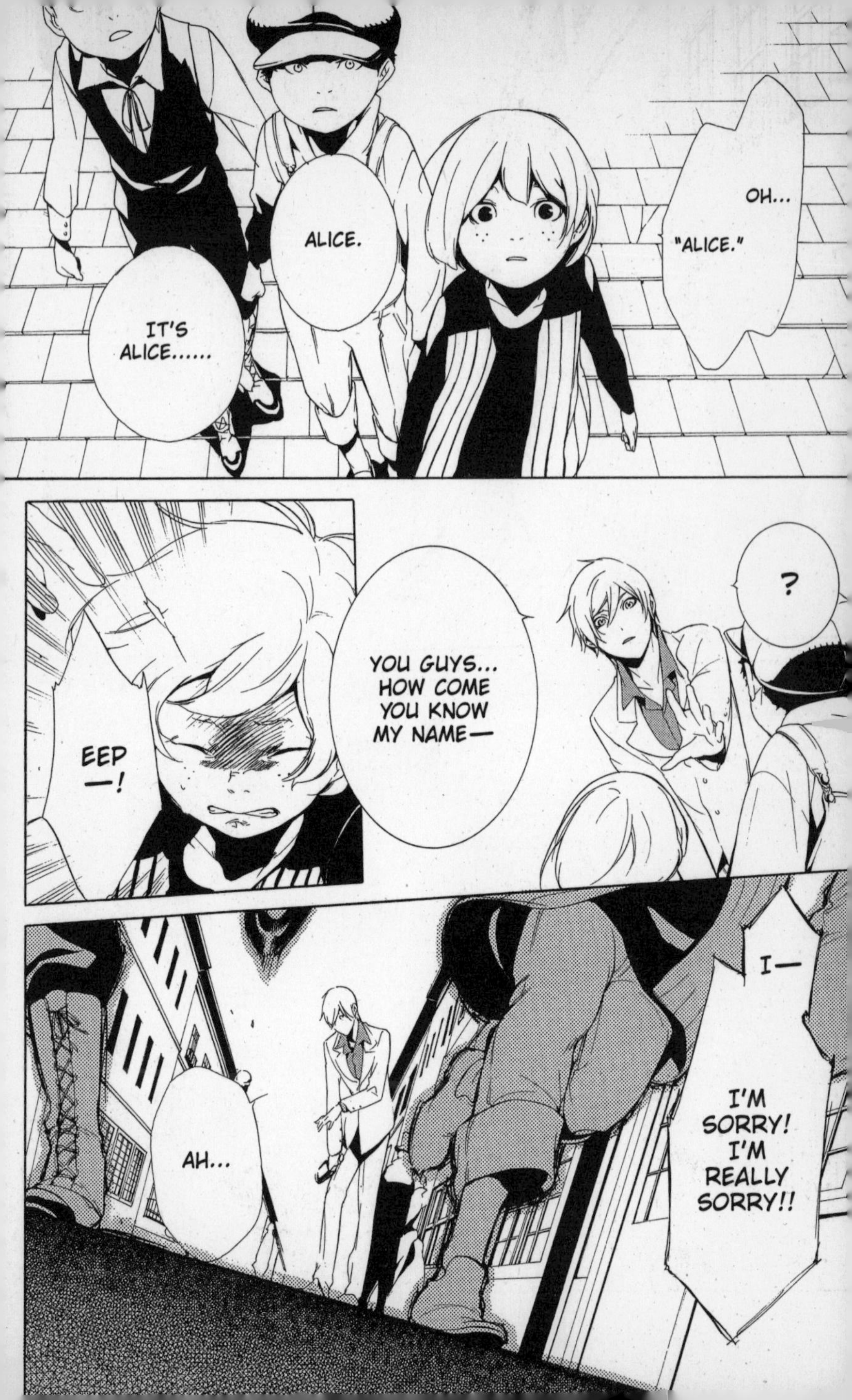
OH... "ALICE."
ALICE.
IT'S ALICE......
?
YOU GUYS... HOW COME YOU KNOW MY NAME—
EEP—!
I—
I'M SORRY! I'M REALLY SORRY!!
AH...

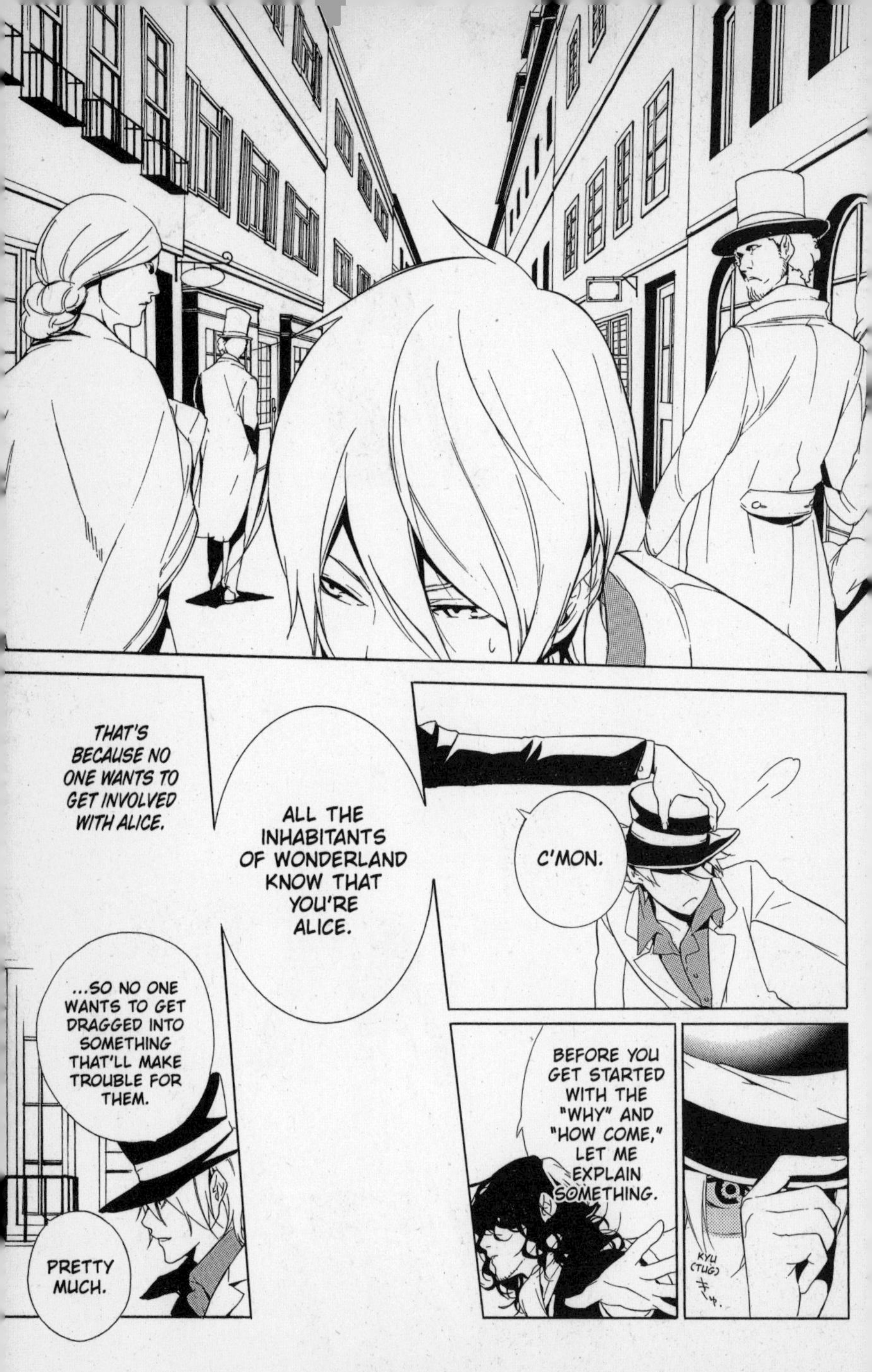
C'MON.
KYU (TUG)
キュ
BEFORE YOU GET STARTED WITH THE "WHY" AND "HOW COME," LET ME EXPLAIN SOMETHING.
ALL THE INHABITANTS OF WONDERLAND KNOW THAT YOU'RE ALICE.
THAT'S BECAUSE NO ONE WANTS TO GET INVOLVED WITH ALICE.
...SO NO ONE WANTS TO GET DRAGGED INTO SOMETHING THAT'LL MAKE TROUBLE FOR THEM.
PRETTY MUCH.

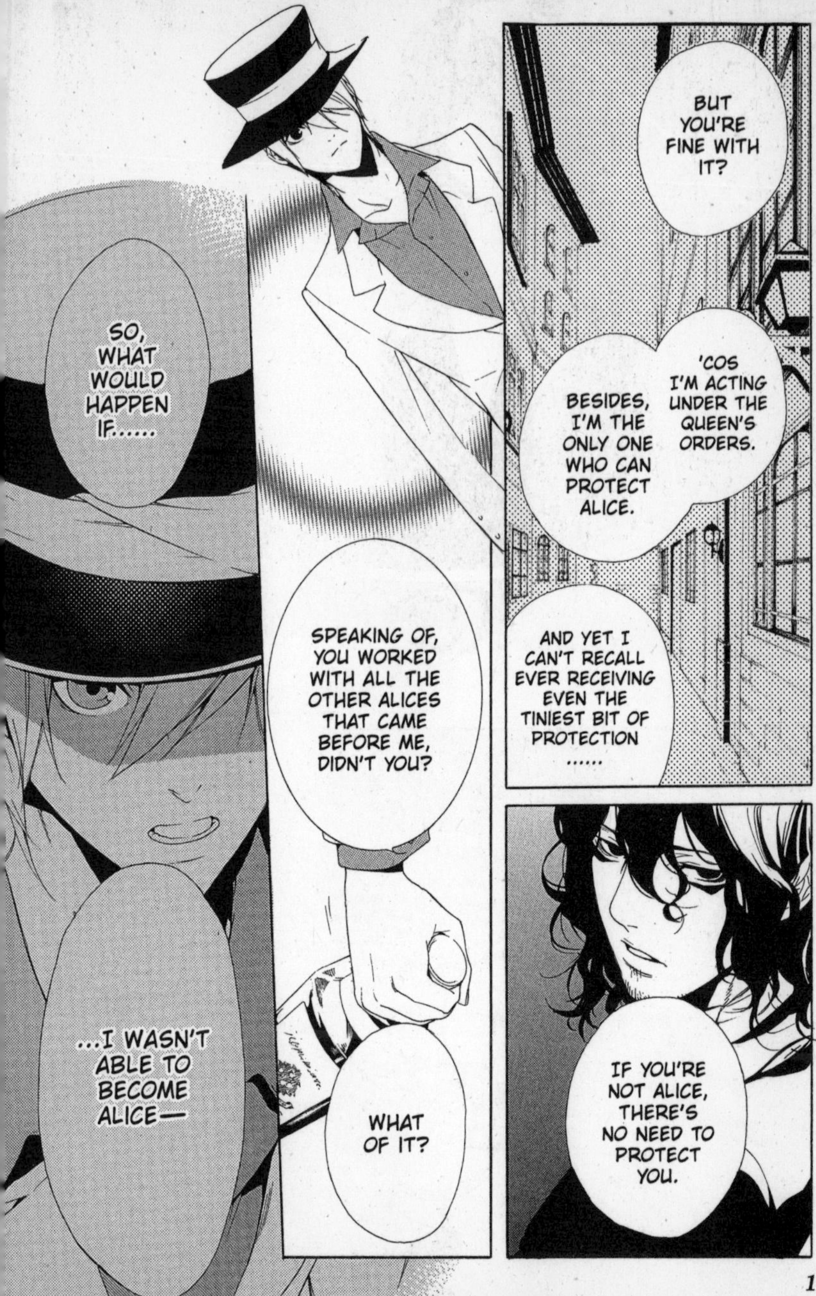
BUT YOU'RE FINE WITH IT?
'COS I'M ACTING UNDER THE QUEEN'S ORDERS.
BESIDES, I'M THE ONLY ONE WHO CAN PROTECT ALICE.
AND YET I CAN'T RECALL EVER RECEIVING EVEN THE TINIEST BIT OF PROTECTION ......
IF YOU'RE NOT ALICE, THERE'S NO NEED TO PROTECT YOU.
SPEAKING OF, YOU WORKED WITH ALL THE OTHER ALICES THAT CAME BEFORE ME, DIDN'T YOU?
WHAT OF IT?
SO, WHAT WOULD HAPPEN IF......
...I WASN'T ABLE TO BECOME ALICE—

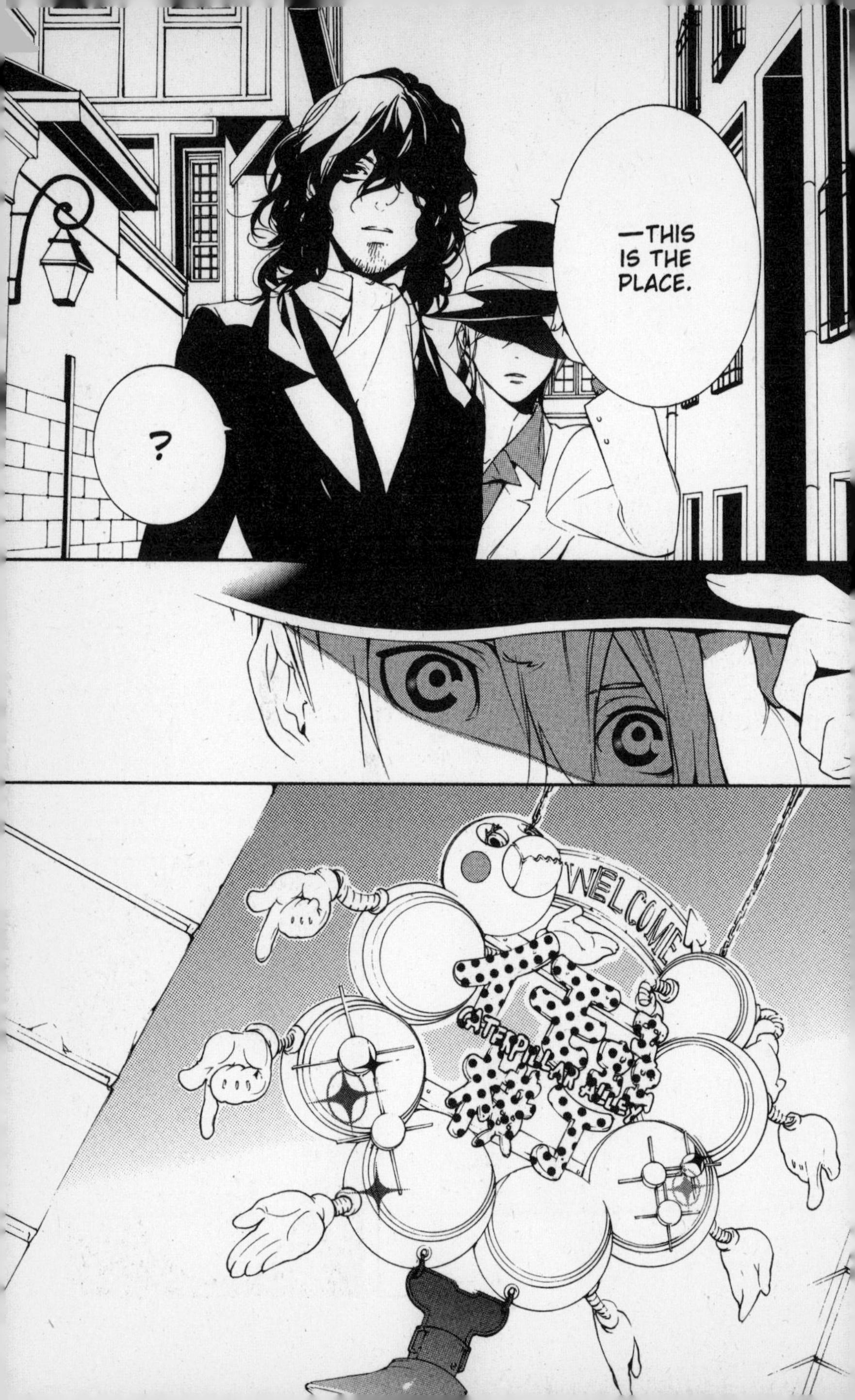
—THIS IS THE PLACE.
?
WELCOME
CATERPILLAR ALLEY

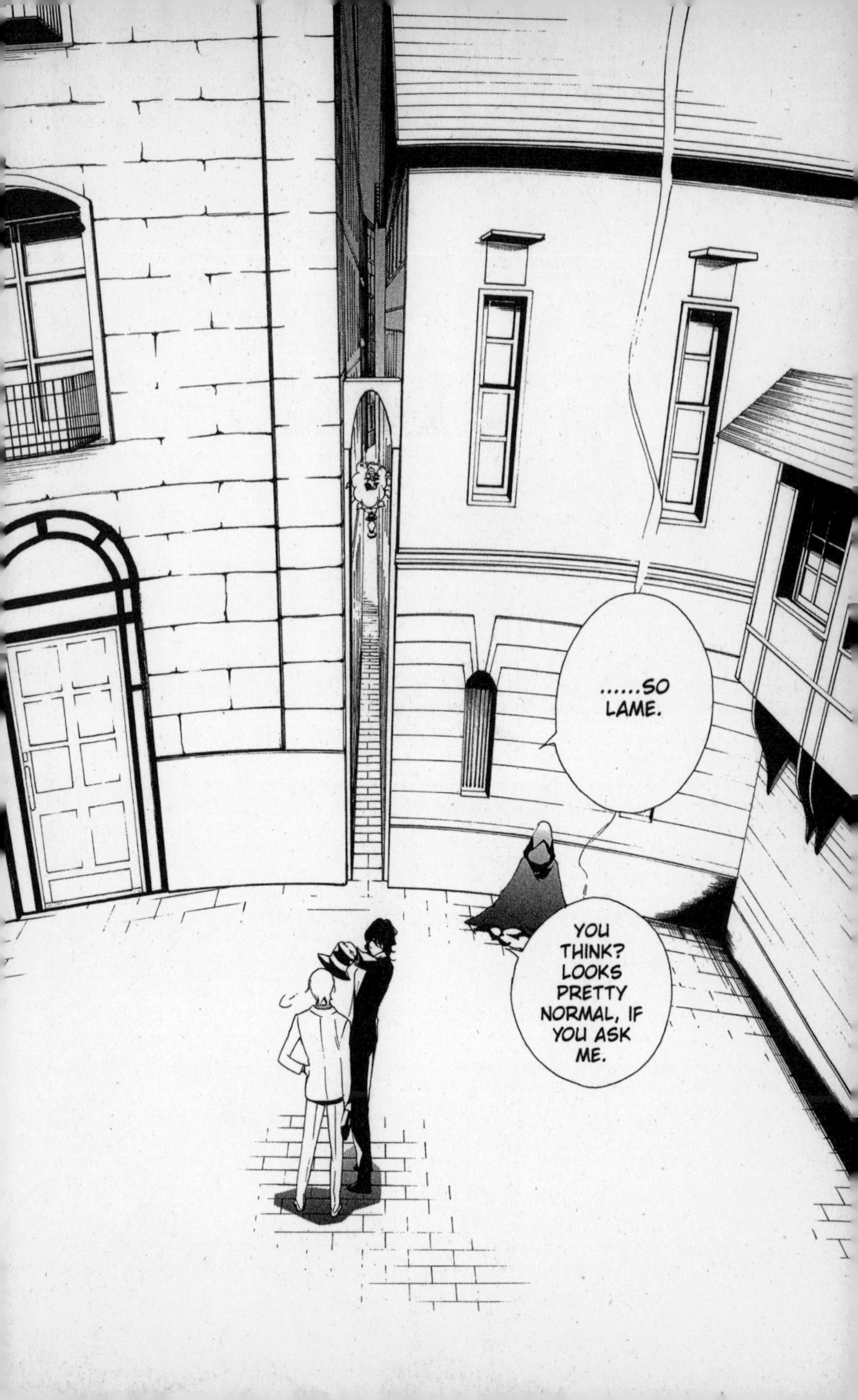
......SO LAME.
YOU THINK? LOOKS PRETTY NORMAL, IF YOU ASK ME.

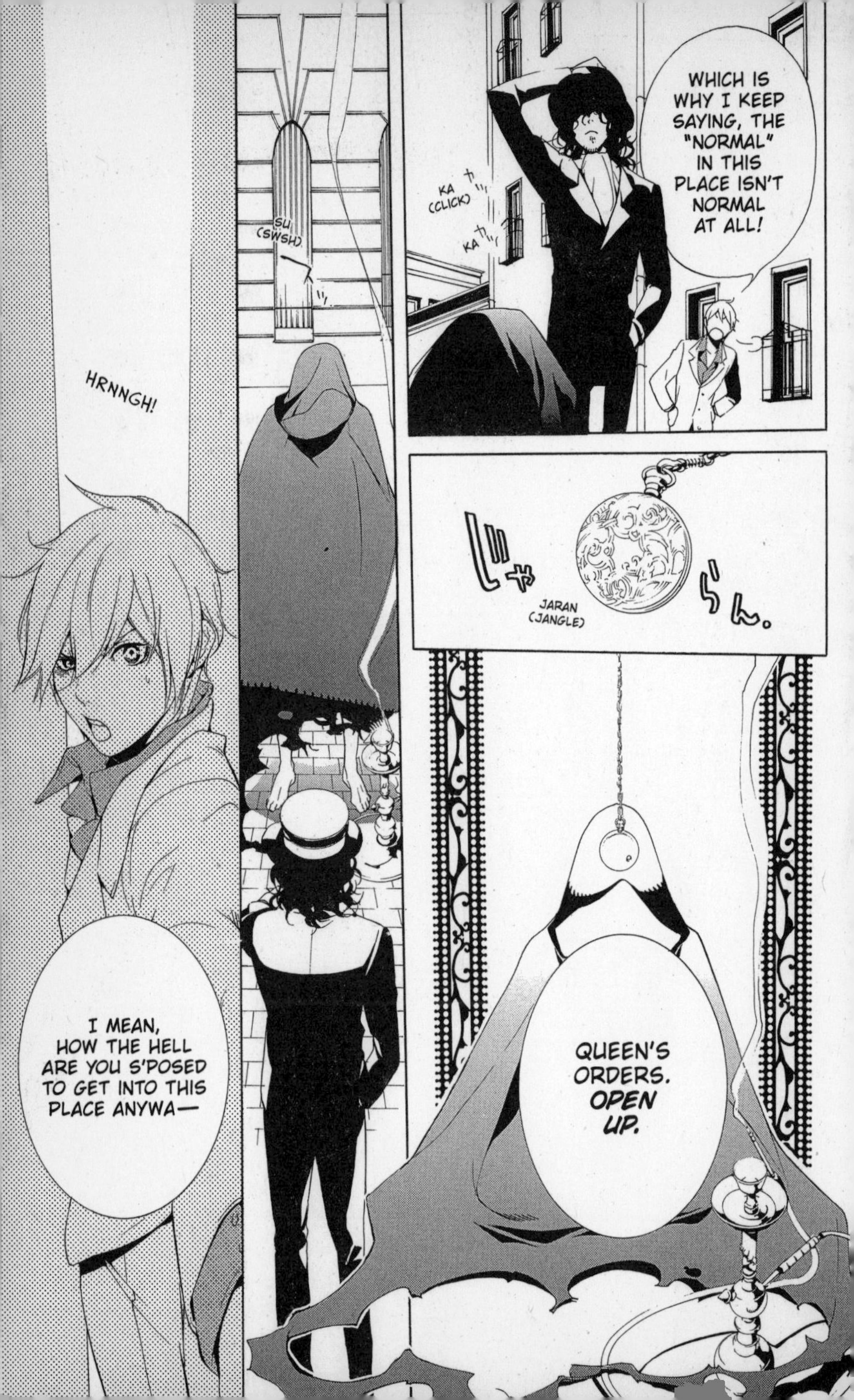
WHICH IS WHY I KEEP SAYING, THE "NORMAL" IN THIS PLACE ISN'T NORMAL AT ALL!
KA (CLICK)
KA
じゃらん。
JARAN (JANGLE)
QUEEN'S ORDERS. OPEN UP.
SU (SWSH)
HRNNGH!
I MEAN, HOW THE HELL ARE YOU S'POSED TO GET INTO THIS PLACE ANYWA—

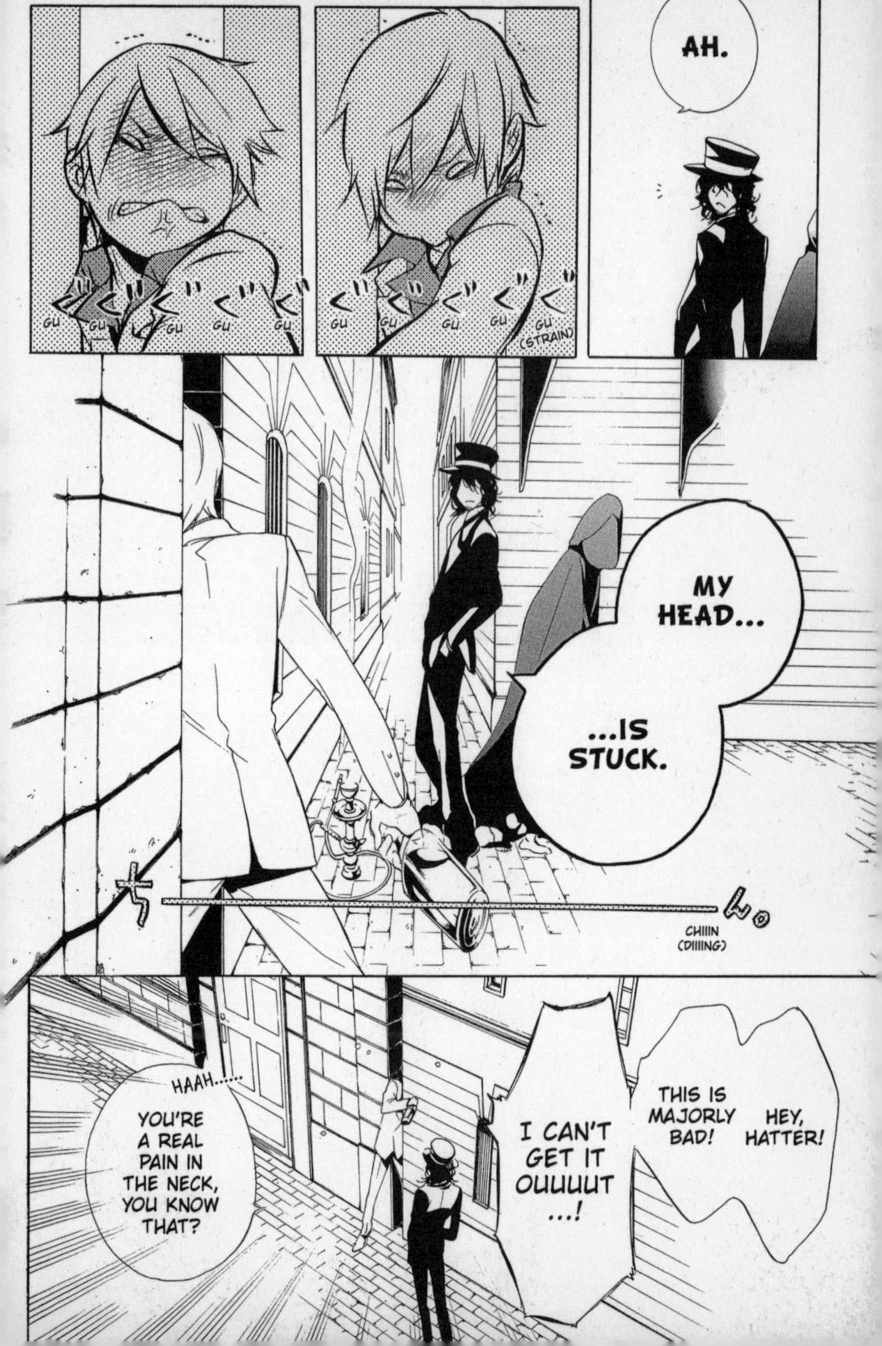
AH.
GU GU GU GU GU (STRAIN)
....
GU GU GU GU GU
MY HEAD...
...IS STUCK.
CHIIIN (DIIIING)
HEY, HATTER!
THIS IS MAJORLY BAD!
I CAN'T GET IT OUUUUT ...!
HAAH......
YOU'RE A REAL PAIN IN THE NECK, YOU KNOW THAT?

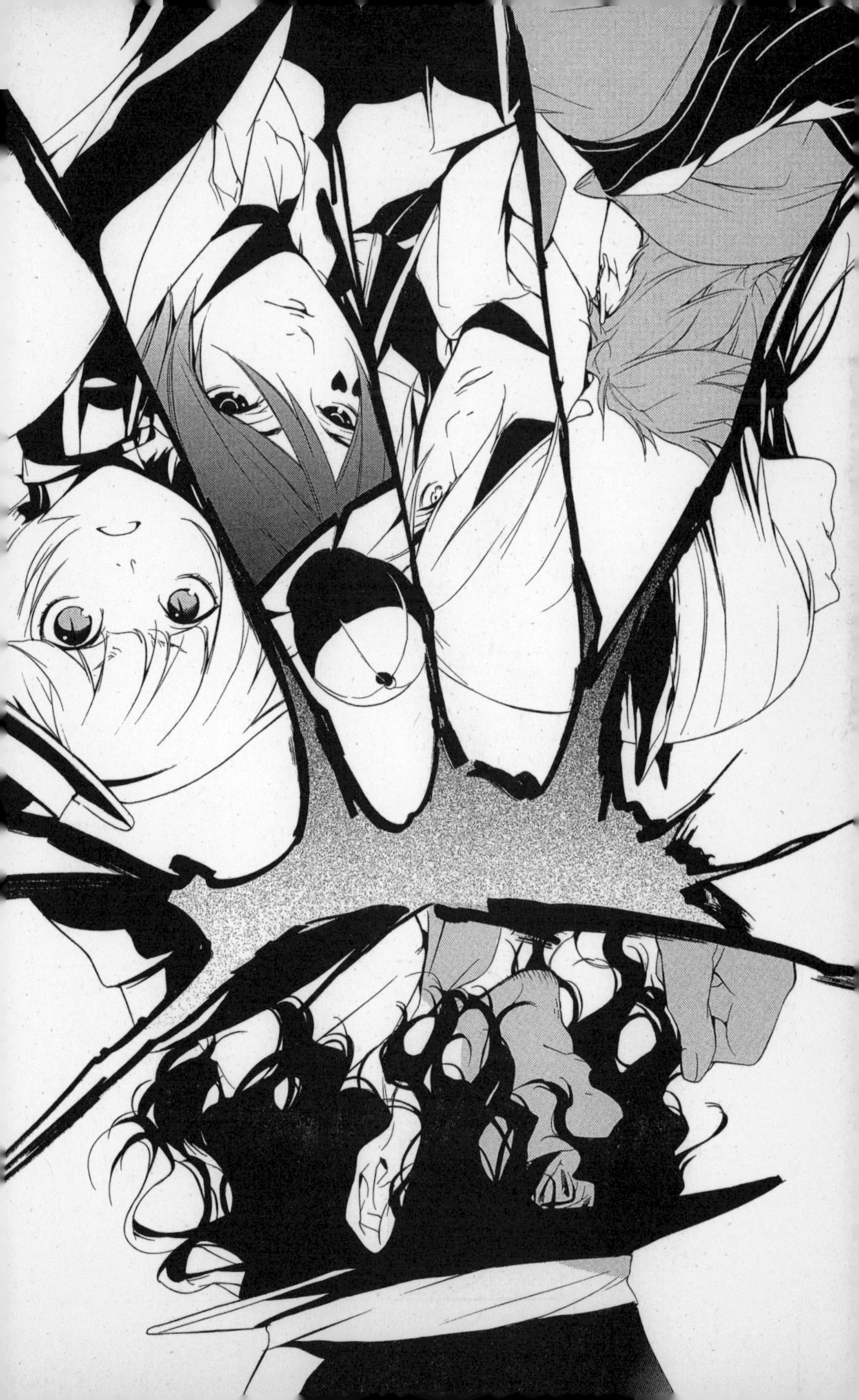

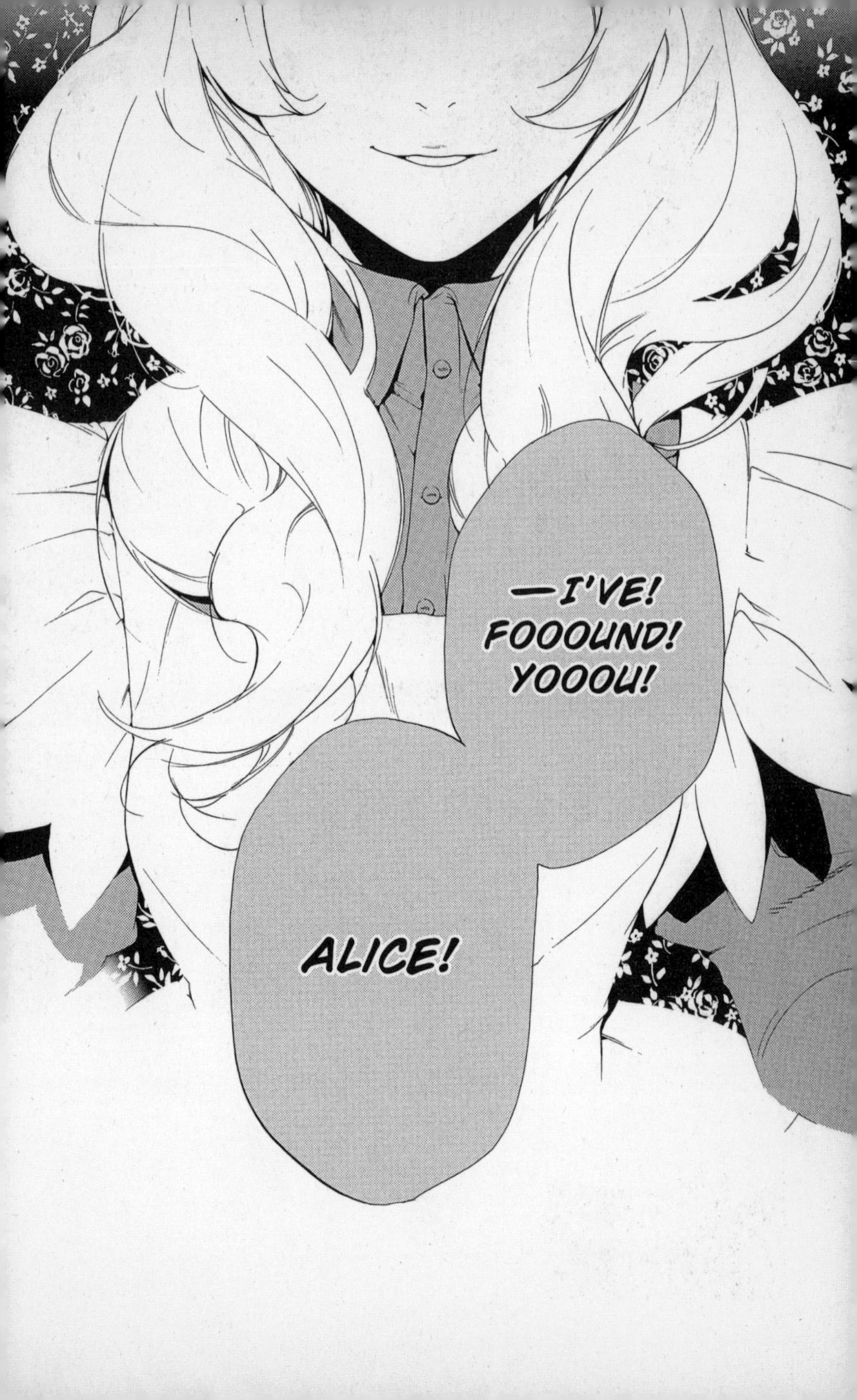
—I'VE! FOOOUND! YOOOU!
ALICE!

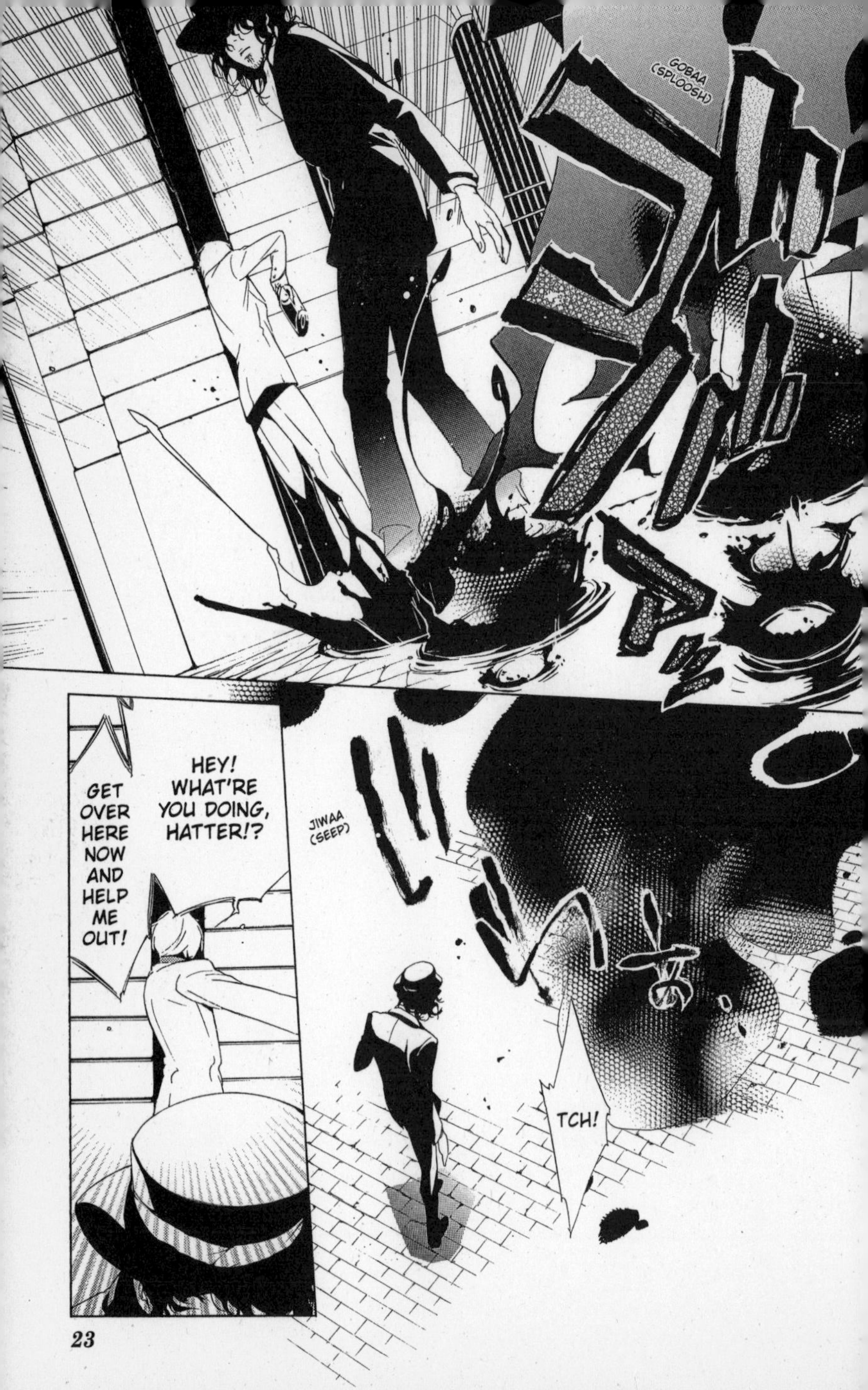
GOBAA (SPLOOSH)
JIWAA (SEEP)
TCH!
HEY! WHAT'RE YOU DOING, HATTER!?
GET OVER HERE NOW AND HELP ME OUT!

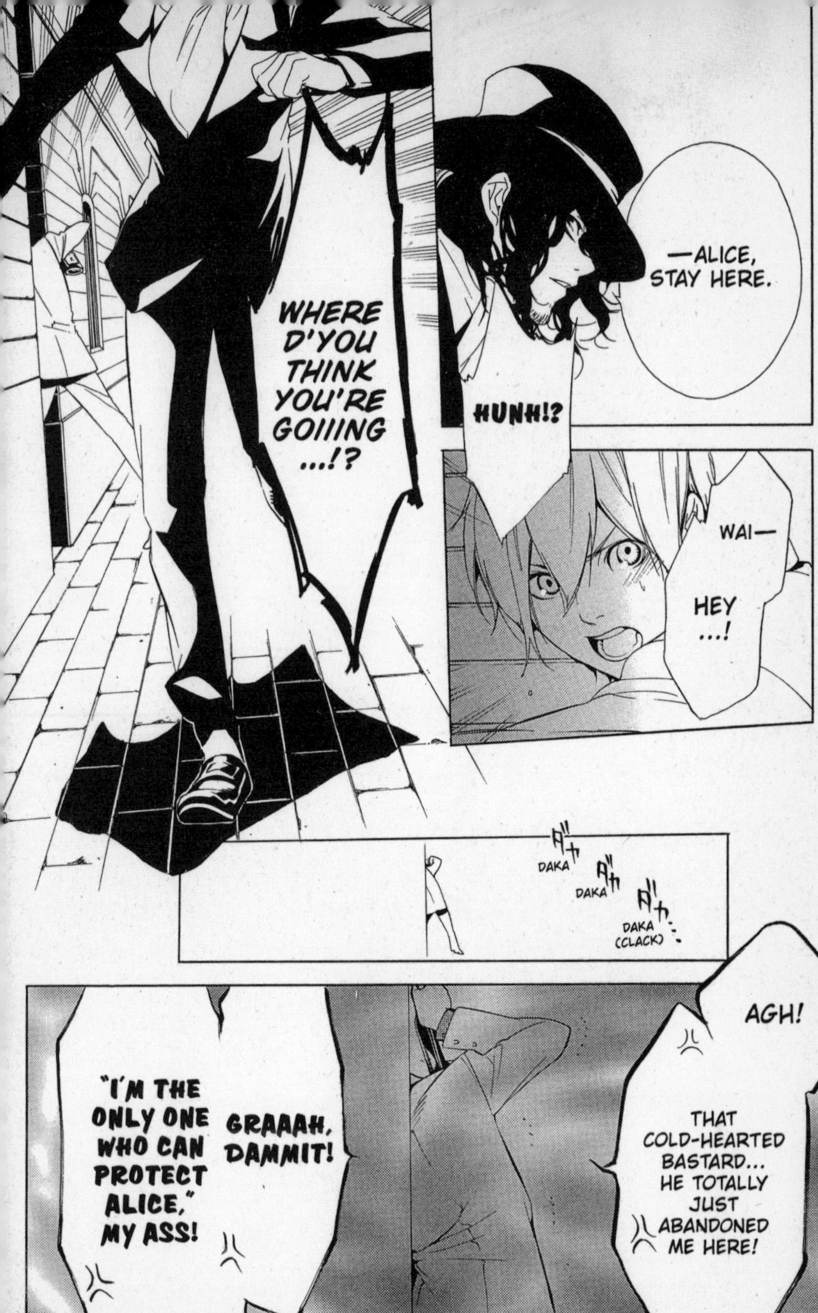
—ALICE, STAY HERE.
HUNH!?
WHERE D'YOU THINK YOU'RE GOIIING ...!?
WAI—
HEY ...!
DAKA
DAKA
DAKA (CLACK)
AGH!
THAT COLD-HEARTED BASTARD... HE TOTALLY JUST ABANDONED ME HERE!
GRAAAH, DAMMIT!
"I'M THE ONLY ONE WHO CAN PROTECT ALICE," MY ASS!

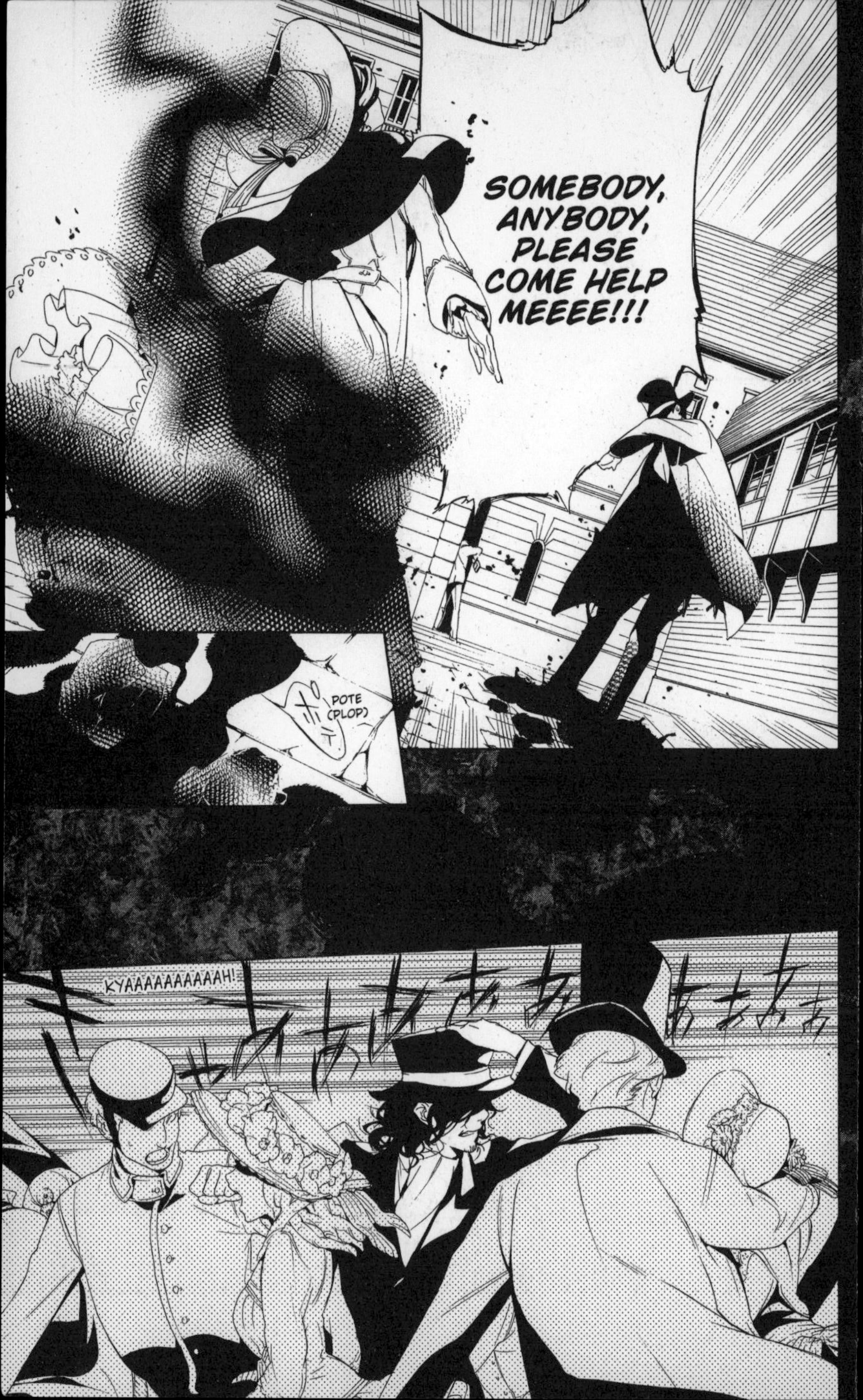
SOMEBODY, ANYBODY, PLEASE COME HELP MEEEE!!!
POTE (PLOP)
KYAAAAAAAAAAH!

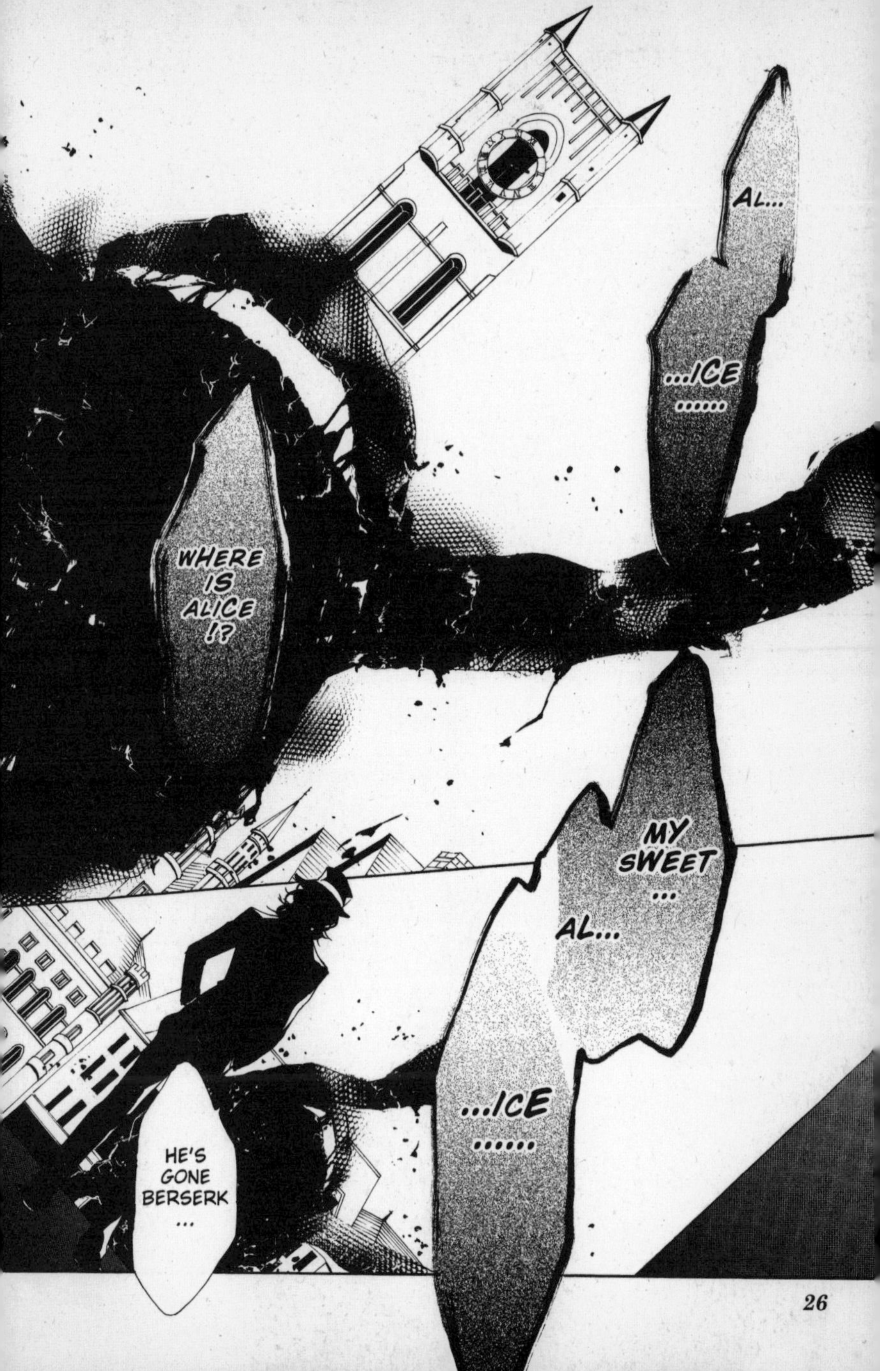
AL...
...ICE ......
WHERE IS ALICE !?
MY SWEET ...
AL...
...ICE ......
HE'S GONE BERSERK ...

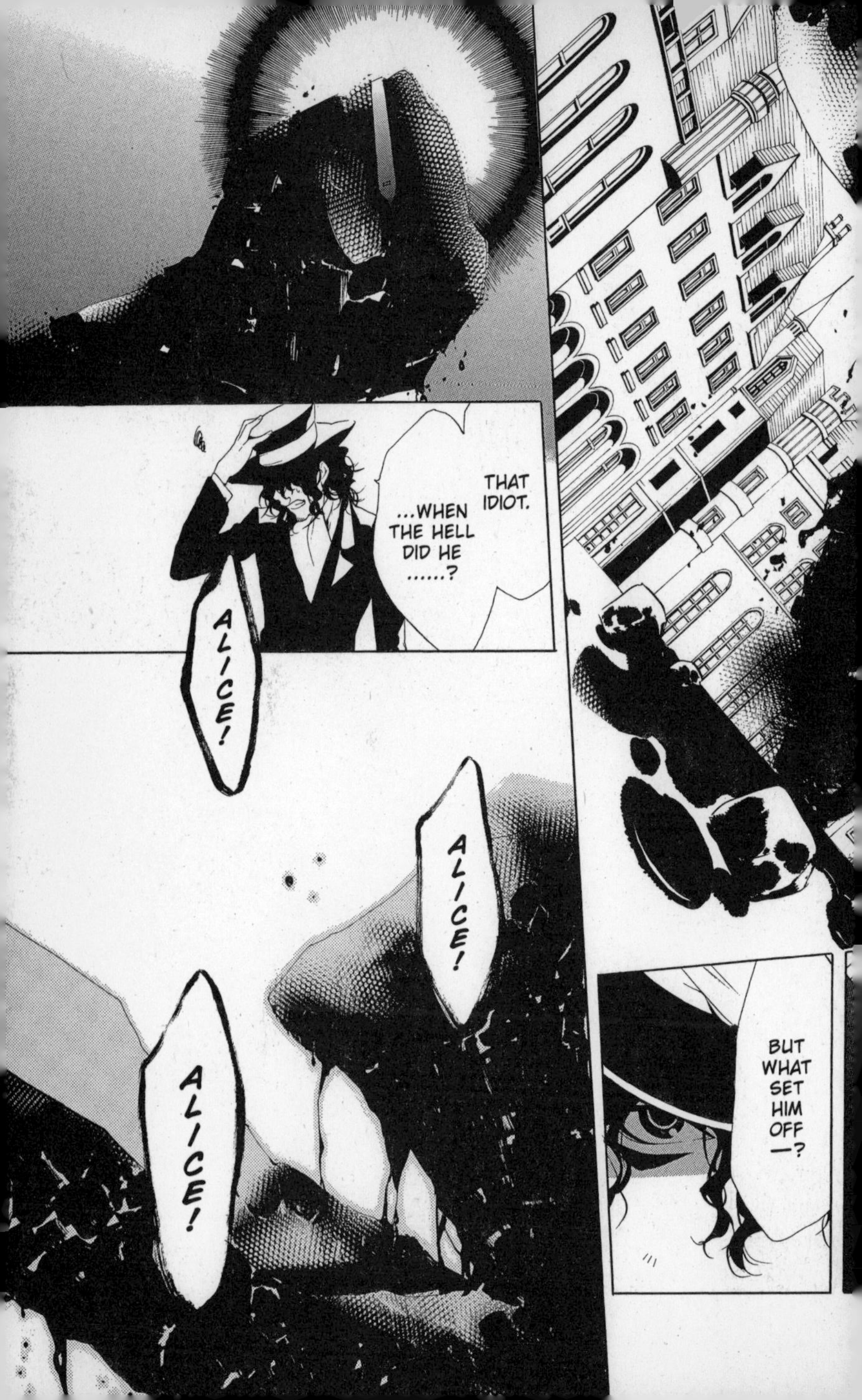
BUT WHAT SET HIM OFF —?
THAT IDIOT.
...WHEN THE HELL DID HE ......?
ALICE!
ALICE!
ALICE!

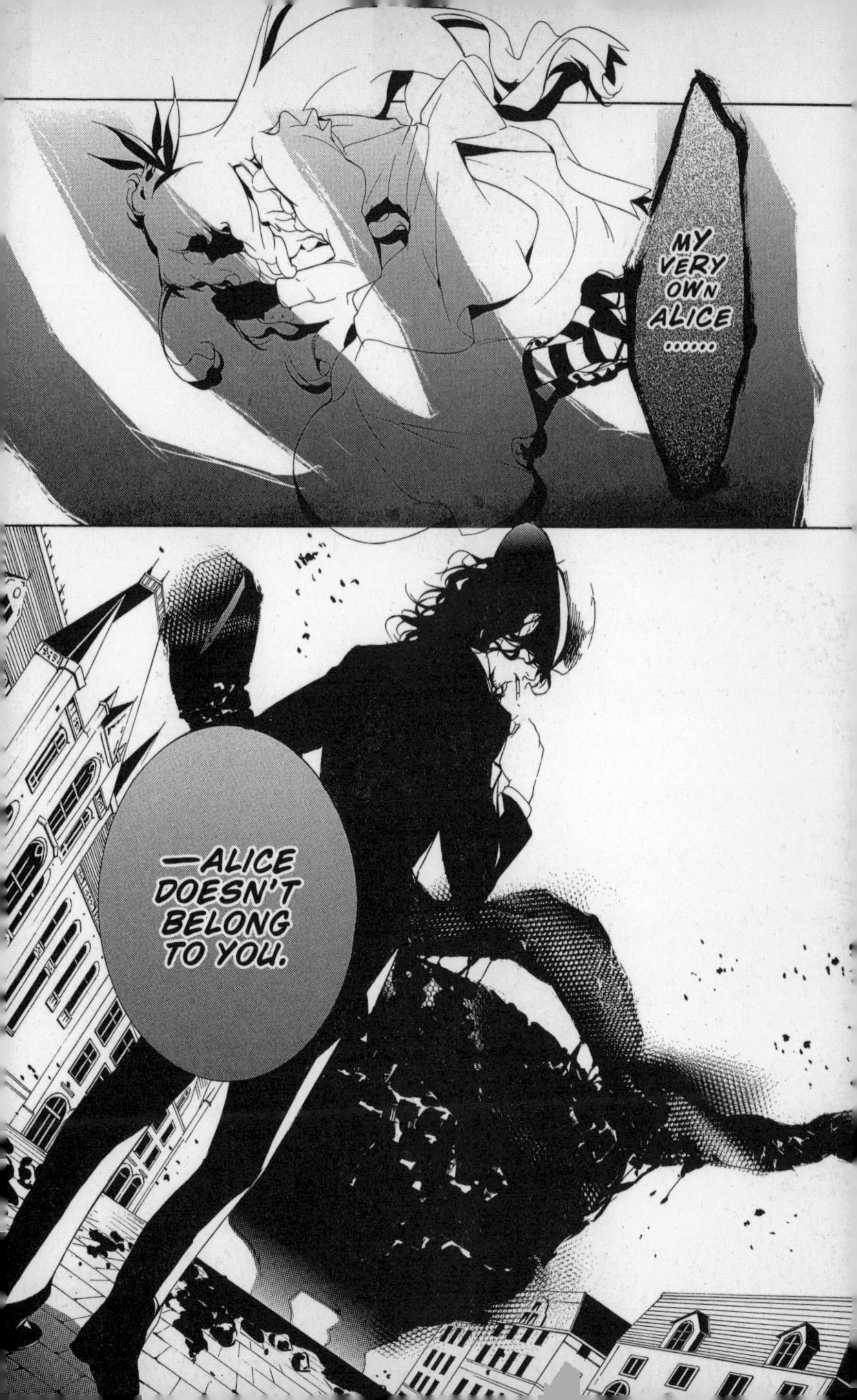
MY VERY OWN ALICE ......
—ALICE DOESN'T BELONG TO YOU.

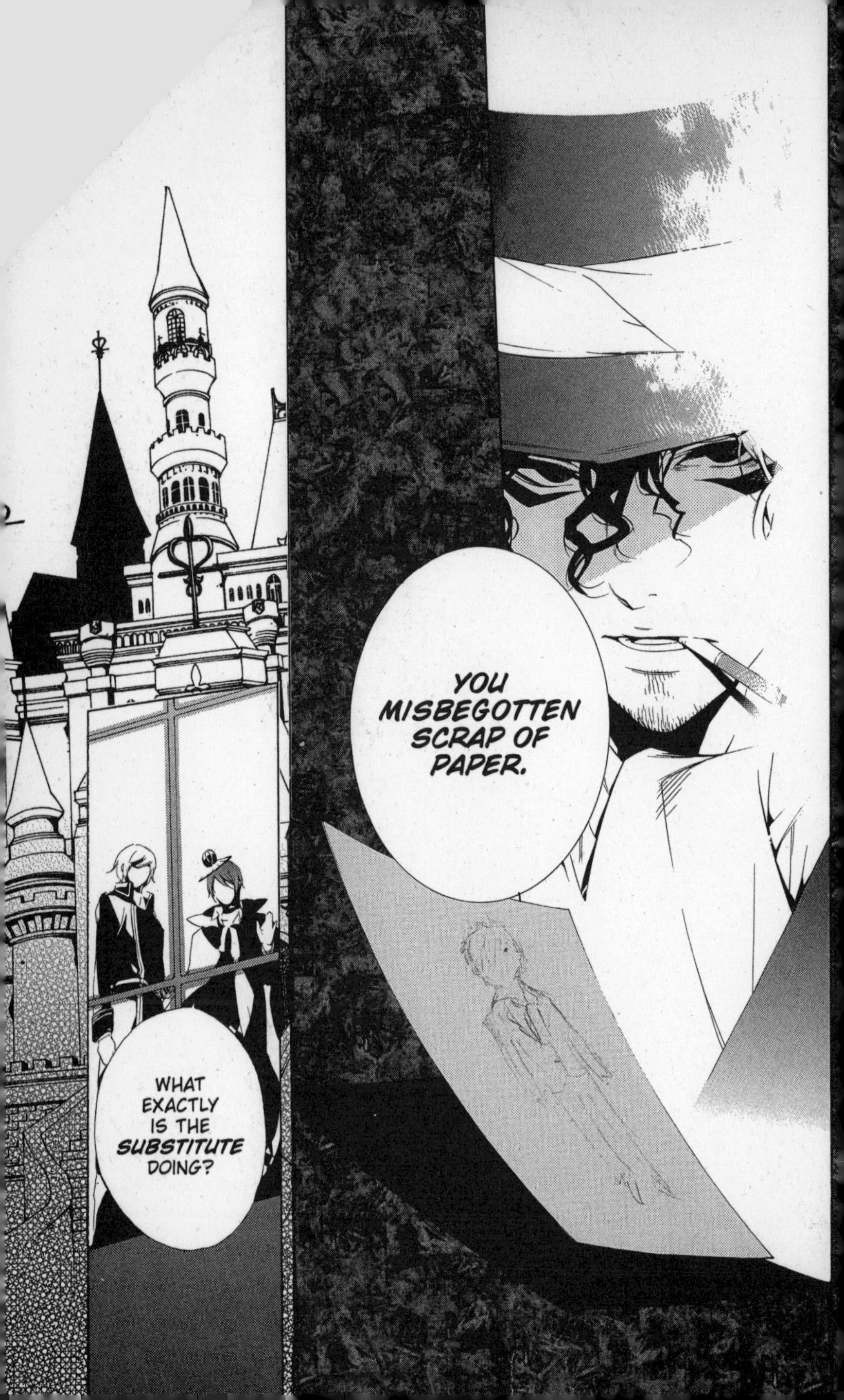
YOU MISBEGOTTEN SCRAP OF PAPER.
WHAT EXACTLY IS THE SUBSTITUTE DOING?

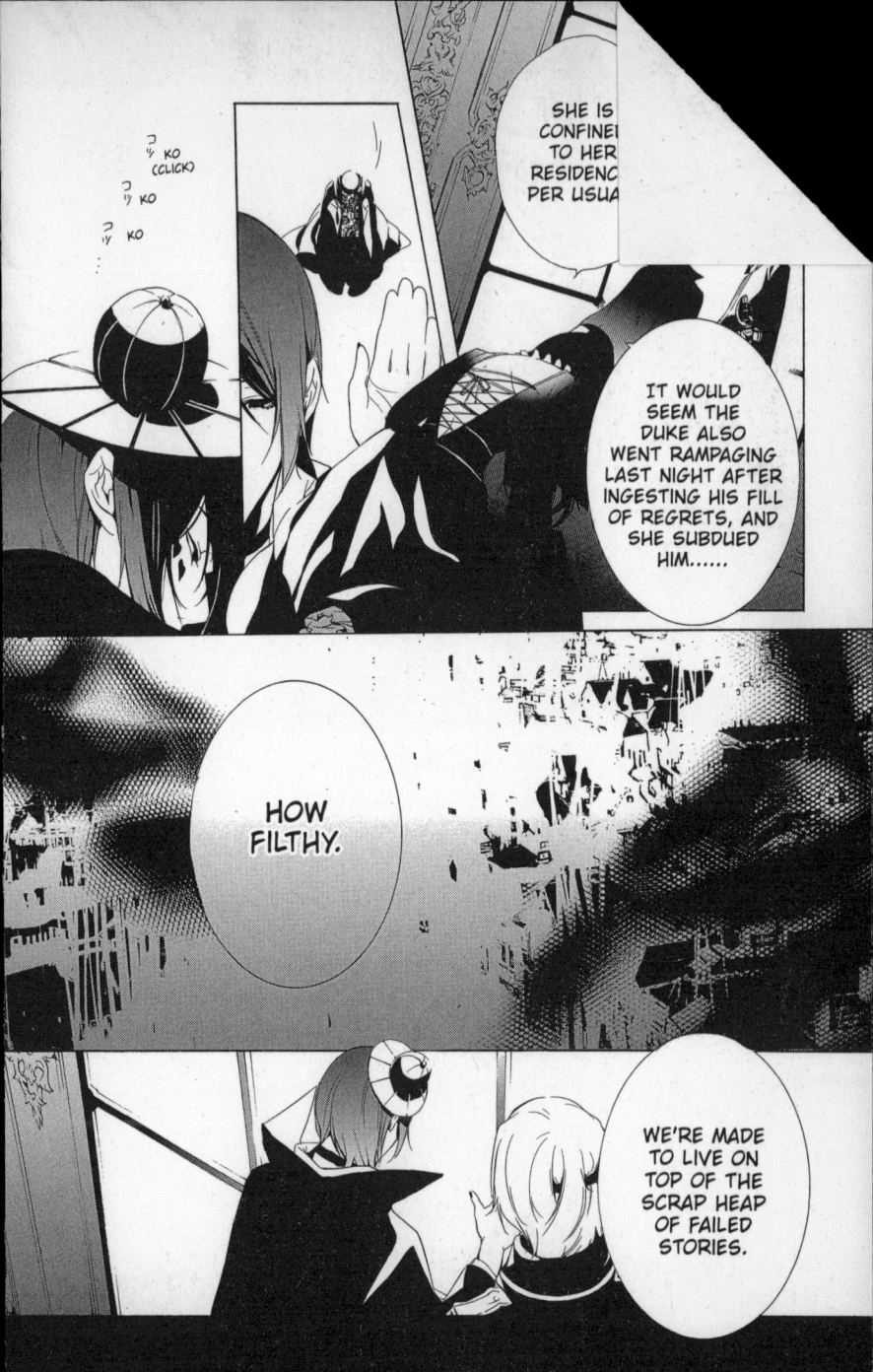

コツ KO
(CLICK)

コツ KO

コツ KO

SHE IS CONFINED TO HER RESIDENCE PER USUAL...

IT WOULD SEEM THE DUKE ALSO WENT RAMPAGING LAST NIGHT AFTER INGESTING HIS FILL OF REGRETS, AND SHE SUBDUED HIM......

HOW FILTHY.

WE'RE MADE TO LIVE ON TOP OF THE SCRAP HEAP OF FAILED STORIES.

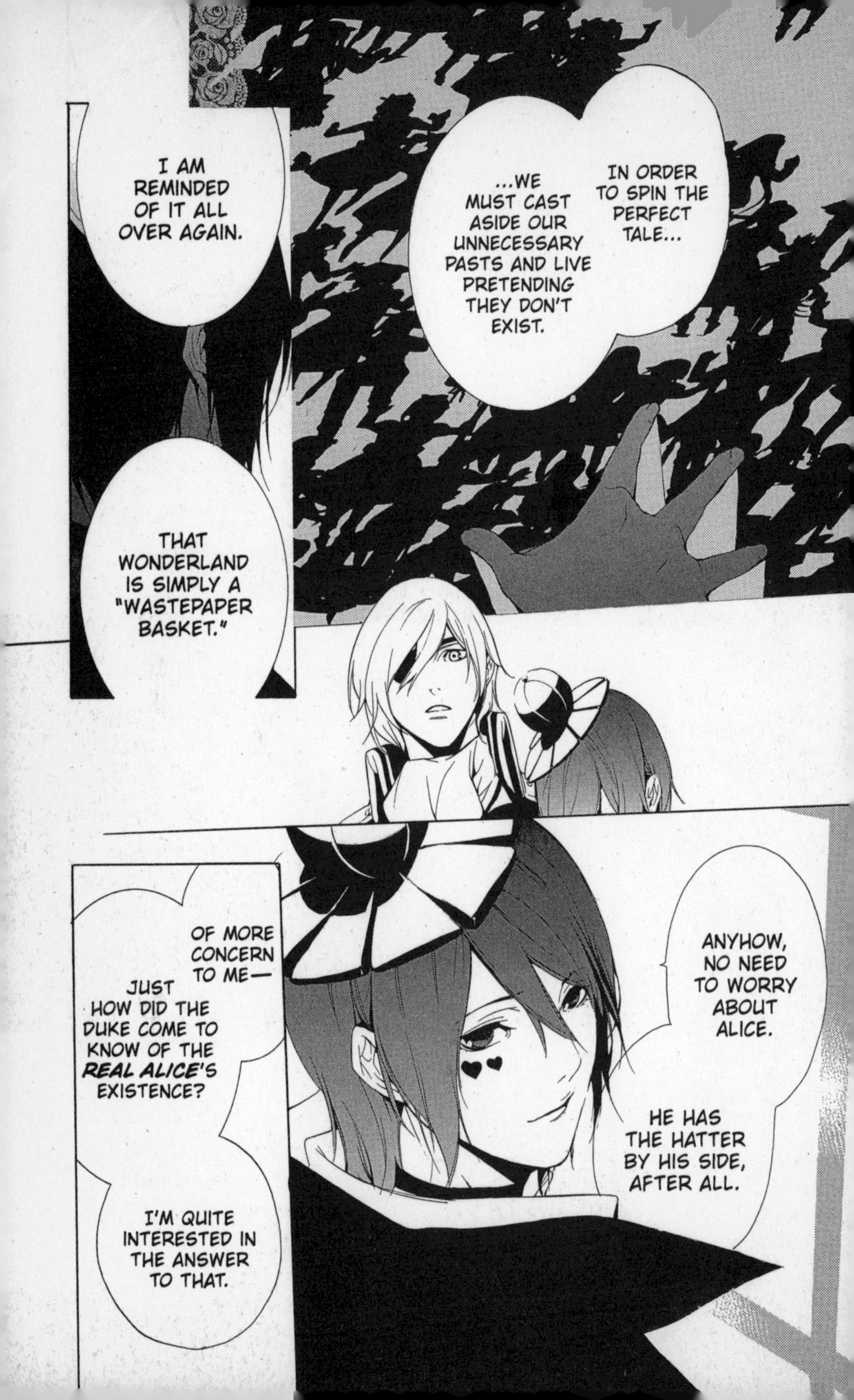
IN ORDER TO SPIN THE PERFECT TALE...
...WE MUST CAST ASIDE OUR UNNECESSARY PASTS AND LIVE PRETENDING THEY DON'T EXIST.
I AM REMINDED OF IT ALL OVER AGAIN.
THAT WONDERLAND IS SIMPLY A "WASTEPAPER BASKET."
ANYHOW, NO NEED TO WORRY ABOUT ALICE.
HE HAS THE HATTER BY HIS SIDE, AFTER ALL.
OF MORE CONCERN TO ME— JUST HOW DID THE DUKE COME TO KNOW OF THE ***REAL ALICE***'S EXISTENCE?
I'M QUITE INTERESTED IN THE ANSWER TO THAT.

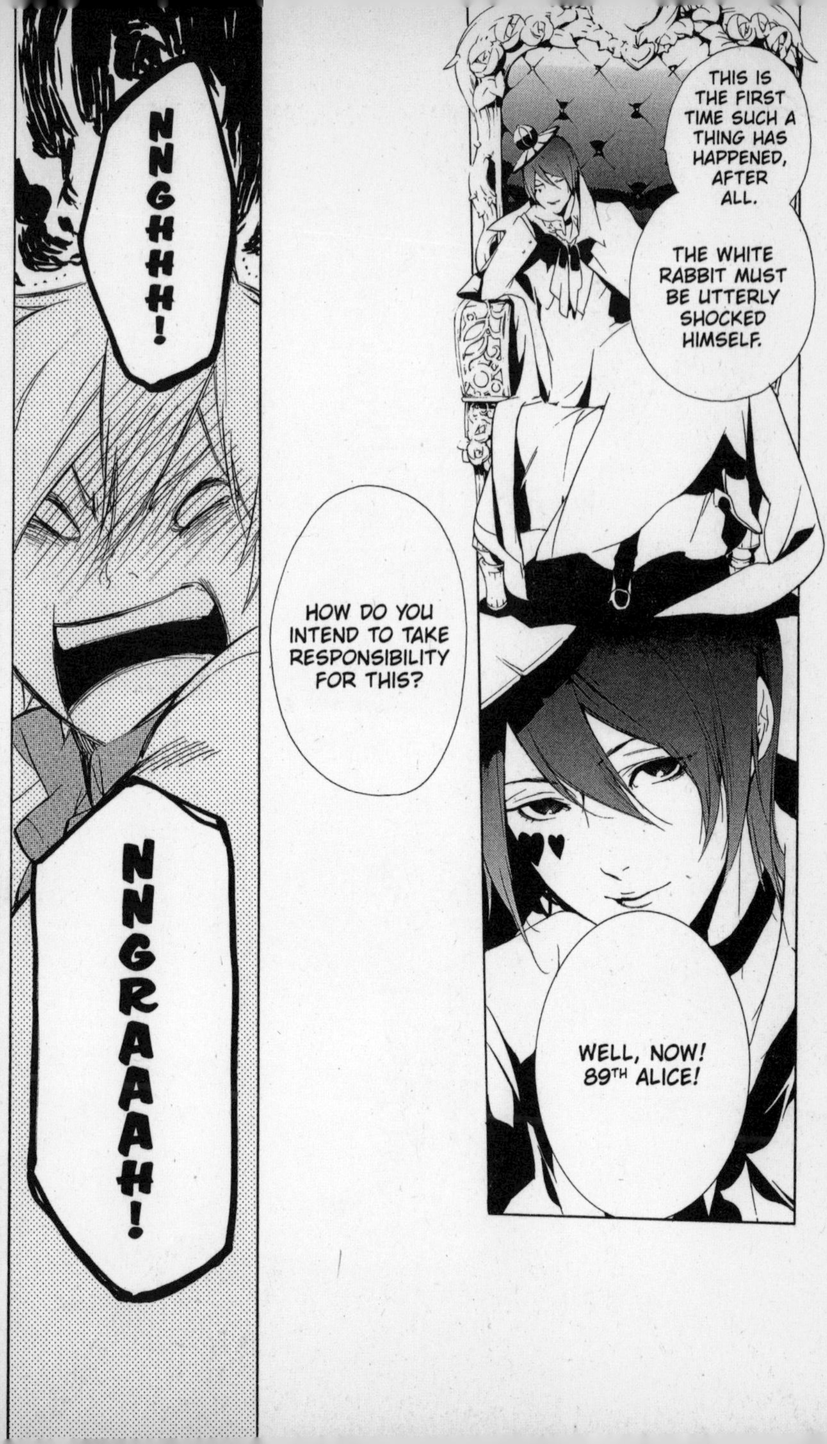
THIS IS THE FIRST TIME SUCH A THING HAS HAPPENED, AFTER ALL.
THE WHITE RABBIT MUST BE UTTERLY SHOCKED HIMSELF.
HOW DO YOU INTEND TO TAKE RESPONSIBILITY FOR THIS?
WELL, NOW! 89TH ALICE!
NNGHHH!
NNGRAAAAH!

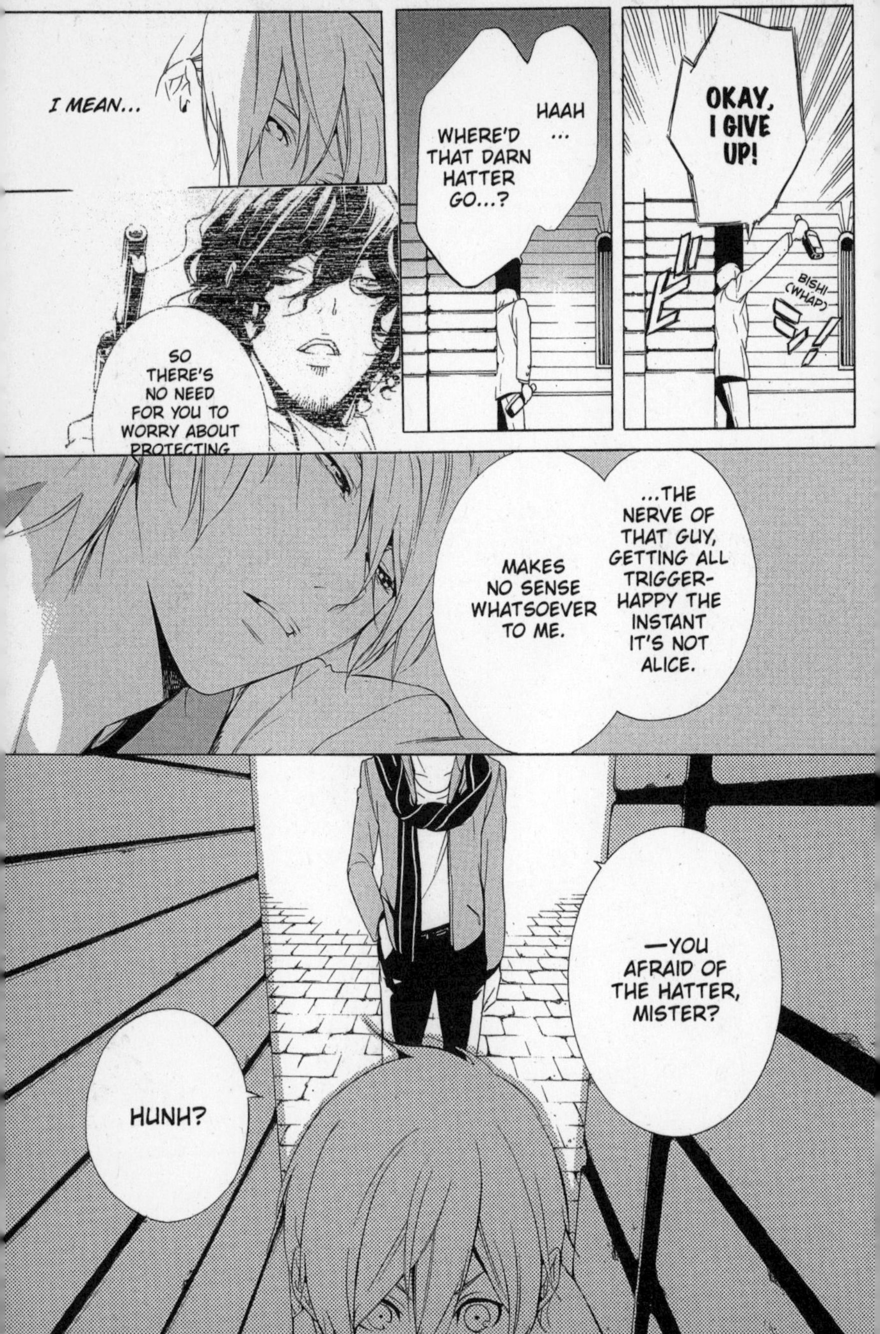
OKAY, I GIVE UP!
BISHI (WHAP)
HAAH ...
WHERE'D THAT DARN HATTER GO...?
I MEAN...
SO THERE'S NO NEED FOR YOU TO WORRY ABOUT PROTECTING
...THE NERVE OF THAT GUY, GETTING ALL TRIGGER-HAPPY THE INSTANT IT'S NOT ALICE.
MAKES NO SENSE WHATSOEVER TO ME.
—YOU AFRAID OF THE HATTER, MISTER?
HUNH?

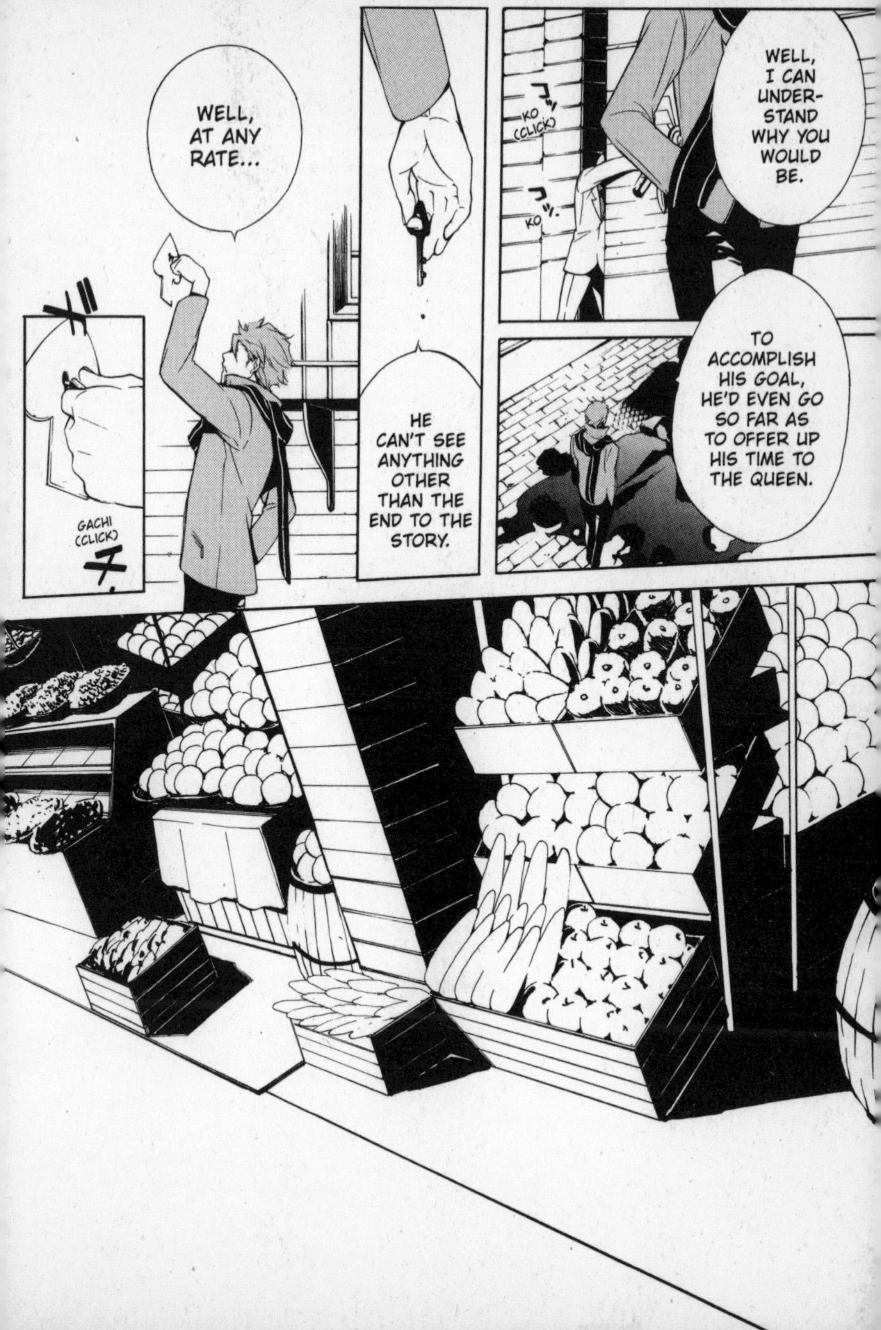
WELL, I CAN UNDER-STAND WHY YOU WOULD BE.
KO (CLICK)
KO
TO ACCOMPLISH HIS GOAL, HE'D EVEN GO SO FAR AS TO OFFER UP HIS TIME TO THE QUEEN.
HE CAN'T SEE ANYTHING OTHER THAN THE END TO THE STORY.
WELL, AT ANY RATE...
GACHI (CLICK)

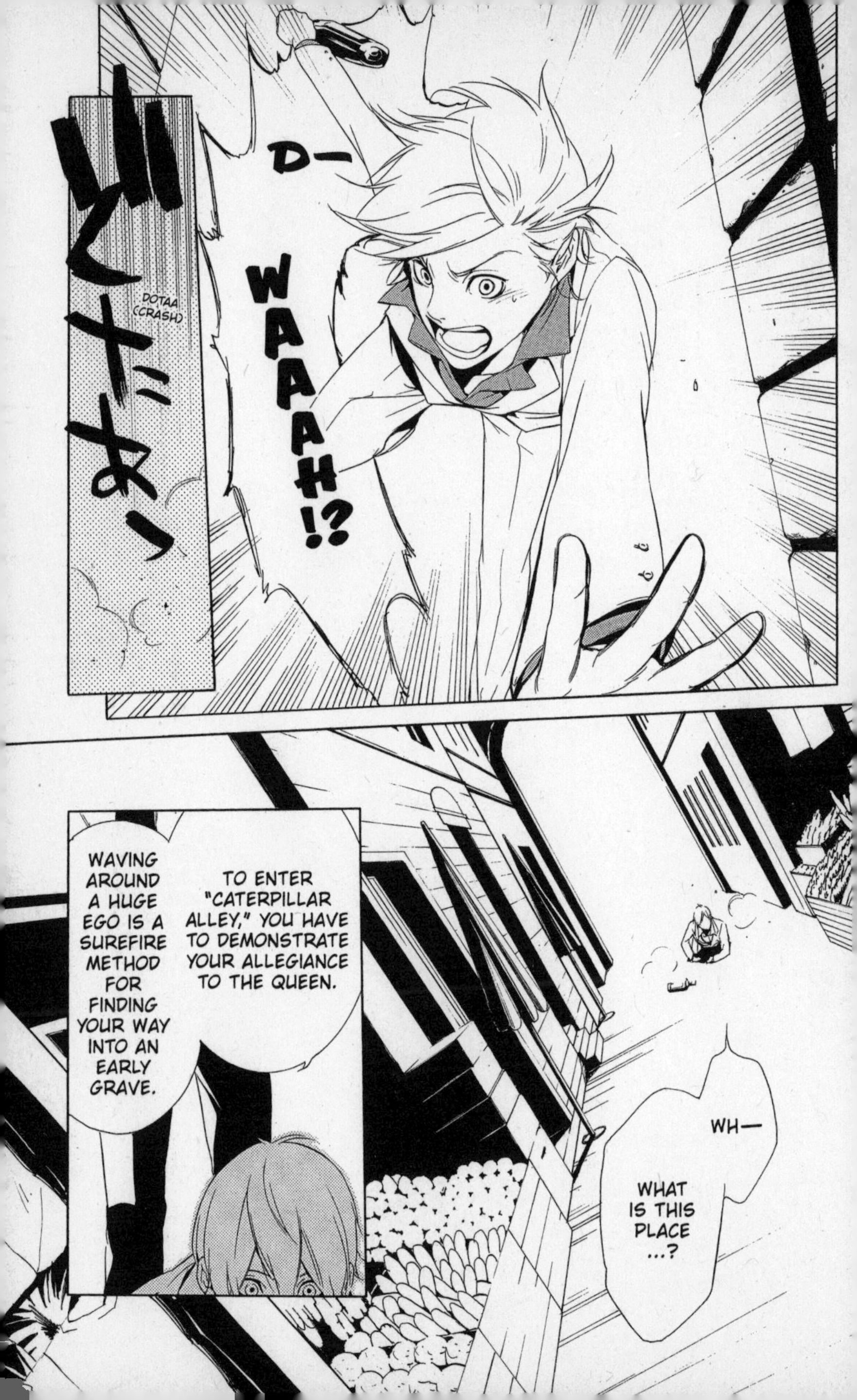
D—
WAAAH!?
どたぁっ
DOTAA (CRASH)
WH—
WHAT IS THIS PLACE ...?
TO ENTER "CATERPILLAR ALLEY," YOU HAVE TO DEMONSTRATE YOUR ALLEGIANCE TO THE QUEEN.
WAVING AROUND A HUGE EGO IS A SUREFIRE METHOD FOR FINDING YOUR WAY INTO AN EARLY GRAVE.

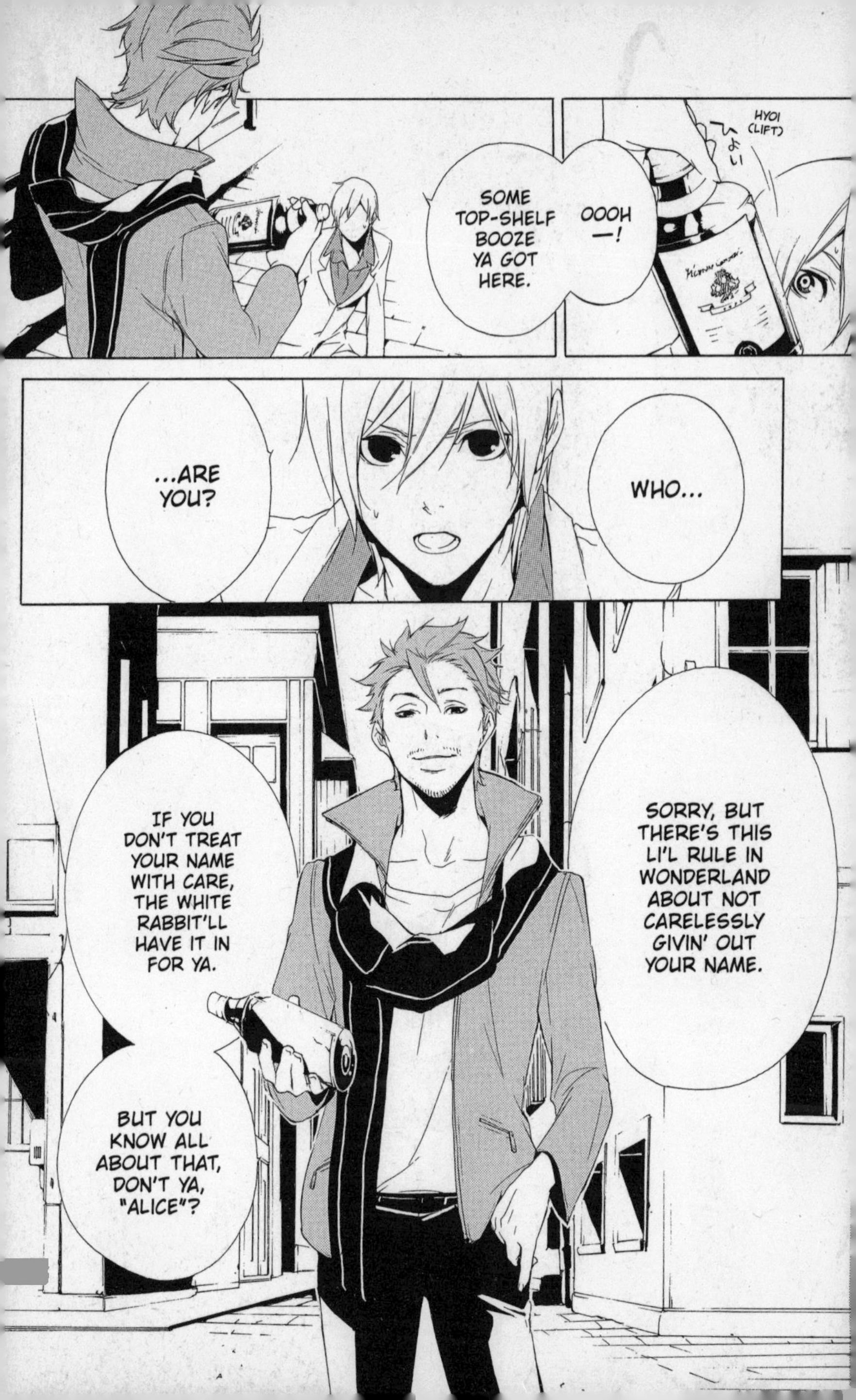
ひょい
HYOI (LIFT)
OOOH—!
SOME TOP-SHELF BOOZE YA GOT HERE.
WHO...
...ARE YOU?
SORRY, BUT THERE'S THIS LI'L RULE IN WONDERLAND ABOUT NOT CARELESSLY GIVIN' OUT YOUR NAME.
IF YOU DON'T TREAT YOUR NAME WITH CARE, THE WHITE RABBIT'LL HAVE IT IN FOR YA.
BUT YOU KNOW ALL ABOUT THAT, DON'T YA, "ALICE"?

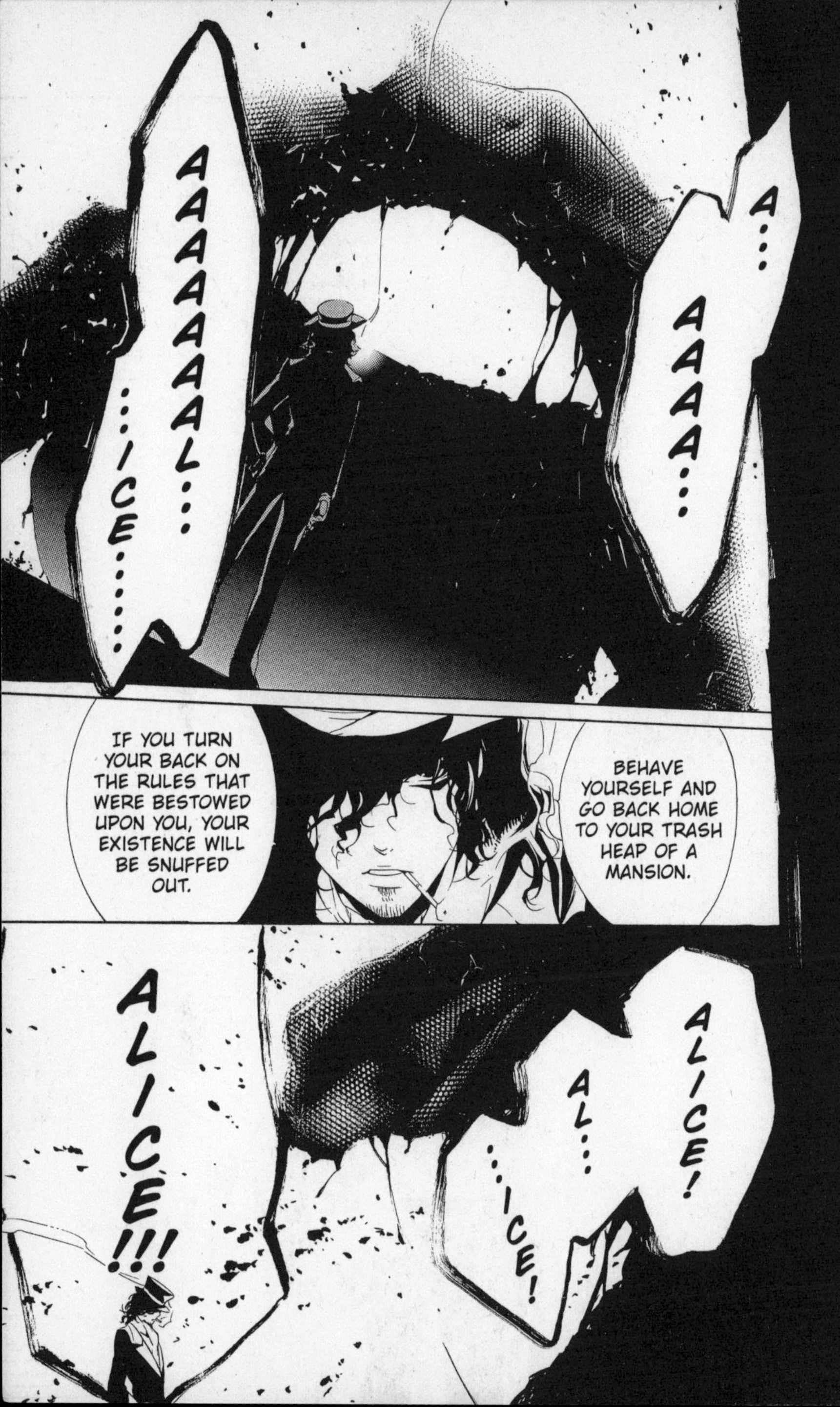
A... AAAA...
AAAAAAAL... ...ICE......
BEHAVE YOURSELF AND GO BACK HOME TO YOUR TRASH HEAP OF A MANSION.
IF YOU TURN YOUR BACK ON THE RULES THAT WERE BESTOWED UPON YOU, YOUR EXISTENCE WILL BE SNUFFED OUT.
ALICE!
AL... ...ICE!
ALICE!!!

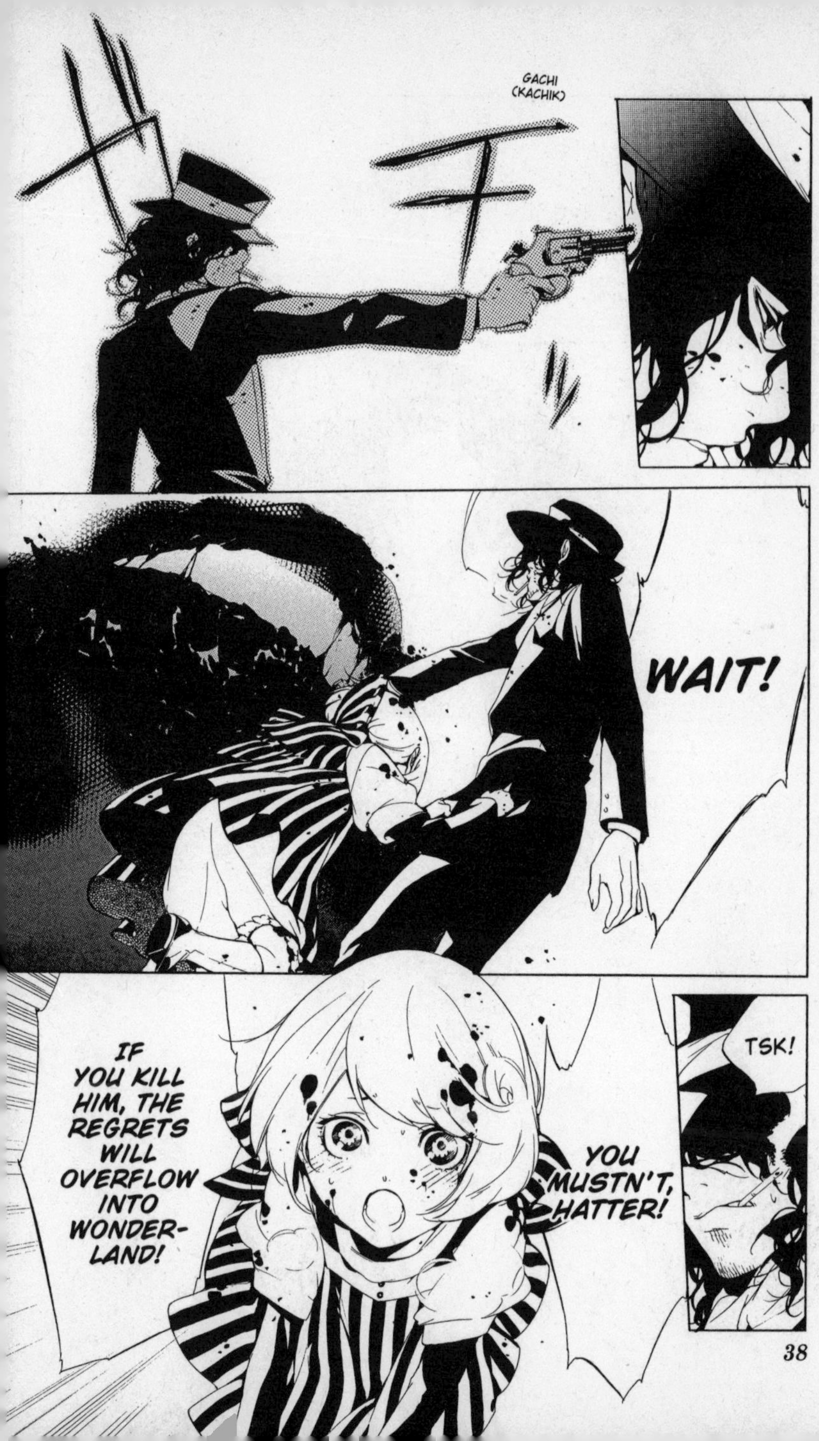
GACHI (KACHIK)
WAIT!
TSK!
YOU MUSTN'T, HATTER!
IF YOU KILL HIM, THE REGRETS WILL OVERFLOW INTO WONDER-LAND!

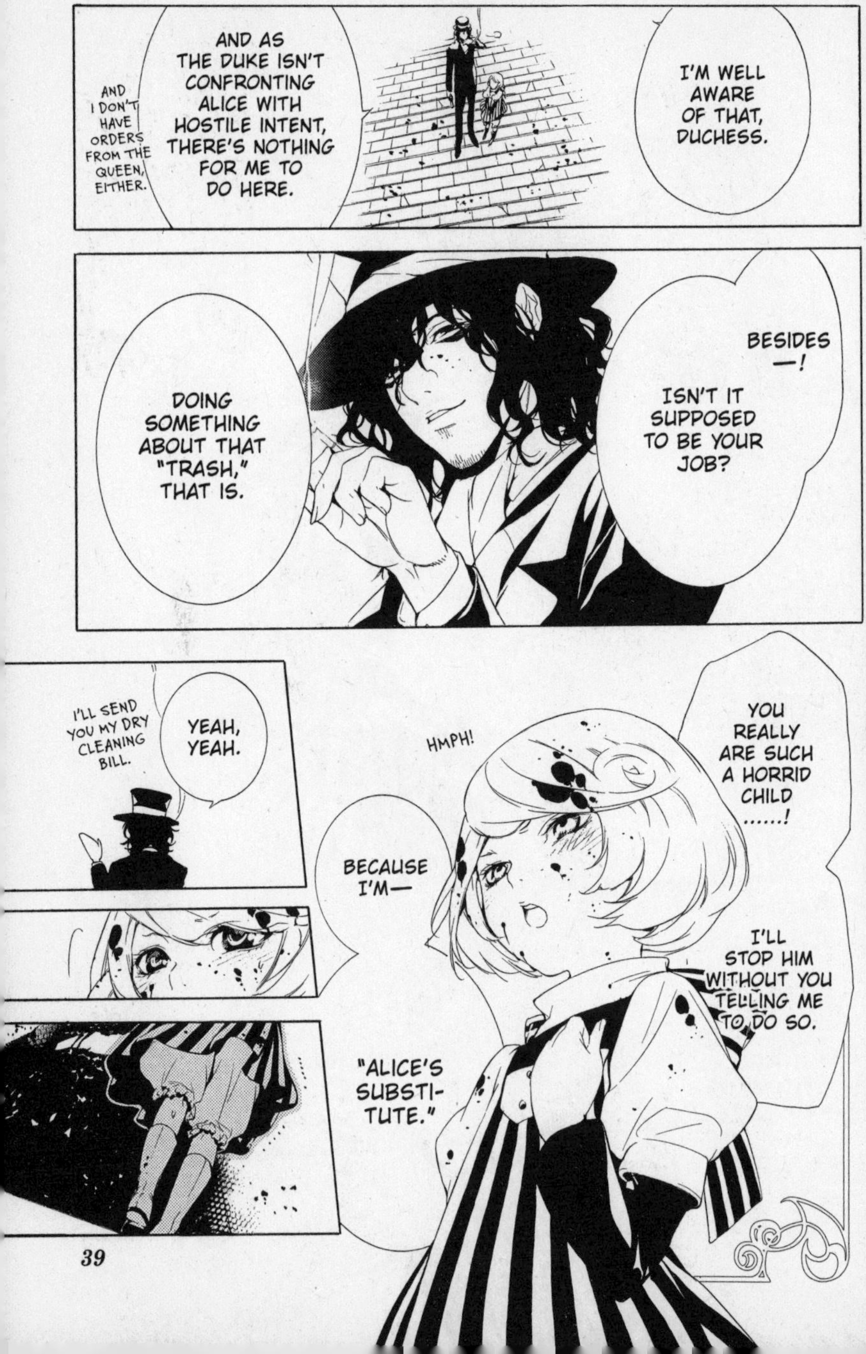
I'M WELL AWARE OF THAT, DUCHESS.
AND AS THE DUKE ISN'T CONFRONTING ALICE WITH HOSTILE INTENT, THERE'S NOTHING FOR ME TO DO HERE.
AND I DON'T HAVE ORDERS FROM THE QUEEN, EITHER.
BESIDES—!
ISN'T IT SUPPOSED TO BE YOUR JOB?
DOING SOMETHING ABOUT THAT "TRASH," THAT IS.
YOU REALLY ARE SUCH A HORRID CHILD......!
HMPH!
I'LL STOP HIM WITHOUT YOU TELLING ME TO DO SO.
BECAUSE I'M—
"ALICE'S SUBSTITUTE."
YEAH, YEAH.
I'LL SEND YOU MY DRY CLEANING BILL.

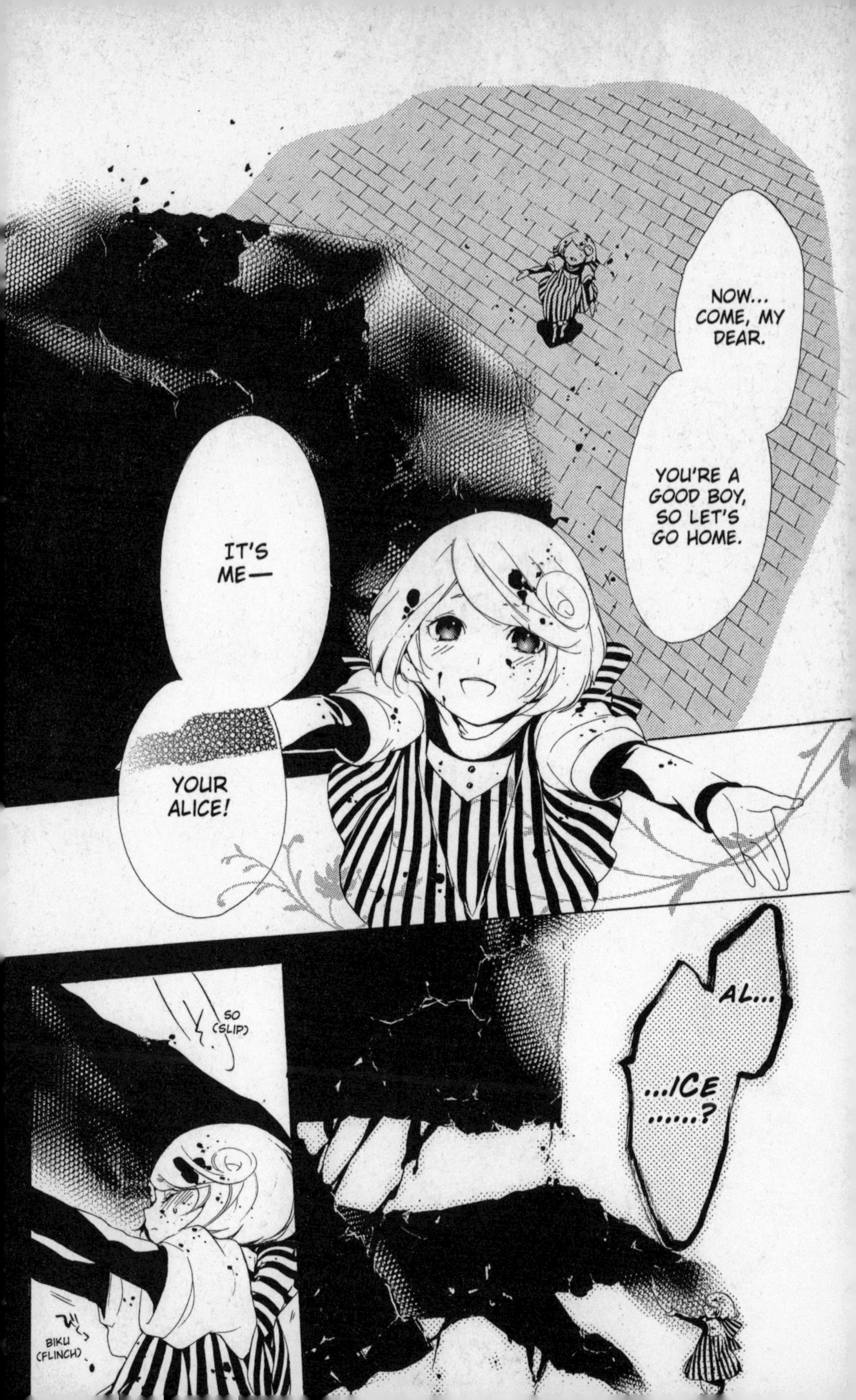
NOW... COME, MY DEAR.
YOU'RE A GOOD BOY, SO LET'S GO HOME.
IT'S ME—
YOUR ALICE!
AL...
...ICE ......?
SO (SLIP)
BIKU (FLINCH)

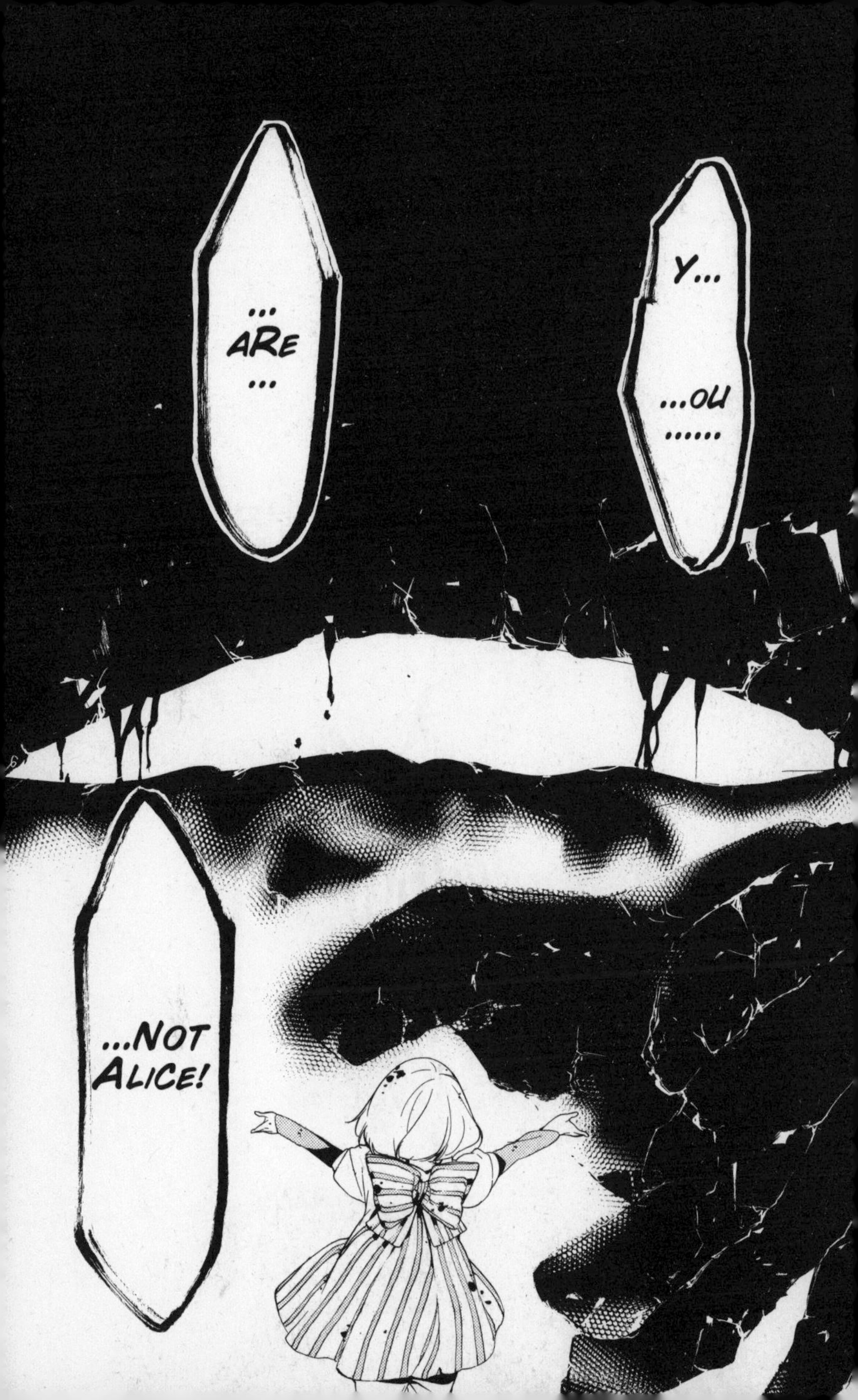
Y... ...ou ......
... ARe ...
...NOT ALICE!

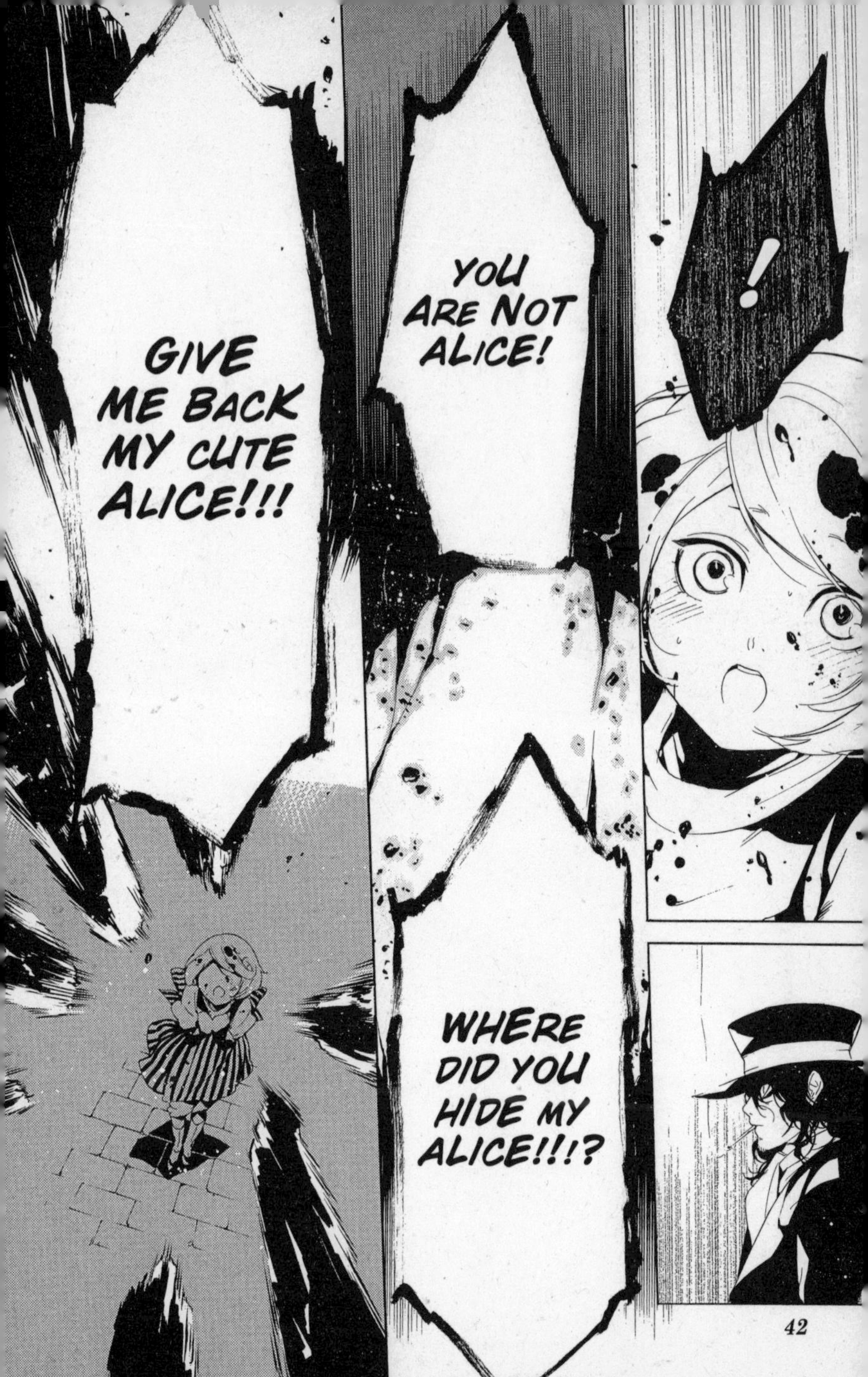
!
YOU ARE NOT ALICE!
WHERE DID YOU HIDE MY ALICE!!!?
GIVE ME BACK MY CUTE ALICE!!!

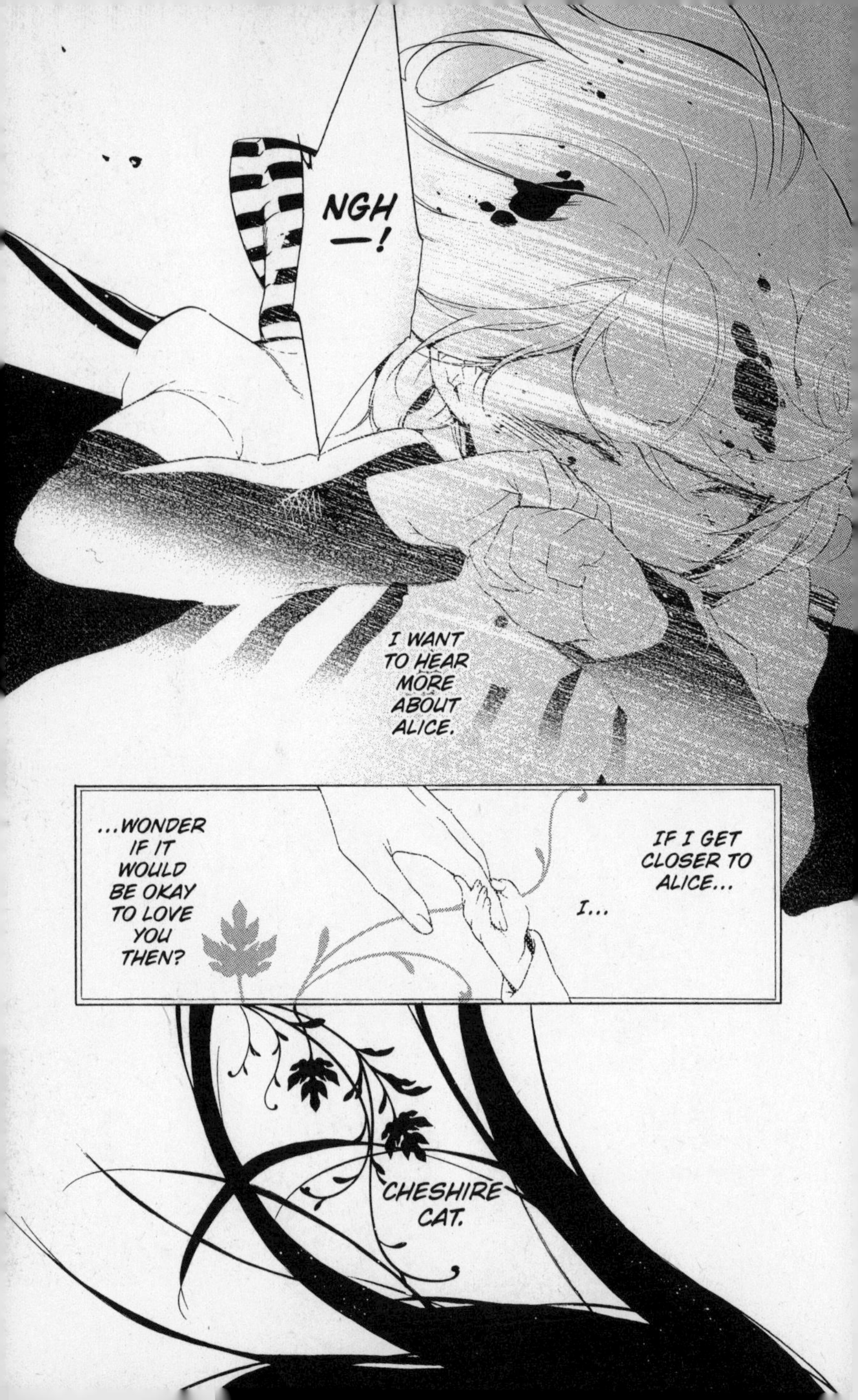
NGH—!
I WANT TO HEAR MORE ABOUT ALICE.
IF I GET CLOSER TO ALICE...
I...
...WONDER IF IT WOULD BE OKAY TO LOVE YOU THEN?
CHESHIRE CAT.

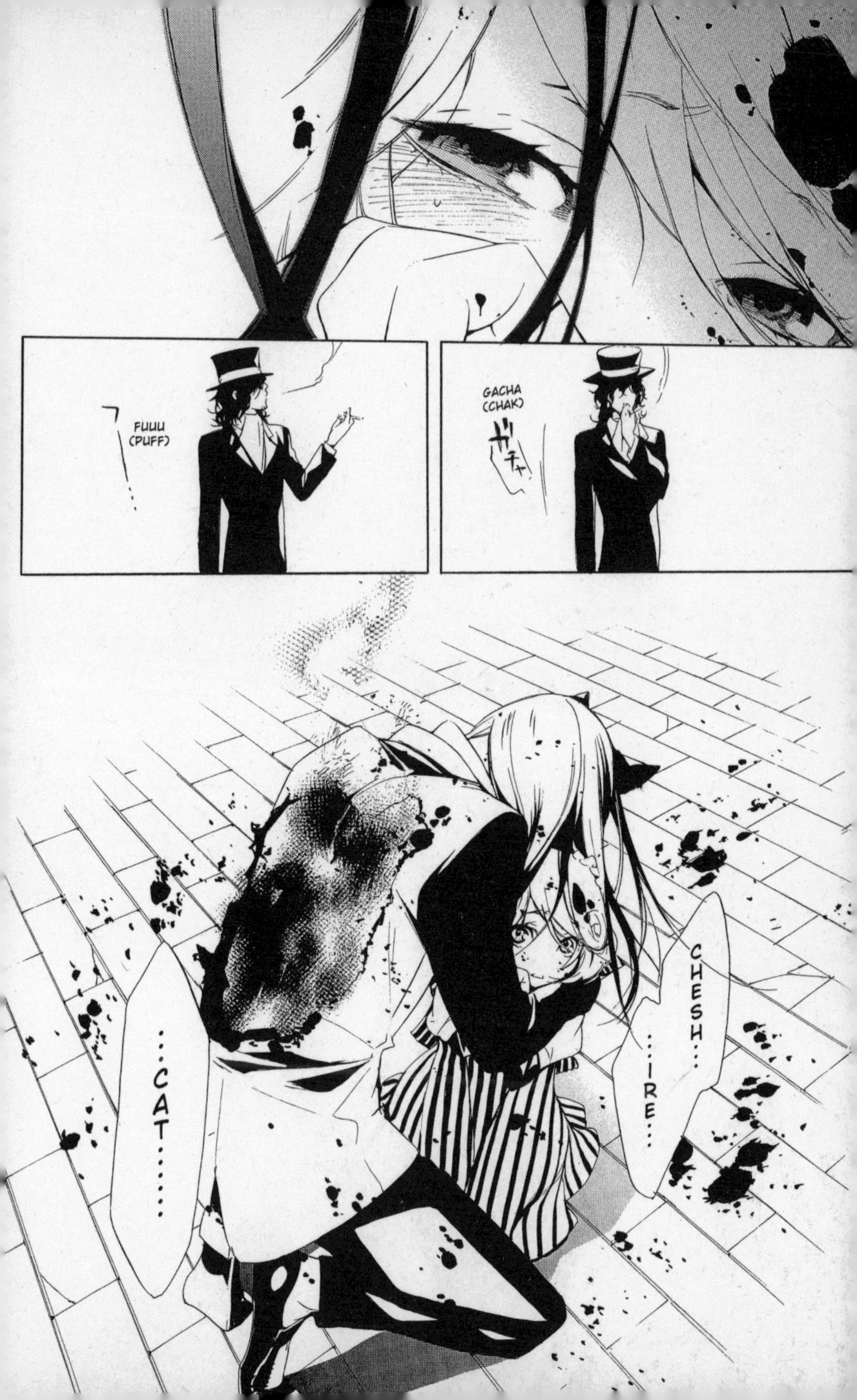
GACHA (CHAK)
ガチャ
FUUU (PUFF)
...
CHESH... ...IRE...
...CAT.....

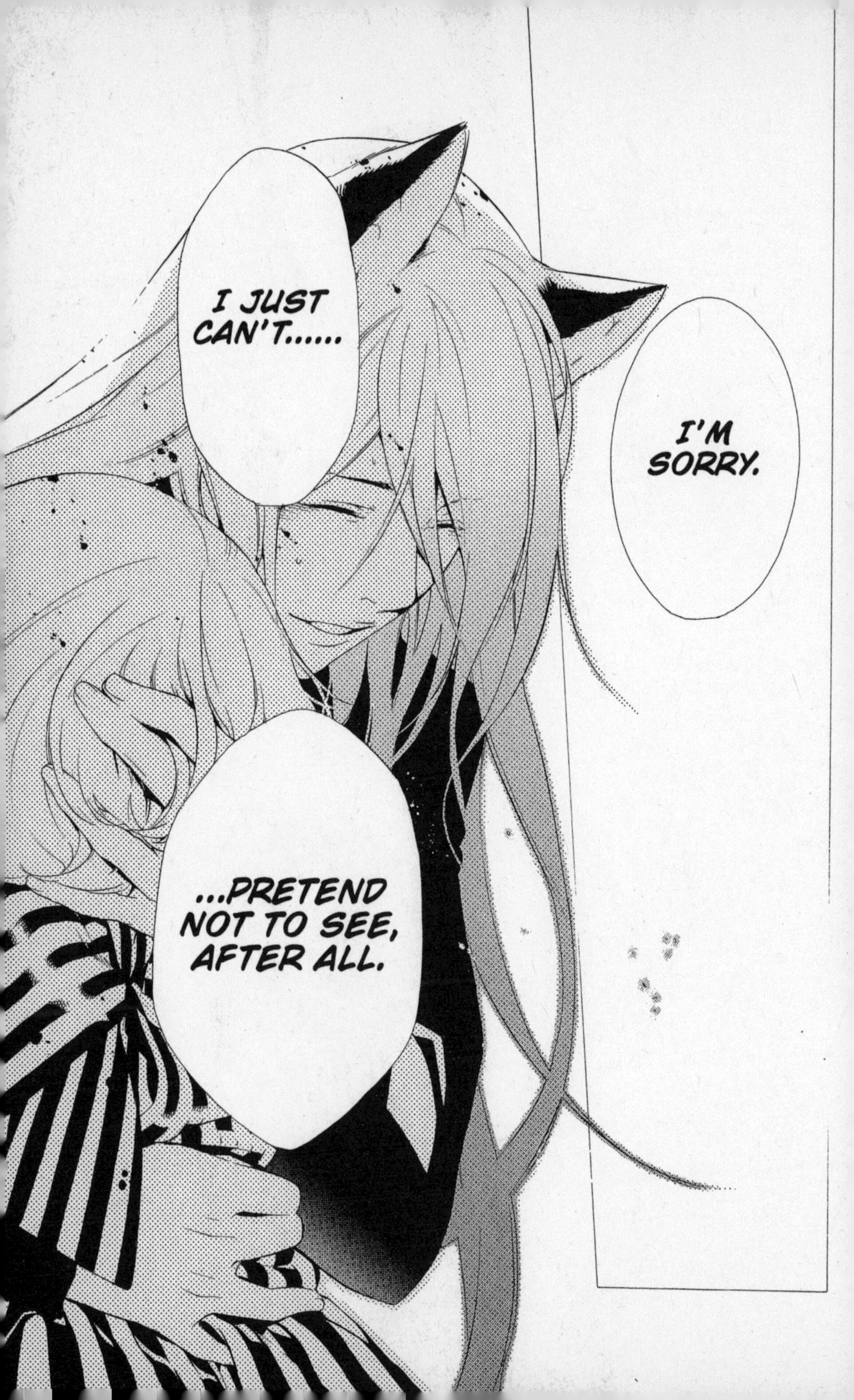
I'M SORRY.
I JUST CAN'T......
...PRETEND NOT TO SEE, AFTER ALL.

Chapter 7
Advice from a Caterpillar.

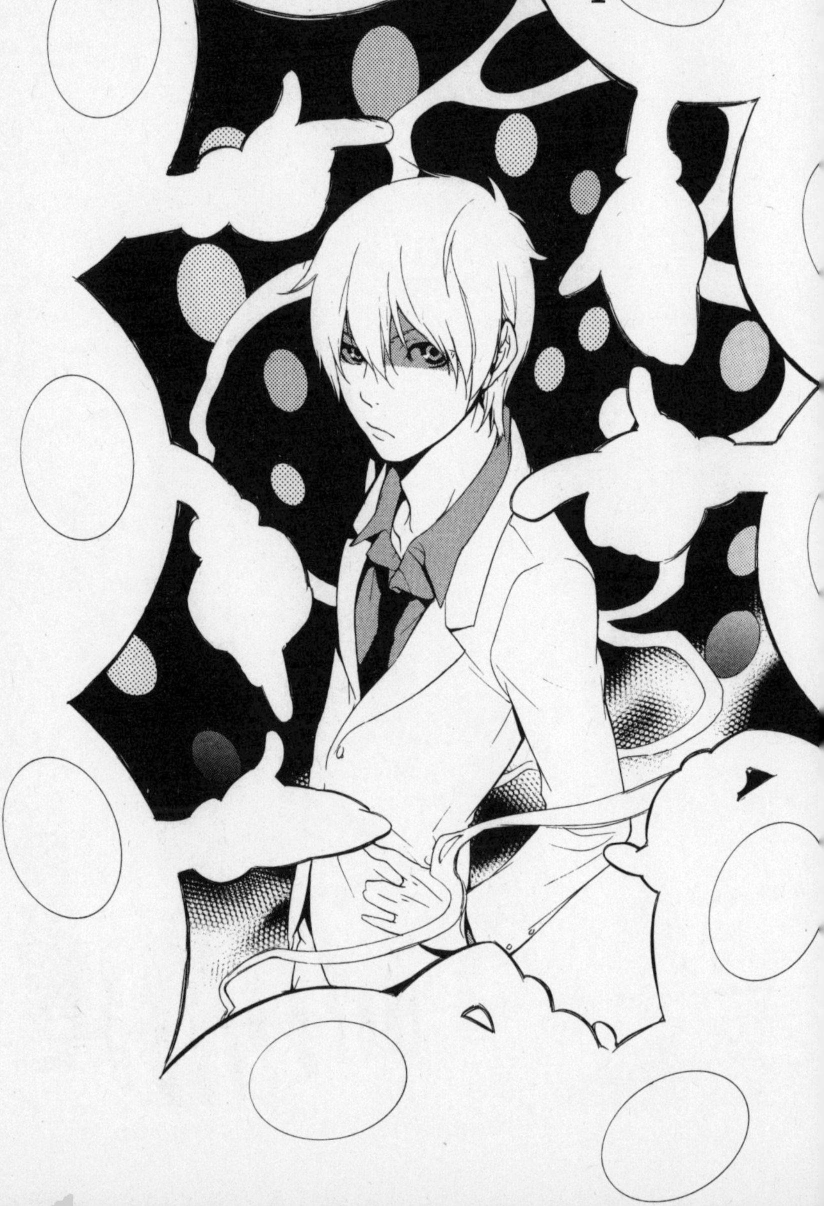

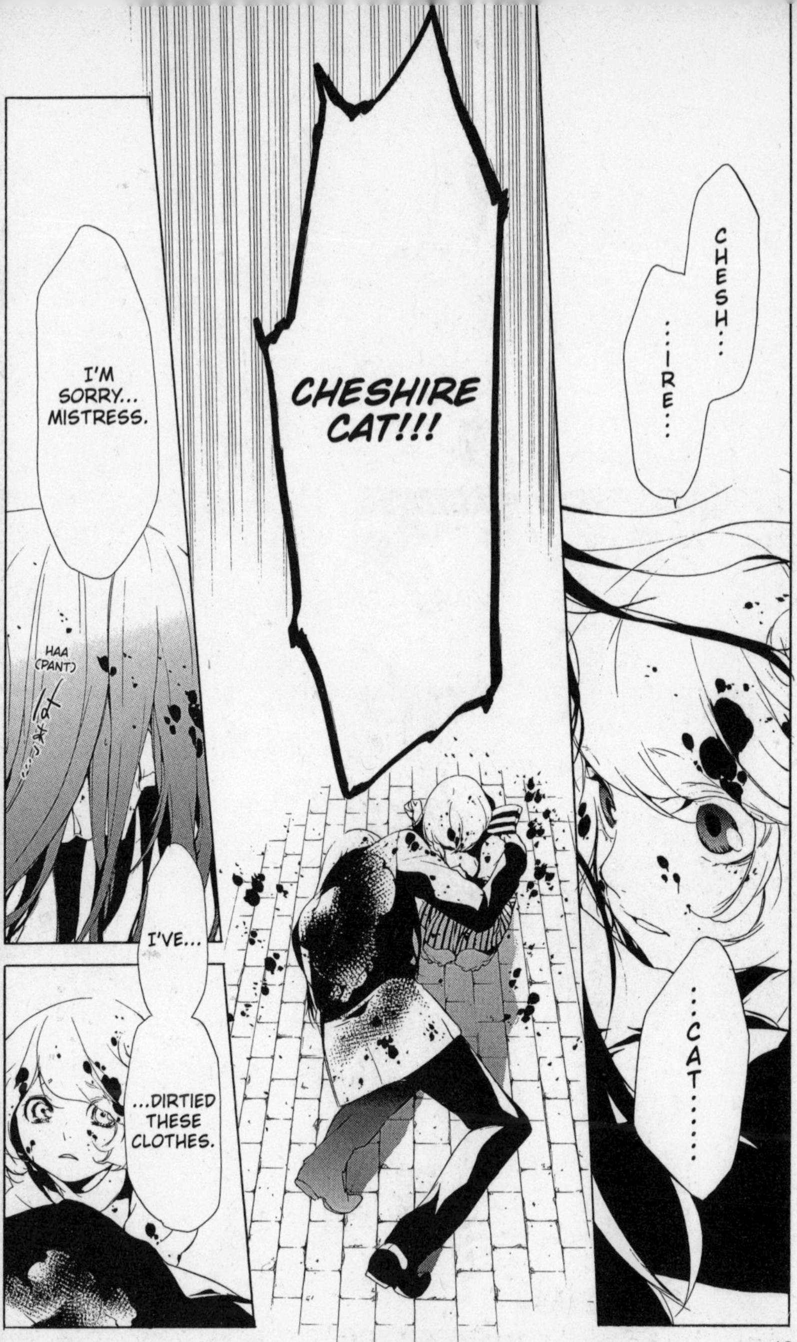
CHESH... ...IRE...
...CAT......
CHESHIRE CAT!!!
I'M SORRY... MISTRESS.
HAA (PANT)
I'VE...
...DIRTIED THESE CLOTHES.

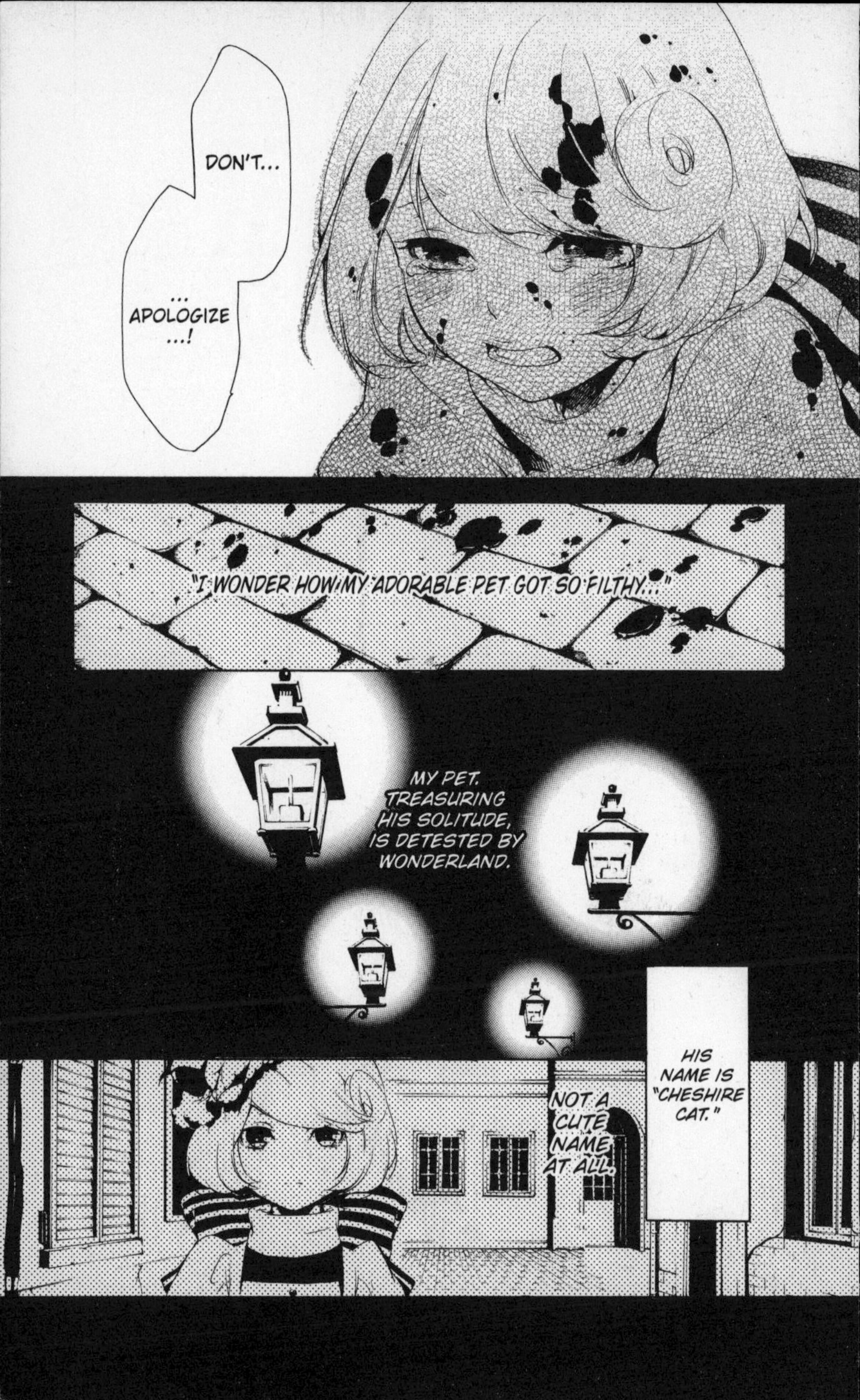
DON'T...
...APOLOGIZE...!
"I WONDER HOW MY ADORABLE PET GOT SO FILTHY..."
MY PET, TREASURING HIS SOLITUDE, IS DETESTED BY WONDERLAND.
HIS NAME IS "CHESHIRE CAT."
NOT A CUTE NAME AT ALL.

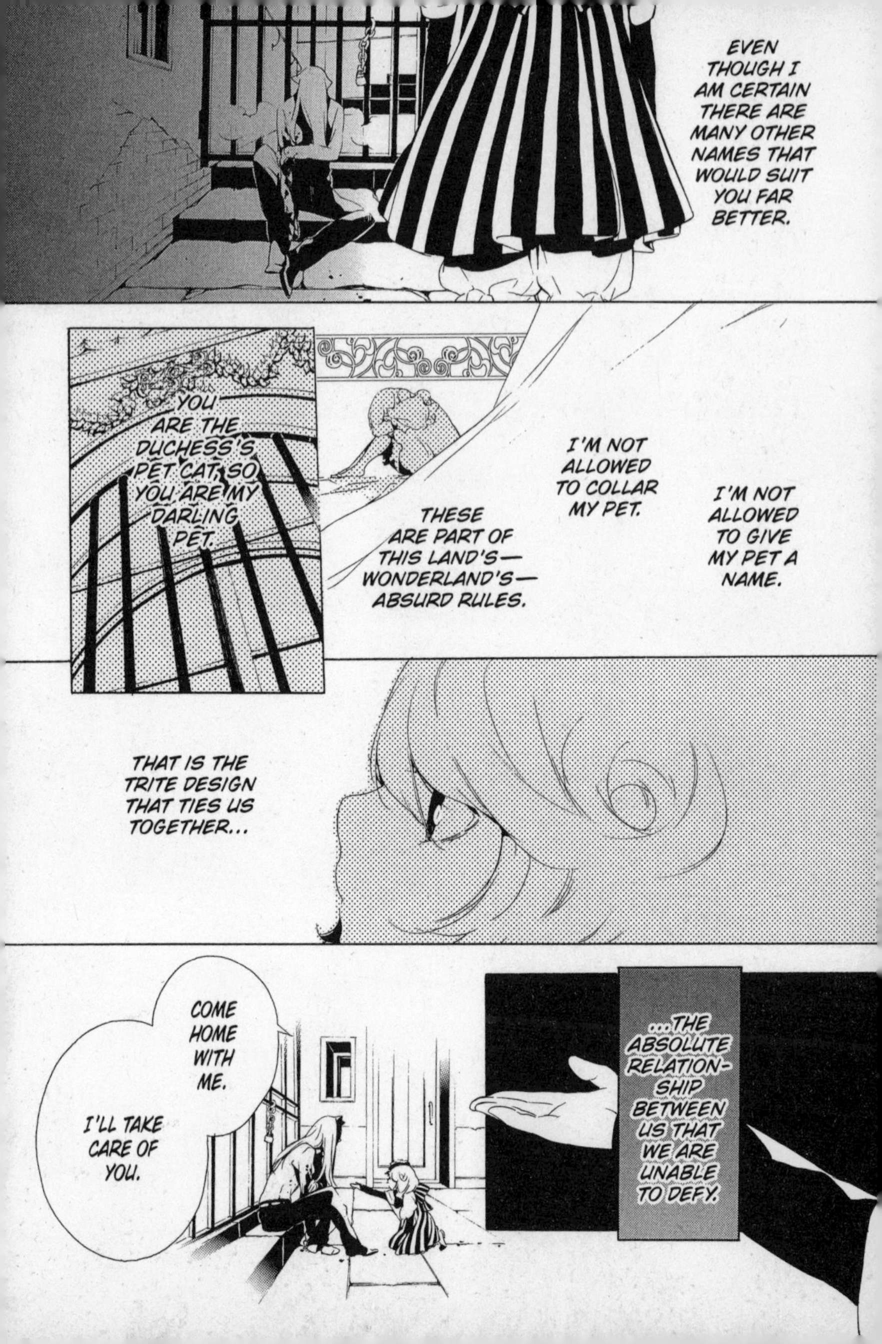
EVEN THOUGH I AM CERTAIN THERE ARE MANY OTHER NAMES THAT WOULD SUIT YOU FAR BETTER.
I'M NOT ALLOWED TO GIVE MY PET A NAME.
I'M NOT ALLOWED TO COLLAR MY PET.
THESE ARE PART OF THIS LAND'S—WONDERLAND'S—ABSURD RULES.
YOU ARE THE DUCHESS'S PET CAT, SO YOU ARE MY DARLING PET.
THAT IS THE TRITE DESIGN THAT TIES US TOGETHER...
...THE ABSOLUTE RELATION-SHIP BETWEEN US THAT WE ARE UNABLE TO DEFY.
COME HOME WITH ME.
I'LL TAKE CARE OF YOU.

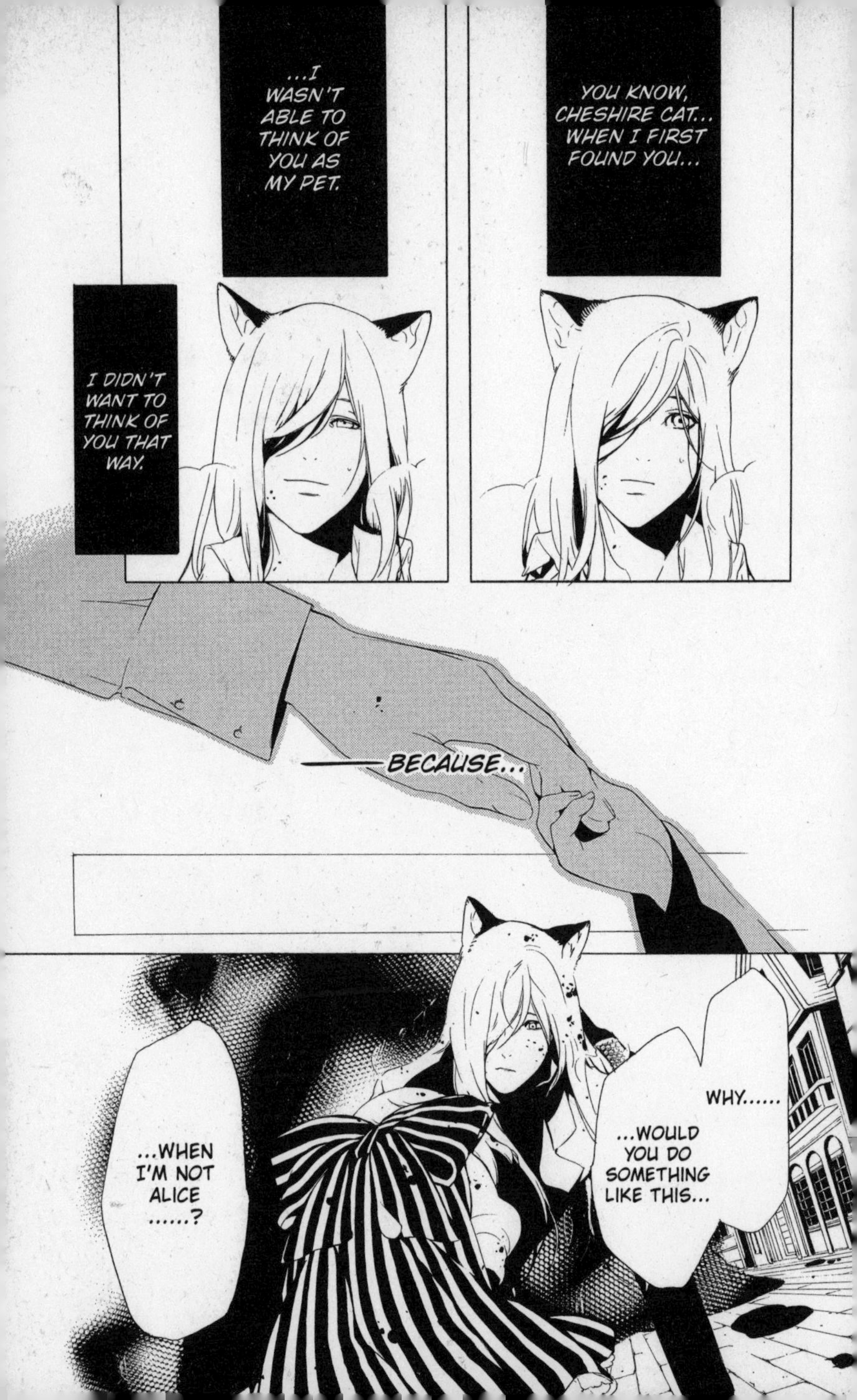
YOU KNOW, CHESHIRE CAT... WHEN I FIRST FOUND YOU...
...I WASN'T ABLE TO THINK OF YOU AS MY PET.
I DIDN'T WANT TO THINK OF YOU THAT WAY.
——BECAUSE...
WHY......
...WOULD YOU DO SOMETHING LIKE THIS...
...WHEN I'M NOT ALICE ......?

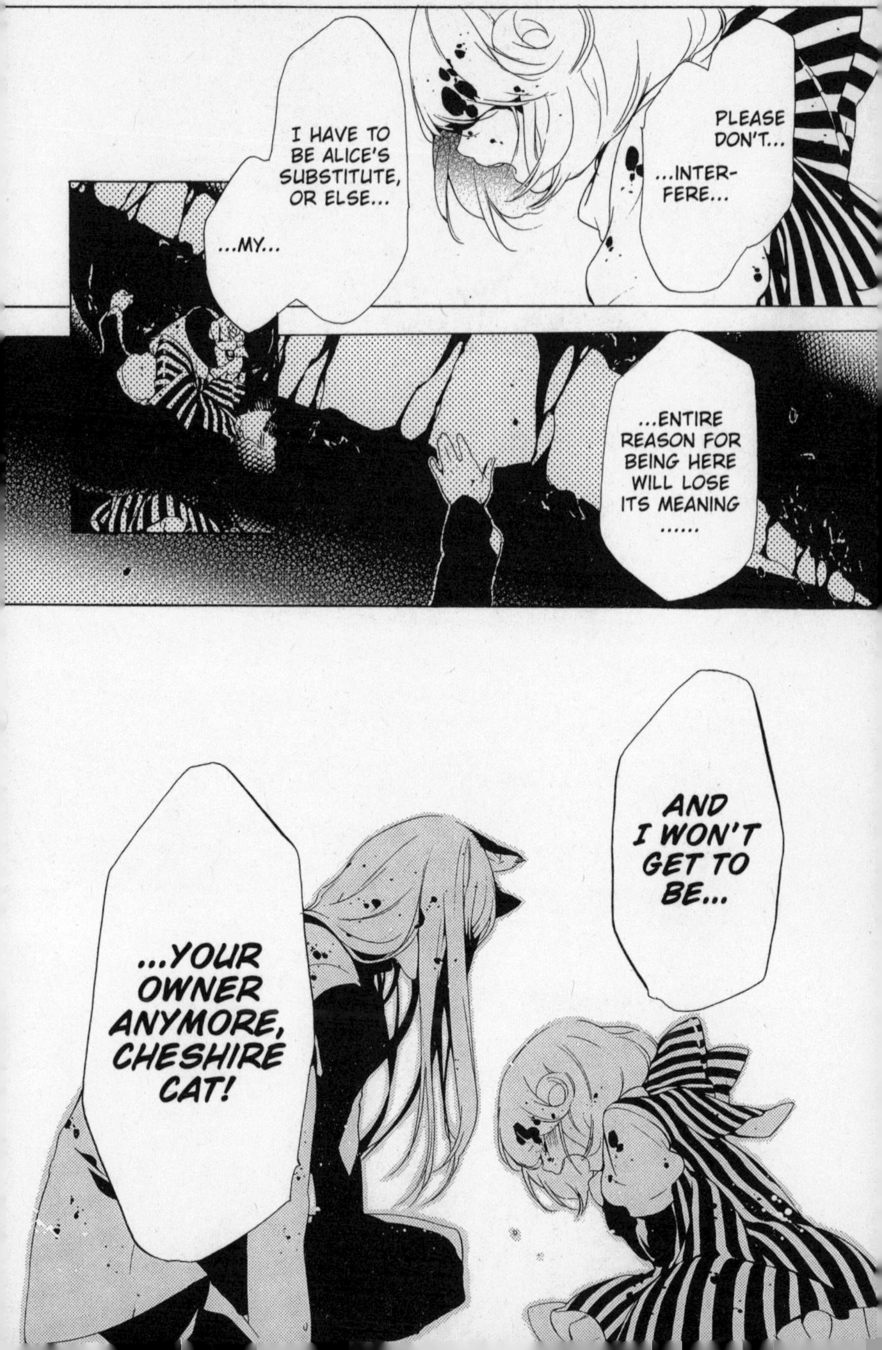
PLEASE DON'T...
...INTER-FERE...
I HAVE TO BE ALICE'S SUBSTITUTE, OR ELSE...
...MY...
...ENTIRE REASON FOR BEING HERE WILL LOSE ITS MEANING ......
AND I WON'T GET TO BE...
...YOUR OWNER ANYMORE, CHESHIRE CAT!

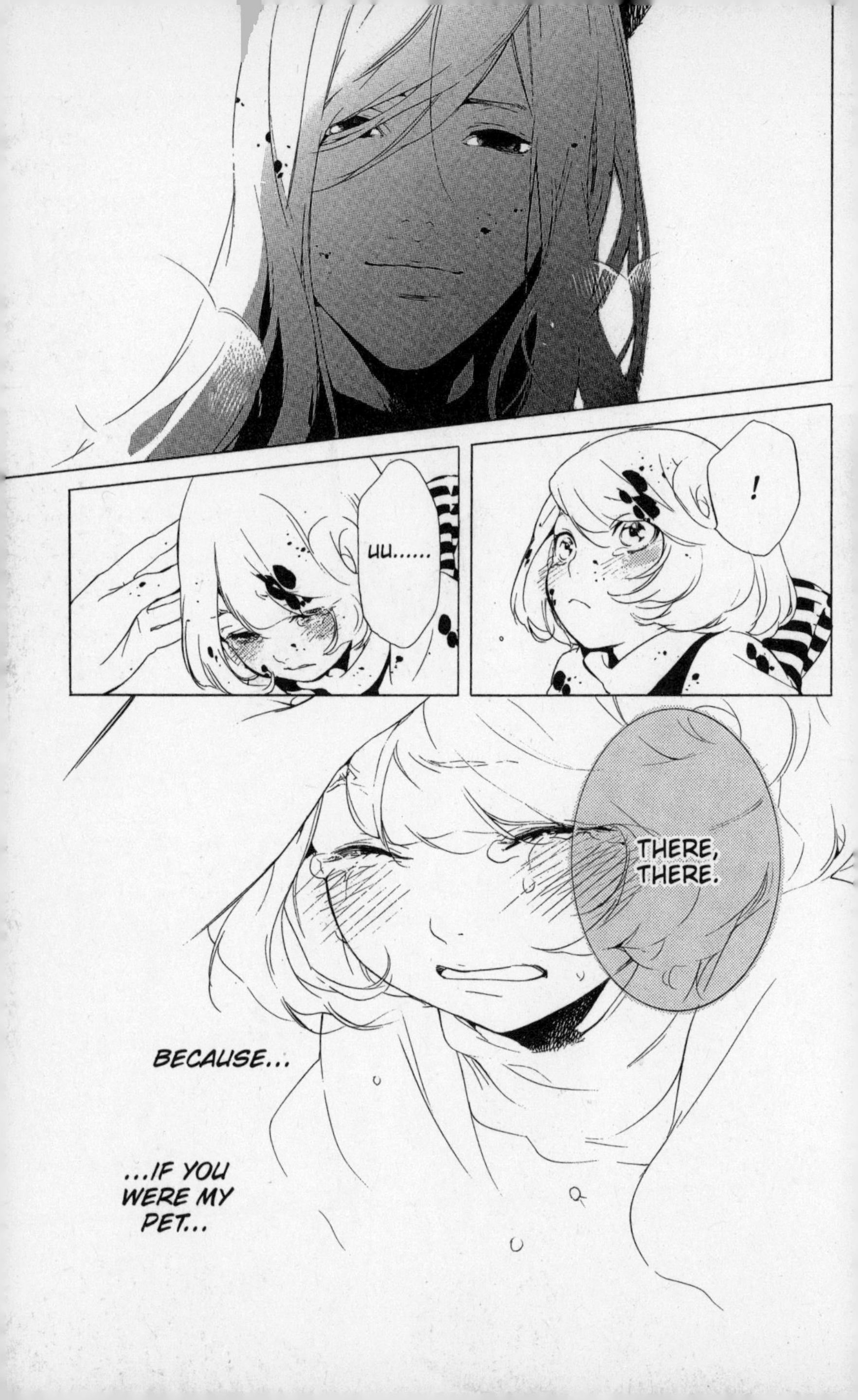
!
uu......
THERE, THERE.
BECAUSE...
...IF YOU WERE MY PET...

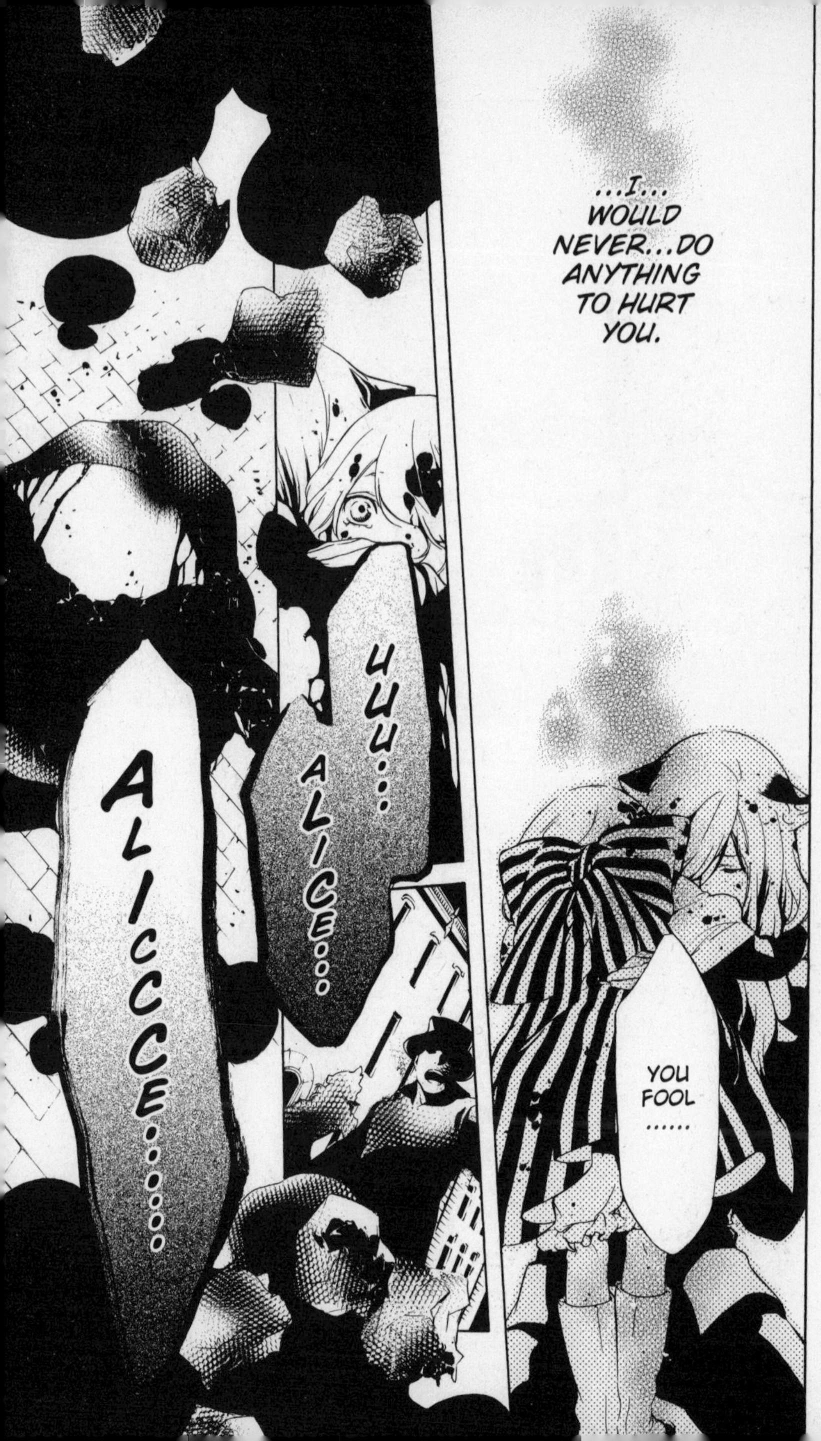
...I... WOULD NEVER...DO ANYTHING TO HURT YOU.
YOU FOOL ......
UUU... ALICE...
ALICCCE......

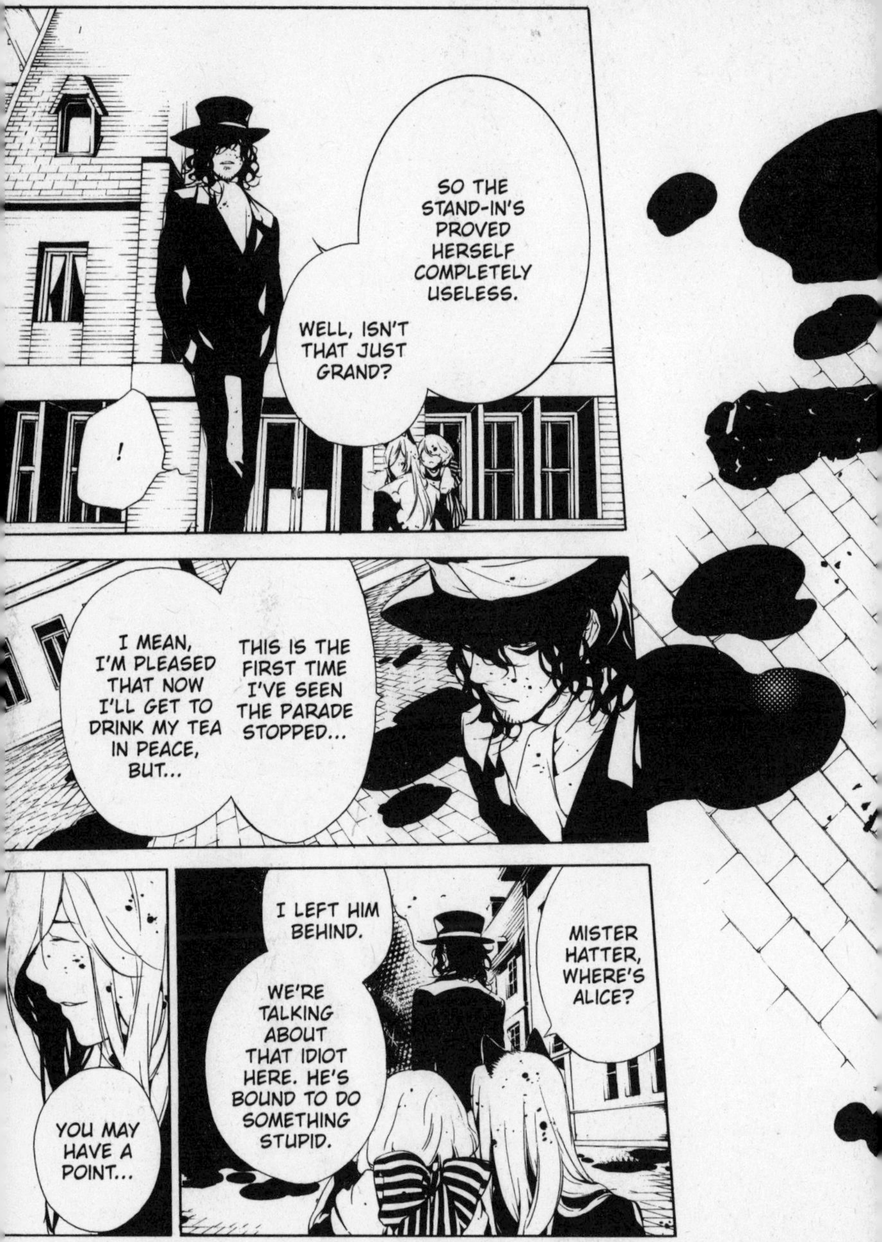
SO THE STAND-IN'S PROVED HERSELF COMPLETELY USELESS.
WELL, ISN'T THAT JUST GRAND?
!
THIS IS THE FIRST TIME I'VE SEEN THE PARADE STOPPED...
I MEAN, I'M PLEASED THAT NOW I'LL GET TO DRINK MY TEA IN PEACE, BUT...
MISTER HATTER, WHERE'S ALICE?
I LEFT HIM BEHIND.
WE'RE TALKING ABOUT THAT IDIOT HERE. HE'S BOUND TO DO SOMETHING STUPID.
YOU MAY HAVE A POINT...

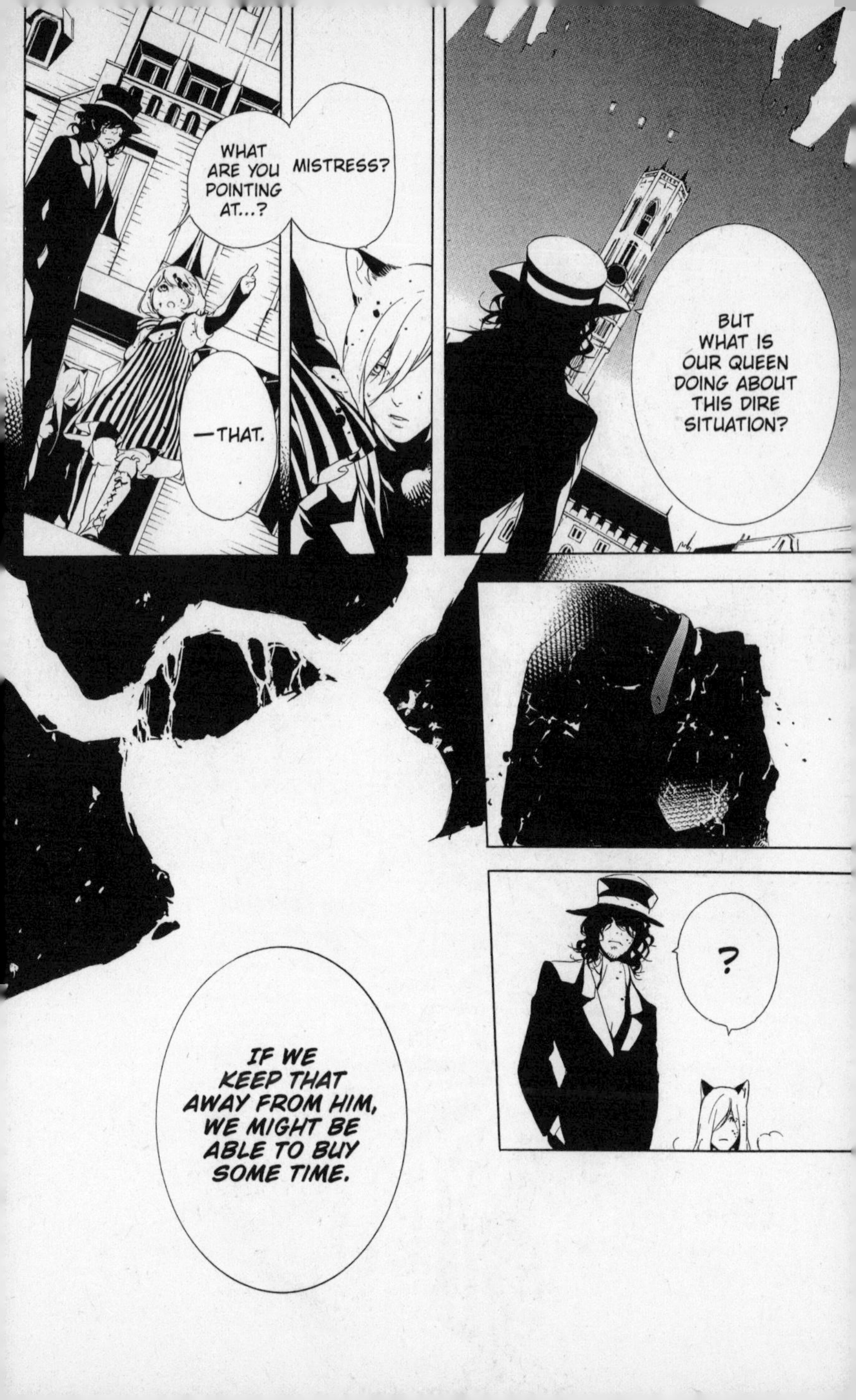
BUT WHAT IS OUR QUEEN DOING ABOUT THIS DIRE SITUATION?
MISTRESS?
WHAT ARE YOU POINTING AT...?
—THAT.
?
IF WE KEEP THAT AWAY FROM HIM, WE MIGHT BE ABLE TO BUY SOME TIME.

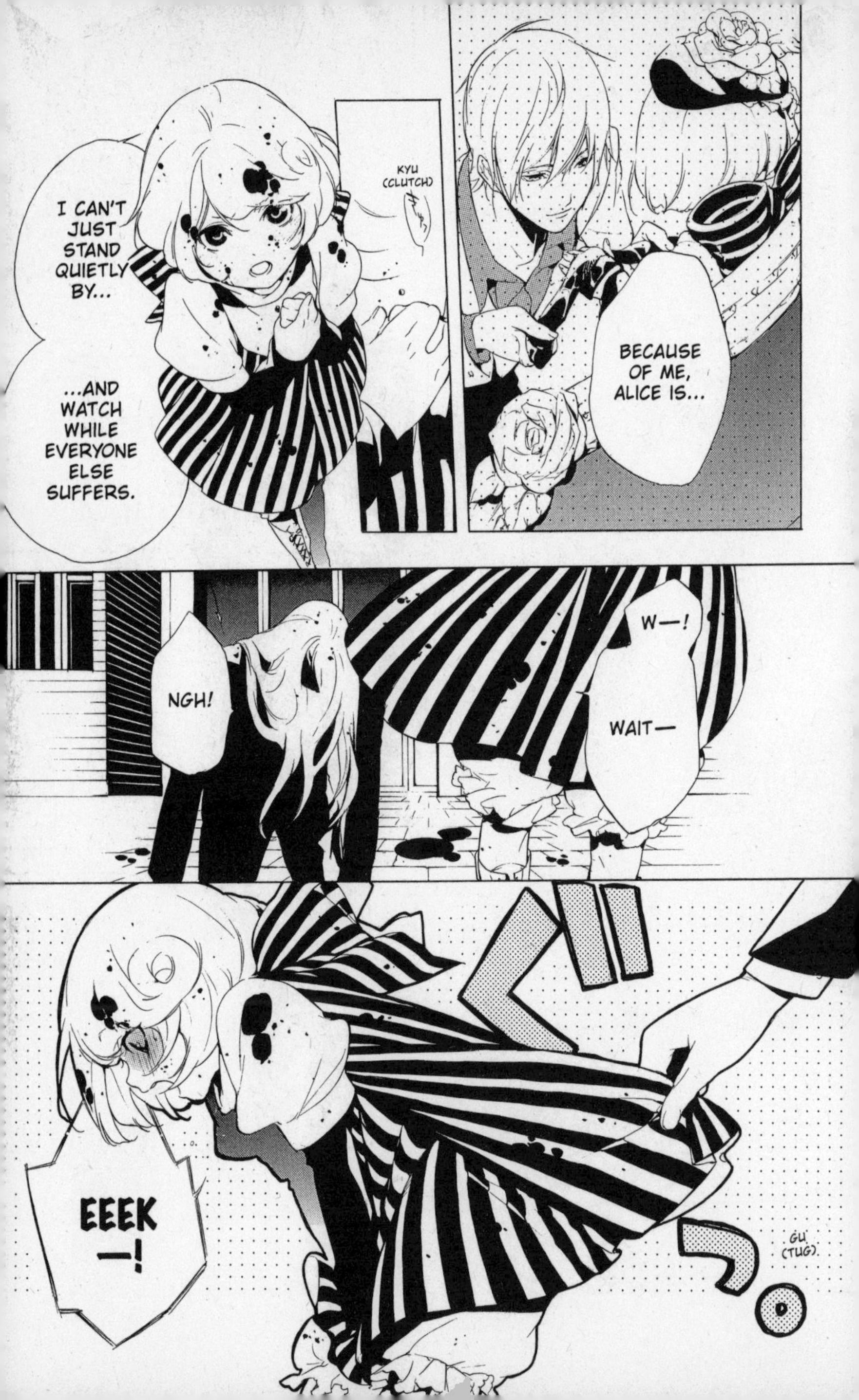
BECAUSE OF ME, ALICE IS...
KYU (CLUTCH)
I CAN'T JUST STAND QUIETLY BY...
...AND WATCH WHILE EVERYONE ELSE SUFFERS.
W—!
WAIT—
NGH!
GU (TUG).
EEEK—!

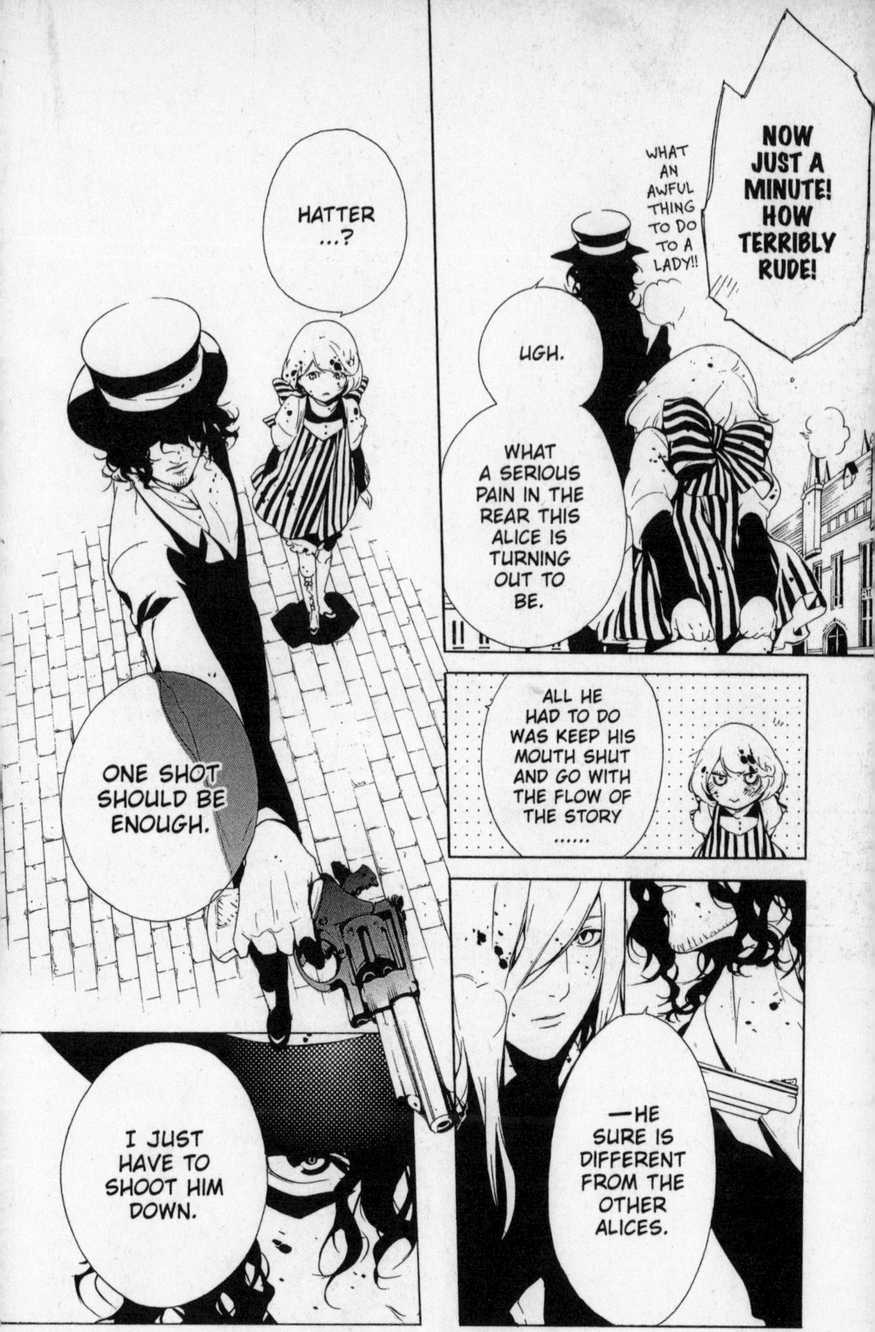
NOW JUST A MINUTE! HOW TERRIBLY RUDE!
WHAT AN AWFUL THING TO DO TO A LADY!!
UGH.
WHAT A SERIOUS PAIN IN THE REAR THIS ALICE IS TURNING OUT TO BE.
ALL HE HAD TO DO WAS KEEP HIS MOUTH SHUT AND GO WITH THE FLOW OF THE STORY ......
—HE SURE IS DIFFERENT FROM THE OTHER ALICES.
HATTER ...?
ONE SHOT SHOULD BE ENOUGH.
I JUST HAVE TO SHOOT HIM DOWN.

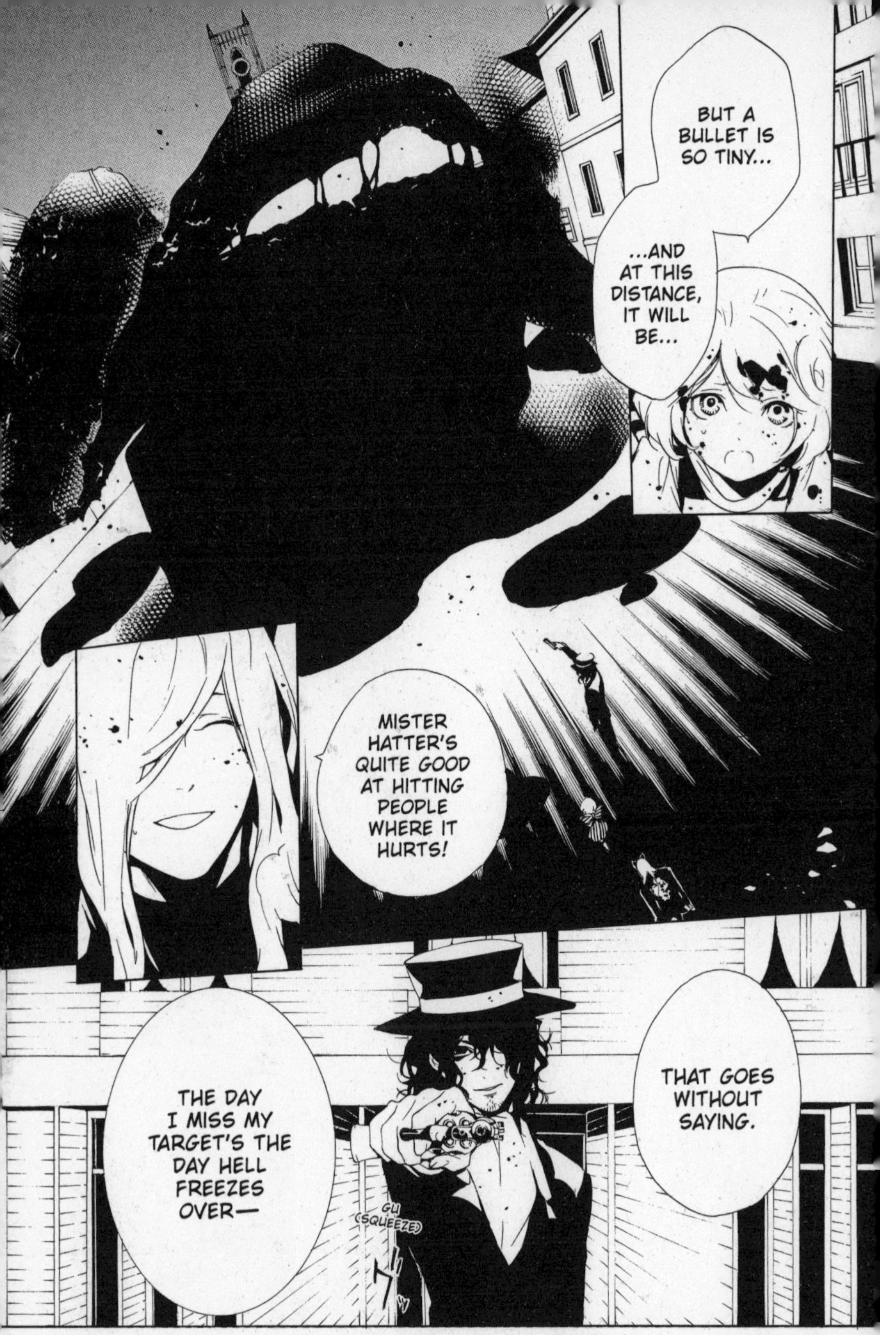
BUT A BULLET IS SO TINY...
...AND AT THIS DISTANCE, IT WILL BE...
MISTER HATTER'S QUITE GOOD AT HITTING PEOPLE WHERE IT HURTS!
THAT GOES WITHOUT SAYING.
THE DAY I MISS MY TARGET'S THE DAY HELL FREEZES OVER—
GU (SQUEEZE)

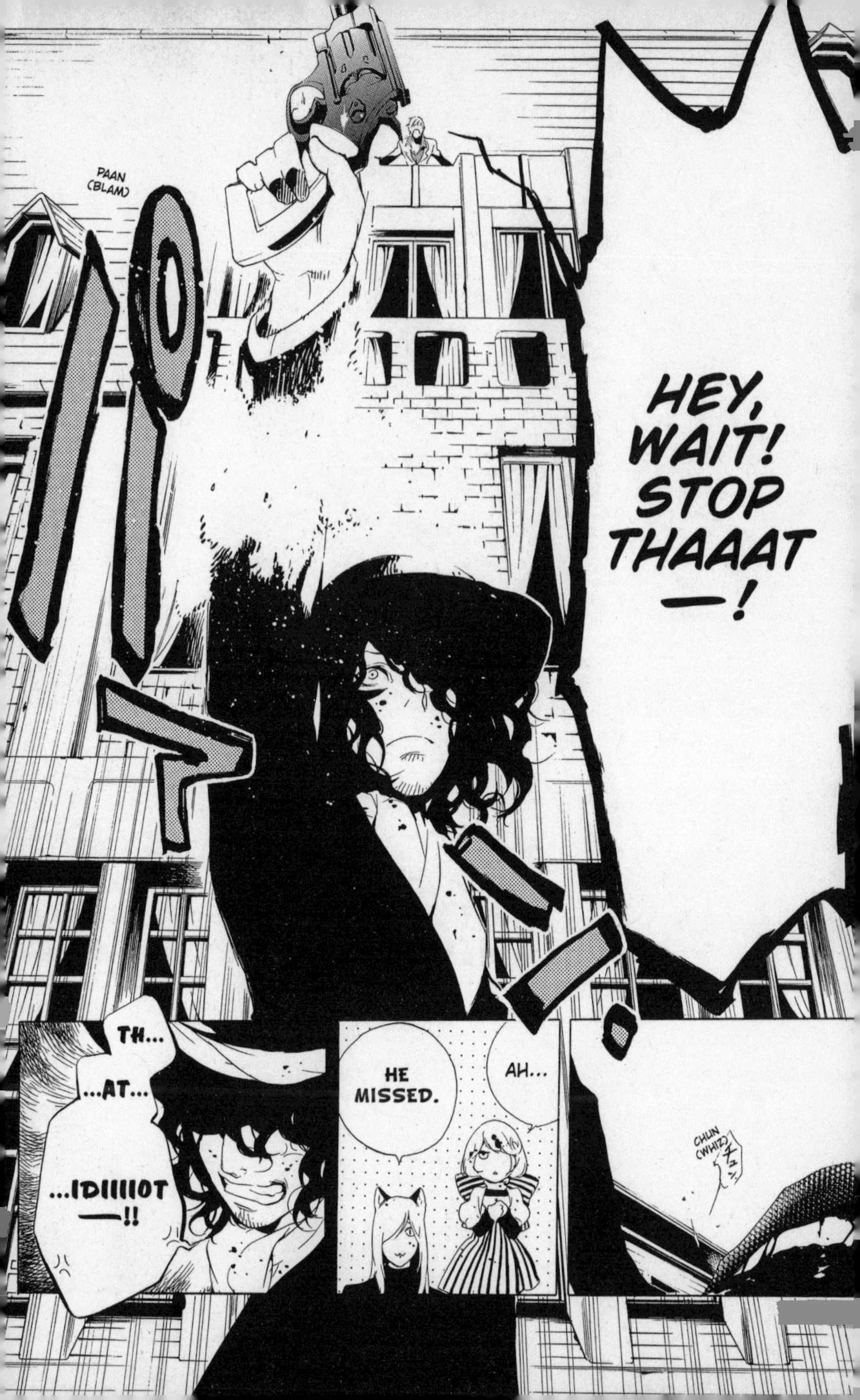
HEY, WAIT! STOP THAAAT—!
PAAN (BLAM)
CHUN (WHIZ)
AH...
HE MISSED.
TH...
...AT...
...IDIIIIOT—!!

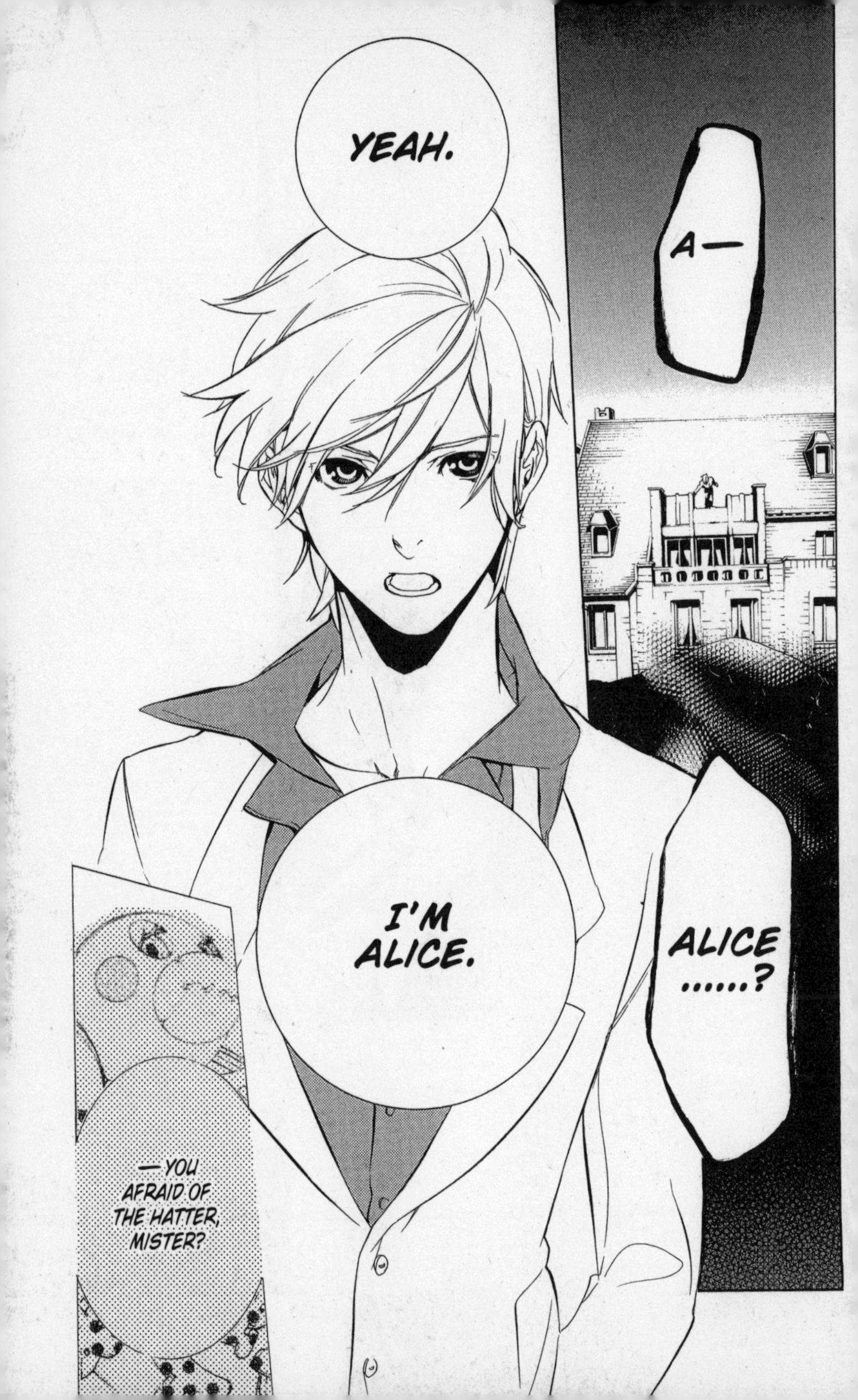
A—
ALICE ......?
YEAH.
I'M ALICE.
—YOU AFRAID OF THE HATTER, MISTER?

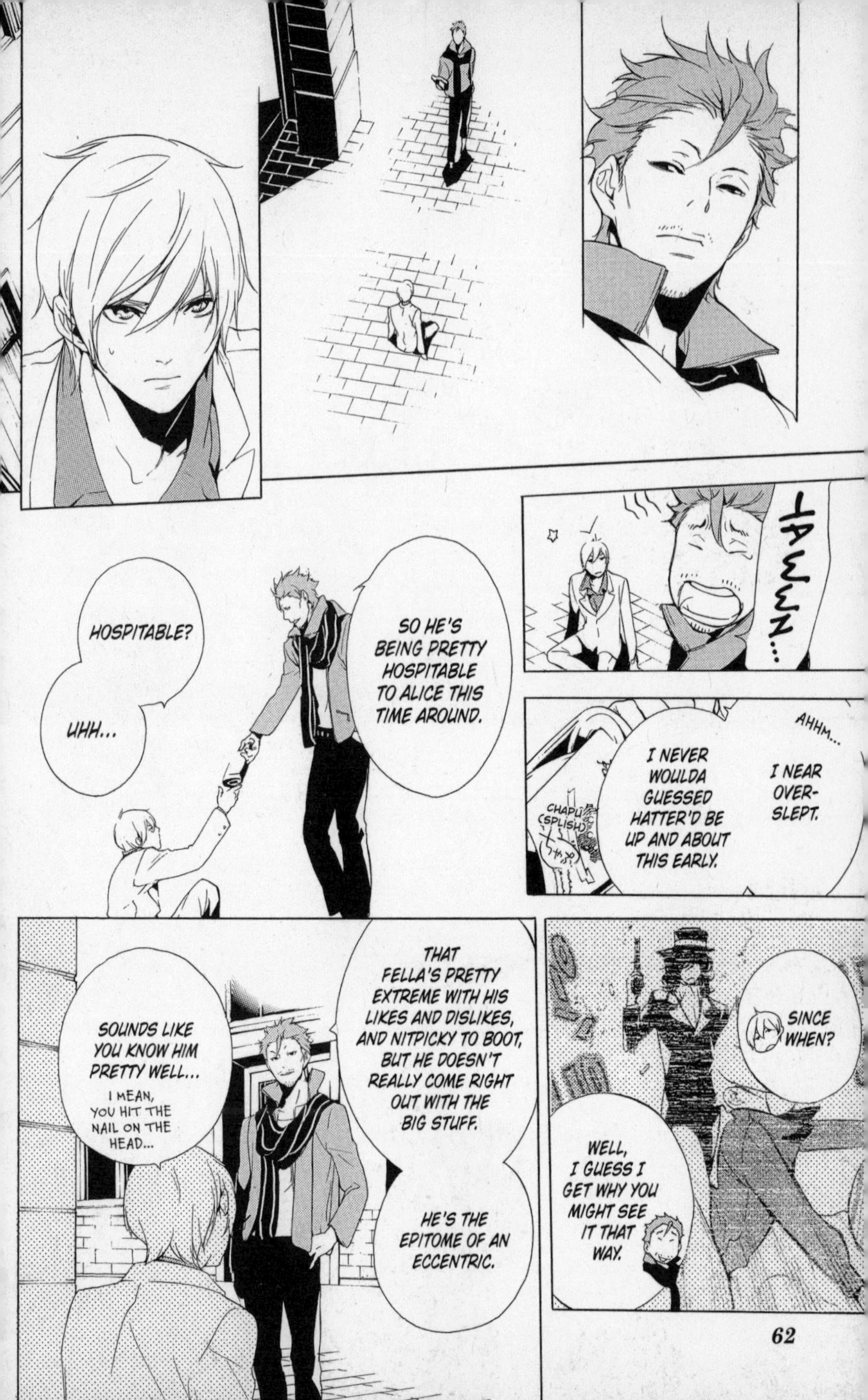
YAWWN...
AHHM...
I NEAR OVER-SLEPT.
I NEVER WOULDA GUESSED HATTER'D BE UP AND ABOUT THIS EARLY.
CHAPU (SPLISH)
SO HE'S BEING PRETTY HOSPITABLE TO ALICE THIS TIME AROUND.
HOSPITABLE?
UHH...
SINCE WHEN?
WELL, I GUESS I GET WHY YOU MIGHT SEE IT THAT WAY.
THAT FELLA'S PRETTY EXTREME WITH HIS LIKES AND DISLIKES, AND NITPICKY TO BOOT, BUT HE DOESN'T REALLY COME RIGHT OUT WITH THE BIG STUFF.
HE'S THE EPITOME OF AN ECCENTRIC.
SOUNDS LIKE YOU KNOW HIM PRETTY WELL...
I MEAN, YOU HIT THE NAIL ON THE HEAD...

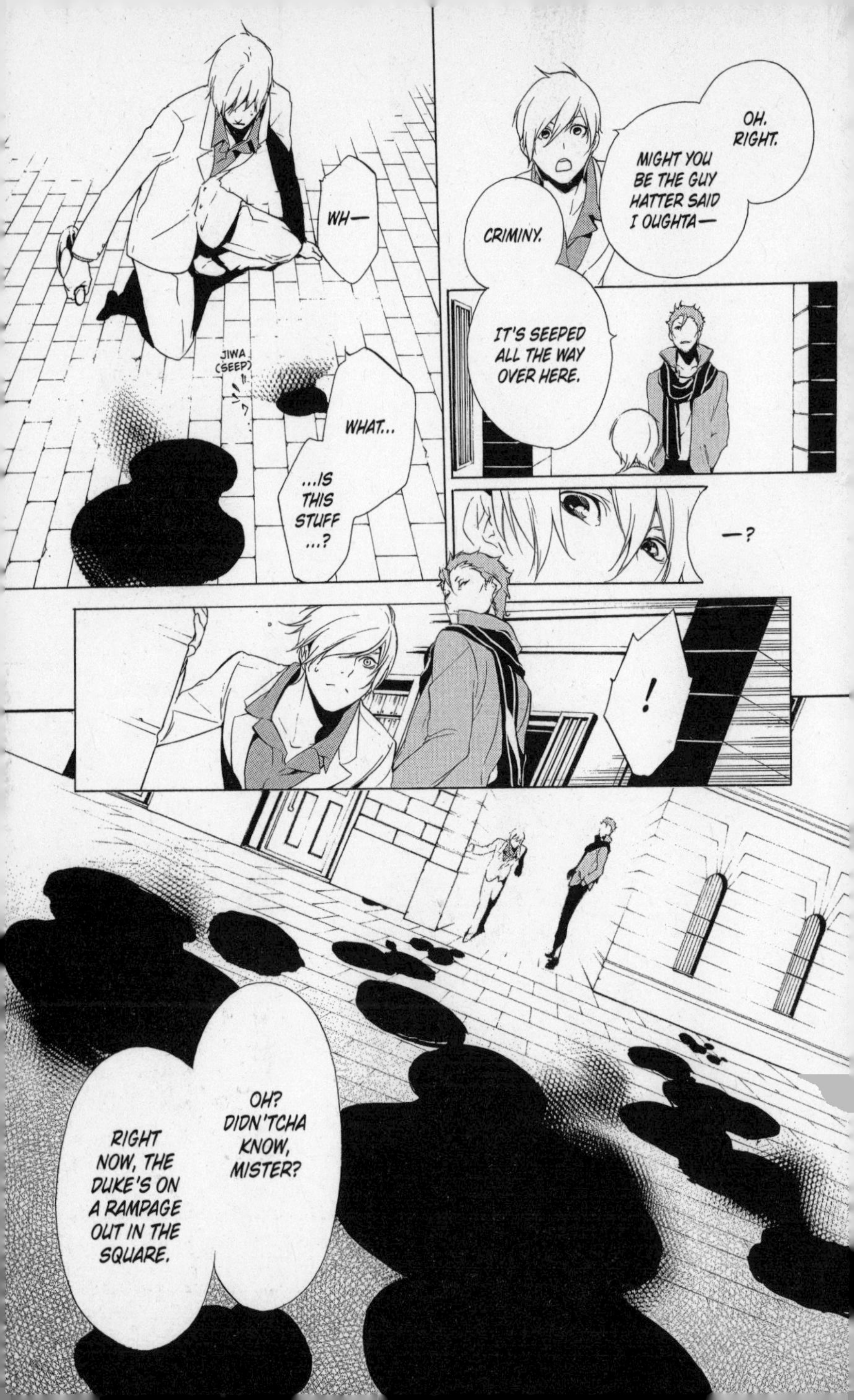
OH. RIGHT.
MIGHT YOU BE THE GUY HATTER SAID I OUGHTA—
CRIMINY.
IT'S SEEPED ALL THE WAY OVER HERE.
—?
WH—
JIWA (SEEP)
WHAT...
...IS THIS STUFF ...?
!
OH? DIDN'TCHA KNOW, MISTER?
RIGHT NOW, THE DUKE'S ON A RAMPAGE OUT IN THE SQUARE.

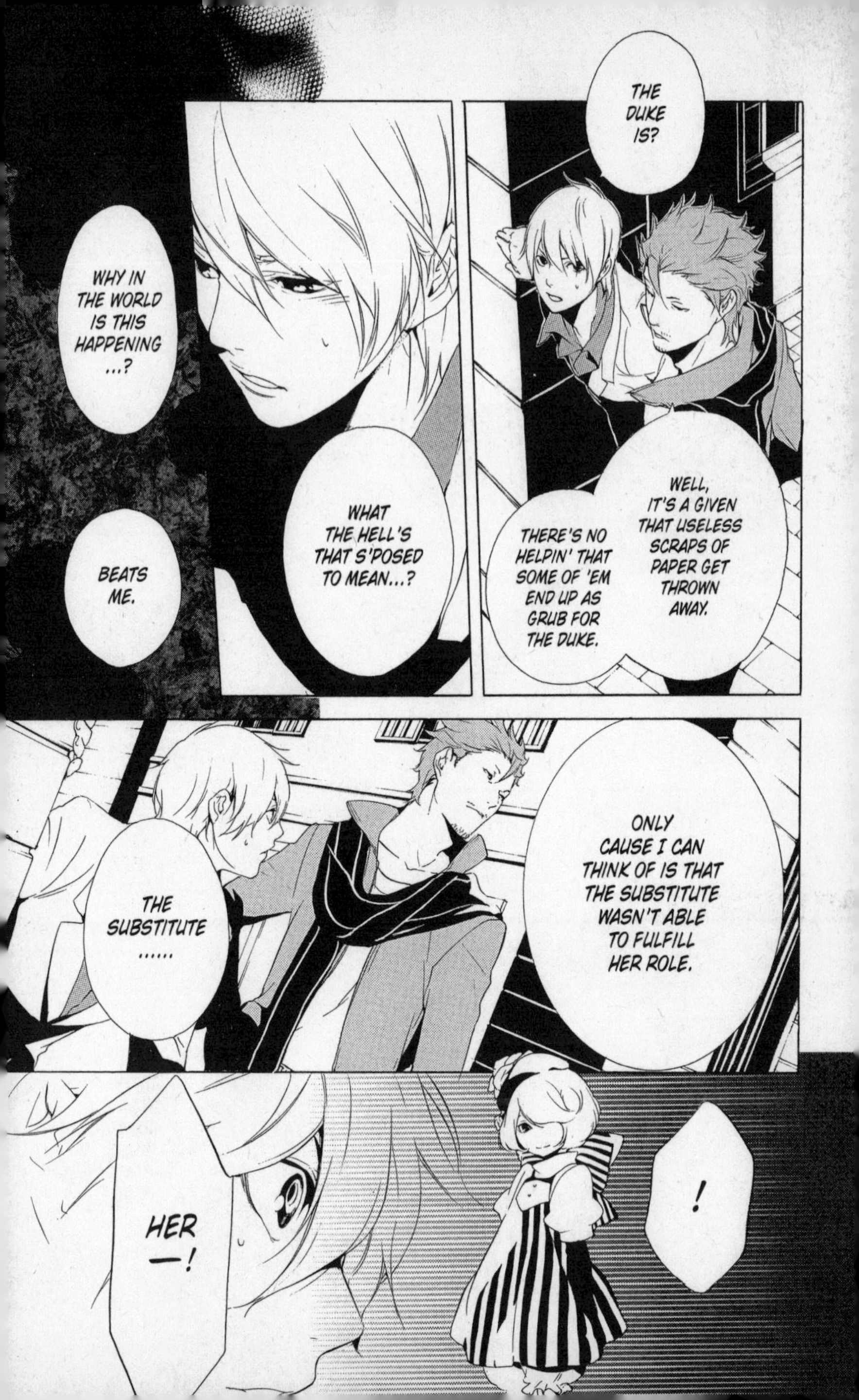
THE DUKE IS?
WELL, IT'S A GIVEN THAT USELESS SCRAPS OF PAPER GET THROWN AWAY.
THERE'S NO HELPIN' THAT SOME OF 'EM END UP AS GRUB FOR THE DUKE.
WHAT THE HELL'S THAT S'POSED TO MEAN...?
WHY IN THE WORLD IS THIS HAPPENING ...?
BEATS ME.
ONLY CAUSE I CAN THINK OF IS THAT THE SUBSTITUTE WASN'T ABLE TO FULFILL HER ROLE.
THE SUBSTITUTE ......
!
HER —!

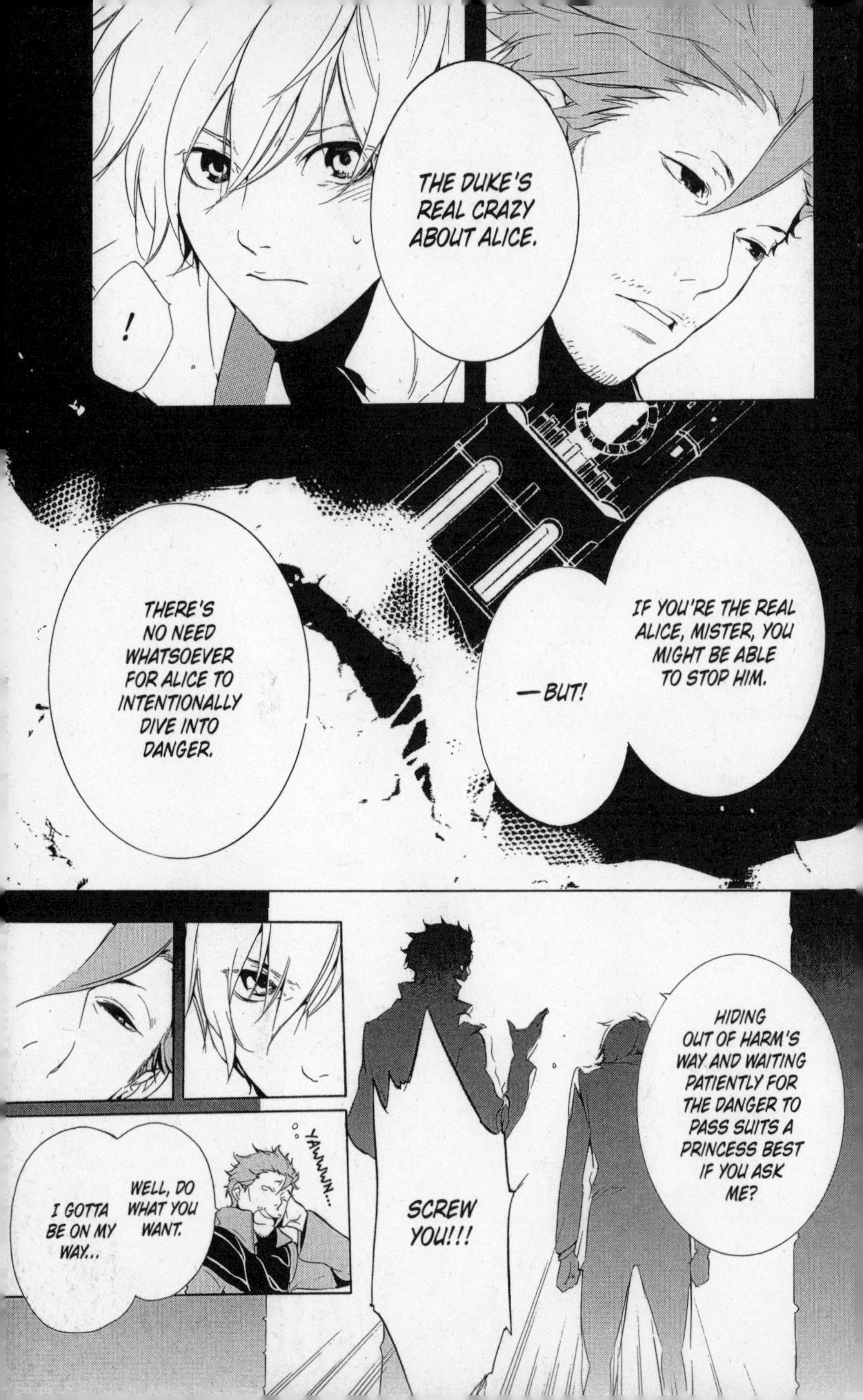
THE DUKE'S REAL CRAZY ABOUT ALICE.
!
IF YOU'RE THE REAL ALICE, MISTER, YOU MIGHT BE ABLE TO STOP HIM.
—BUT!
THERE'S NO NEED WHATSOEVER FOR ALICE TO INTENTIONALLY DIVE INTO DANGER.
HIDING OUT OF HARM'S WAY AND WAITING PATIENTLY FOR THE DANGER TO PASS SUITS A PRINCESS BEST IF YOU ASK ME?
SCREW YOU!!!
YAWWWN...
WELL, DO WHAT YOU WANT.
I GOTTA BE ON MY WAY...

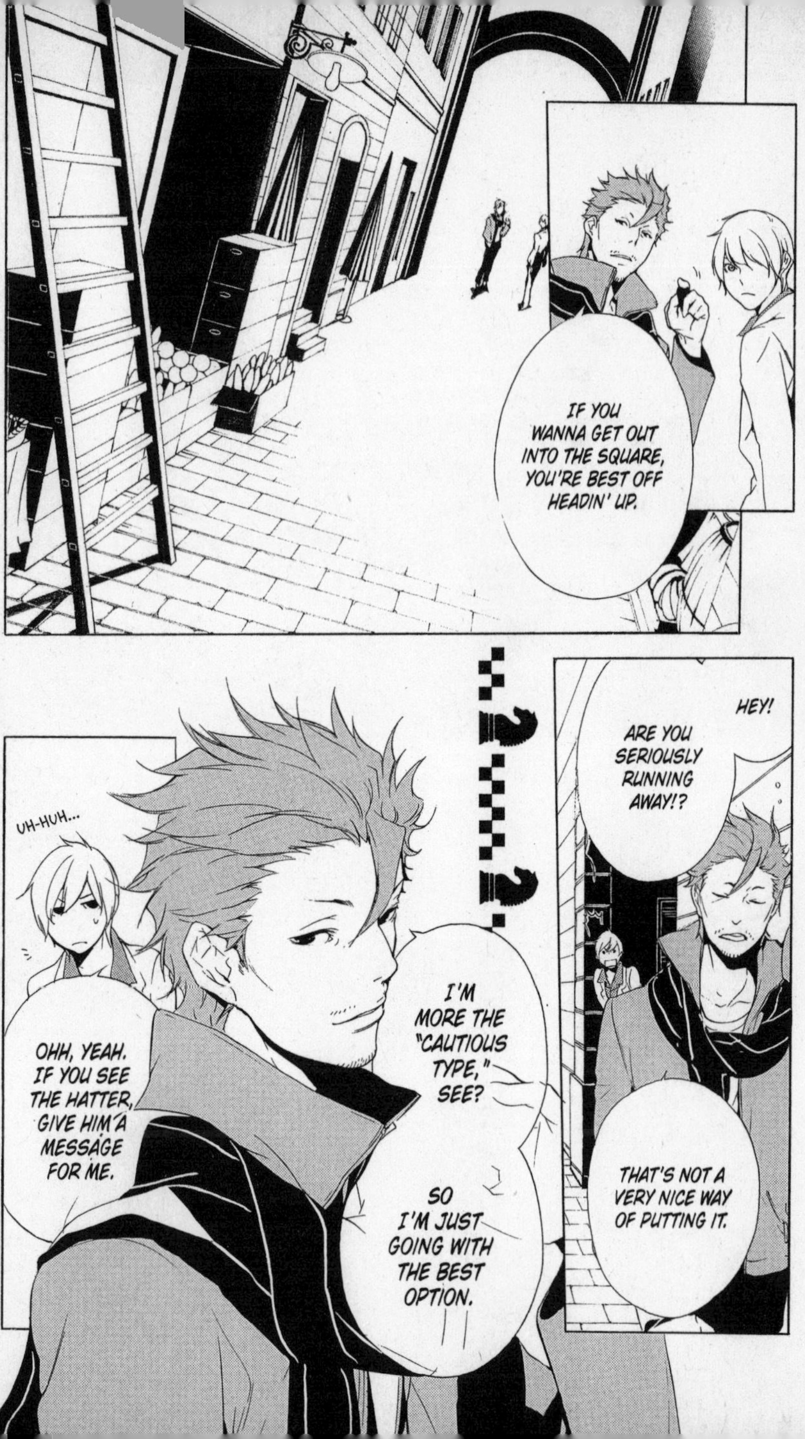
IF YOU WANNA GET OUT INTO THE SQUARE, YOU'RE BEST OFF HEADIN' UP.
HEY!
ARE YOU SERIOUSLY RUNNING AWAY!?
THAT'S NOT A VERY NICE WAY OF PUTTING IT.
I'M MORE THE "CAUTIOUS TYPE," SEE?
SO I'M JUST GOING WITH THE BEST OPTION.
UH-HUH...
OHH, YEAH. IF YOU SEE THE HATTER, GIVE HIM A MESSAGE FOR ME.

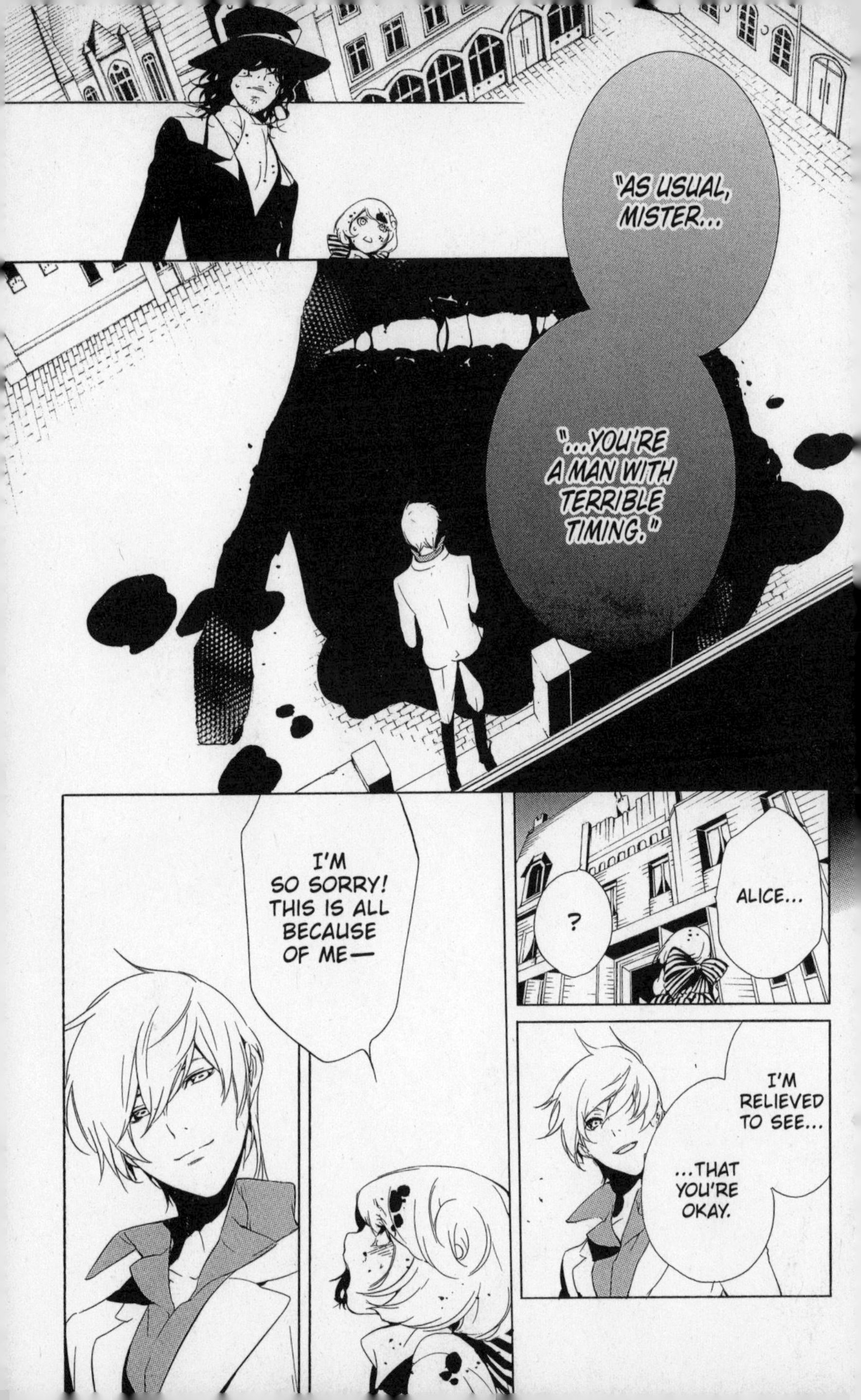
"AS USUAL, MISTER...
"...YOU'RE A MAN WITH TERRIBLE TIMING."
ALICE...
?
I'M RELIEVED TO SEE...
...THAT YOU'RE OKAY.
I'M SO SORRY! THIS IS ALL BECAUSE OF ME—

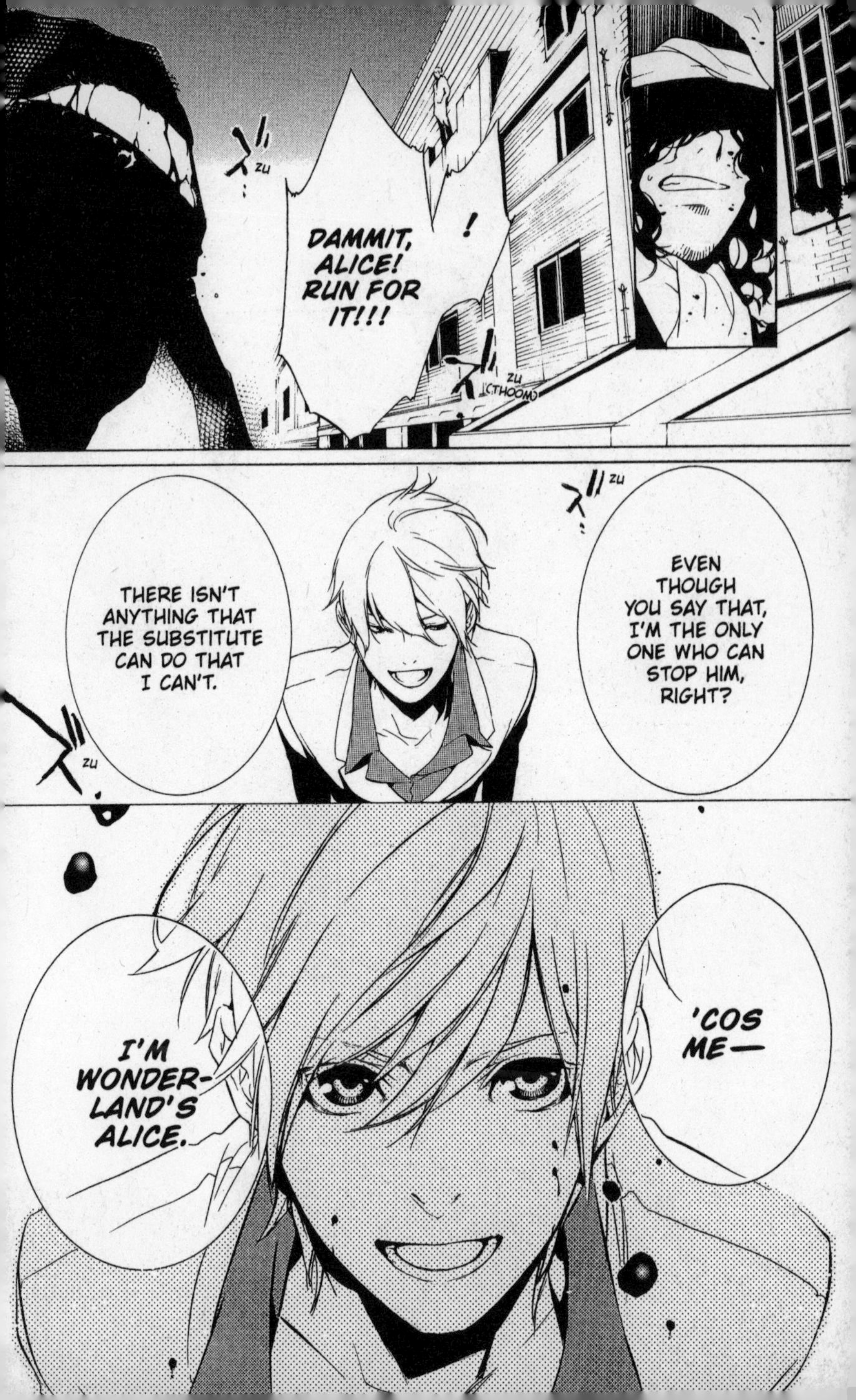
ZU (THOOM)
!
DAMMIT, ALICE! RUN FOR IT!!!
ZU
ZU
EVEN THOUGH YOU SAY THAT, I'M THE ONLY ONE WHO CAN STOP HIM, RIGHT?
THERE ISN'T ANYTHING THAT THE SUBSTITUTE CAN DO THAT I CAN'T.
ZU
'COS ME—
I'M WONDERLAND'S ALICE.

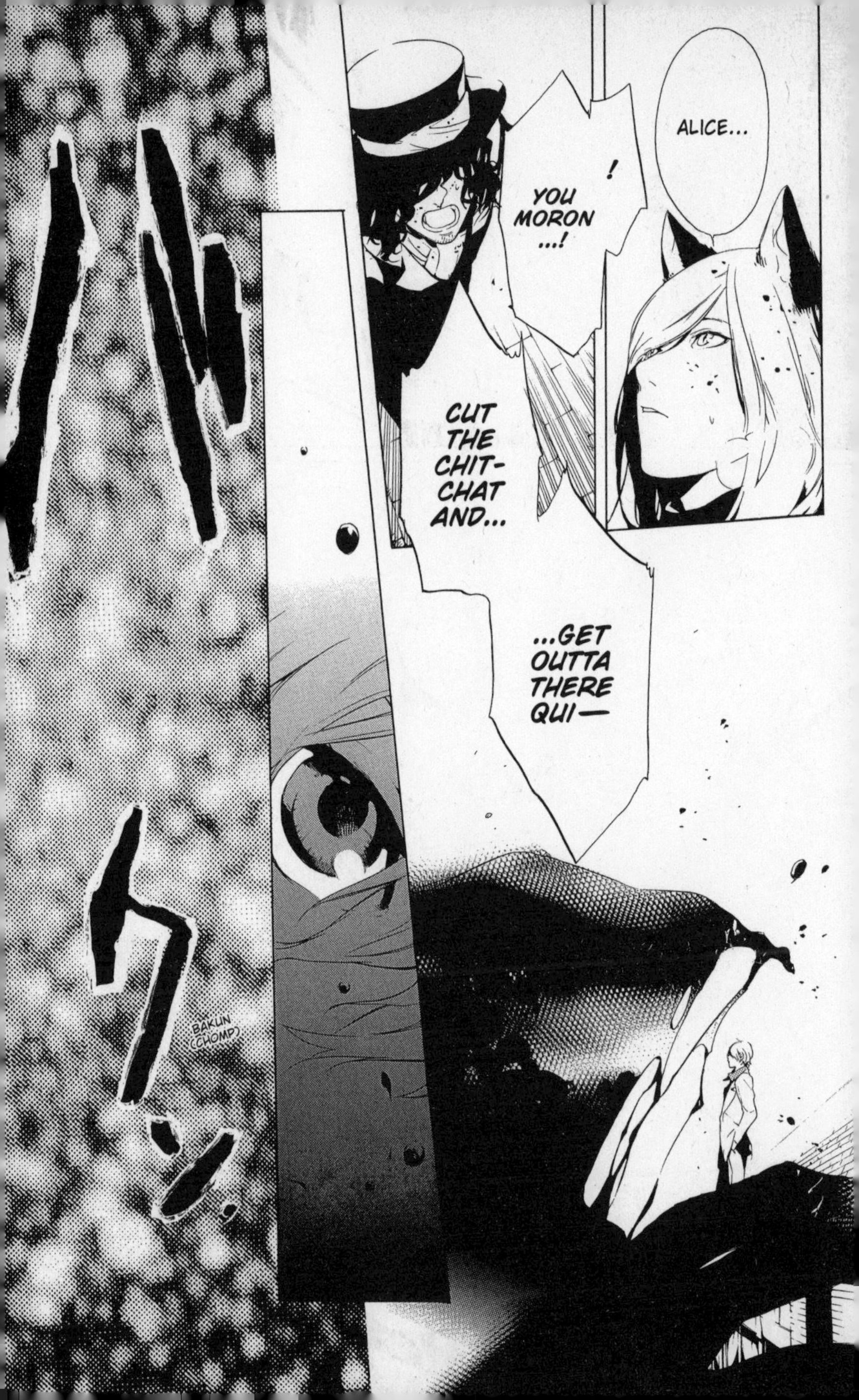
ALICE...
!
YOU MORON ...!
CUT THE CHIT-CHAT AND...
...GET OUTTA THERE QUI—
BAKUN (CHOMP)

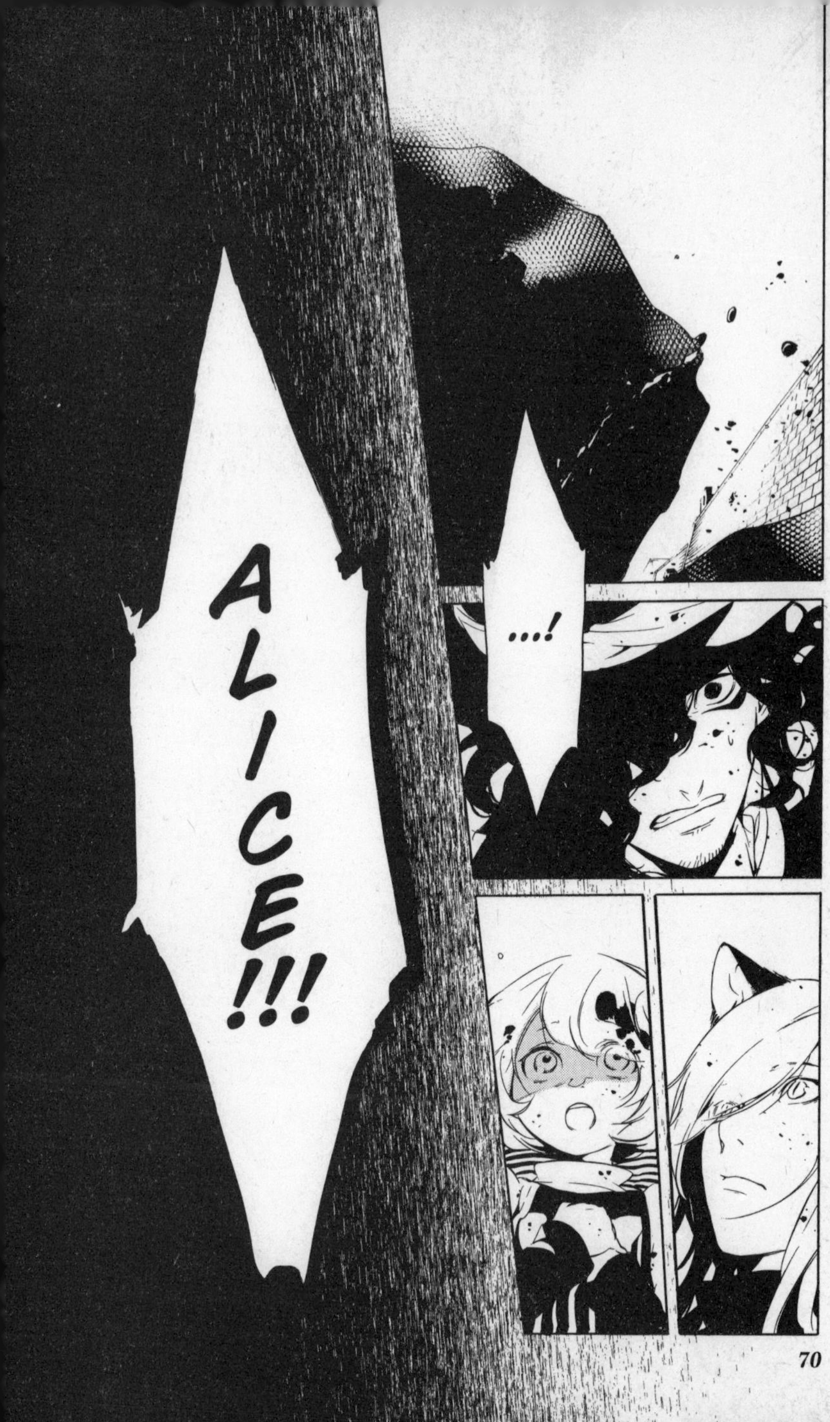
...!
ALICE!!!

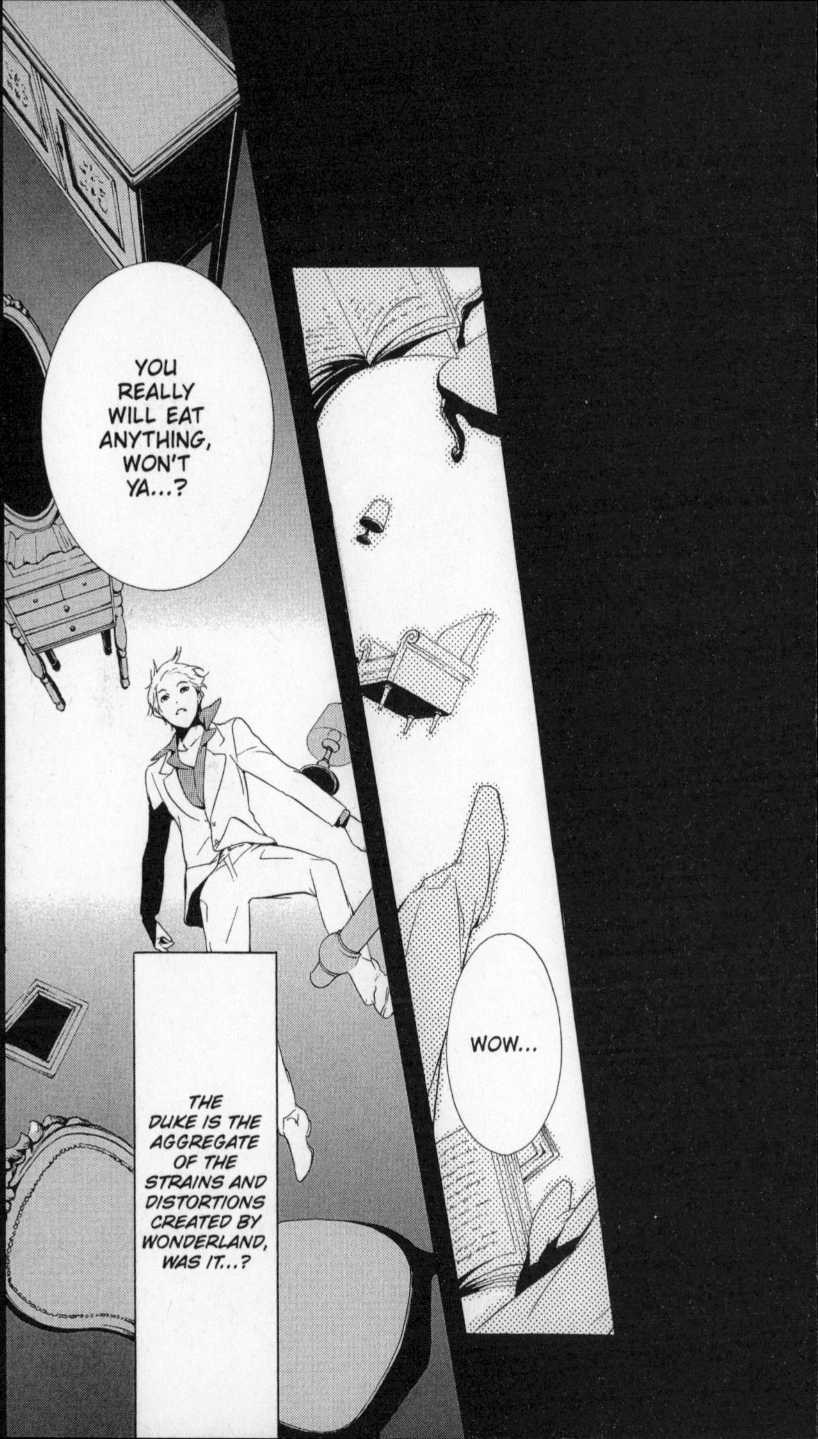
WOW...
YOU REALLY WILL EAT ANYTHING, WON'T YA...?
THE DUKE IS THE AGGREGATE OF THE STRAINS AND DISTORTIONS CREATED BY WONDERLAND, WAS IT...?

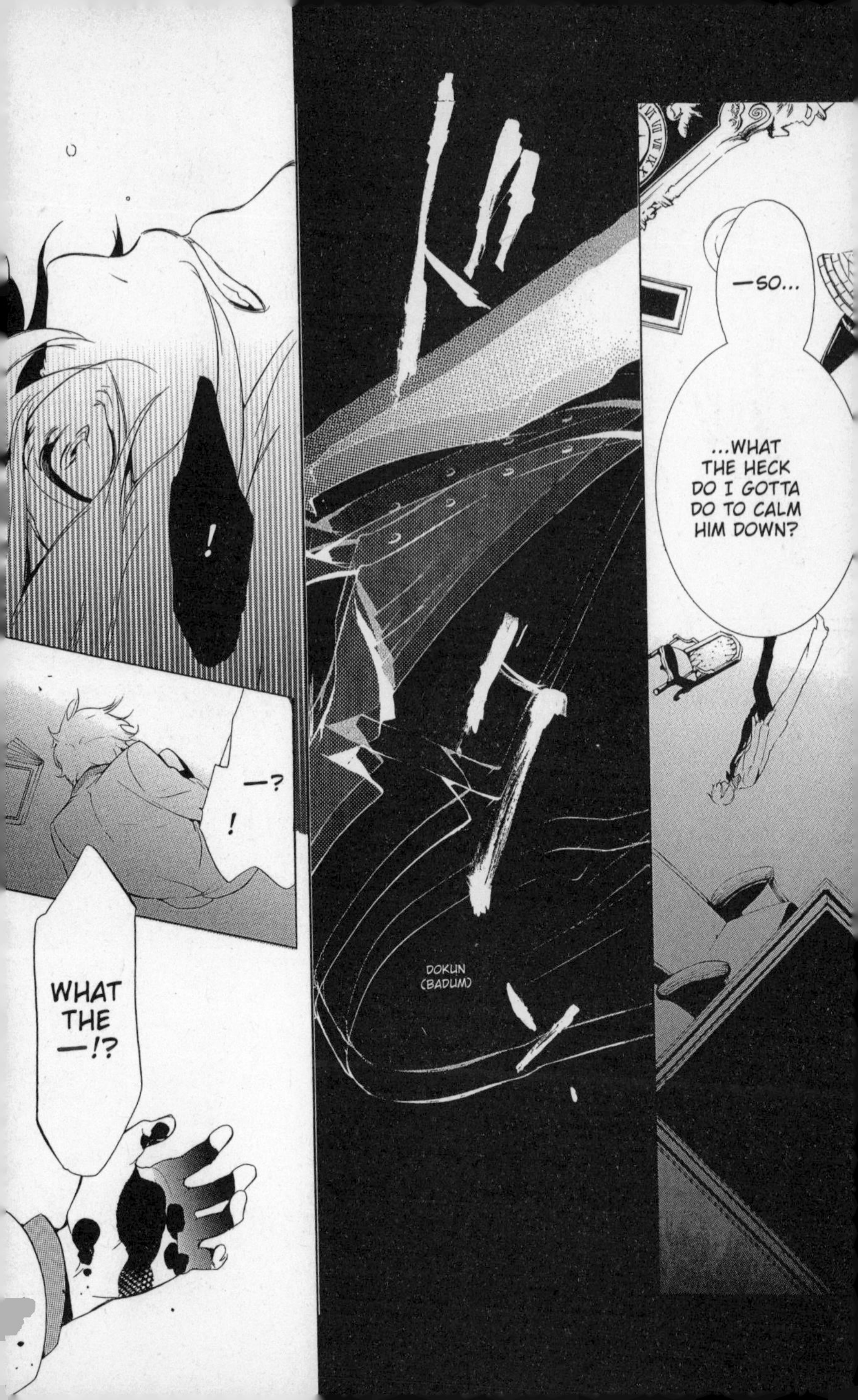
—SO...
...WHAT THE HECK DO I GOTTA DO TO CALM HIM DOWN?
DOKUN (BADUM)
!
—?
!
WHAT THE —!?

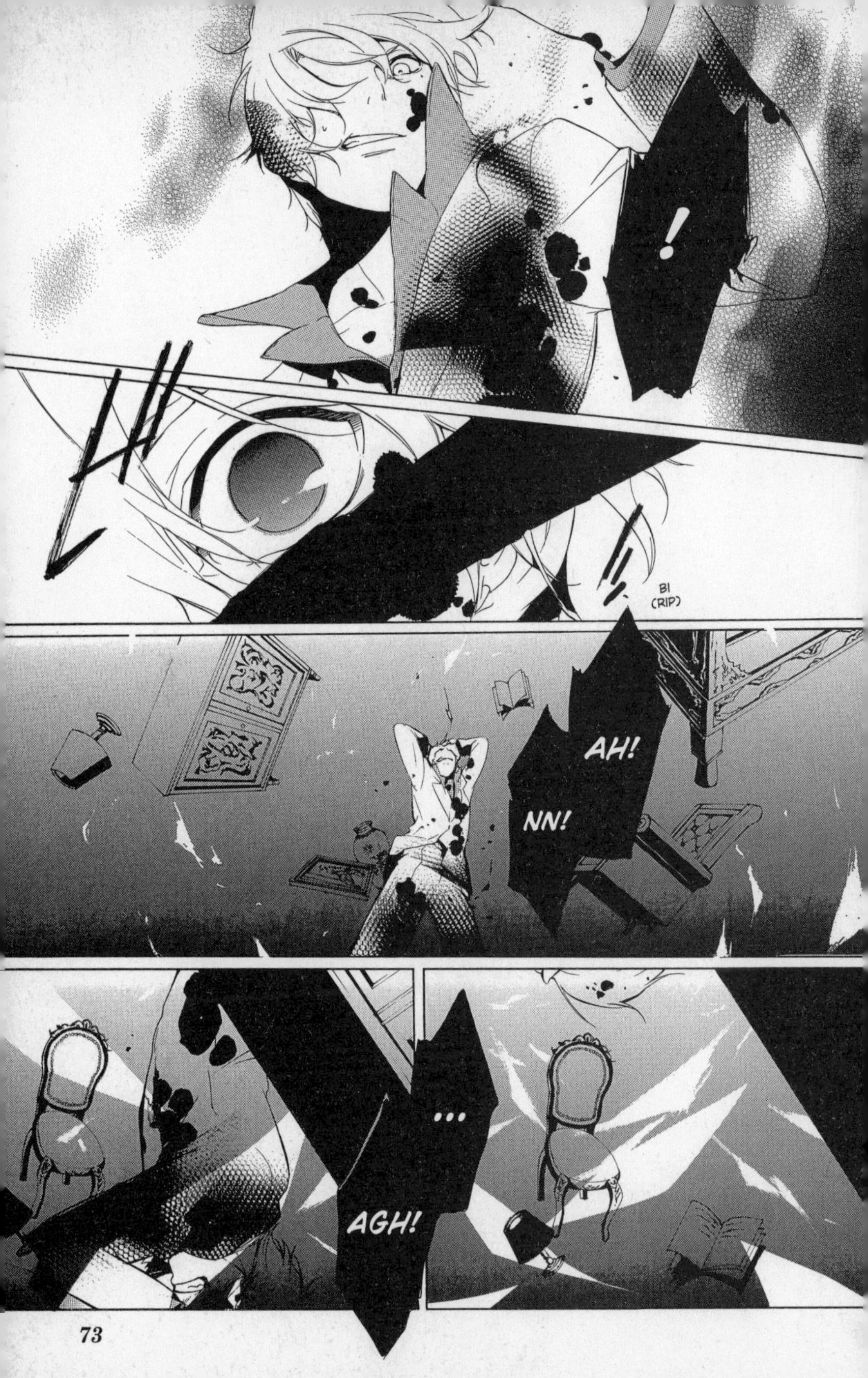
!
BI
(RIP)
AH!
NN!
...
AGH!

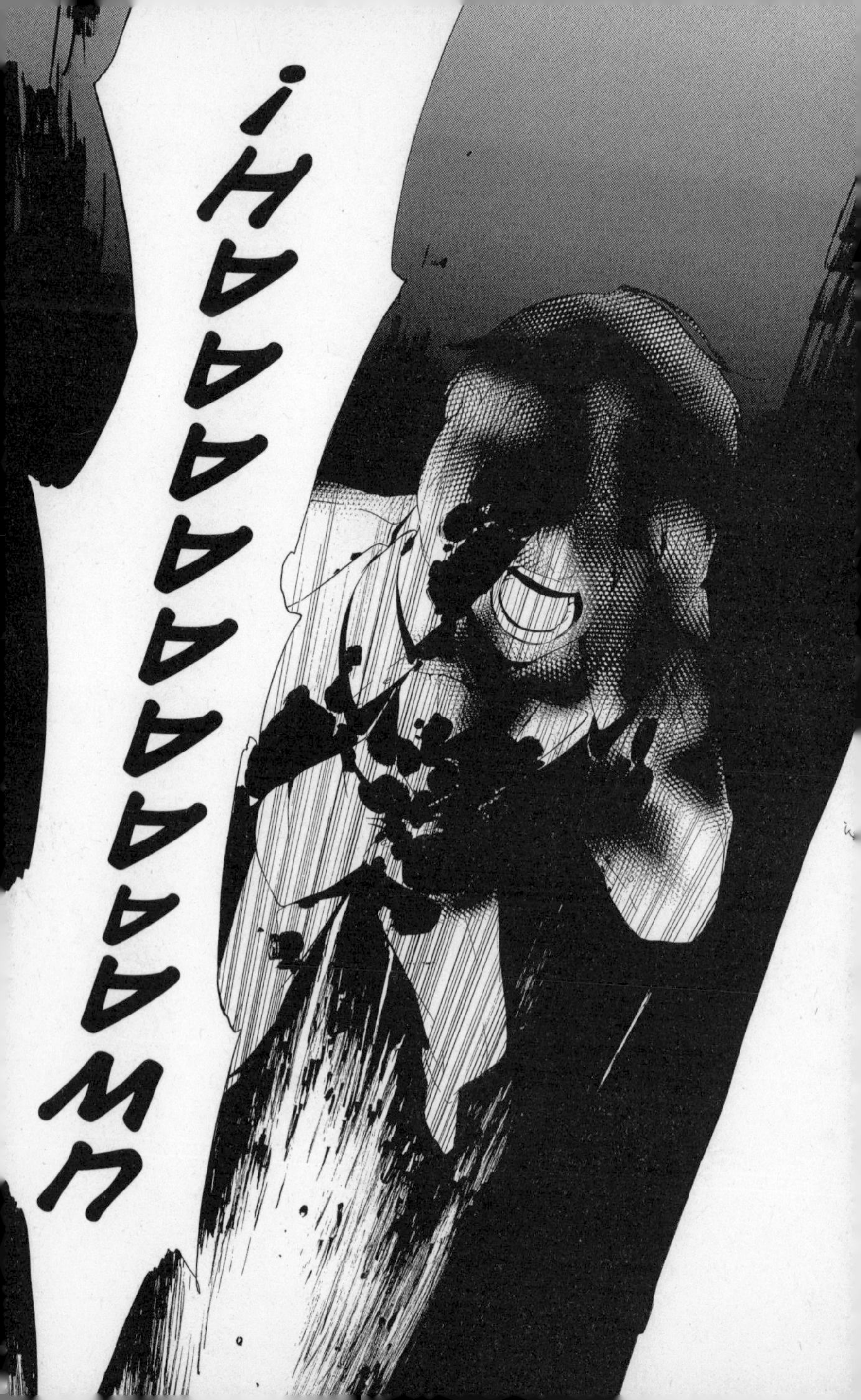
GWAAAAAAAAAH!

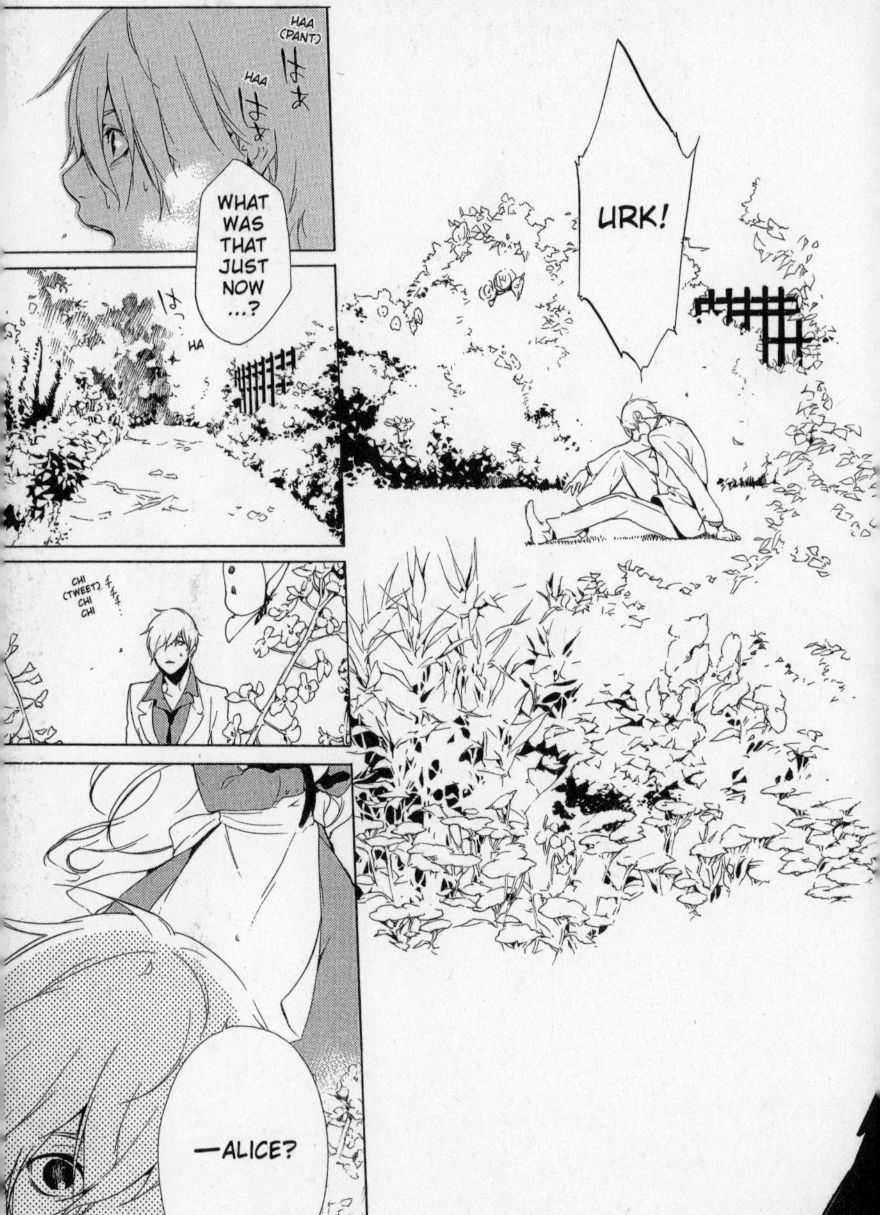
URK!
HAA (PANT) はぁ
HAA はぁ
WHAT WAS THAT JUST NOW ...?
HA はっ
CHI (TWEET) CHI CHI チチチ...
—ALICE?

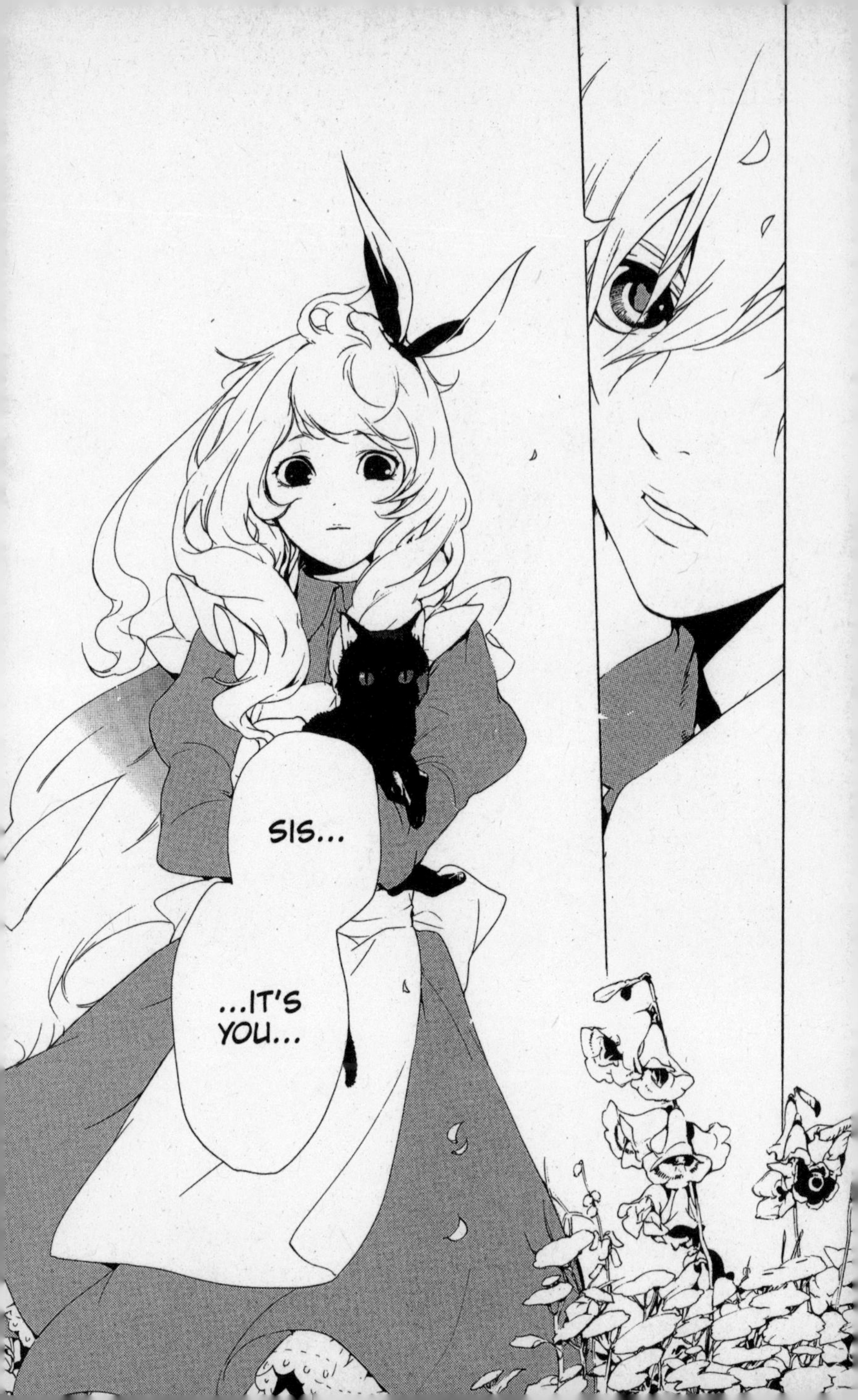
SIS...
...IT'S YOU...

Chapter 8

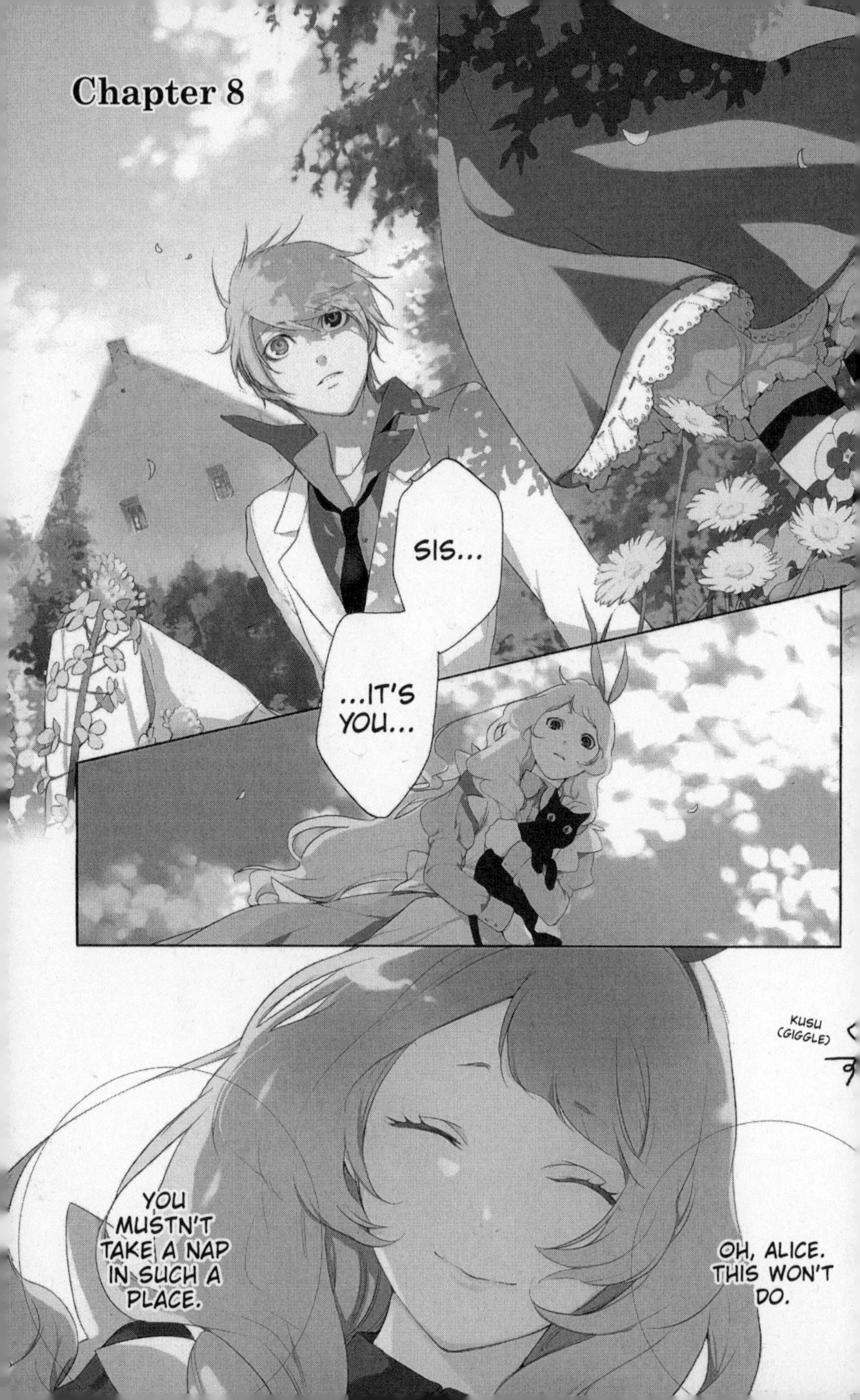
SIS...
...IT'S YOU...
KUSU (GIGGLE)
OH, ALICE. THIS WON'T DO.
YOU MUSTN'T TAKE A NAP IN SUCH A PLACE.

Chapter 8 BAD END.

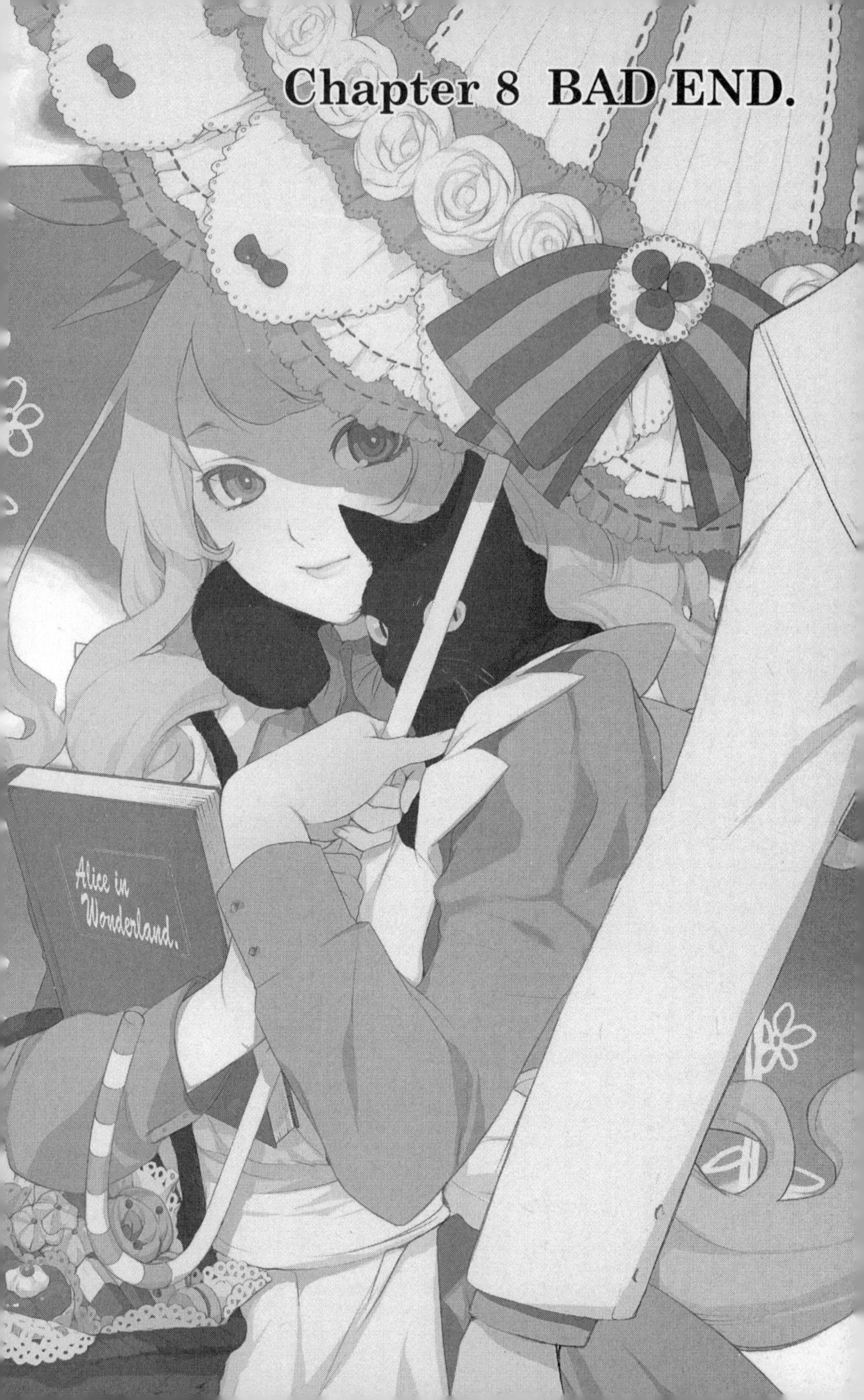
Alice in Wonderland.

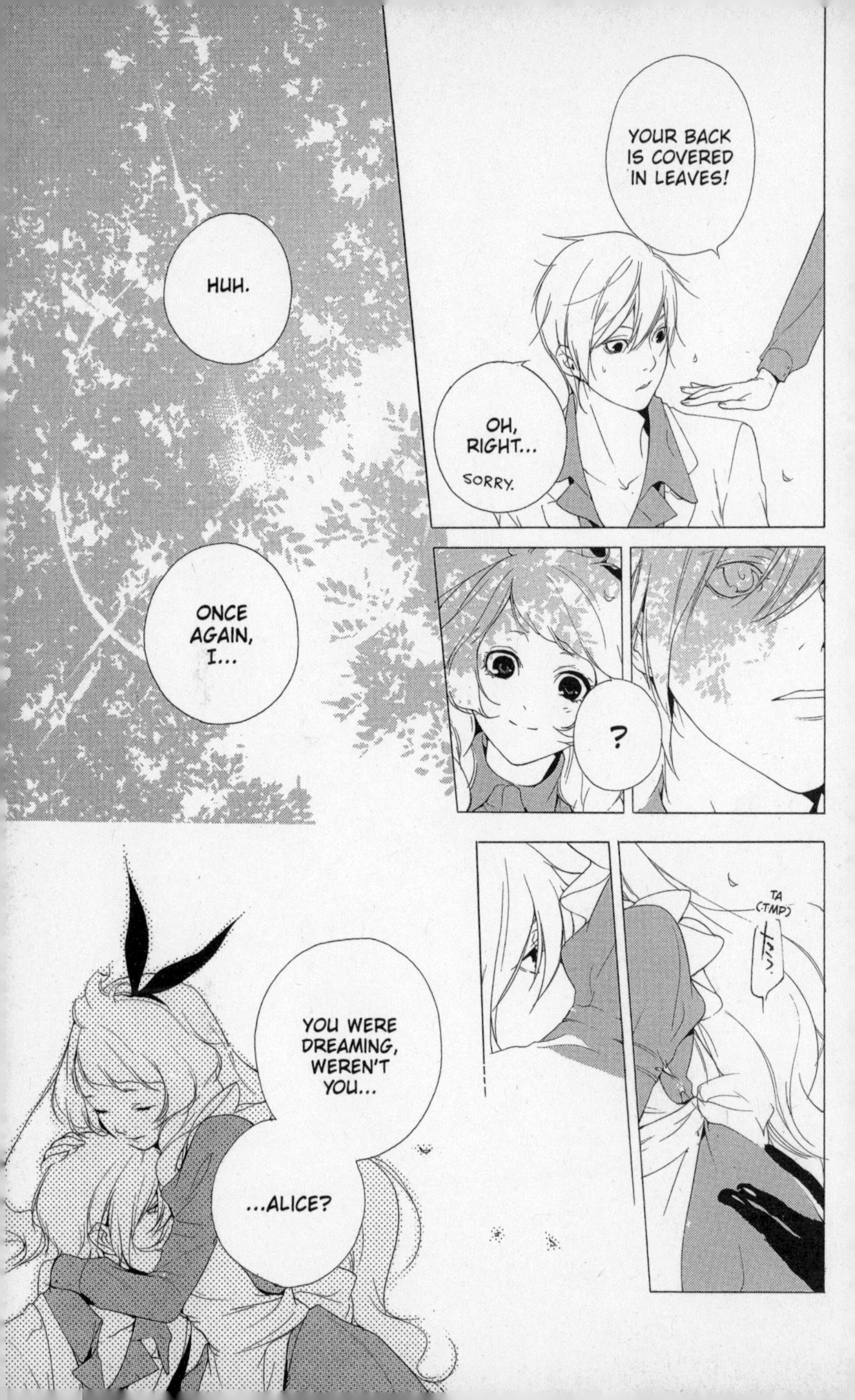
YOUR BACK IS COVERED IN LEAVES!
OH, RIGHT...
SORRY.
HUH.
ONCE AGAIN, I...
?
TA (TMP)
YOU WERE DREAMING, WEREN'T YOU...
...ALICE?

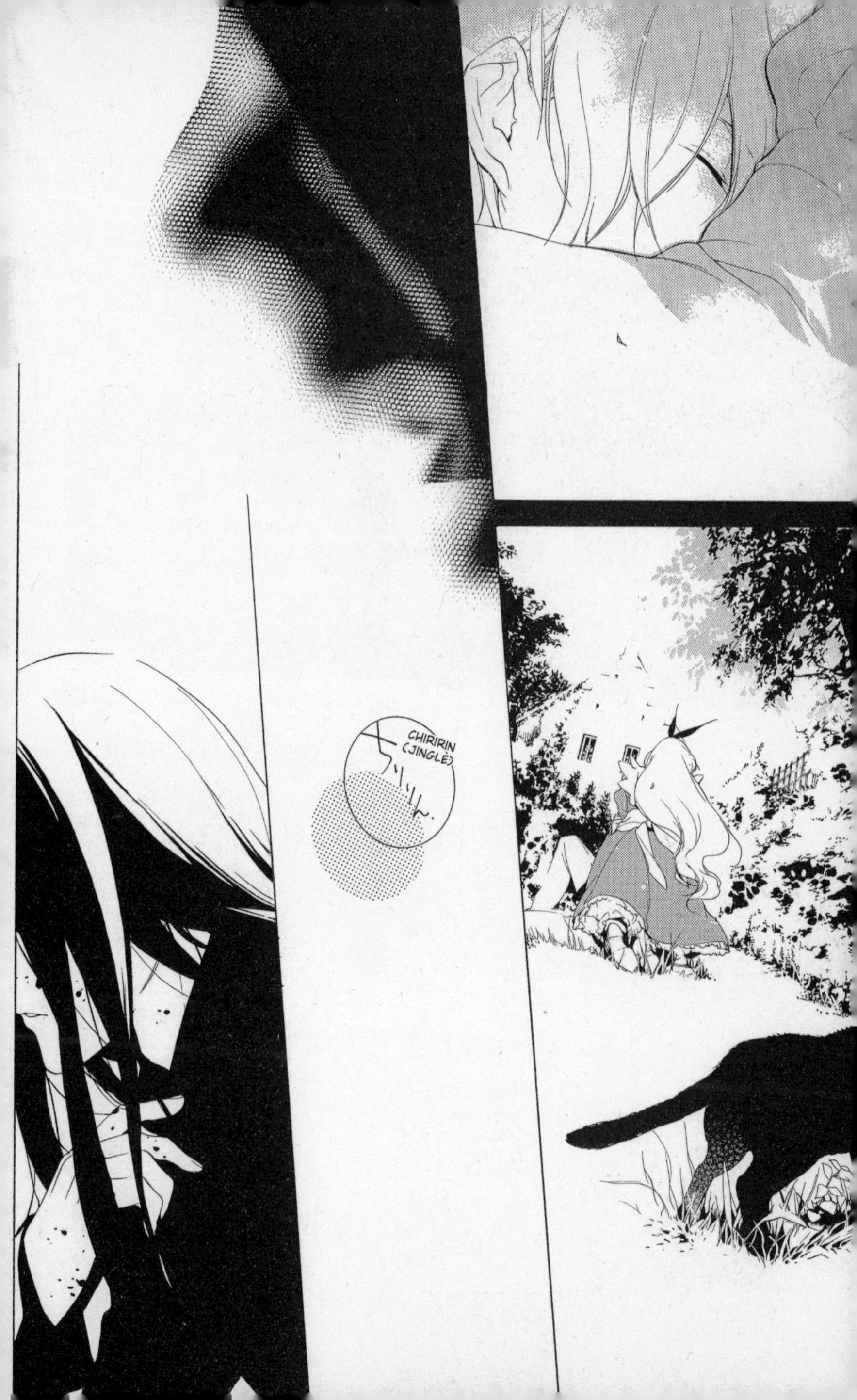

CHIRIRIN (JINGLE)

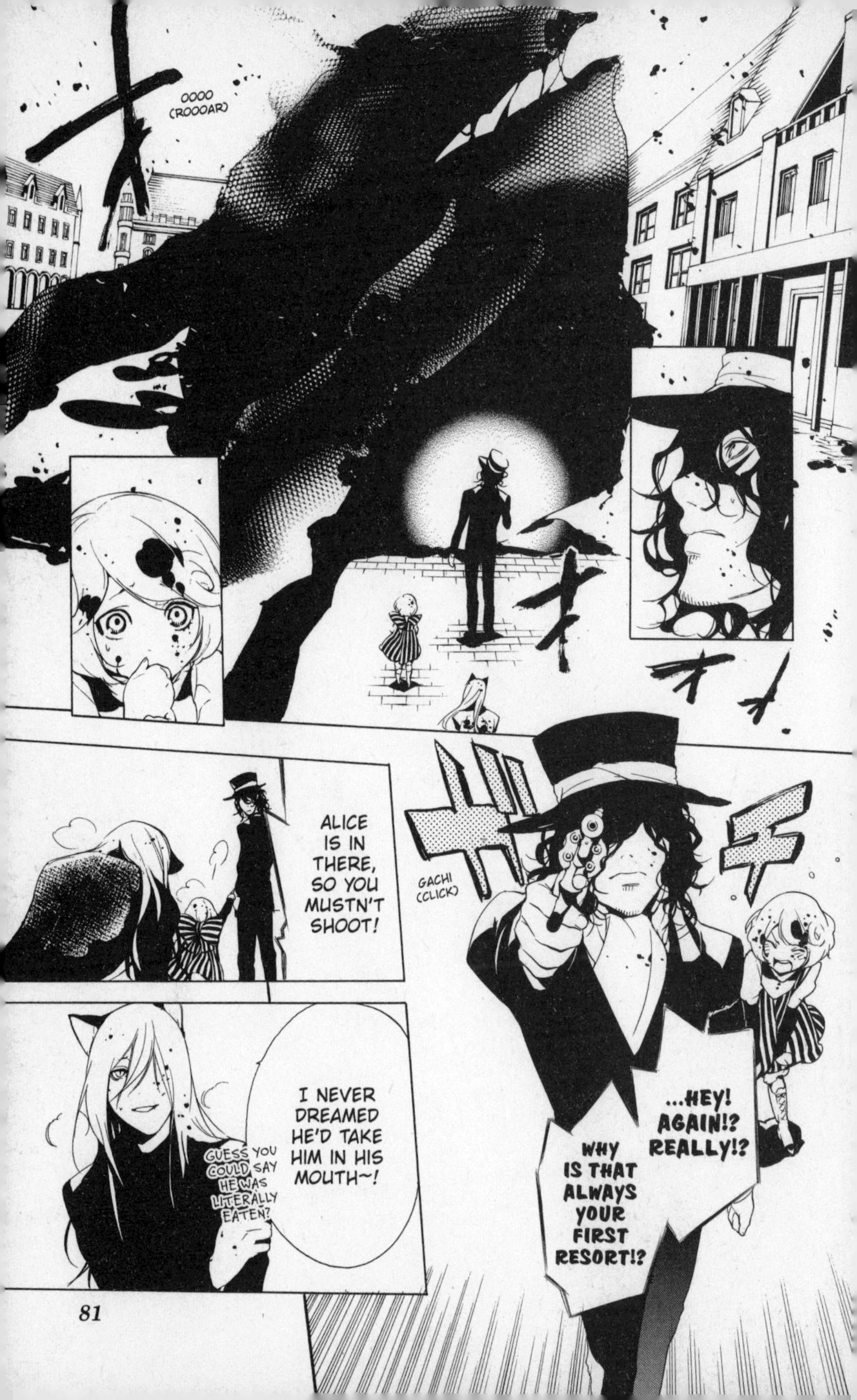
OOOO (ROOOAR)
GACHI (CLICK)
...HEY! AGAIN!? REALLY!?
WHY IS THAT ALWAYS YOUR FIRST RESORT!?
ALICE IS IN THERE, SO YOU MUSTN'T SHOOT!
I NEVER DREAMED HE'D TAKE HIM IN HIS MOUTH~!
GUESS YOU COULD SAY HE WAS LITERALLY EATEN?

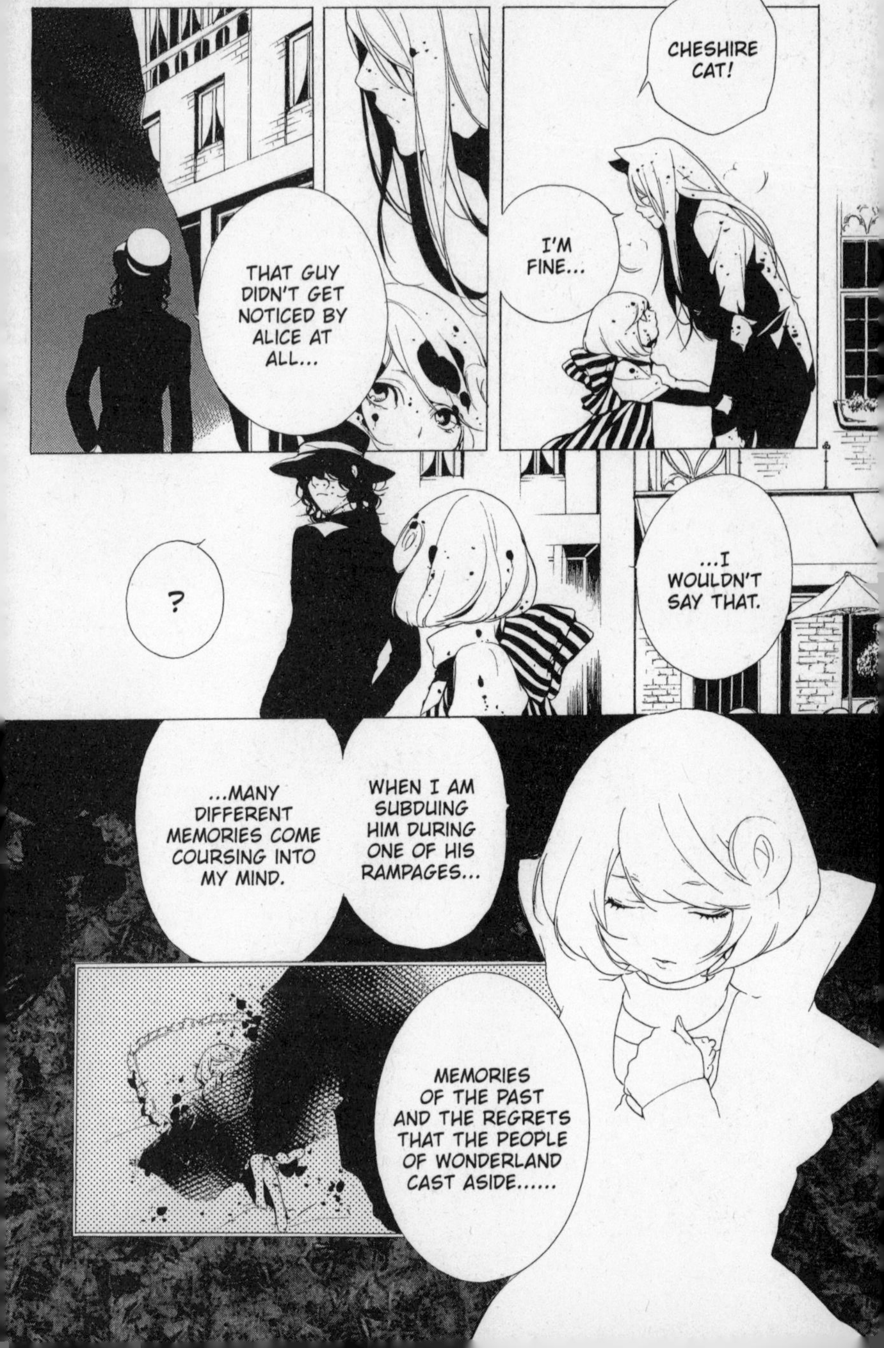
CHESHIRE CAT!
I'M FINE...
THAT GUY DIDN'T GET NOTICED BY ALICE AT ALL...
...I WOULDN'T SAY THAT.
?
WHEN I AM SUBDUING HIM DURING ONE OF HIS RAMPAGES...
...MANY DIFFERENT MEMORIES COME COURSING INTO MY MIND.
MEMORIES OF THE PAST AND THE REGRETS THAT THE PEOPLE OF WONDERLAND CAST ASIDE......

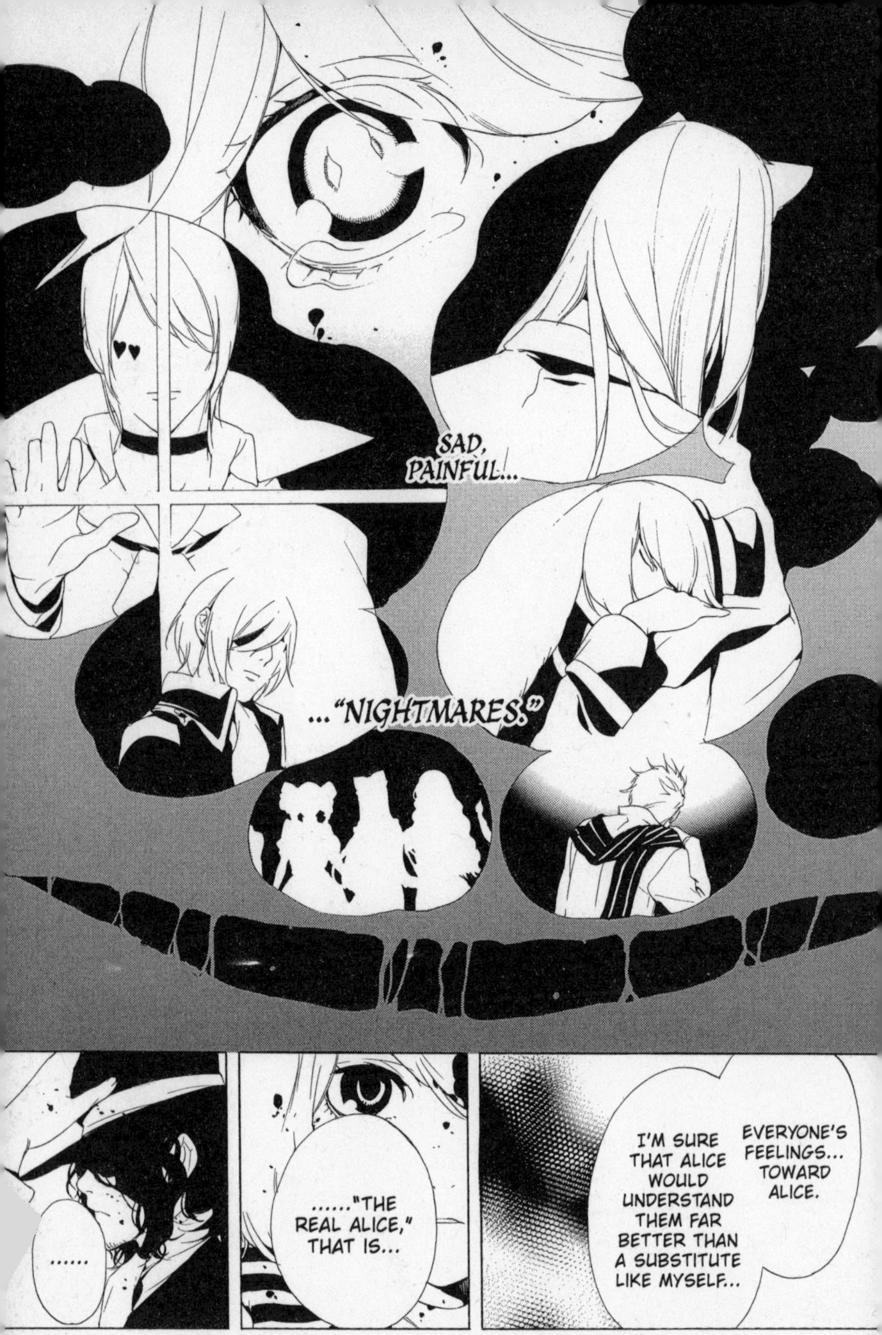
SAD, PAINFUL...
..."NIGHTMARES."
EVERYONE'S FEELINGS... TOWARD ALICE.
I'M SURE THAT ALICE WOULD UNDERSTAND THEM FAR BETTER THAN A SUBSTITUTE LIKE MYSELF...
......"THE REAL ALICE," THAT IS...
......

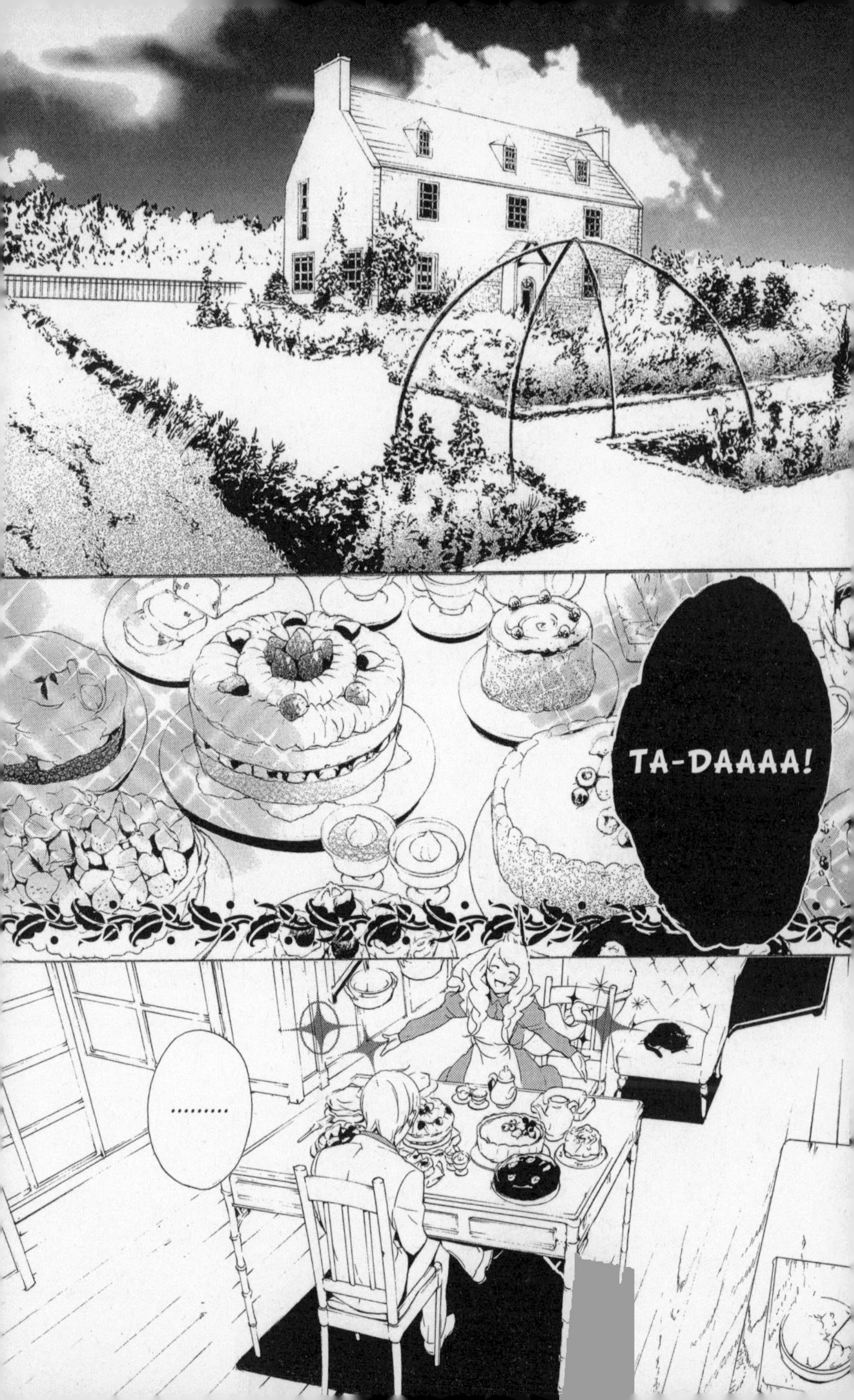
TA-DAAAA!
....

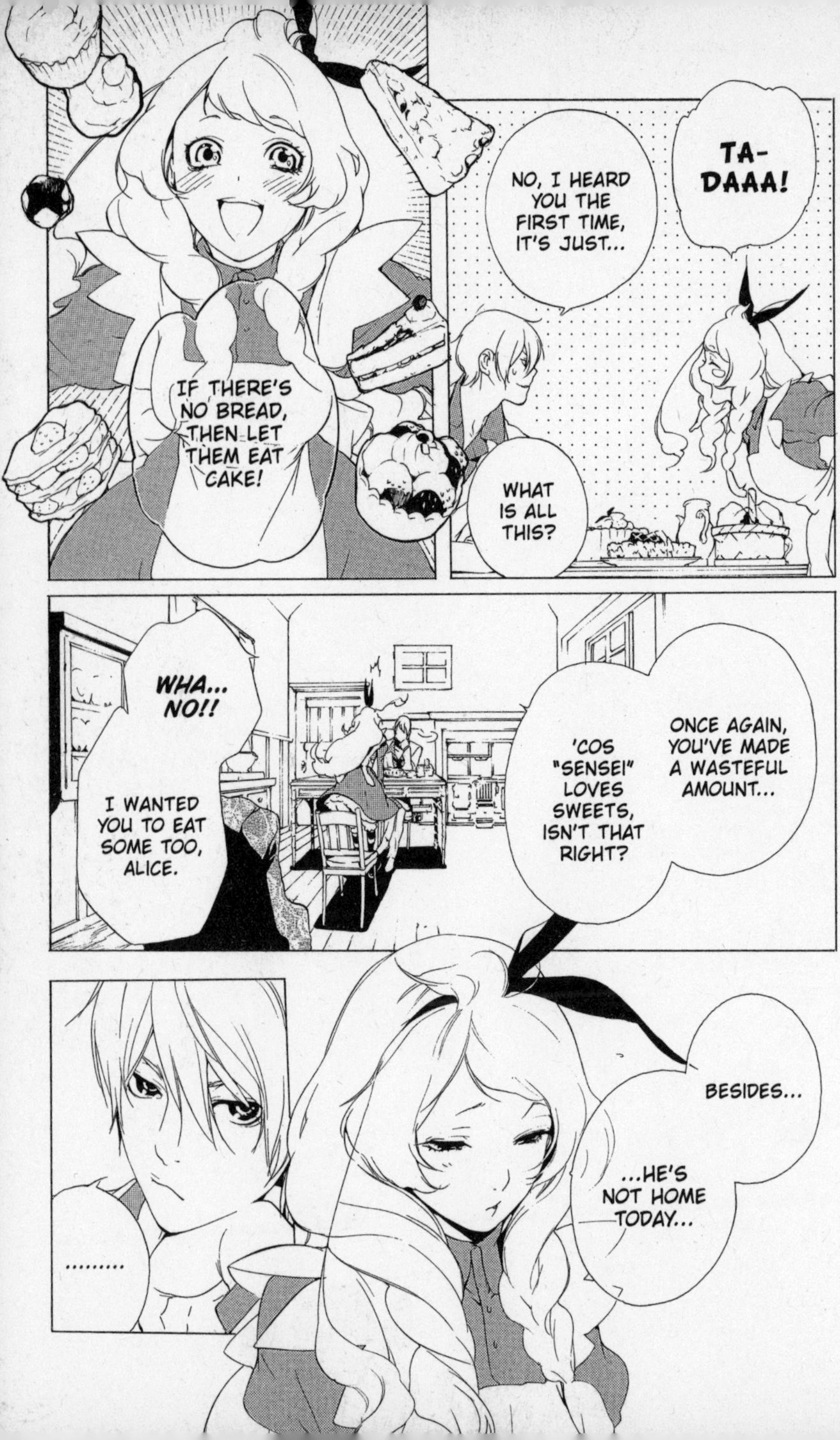
TA-
DAAA!
NO, I HEARD YOU THE FIRST TIME, IT'S JUST...
WHAT IS ALL THIS?
IF THERE'S NO BREAD, THEN LET THEM EAT CAKE!
ONCE AGAIN, YOU'VE MADE A WASTEFUL AMOUNT...
'COS "SENSEI" LOVES SWEETS, ISN'T THAT RIGHT?
WHA... NO!!
I WANTED YOU TO EAT SOME TOO, ALICE.
BESIDES...
...HE'S NOT HOME TODAY...
....

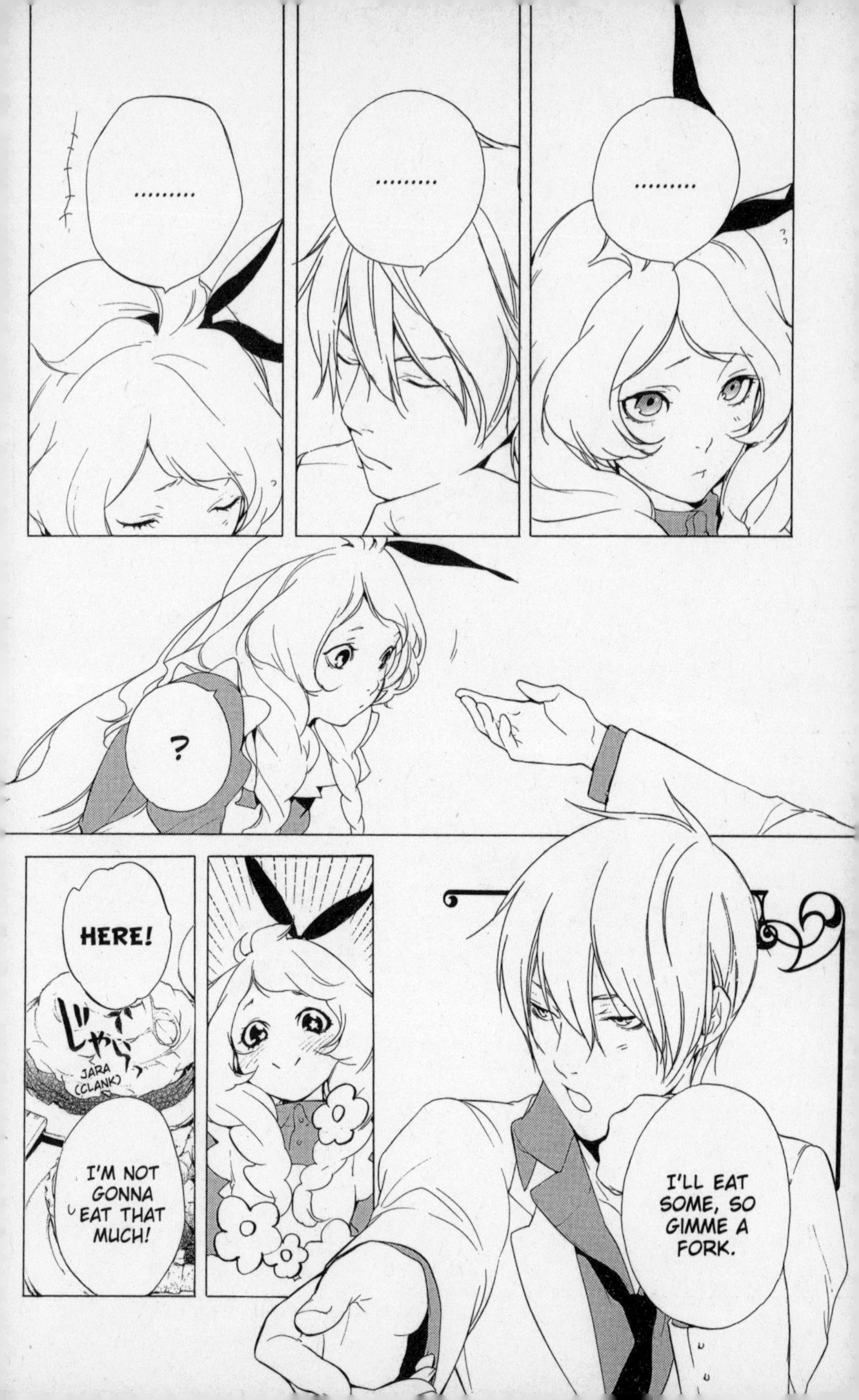
....
....
....
?
I'LL EAT SOME, SO GIMME A FORK.
HERE!
JARA (CLANK)
I'M NOT GONNA EAT THAT MUCH!

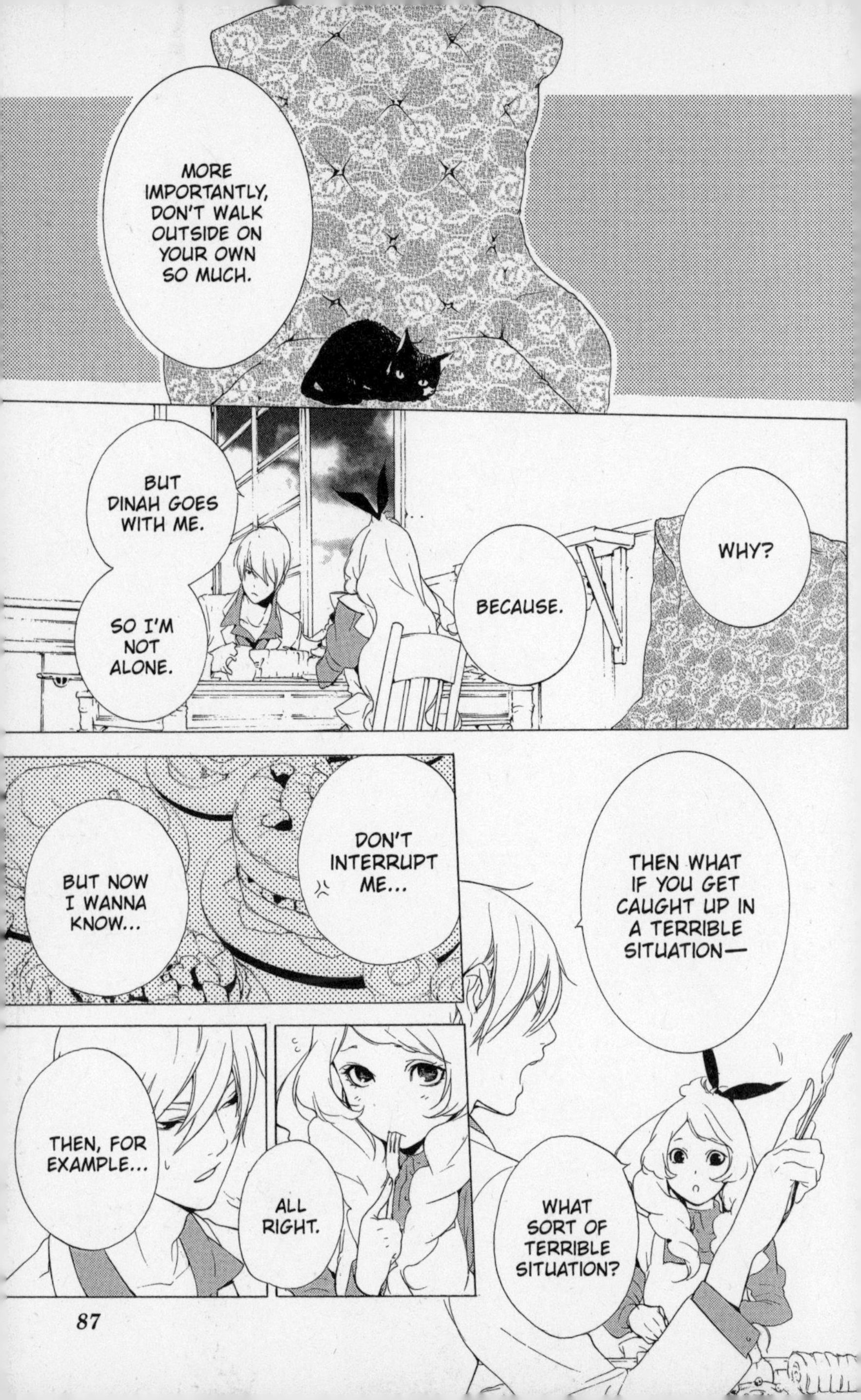
MORE IMPORTANTLY, DON'T WALK OUTSIDE ON YOUR OWN SO MUCH.
WHY?
BECAUSE.
BUT DINAH GOES WITH ME.
SO I'M NOT ALONE.
THEN WHAT IF YOU GET CAUGHT UP IN A TERRIBLE SITUATION—
WHAT SORT OF TERRIBLE SITUATION?
DON'T INTERRUPT ME...
BUT NOW I WANNA KNOW...
ALL RIGHT.
THEN, FOR EXAMPLE...

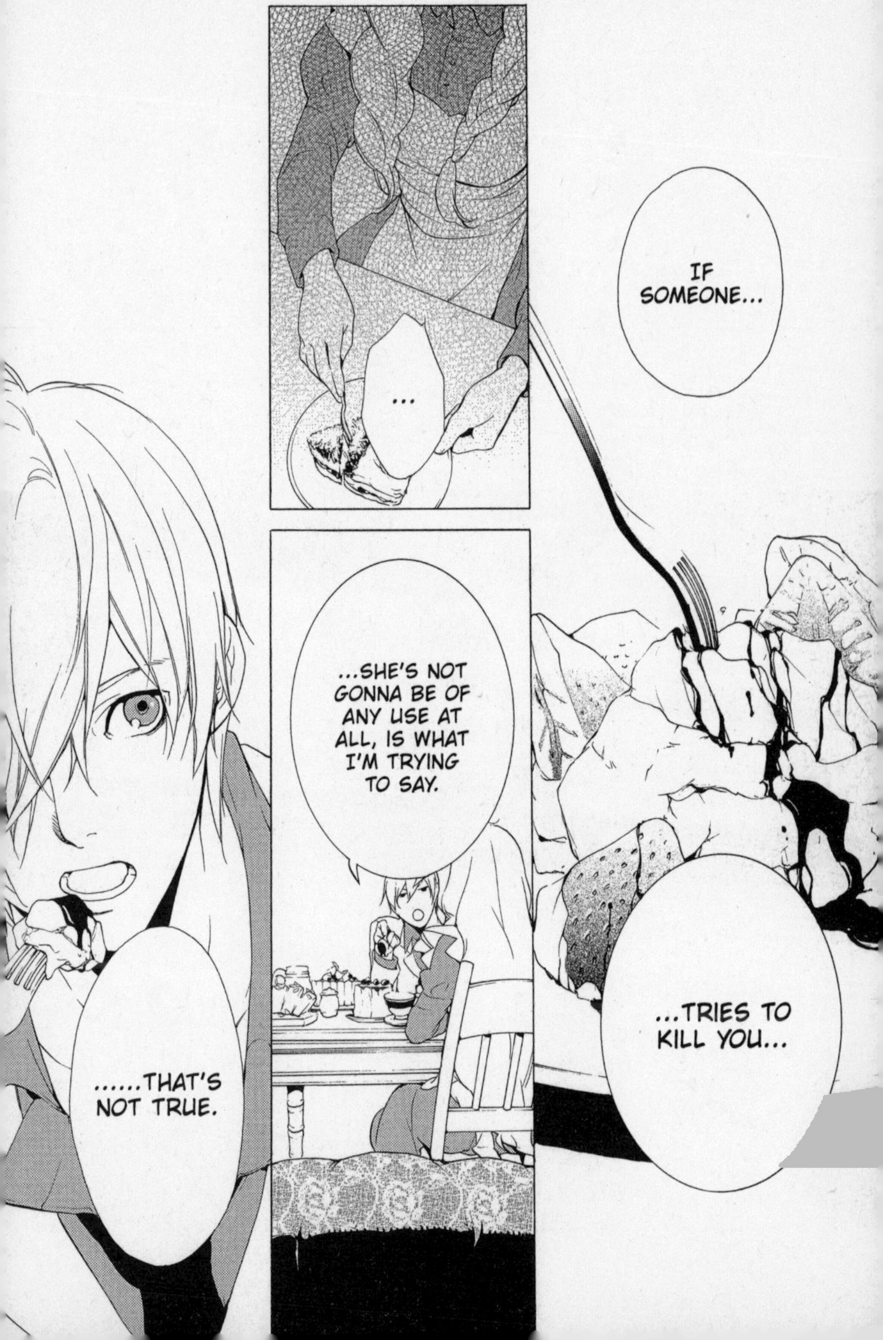
IF SOMEONE...
...TRIES TO KILL YOU...
...
...SHE'S NOT GONNA BE OF ANY USE AT ALL, IS WHAT I'M TRYING TO SAY.
......THAT'S NOT TRUE.

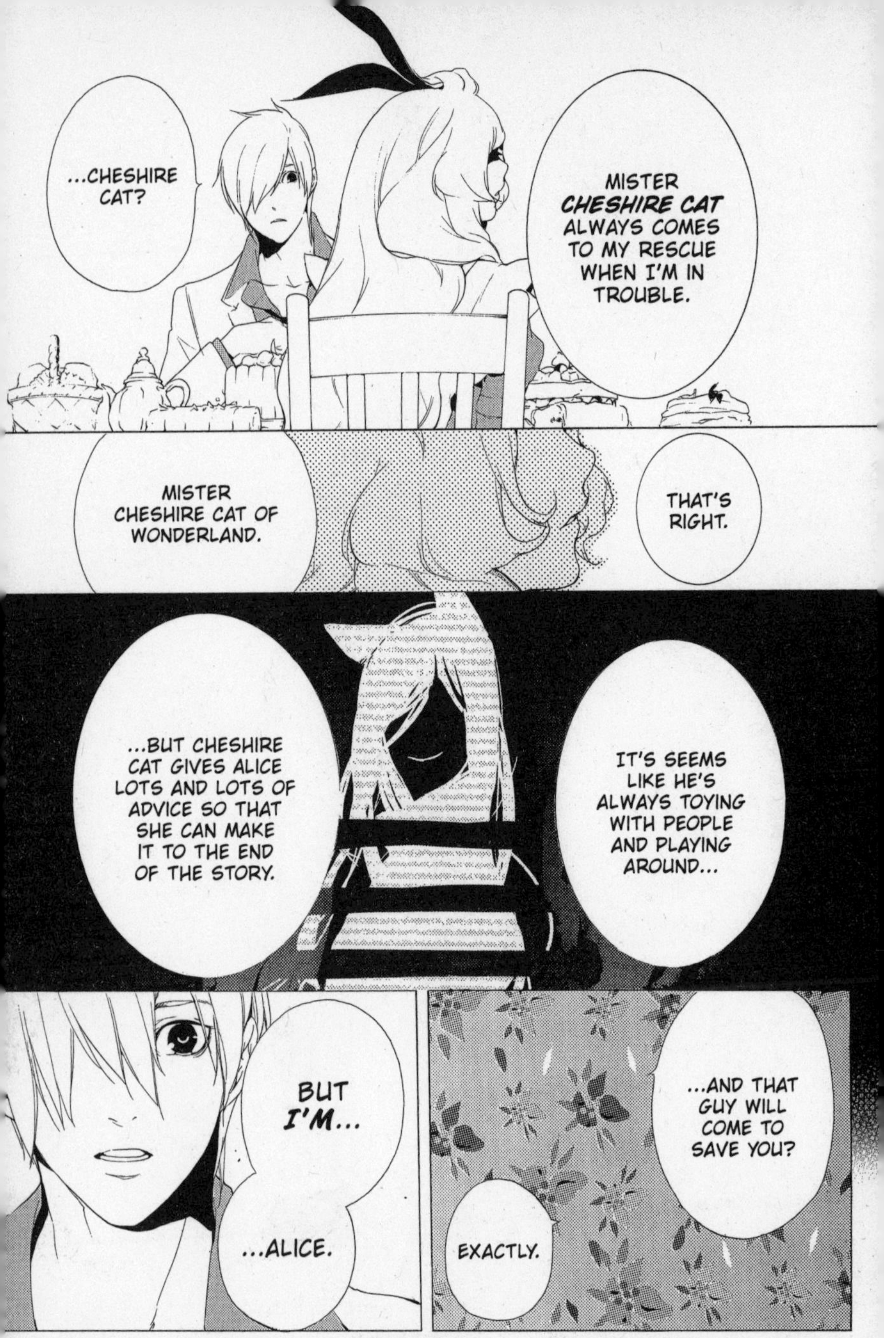
MISTER **CHESHIRE CAT** ALWAYS COMES TO MY RESCUE WHEN I'M IN TROUBLE.
...CHESHIRE CAT?
THAT'S RIGHT.
MISTER CHESHIRE CAT OF WONDERLAND.
IT'S SEEMS LIKE HE'S ALWAYS TOYING WITH PEOPLE AND PLAYING AROUND...
...BUT CHESHIRE CAT GIVES ALICE LOTS AND LOTS OF ADVICE SO THAT SHE CAN MAKE IT TO THE END OF THE STORY.
...AND THAT GUY WILL COME TO SAVE YOU?
EXACTLY.
BUT *I'M*...
...ALICE.

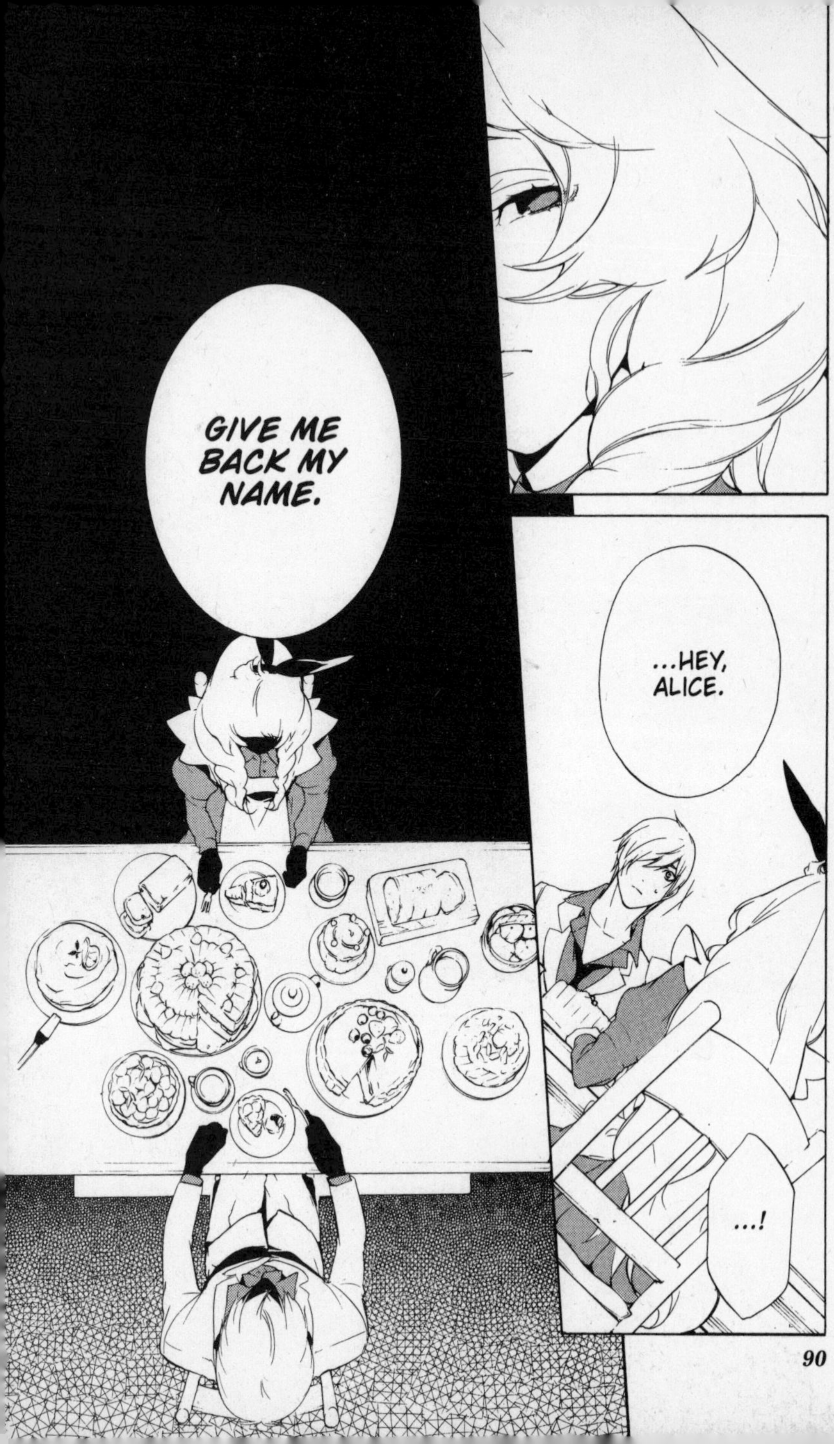
...HEY, ALICE.
...!
GIVE ME BACK MY NAME.

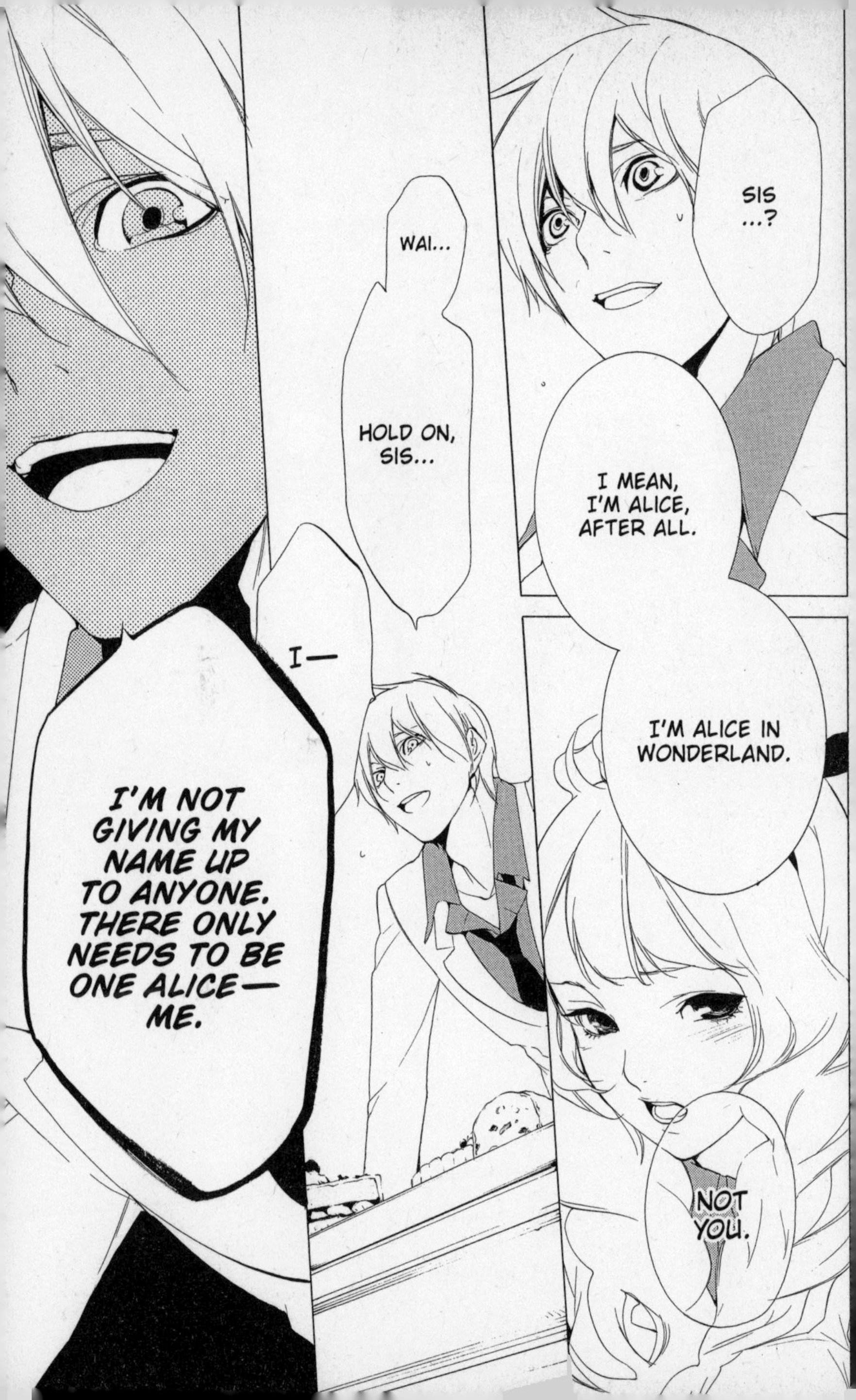
SIS ...?
I MEAN, I'M ALICE, AFTER ALL.
I'M ALICE IN WONDERLAND.
NOT YOU.
WAI...
HOLD ON, SIS...
I—
I'M NOT GIVING MY NAME UP TO ANYONE. THERE ONLY NEEDS TO BE ONE ALICE— ME.

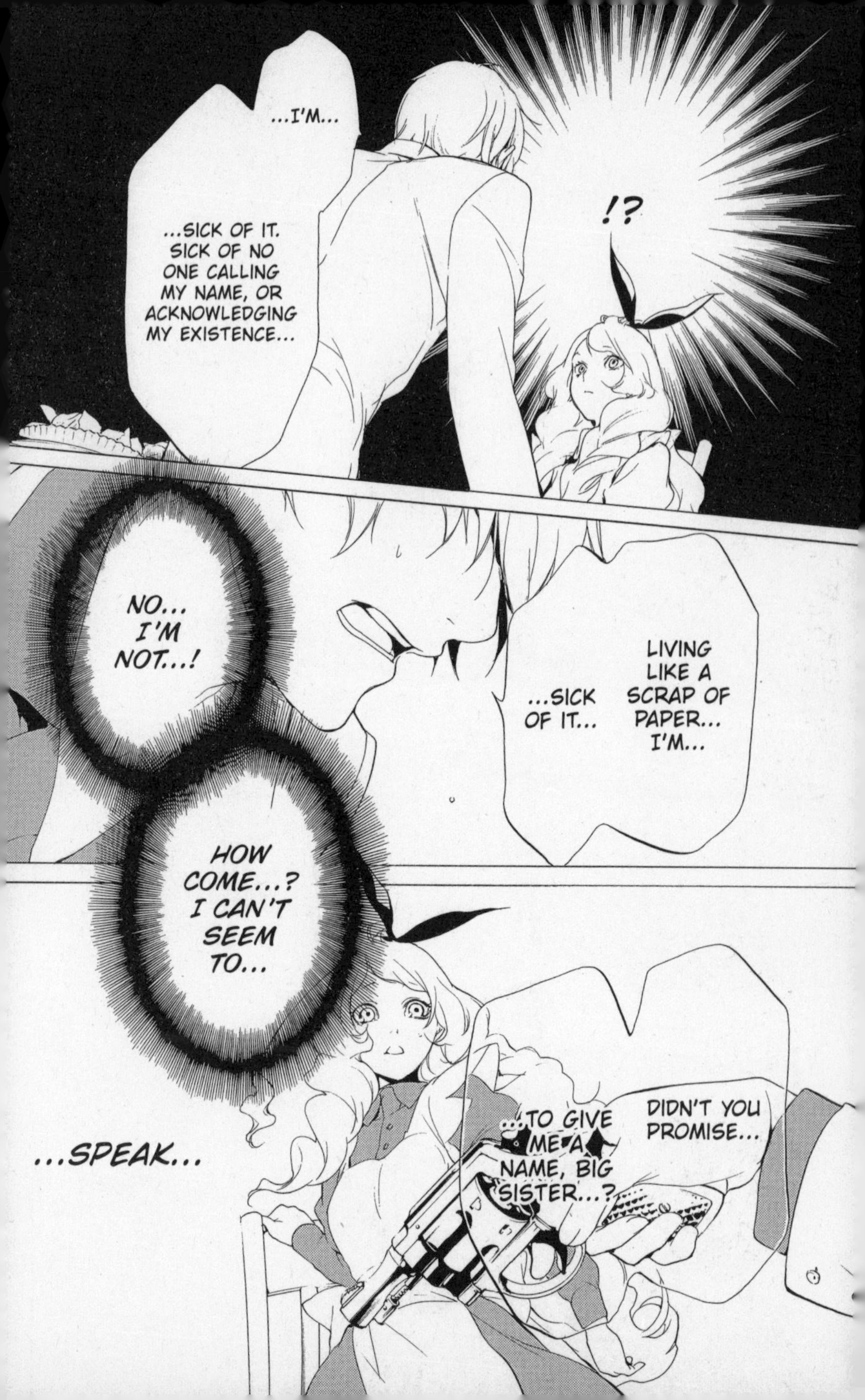
...I'M...
...SICK OF IT. SICK OF NO ONE CALLING MY NAME, OR ACKNOWLEDGING MY EXISTENCE...
!?
LIVING LIKE A SCRAP OF PAPER... I'M...
...SICK OF IT...
NO... I'M NOT...!
HOW COME...? I CAN'T SEEM TO...
DIDN'T YOU PROMISE...
...TO GIVE ME A NAME, BIG SISTER...?
...SPEAK...

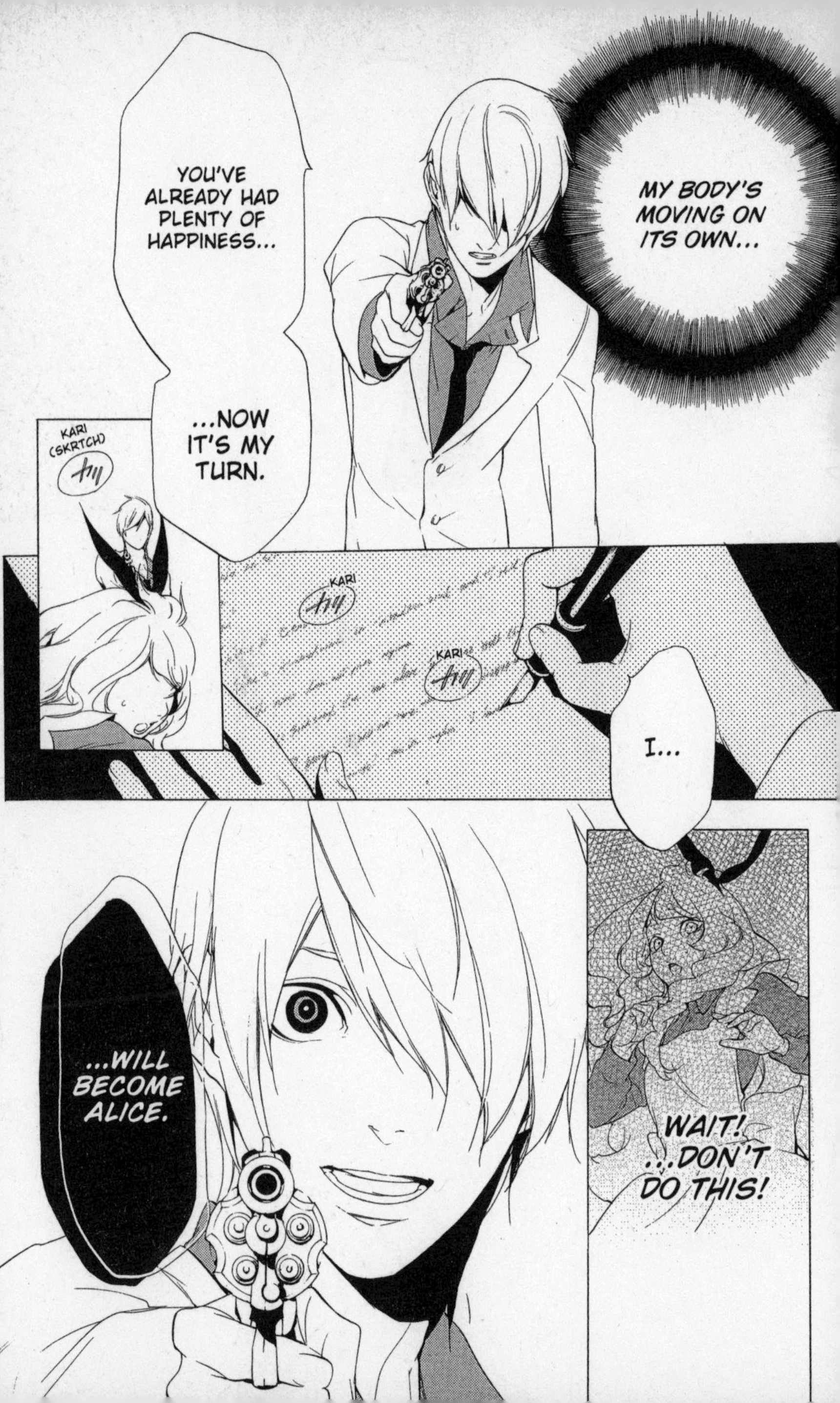
MY BODY'S MOVING ON ITS OWN...
YOU'VE ALREADY HAD PLENTY OF HAPPINESS...
...NOW IT'S MY TURN.
KARI (SKRTCH)
KARI
KARI
I...
WAIT! ...DON'T DO THIS!
...WILL BECOME ALICE.

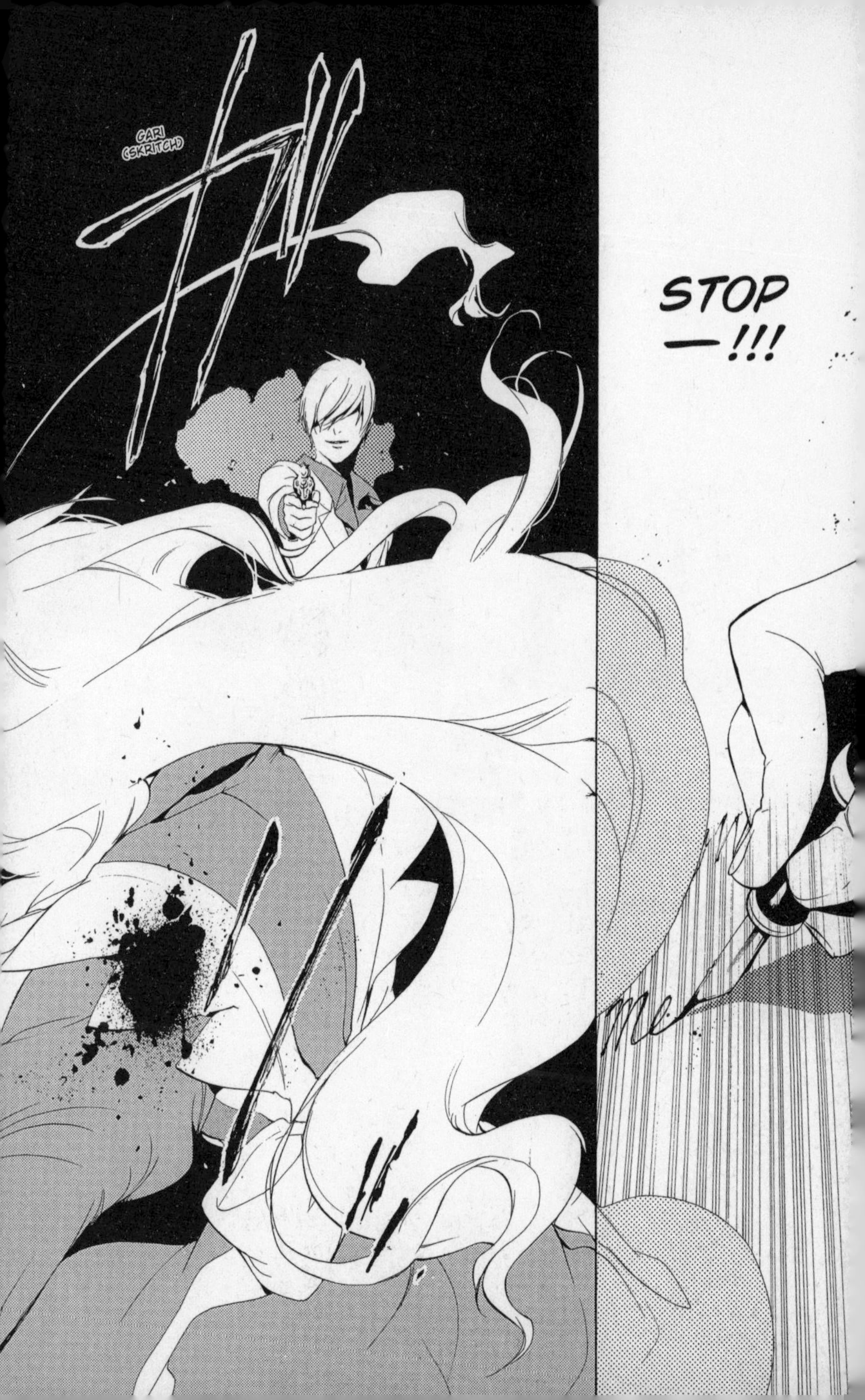
STOP—!!!
GARI
(SKRITCH)

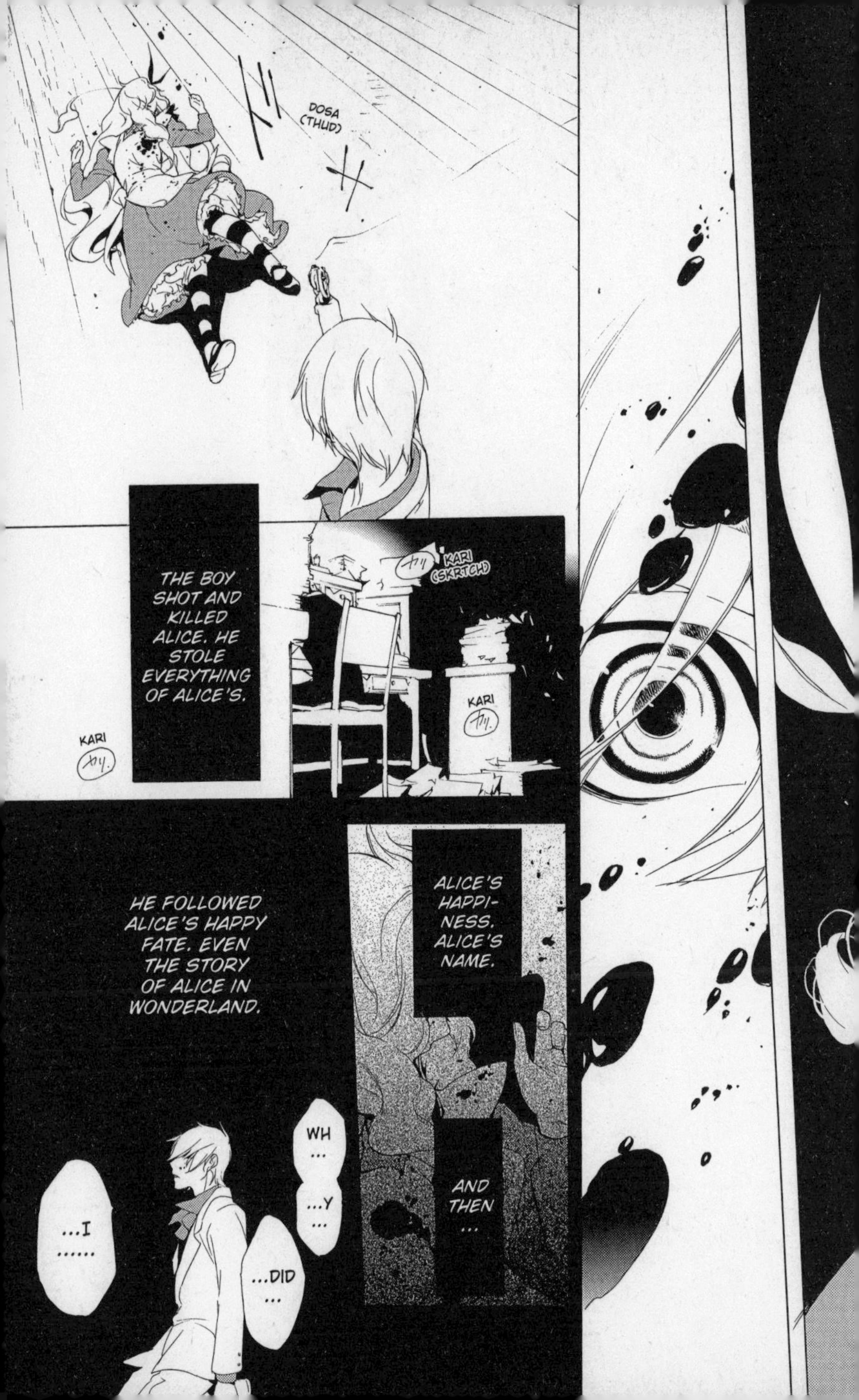
DOSA (THUD)
KARI (SKRTCH)
KARI
THE BOY SHOT AND KILLED ALICE. HE STOLE EVERYTHING OF ALICE'S.
KARI
ALICE'S HAPPI-NESS. ALICE'S NAME.
AND THEN ...
HE FOLLOWED ALICE'S HAPPY FATE. EVEN THE STORY OF ALICE IN WONDERLAND.
WH ...
...Y ...
...DID ...
...I ......

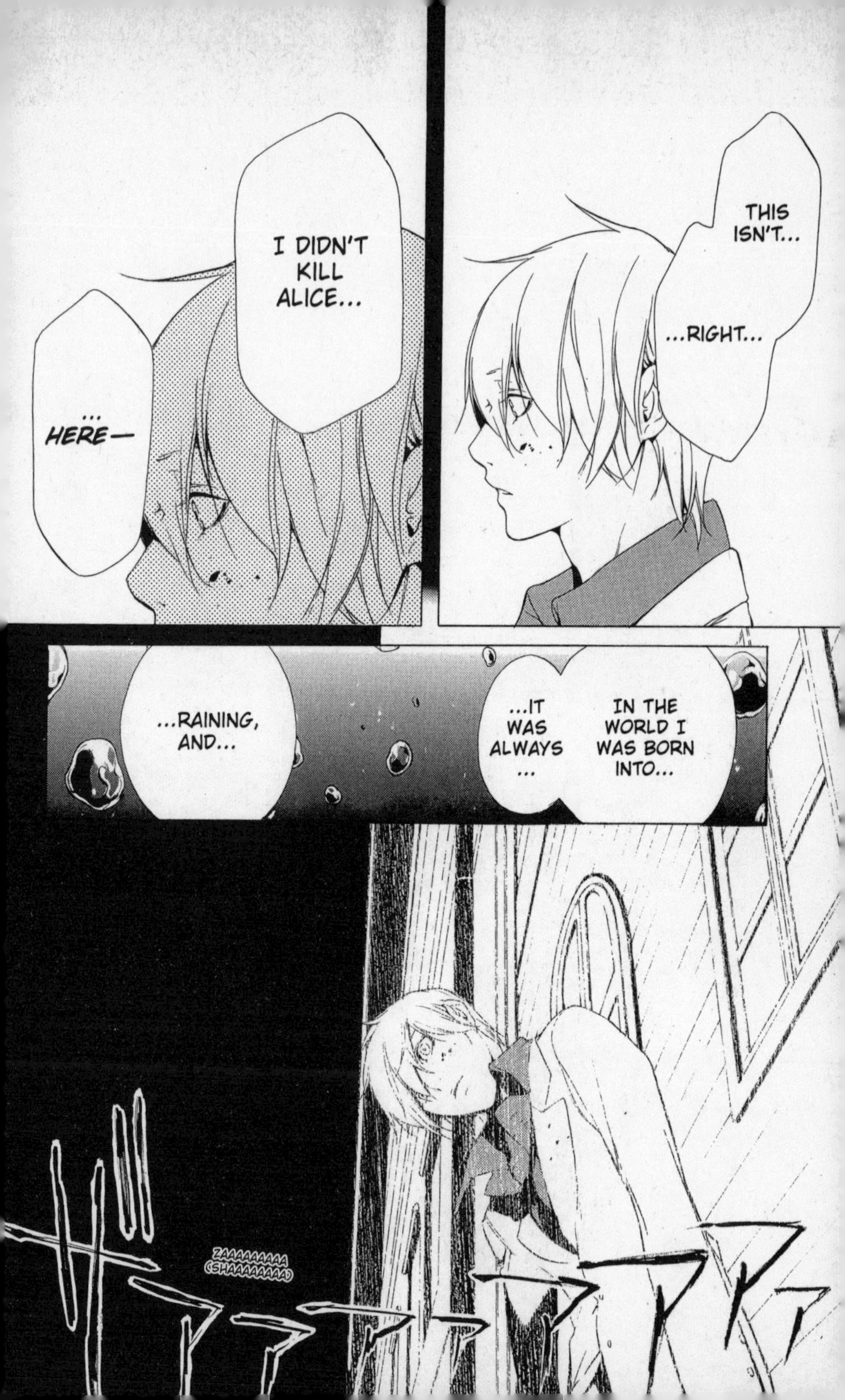
THIS ISN'T...
...RIGHT...
I DIDN'T KILL ALICE...
...HERE—
IN THE WORLD I WAS BORN INTO...
...IT WAS ALWAYS ...
...RAINING, AND...
ZAAAAAAAAA (SHAAAAAAAAA)

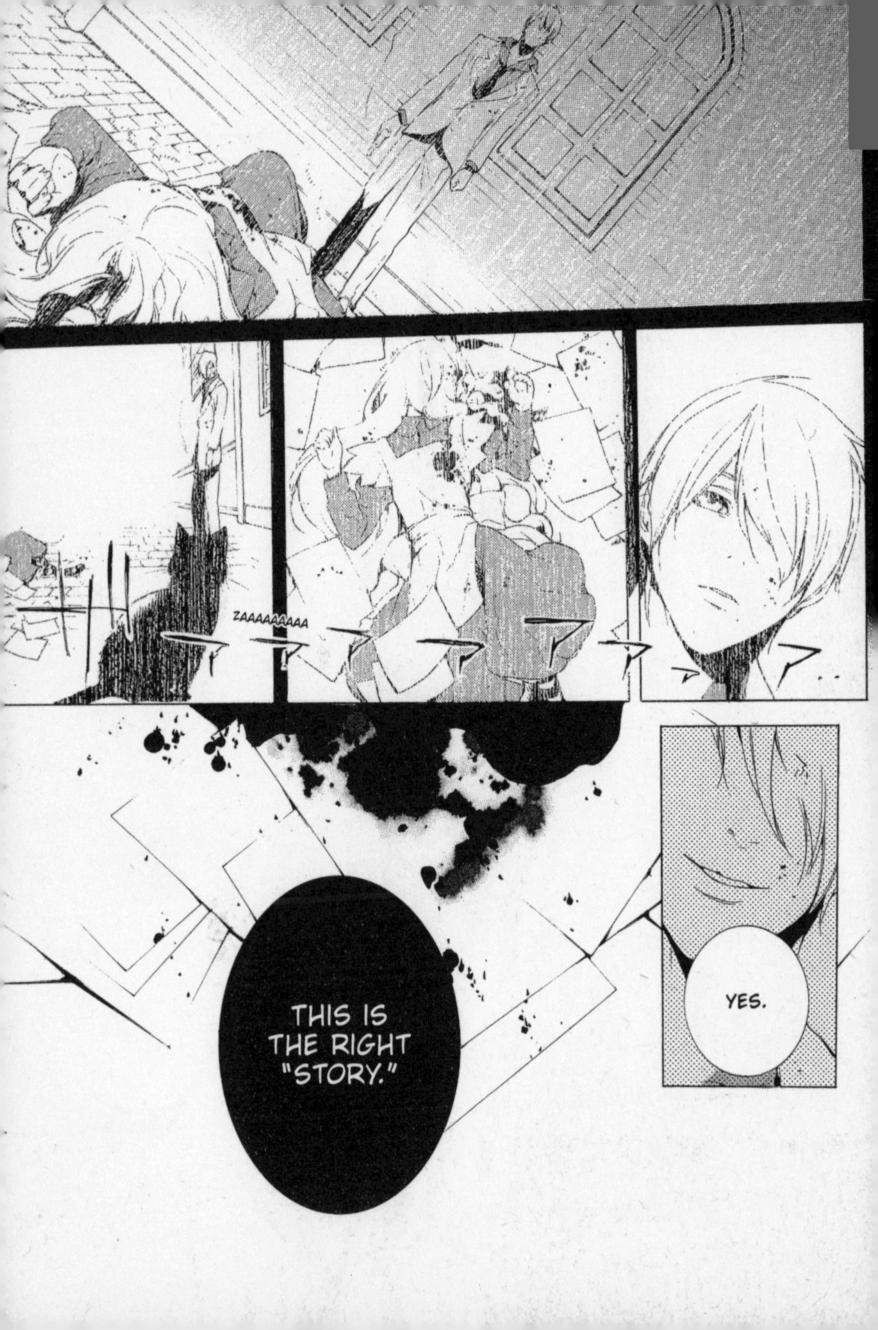
ZAAAAAAAAA
YES.
THIS IS THE RIGHT "STORY."

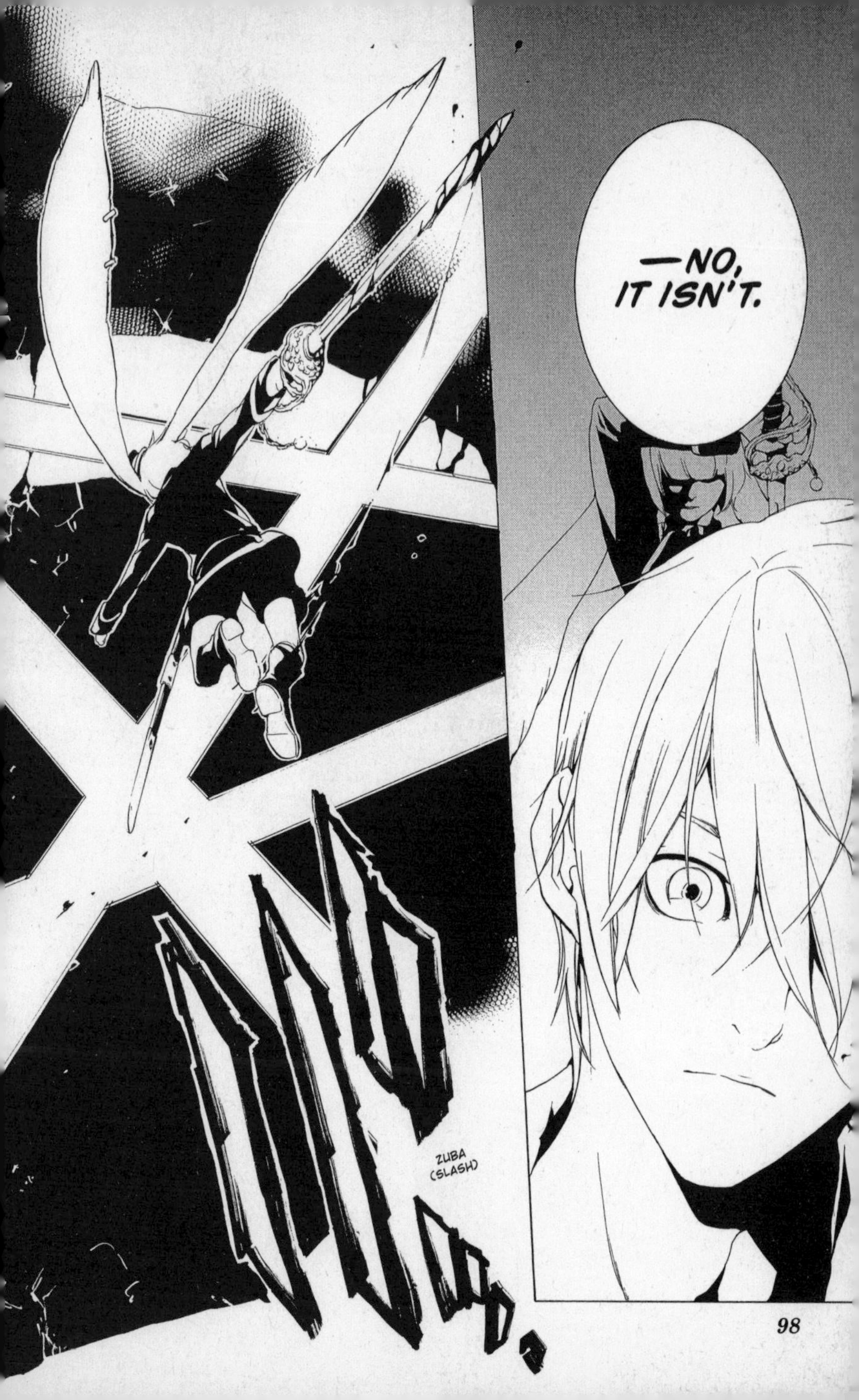
—NO, IT ISN'T.
ZUBA (SLASH)

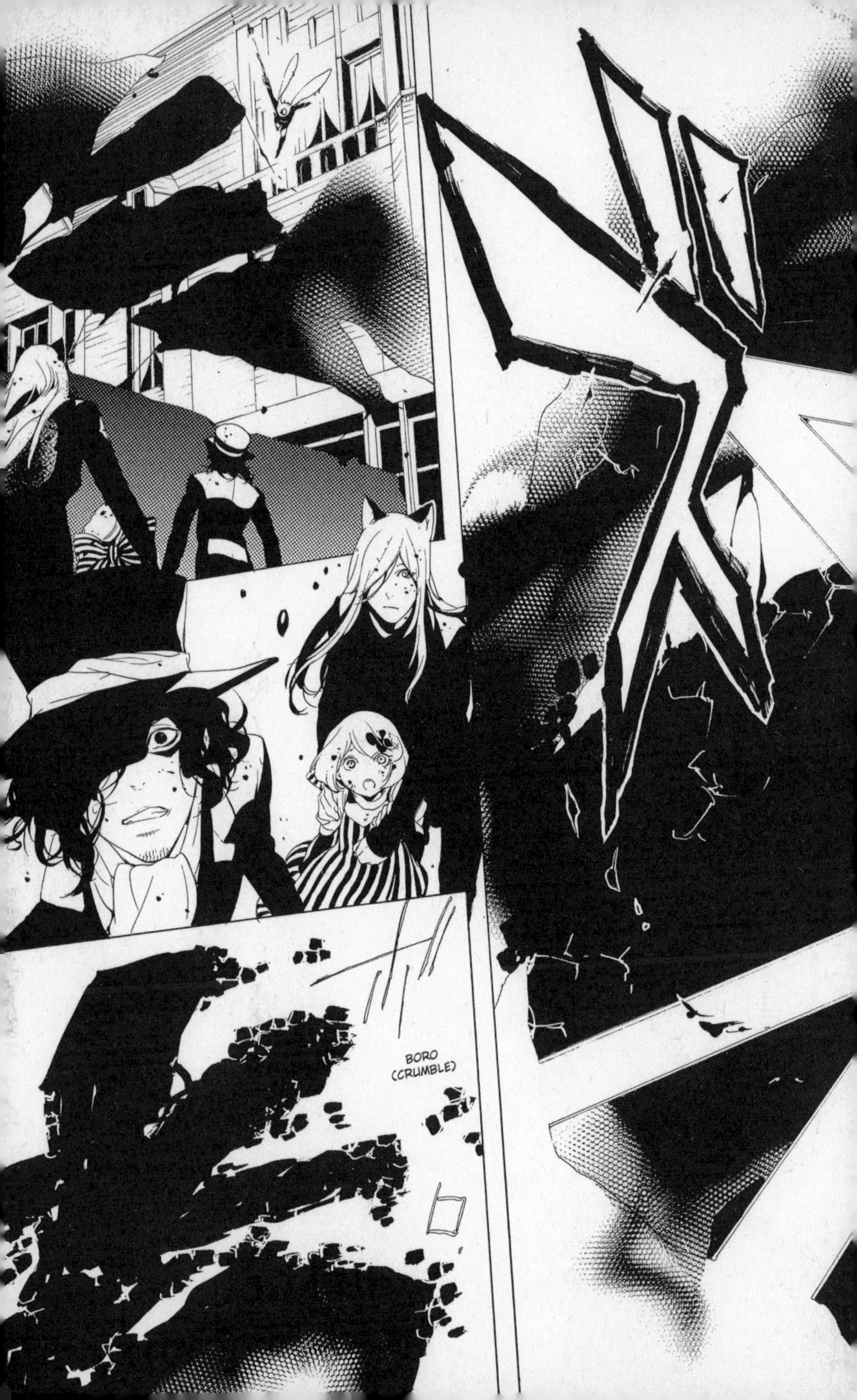
BORO
(CRUMBLE)

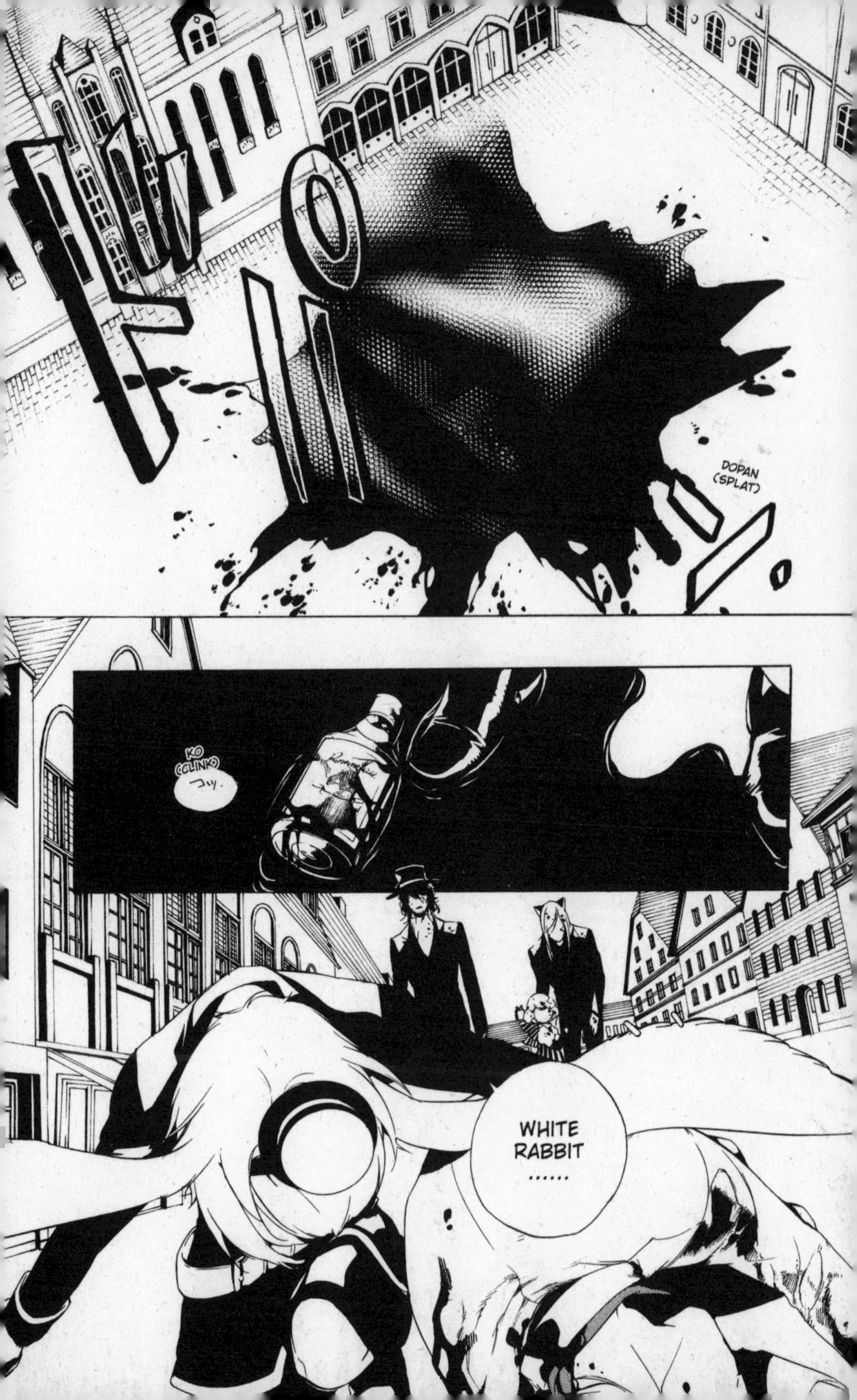
DOPAN (SPLAT)
KO (CLINK)
コッ.
WHITE RABBIT ......

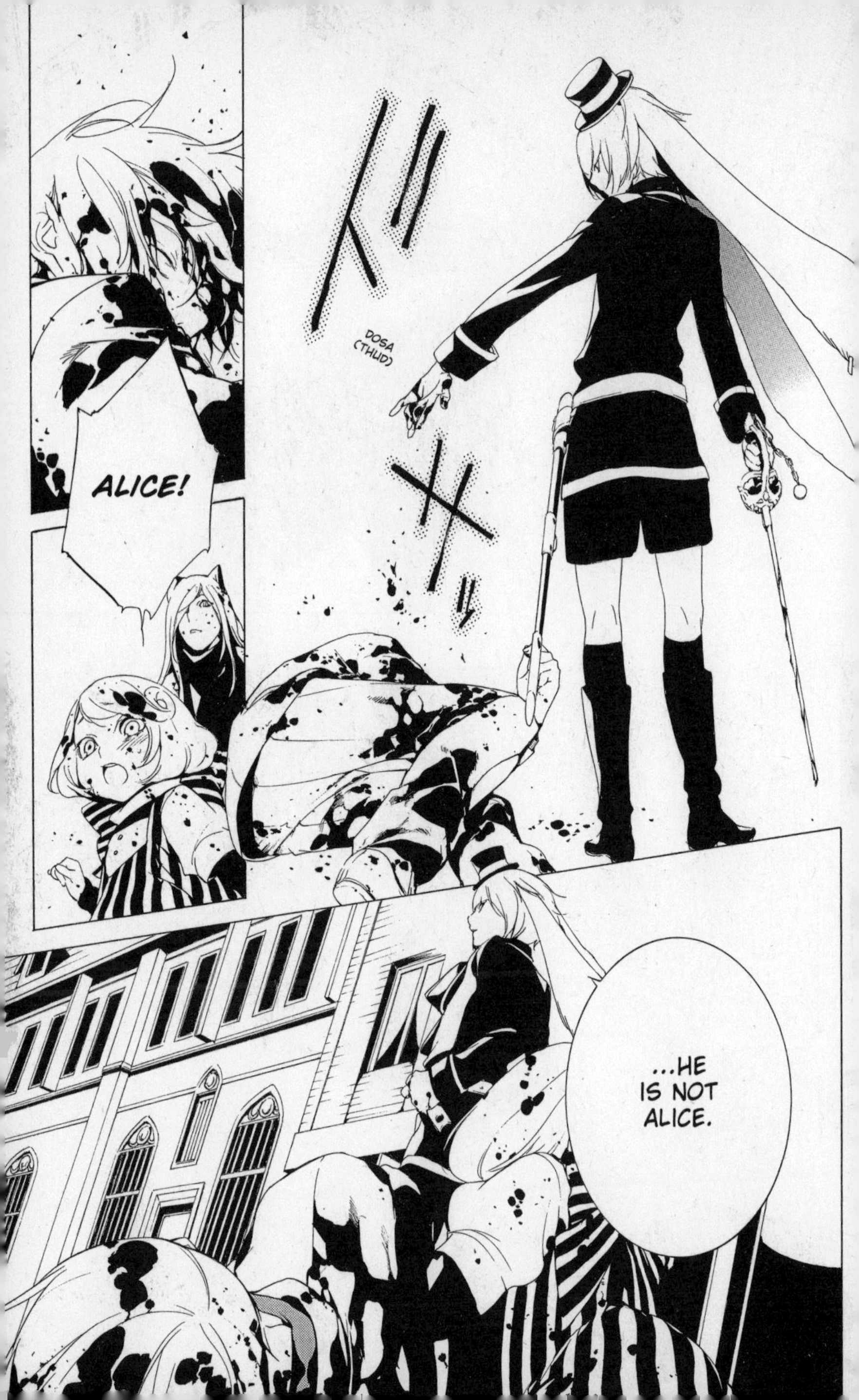
DOSA (THUD)
ALICE!
...HE IS NOT ALICE.

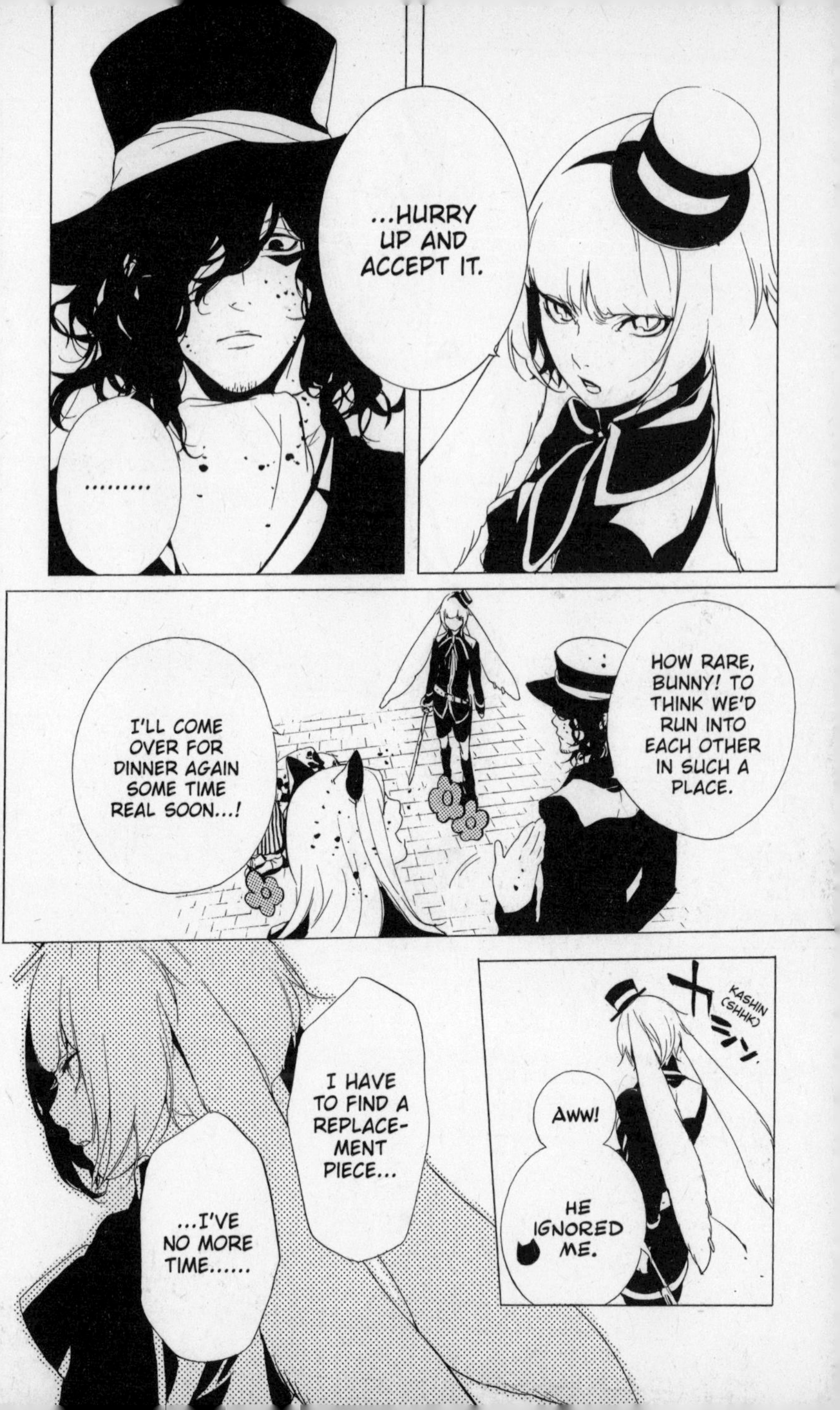
...HURRY UP AND ACCEPT IT.
....
HOW RARE, BUNNY! TO THINK WE'D RUN INTO EACH OTHER IN SUCH A PLACE.
I'LL COME OVER FOR DINNER AGAIN SOME TIME REAL SOON...!
KASHIN (SHHK)
AWW!
HE IGNORED ME.
I HAVE TO FIND A REPLACE-MENT PIECE...
...I'VE NO MORE TIME......

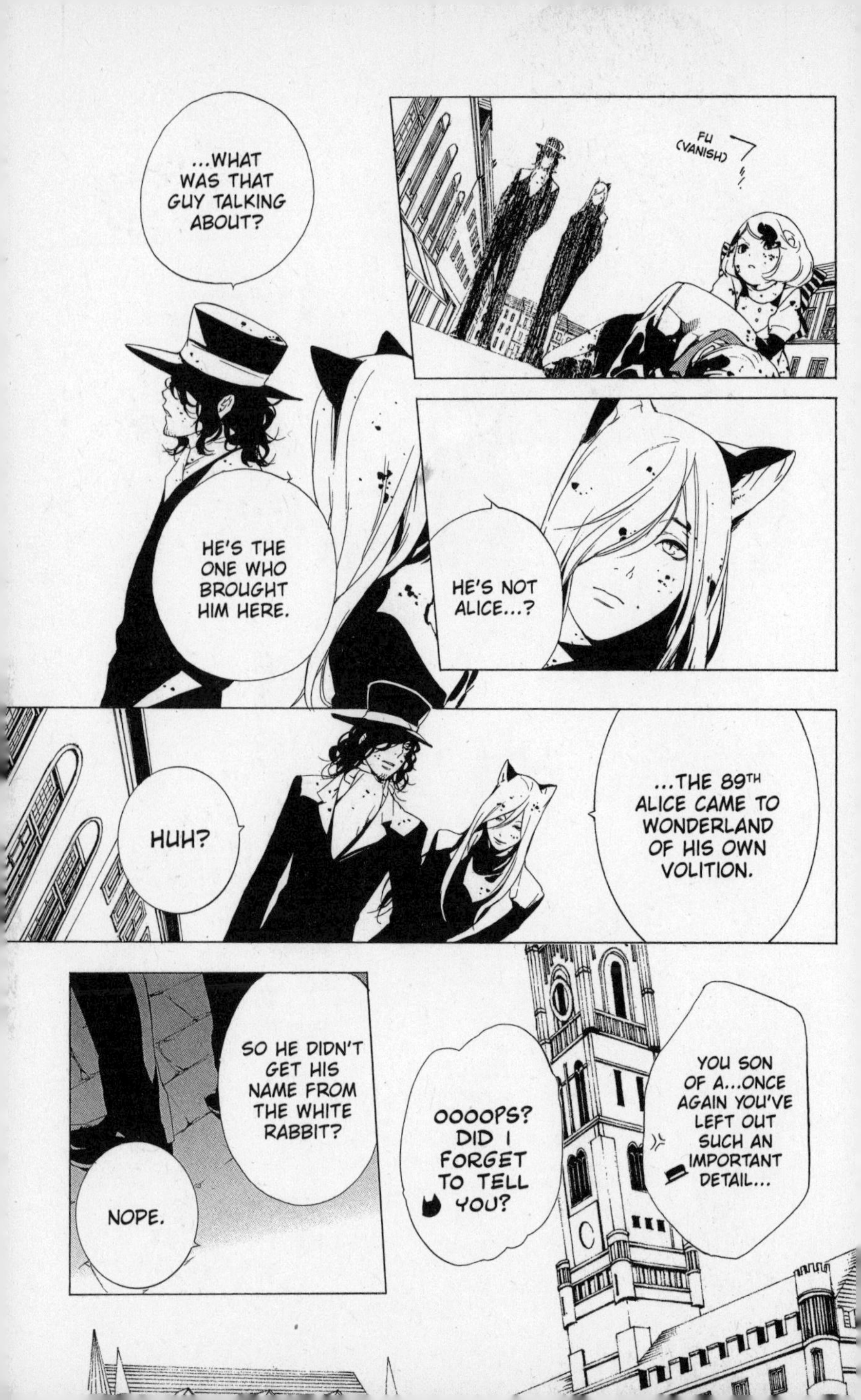
FU (VANISH)
...WHAT WAS THAT GUY TALKING ABOUT?
HE'S NOT ALICE...?
HE'S THE ONE WHO BROUGHT HIM HERE.
...THE 89TH ALICE CAME TO WONDERLAND OF HIS OWN VOLITION.
HUH?
YOU SON OF A...ONCE AGAIN YOU'VE LEFT OUT SUCH AN IMPORTANT DETAIL...
OOOOPS? DID I FORGET TO TELL YOU?
SO HE DIDN'T GET HIS NAME FROM THE WHITE RABBIT?
NOPE.

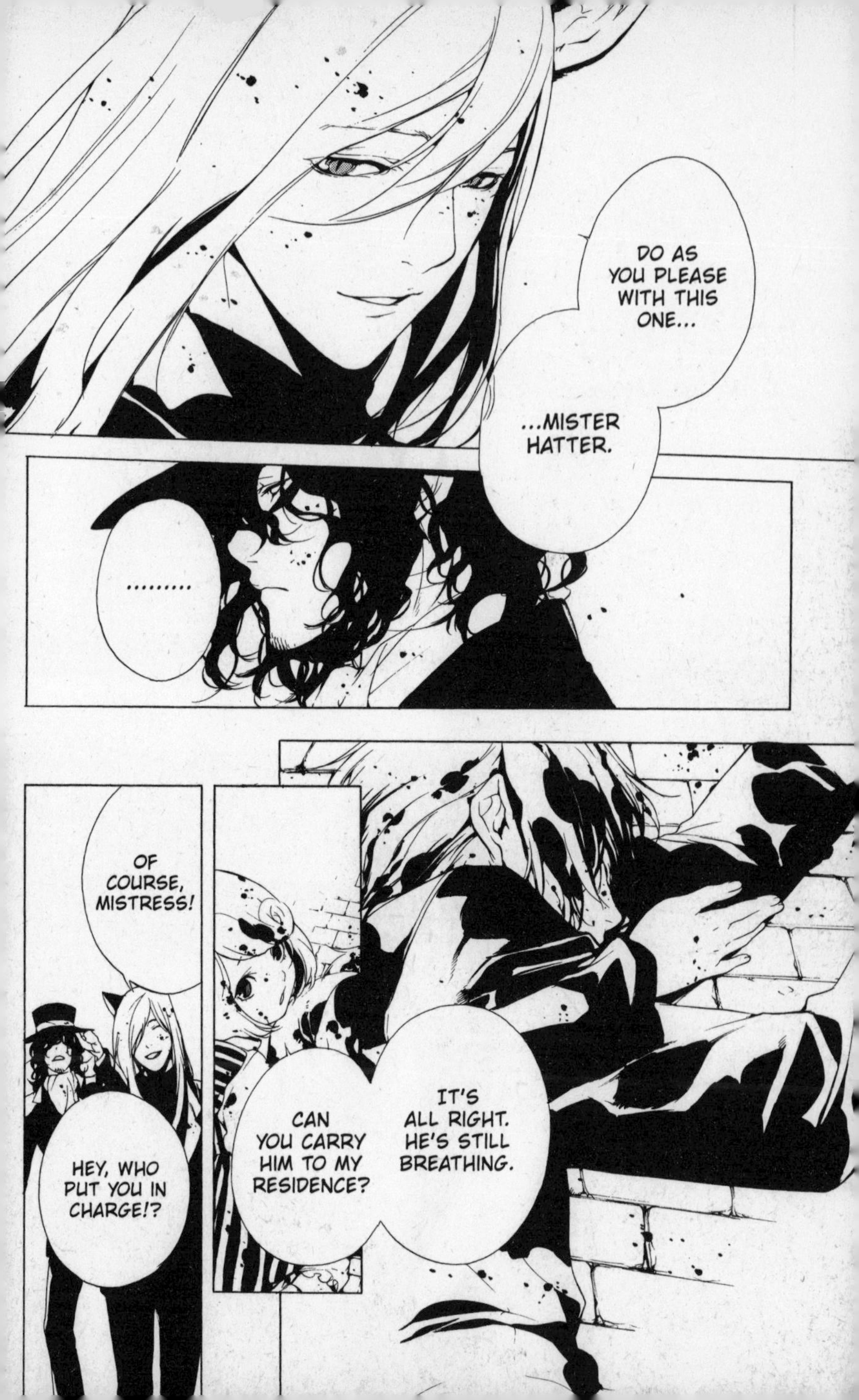
DO AS YOU PLEASE WITH THIS ONE...
...MISTER HATTER.
....
IT'S ALL RIGHT. HE'S STILL BREATHING.
CAN YOU CARRY HIM TO MY RESIDENCE?
OF COURSE, MISTRESS!
HEY, WHO PUT YOU IN CHARGE!?

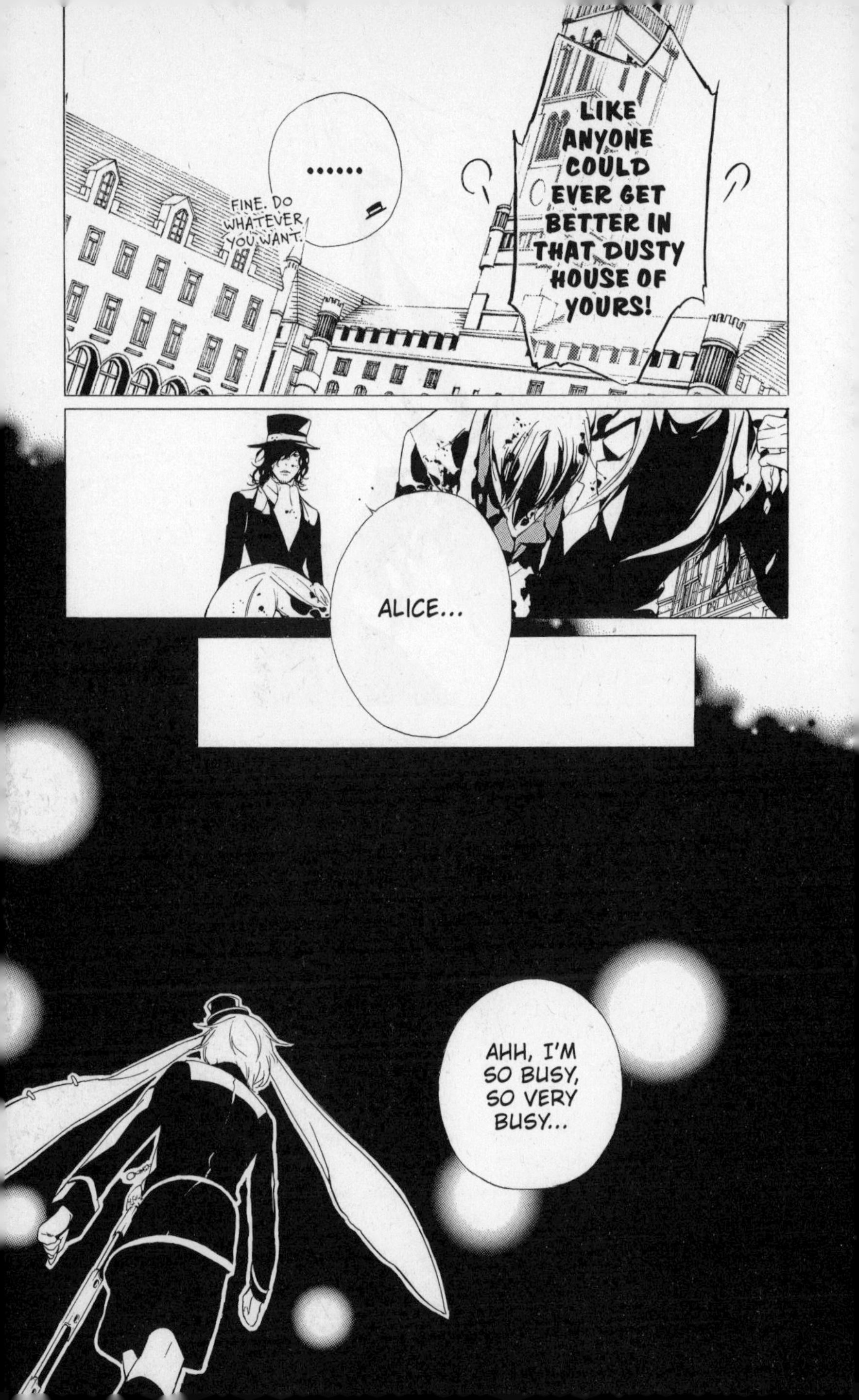
LIKE ANYONE COULD EVER GET BETTER IN THAT DUSTY HOUSE OF YOURS!
......
FINE. DO WHATEVER YOU WANT.
ALICE...
AHH, I'M SO BUSY, SO VERY BUSY...

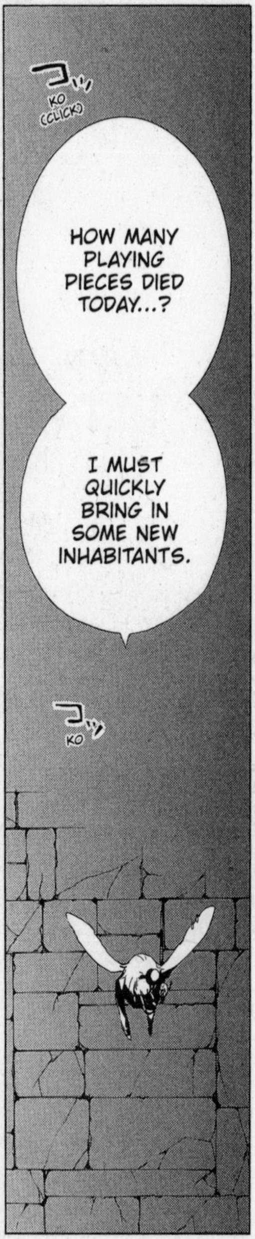
KO (CLICK)
HOW MANY PLAYING PIECES DIED TODAY...?
I MUST QUICKLY BRING IN SOME NEW INHABITANTS.
KO

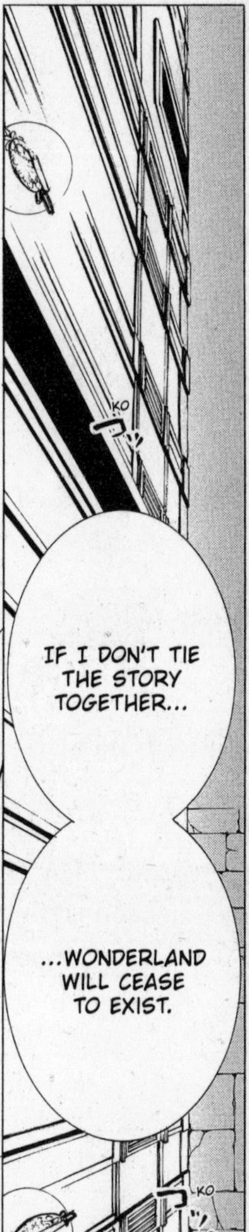
KO
IF I DON'T TIE THE STORY TOGETHER...
...WONDERLAND WILL CEASE TO EXIST.
KO

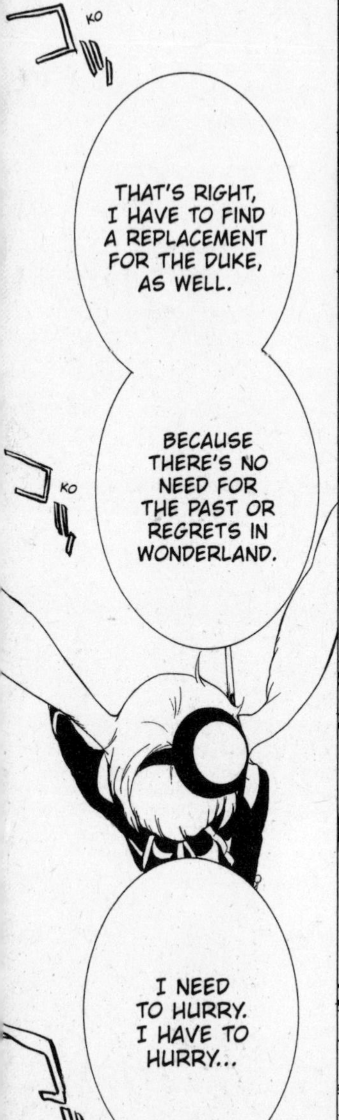
KO
THAT'S RIGHT, I HAVE TO FIND A REPLACEMENT FOR THE DUKE, AS WELL.
BECAUSE THERE'S NO NEED FOR THE PAST OR REGRETS IN WONDERLAND.
KO
I NEED TO HURRY. I HAVE TO HURRY...
KO

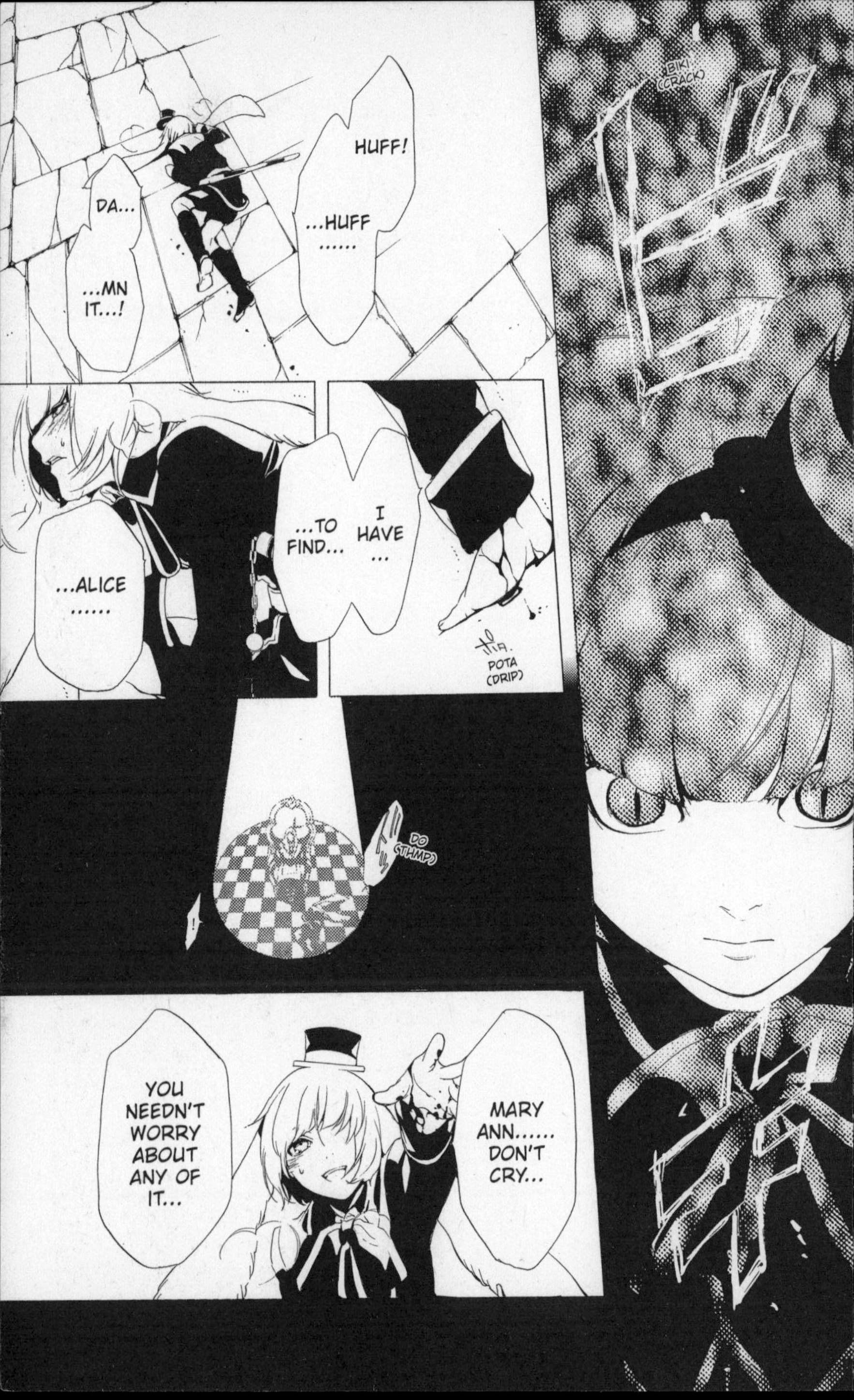
BIKI (CRACK)
HUFF!
...HUFF ......
DA...
...MN IT...!
I HAVE ...
...TO FIND...
POTA (DRIP)
...ALICE ......
DO (THMP)
!
MARY ANN...... DON'T CRY...
YOU NEEDN'T WORRY ABOUT ANY OF IT...

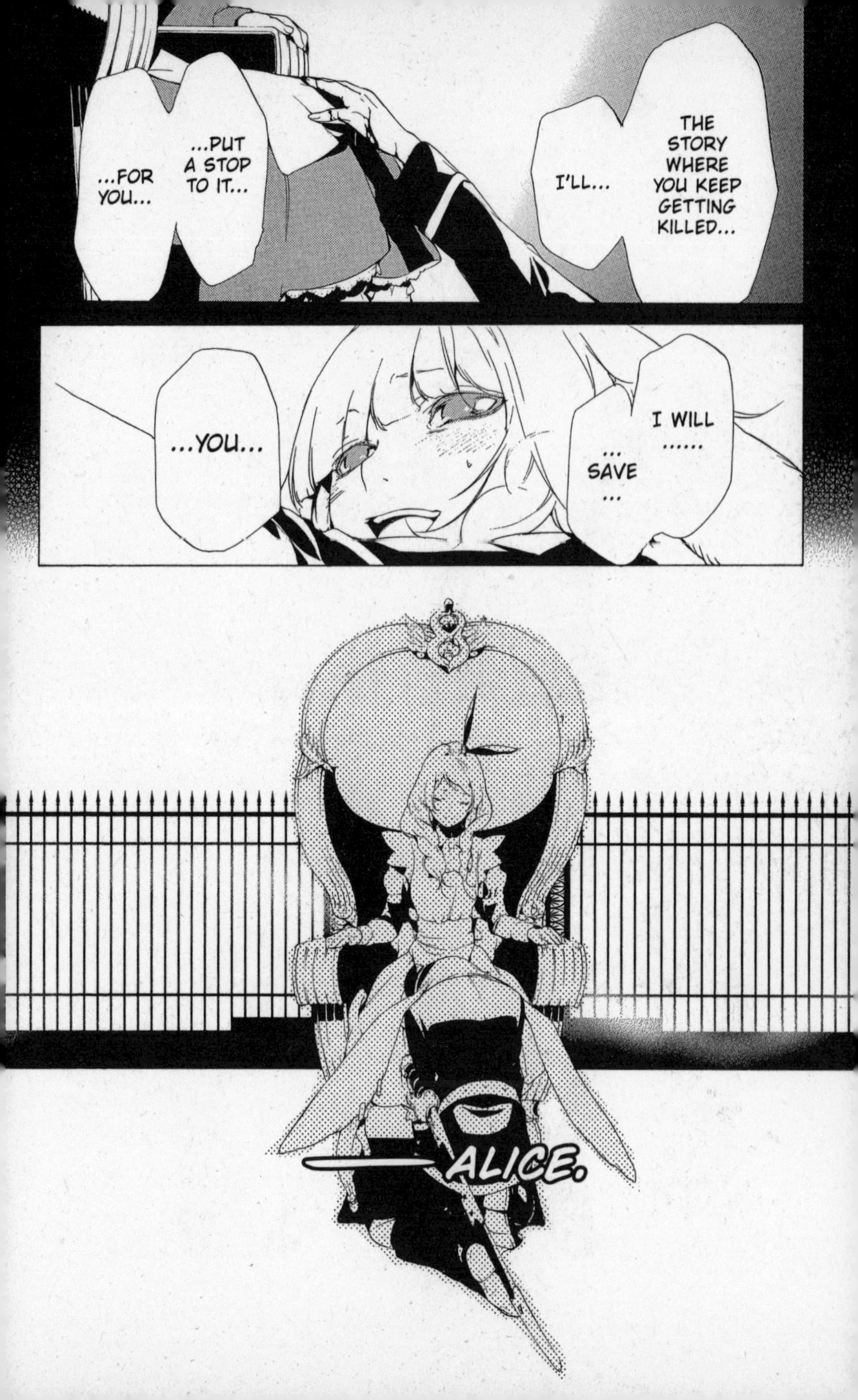
THE STORY WHERE YOU KEEP GETTING KILLED...
I'LL...
...PUT A STOP TO IT...
...FOR YOU...
I WILL ......
... SAVE ...
...YOU...
—ALICE.

Chapter 9 Bubblegum Music.

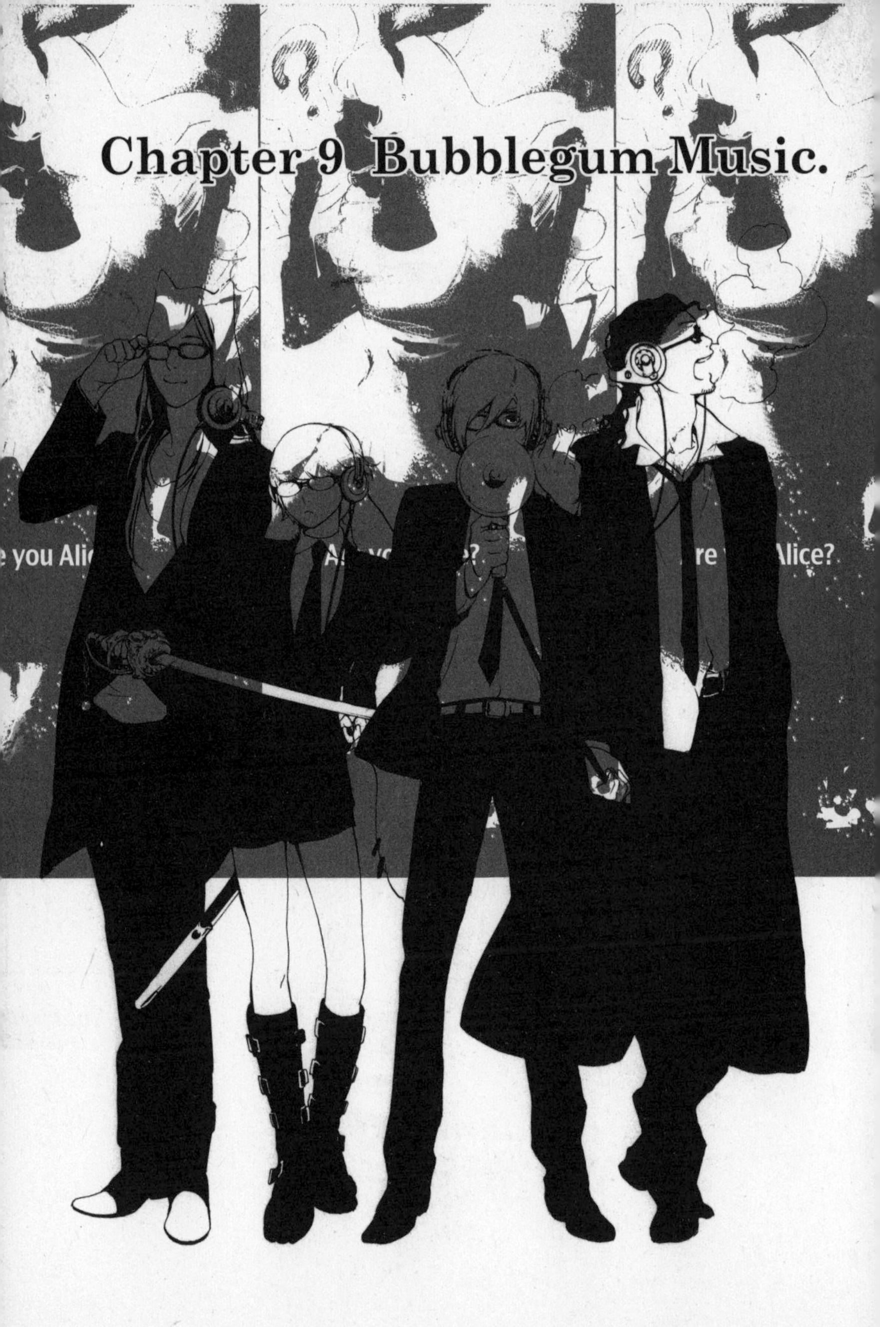
e you Ali
A yo e?
re Alice?

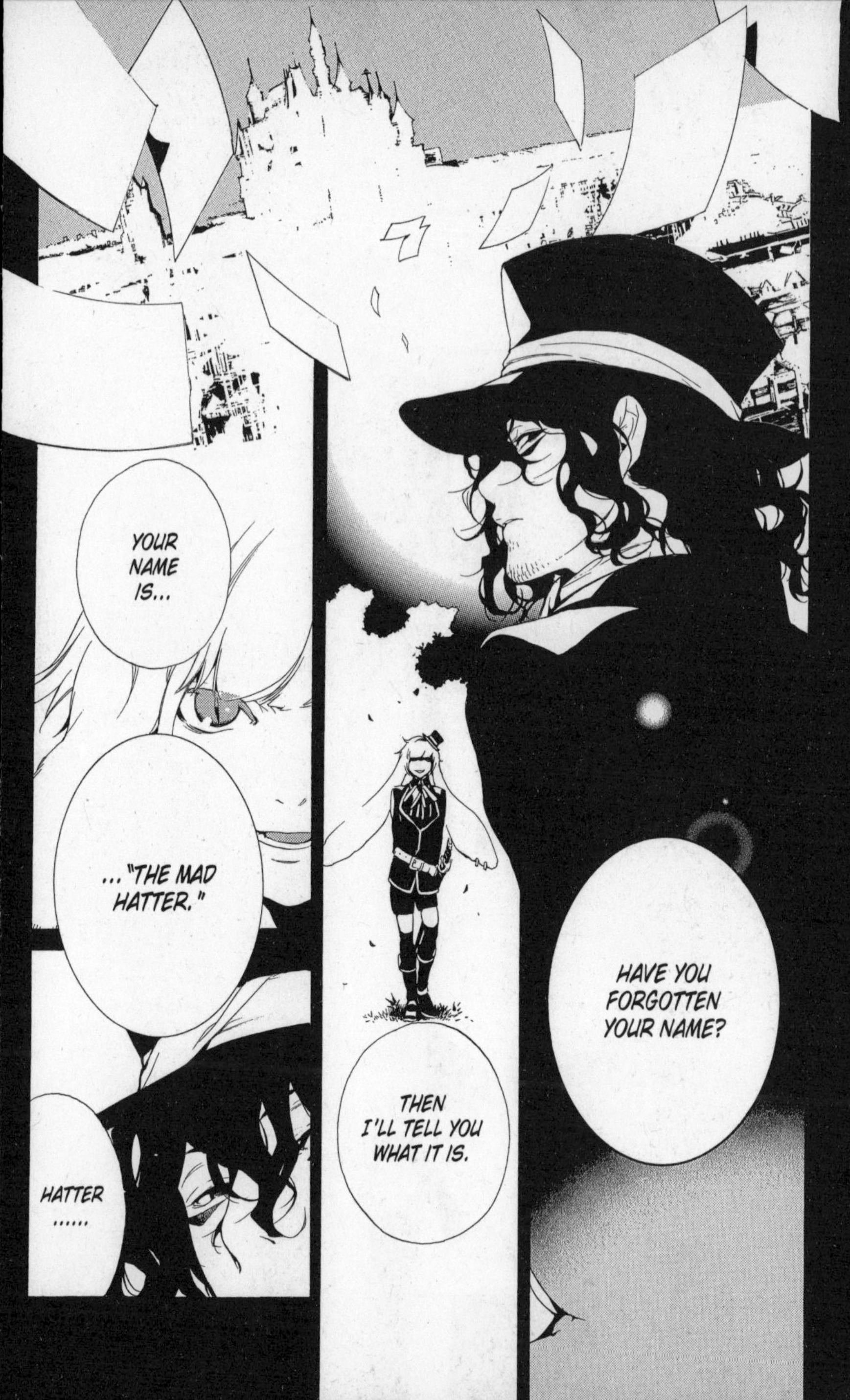
HAVE YOU FORGOTTEN YOUR NAME?
THEN I'LL TELL YOU WHAT IT IS.
YOUR NAME IS...
..."THE MAD HATTER."
HATTER ......

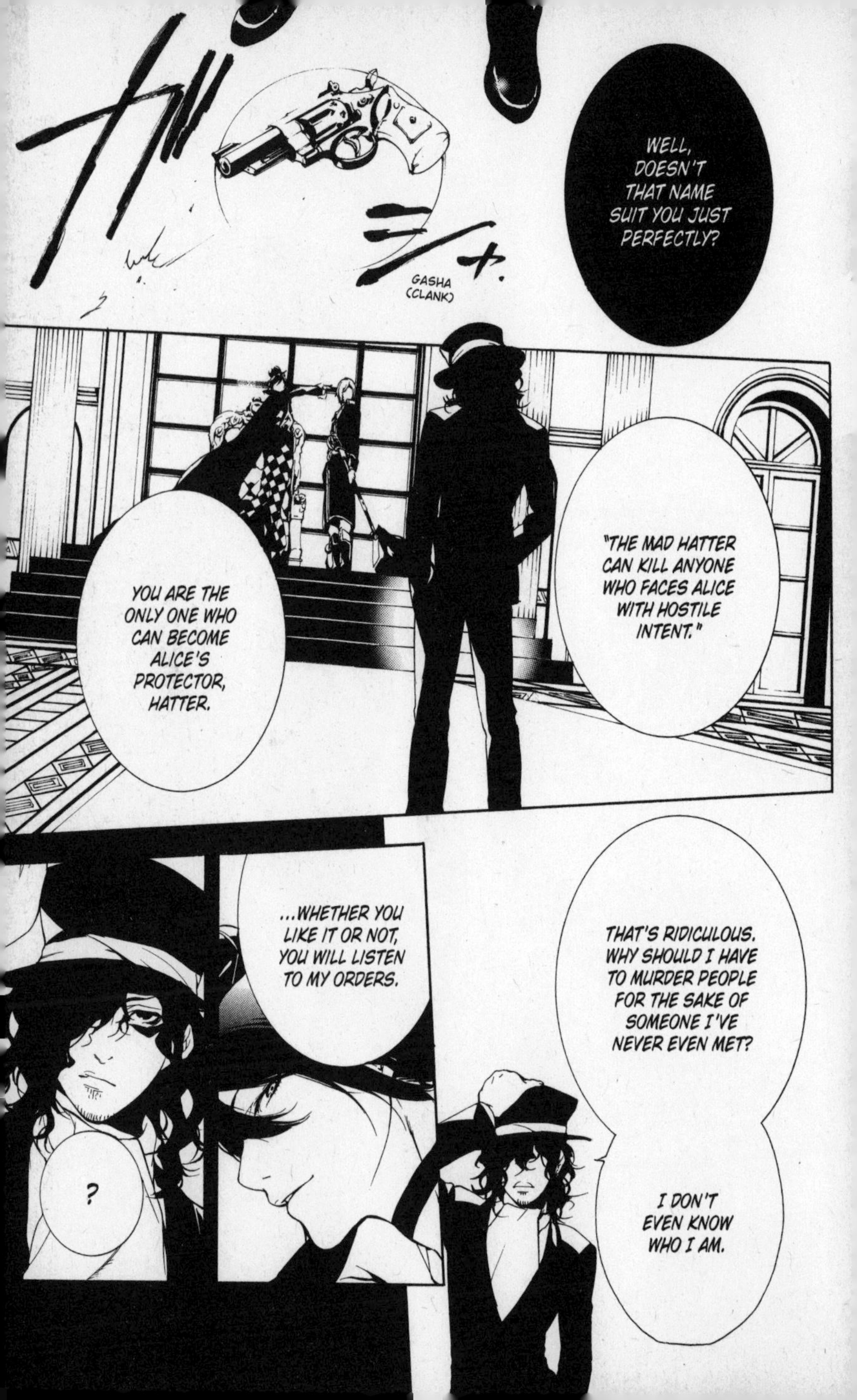
WELL, DOESN'T THAT NAME SUIT YOU JUST PERFECTLY?
GASHA (CLANK)
"THE MAD HATTER CAN KILL ANYONE WHO FACES ALICE WITH HOSTILE INTENT."
YOU ARE THE ONLY ONE WHO CAN BECOME ALICE'S PROTECTOR, HATTER.
THAT'S RIDICULOUS. WHY SHOULD I HAVE TO MURDER PEOPLE FOR THE SAKE OF SOMEONE I'VE NEVER EVEN MET?
I DON'T EVEN KNOW WHO I AM.
...WHETHER YOU LIKE IT OR NOT, YOU WILL LISTEN TO MY ORDERS.
?

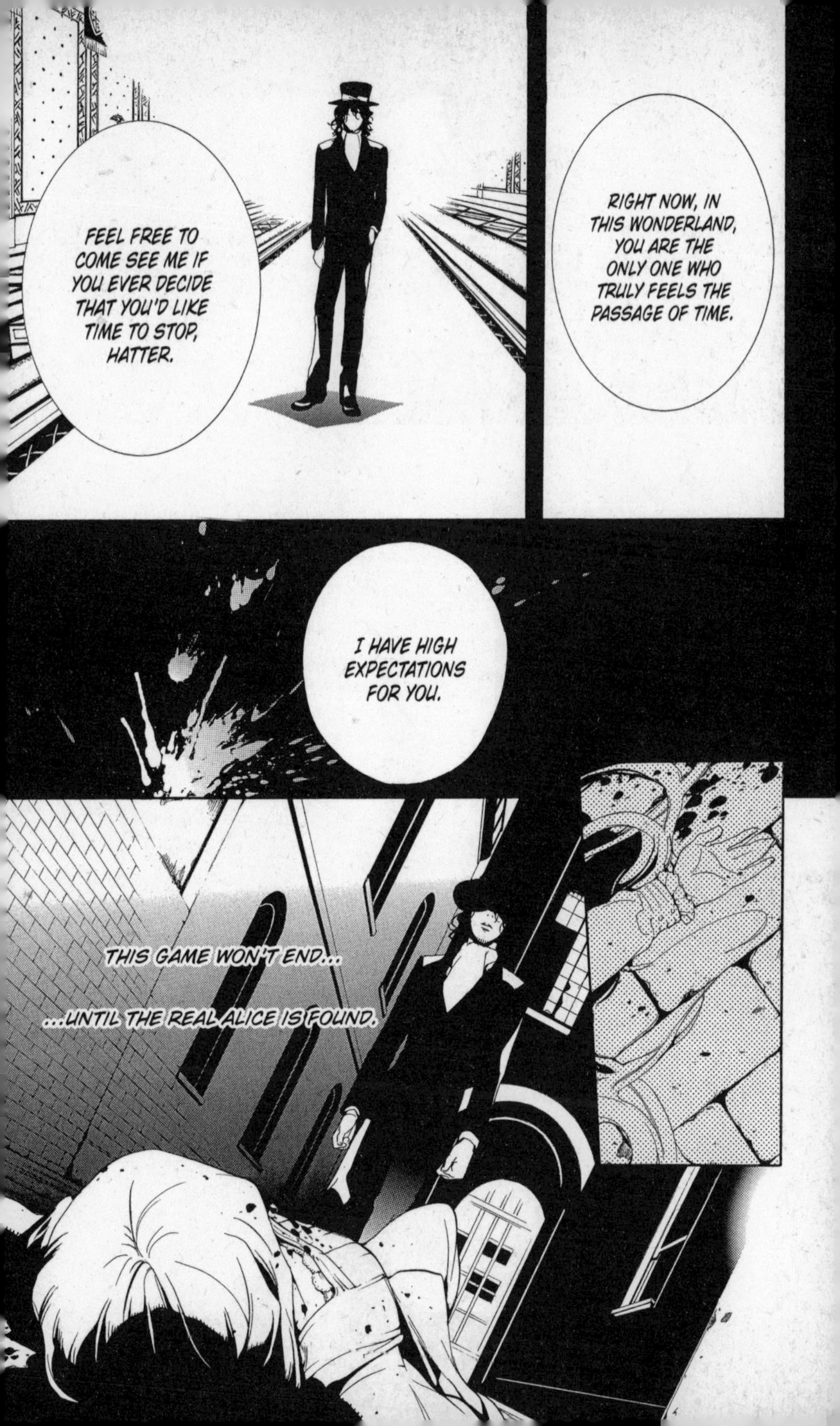
RIGHT NOW, IN THIS WONDERLAND, YOU ARE THE ONLY ONE WHO TRULY FEELS THE PASSAGE OF TIME.
FEEL FREE TO COME SEE ME IF YOU EVER DECIDE THAT YOU'D LIKE TIME TO STOP, HATTER.
I HAVE HIGH EXPECTATIONS FOR YOU.
THIS GAME WON'T END...
...UNTIL THE REAL ALICE IS FOUND.

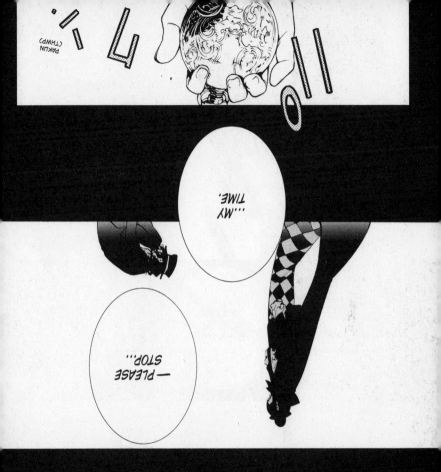

PAKUN (THWP)

"...MY TIME,

—PLEASE STOP...

WHERE IS...THE REAL...ALICE?

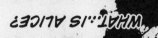

WHAT...IS ALICE?

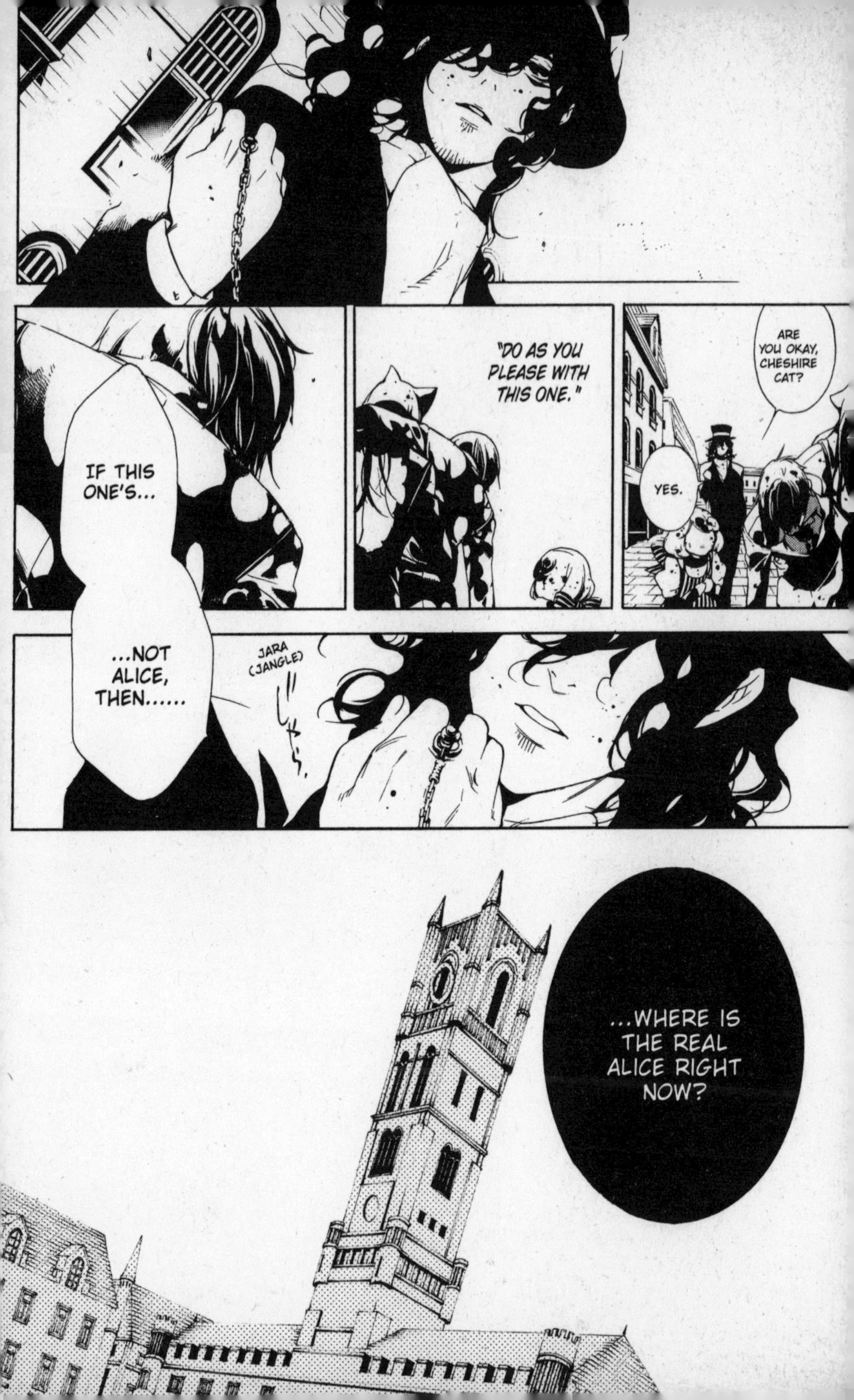
...
...
ARE YOU OKAY, CHESHIRE CAT?
YES.
"DO AS YOU PLEASE WITH THIS ONE."
IF THIS ONE'S...
...NOT ALICE, THEN......
JARA (JANGLE)
...WHERE IS THE REAL ALICE RIGHT NOW?

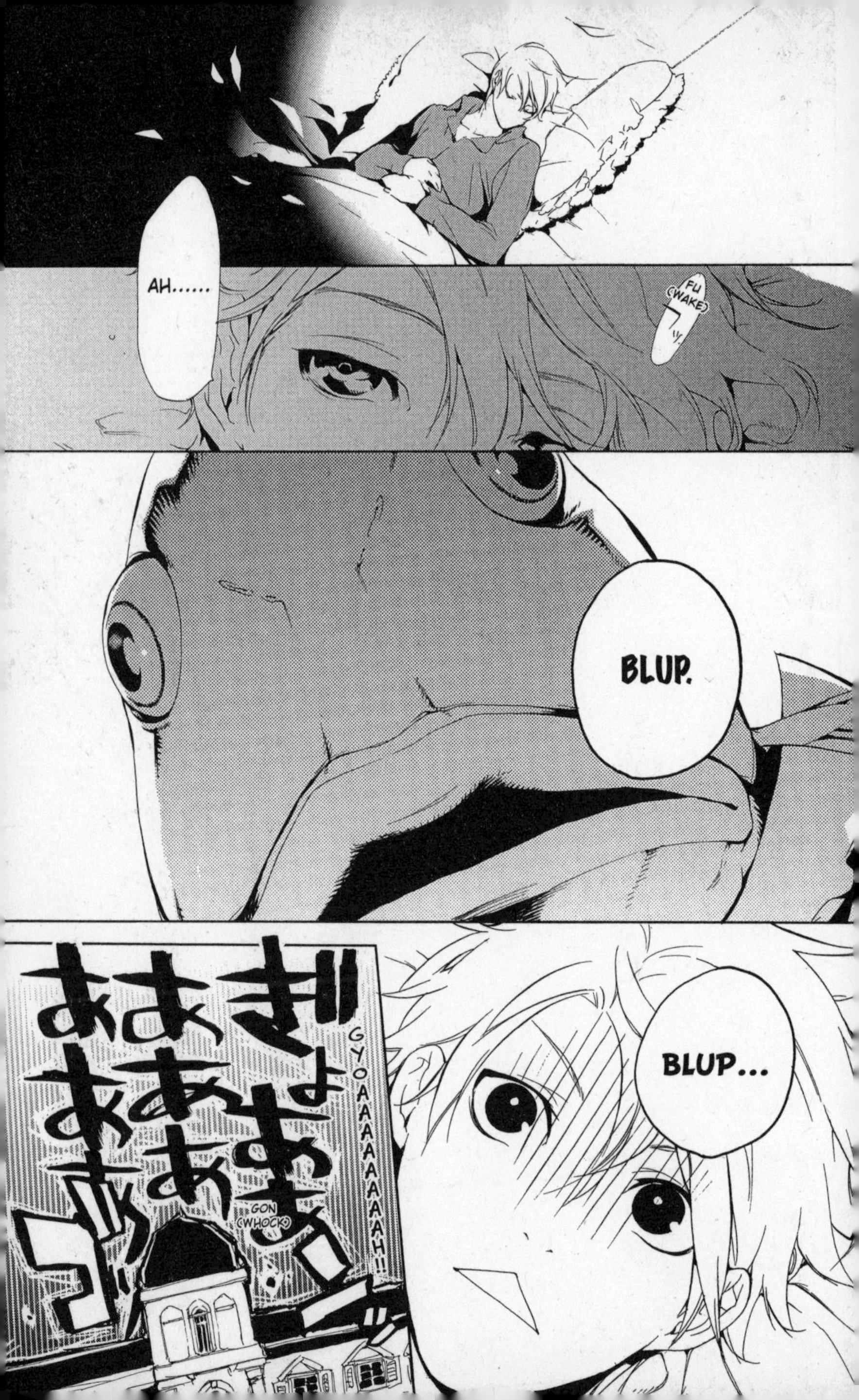
FU (WAKE)
AH......
BLUP.
BLUP...
GYOAAAAAAAAAAH!!
GON (WHOCK)

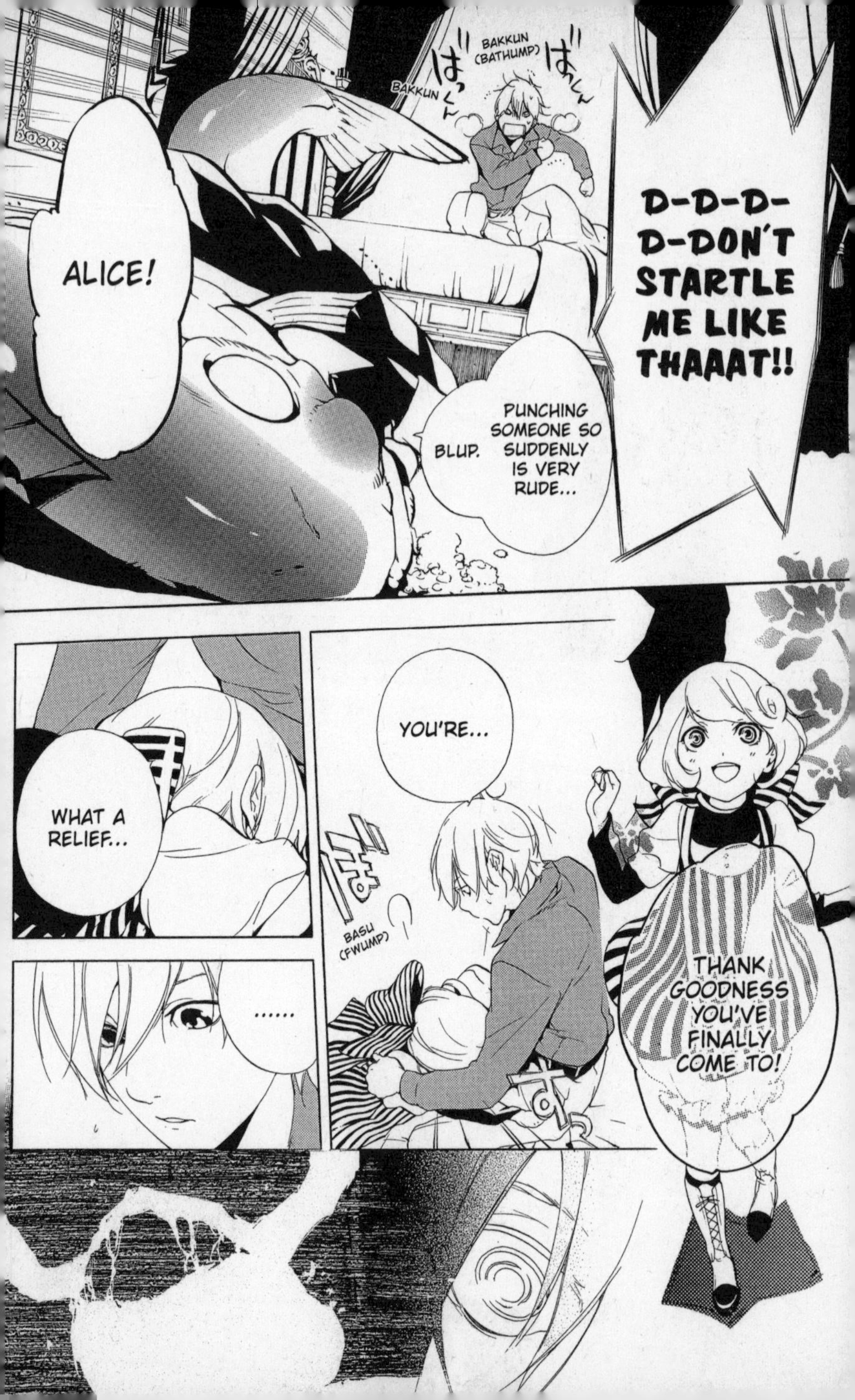
BAKKUN (BATHUMP)
BAKKUN
D-D-D-D-DON'T STARTLE ME LIKE THAAAT!!
ALICE!
PUNCHING SOMEONE SO SUDDENLY IS VERY RUDE...
BLUP.
THANK GOODNESS YOU'VE FINALLY COME TO!
YOU'RE...
BASU (FWUMP)
WHAT A RELIEF...
......

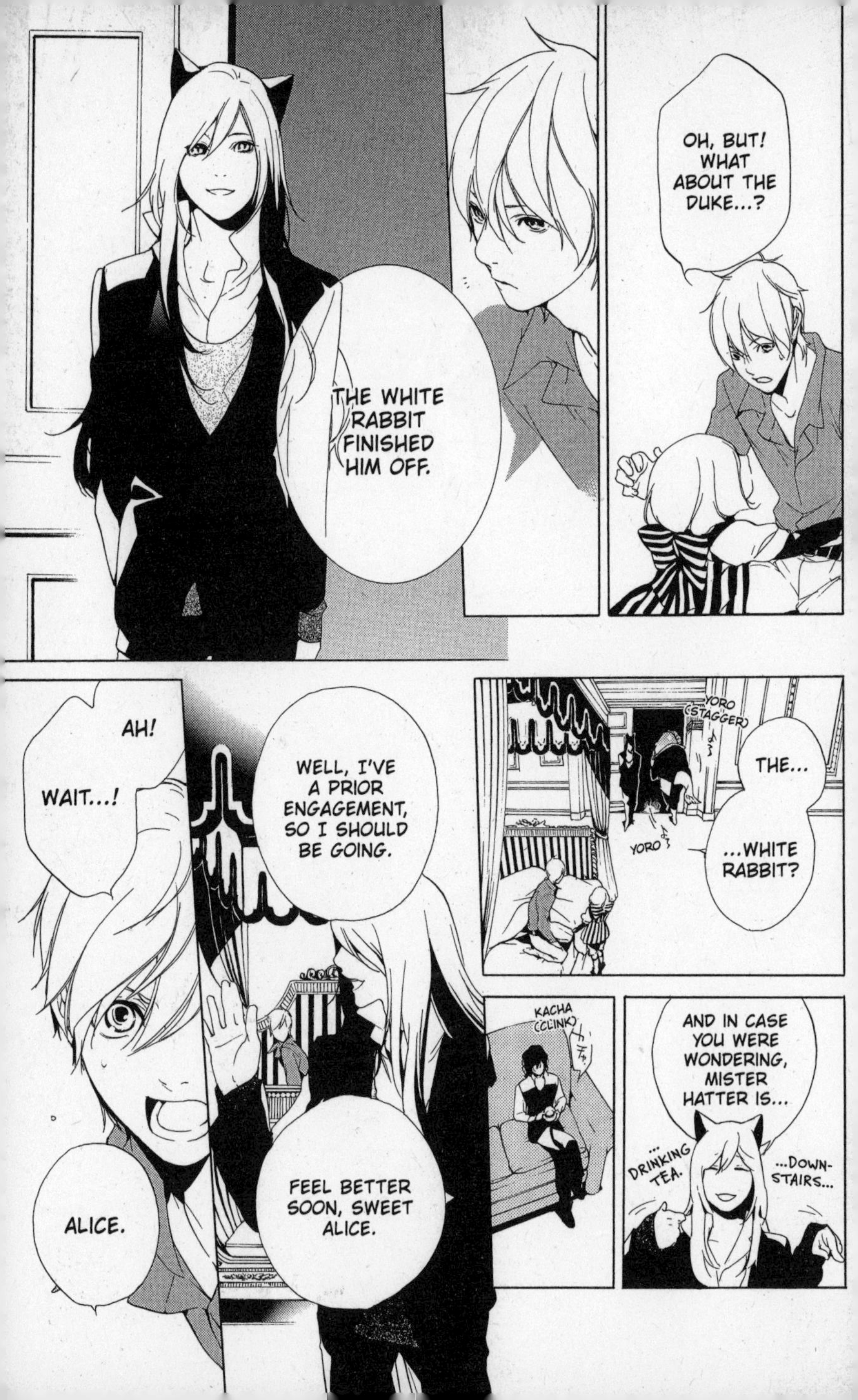
OH, BUT! WHAT ABOUT THE DUKE...?
THE WHITE RABBIT FINISHED HIM OFF.
THE...
YORO (STAGGER)
YORO
...WHITE RABBIT?
AND IN CASE YOU WERE WONDERING, MISTER HATTER IS...
...DOWN-STAIRS...
...DRINKING TEA.
KACHA (CLINK)
WELL, I'VE A PRIOR ENGAGEMENT, SO I SHOULD BE GOING.
FEEL BETTER SOON, SWEET ALICE.
AH!
WAIT...!
ALICE.

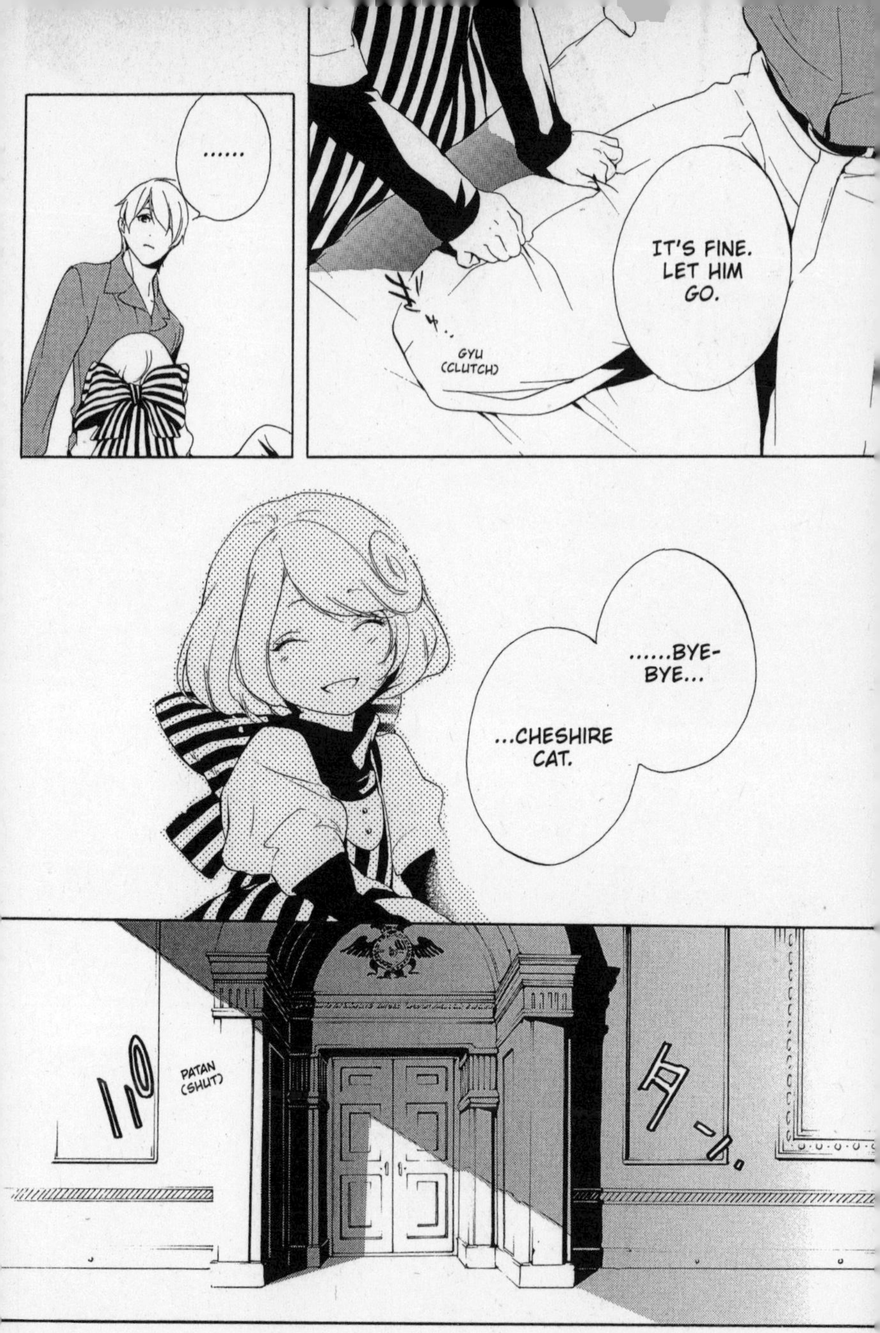
IT'S FINE. LET HIM GO.
GYU (CLUTCH)
......
......BYE-BYE...
...CHESHIRE CAT.
PATAN (SHUT)

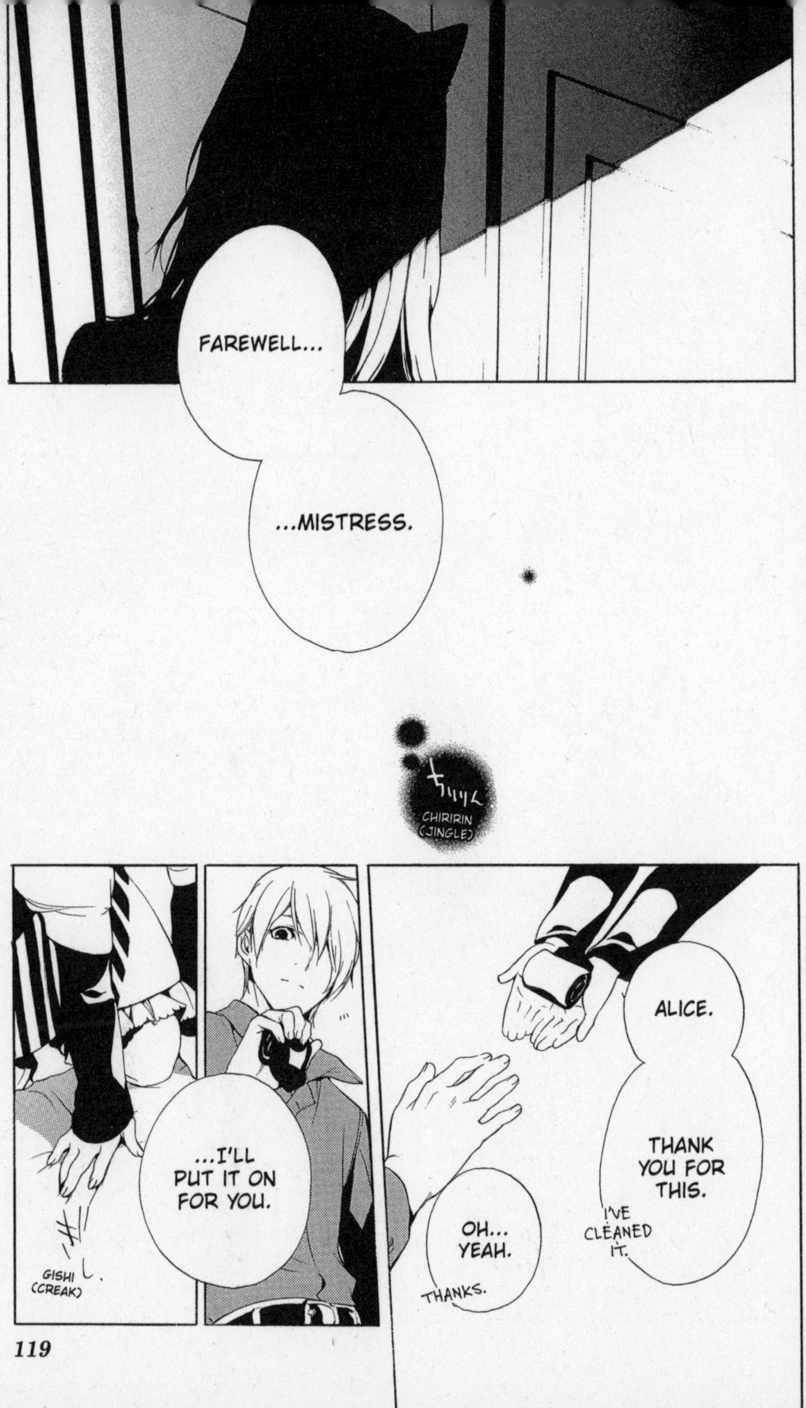
FAREWELL...
...MISTRESS.
CHIRIRIN (JINGLE)
ALICE.
THANK YOU FOR THIS.
I'VE CLEANED IT.
OH... YEAH.
THANKS.
...I'LL PUT IT ON FOR YOU.
GISHI (CREAK)

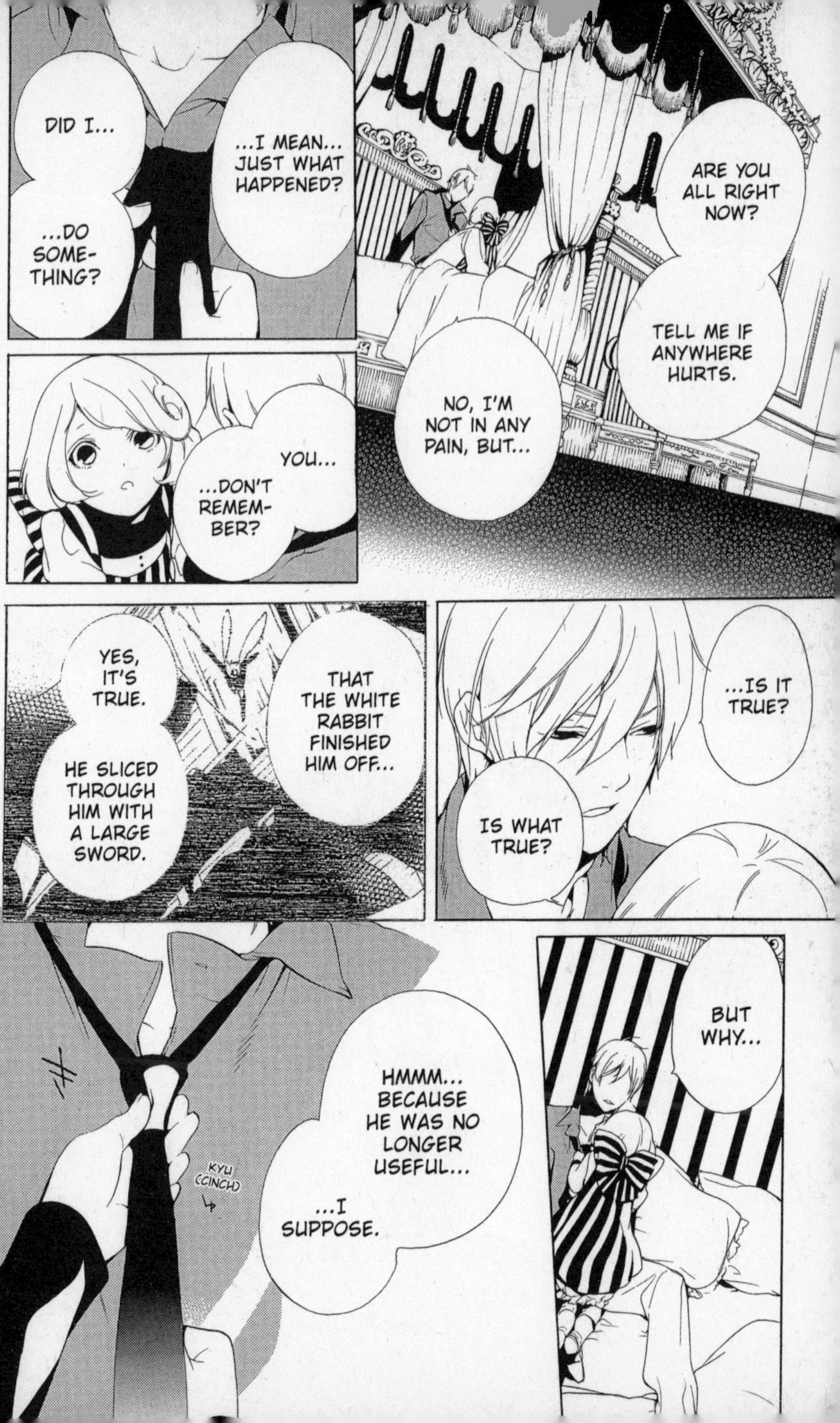
ARE YOU ALL RIGHT NOW?
TELL ME IF ANYWHERE HURTS.
NO, I'M NOT IN ANY PAIN, BUT...
DID I...
...DO SOME-THING?
...I MEAN... JUST WHAT HAPPENED?
YOU...
...DON'T REMEM-BER?
...IS IT TRUE?
IS WHAT TRUE?
THAT THE WHITE RABBIT FINISHED HIM OFF...
YES, IT'S TRUE.
HE SLICED THROUGH HIM WITH A LARGE SWORD.
BUT WHY...
HMMM... BECAUSE HE WAS NO LONGER USEFUL...
...I SUPPOSE.
KYU (CINCH)

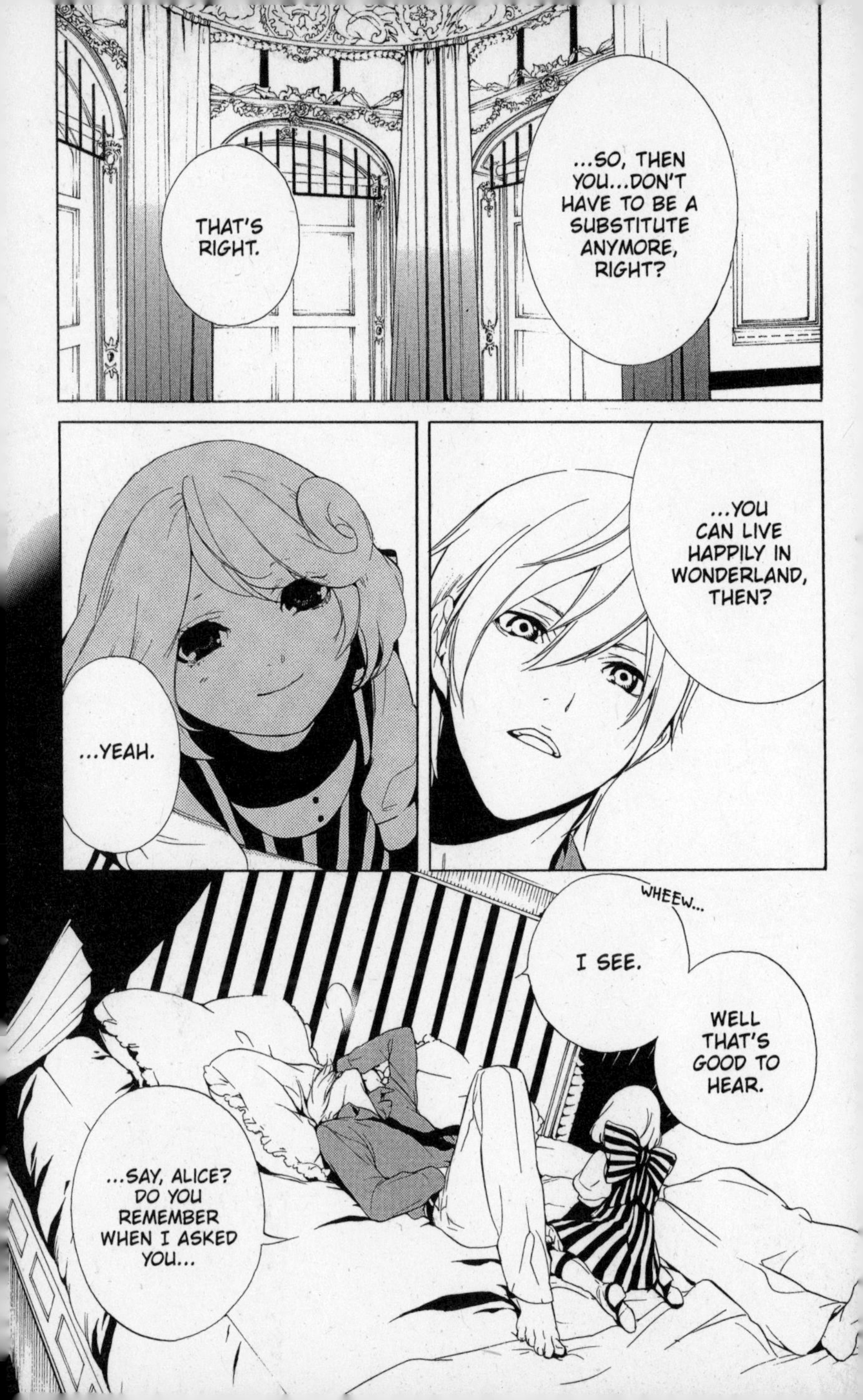
...SO, THEN YOU...DON'T HAVE TO BE A SUBSTITUTE ANYMORE, RIGHT?
THAT'S RIGHT.
...YOU CAN LIVE HAPPILY IN WONDERLAND, THEN?
...YEAH.
WHEEW...
I SEE.
WELL THAT'S GOOD TO HEAR.
...SAY, ALICE? DO YOU REMEMBER WHEN I ASKED YOU...

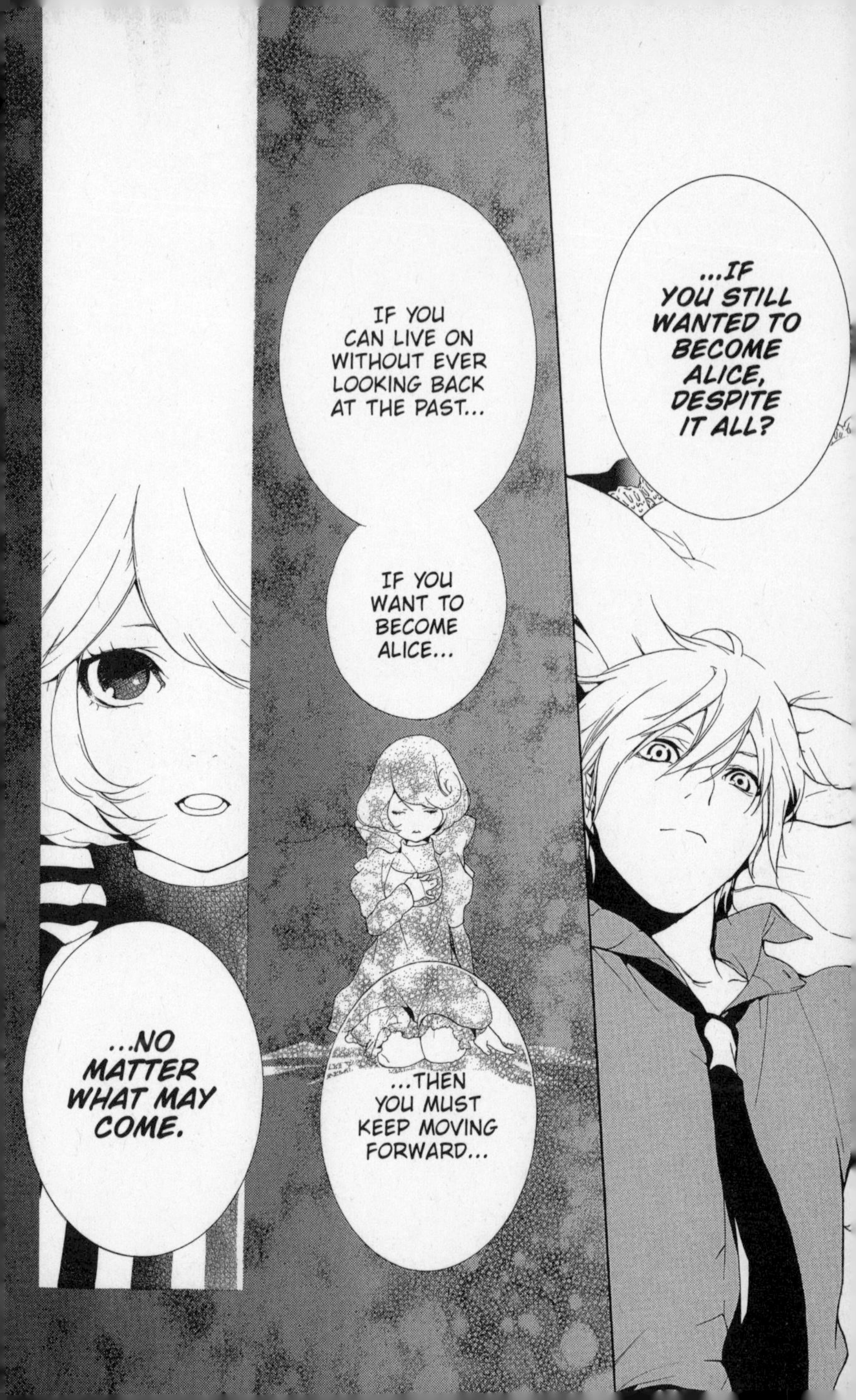
...IF YOU STILL WANTED TO BECOME ALICE, DESPITE IT ALL?
IF YOU CAN LIVE ON WITHOUT EVER LOOKING BACK AT THE PAST...
IF YOU WANT TO BECOME ALICE...
...THEN YOU MUST KEEP MOVING FORWARD...
...NO MATTER WHAT MAY COME.

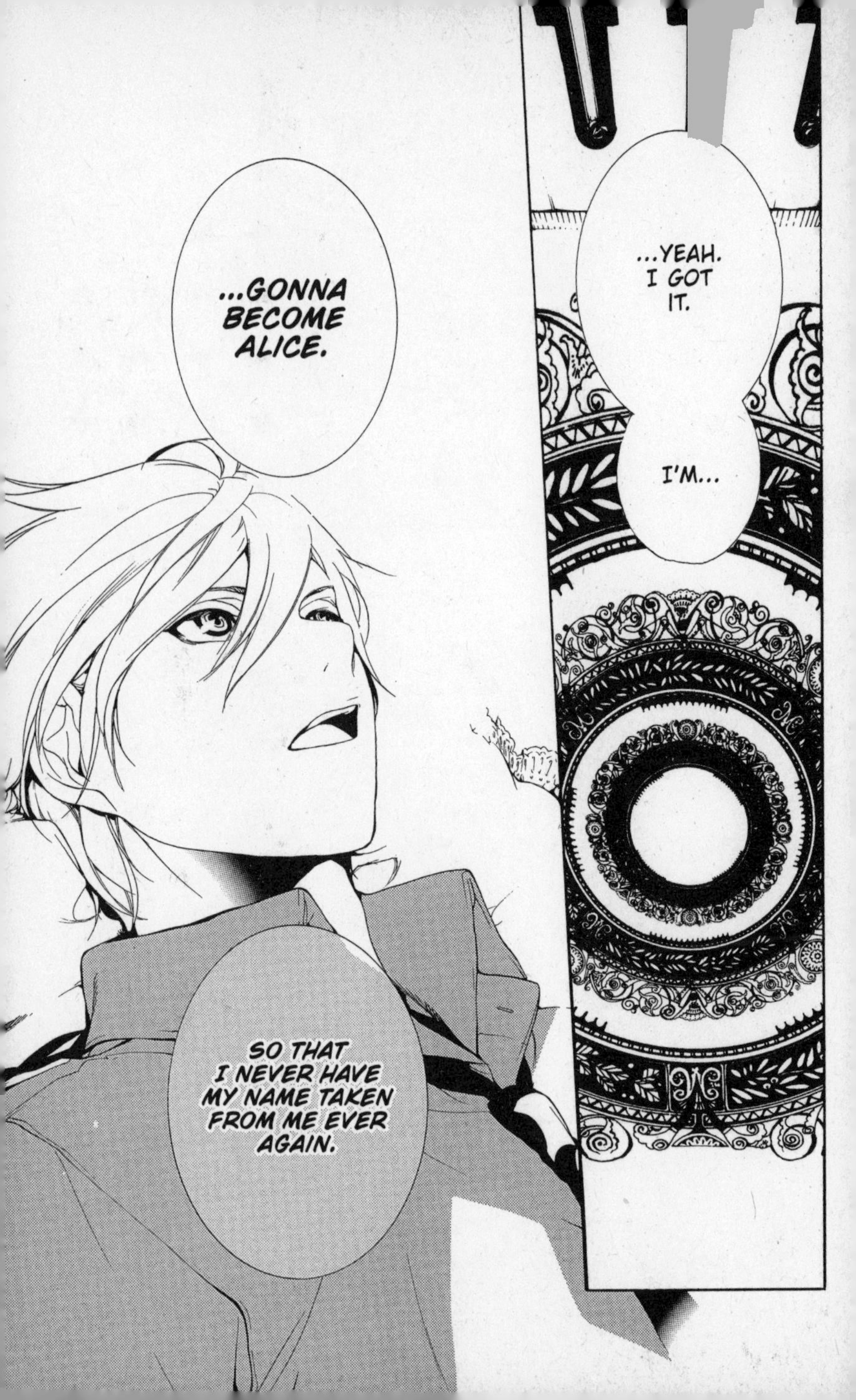
...YEAH. I GOT IT.
I'M...
...GONNA BECOME ALICE.
SO THAT I NEVER HAVE MY NAME TAKEN FROM ME EVER AGAIN.

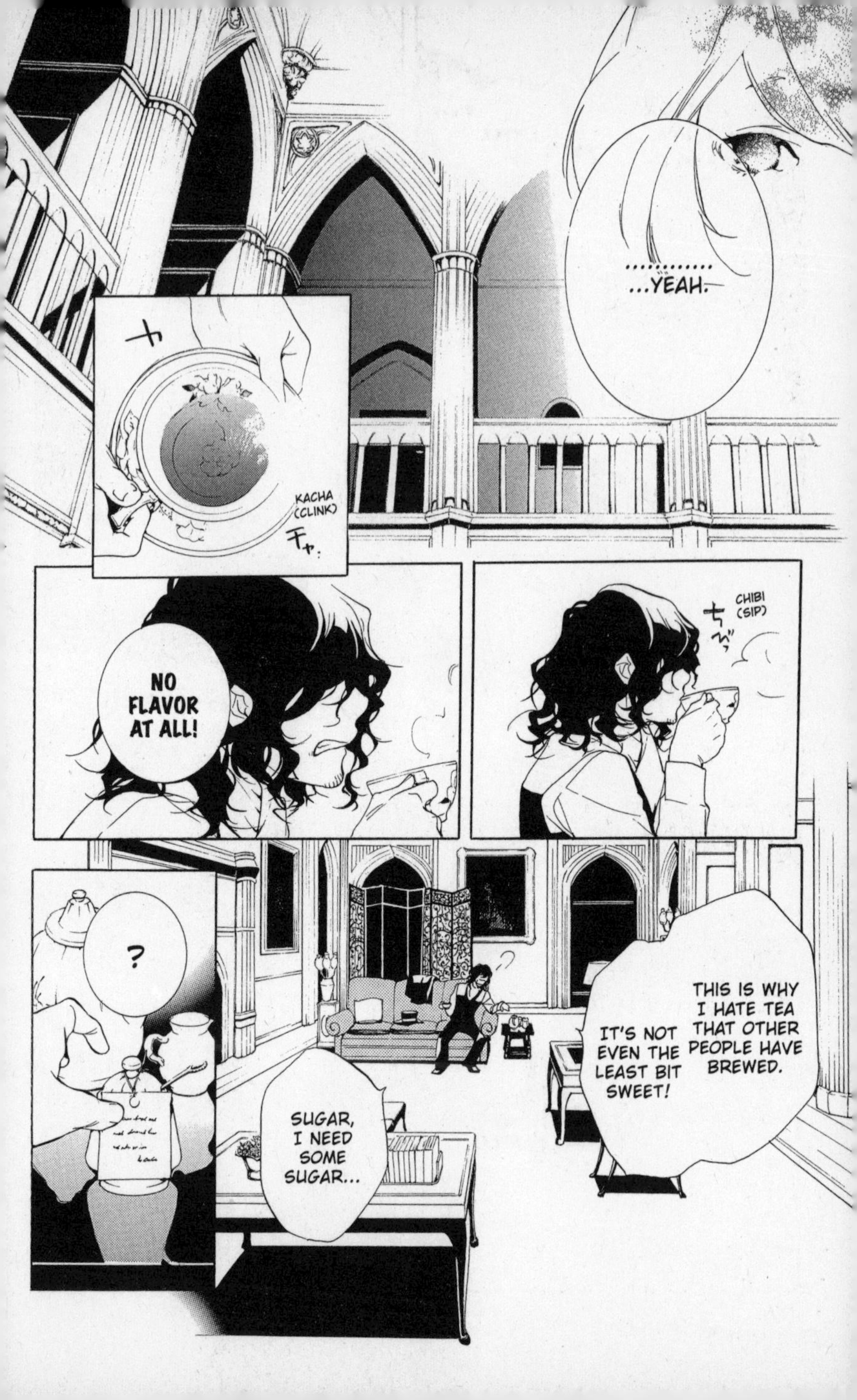
....
...YEAH.
KACHA (CLINK)
CHIBI (SIP)
NO FLAVOR AT ALL!
THIS IS WHY I HATE TEA THAT OTHER PEOPLE HAVE BREWED.
IT'S NOT EVEN THE LEAST BIT SWEET!
SUGAR, I NEED SOME SUGAR...
?

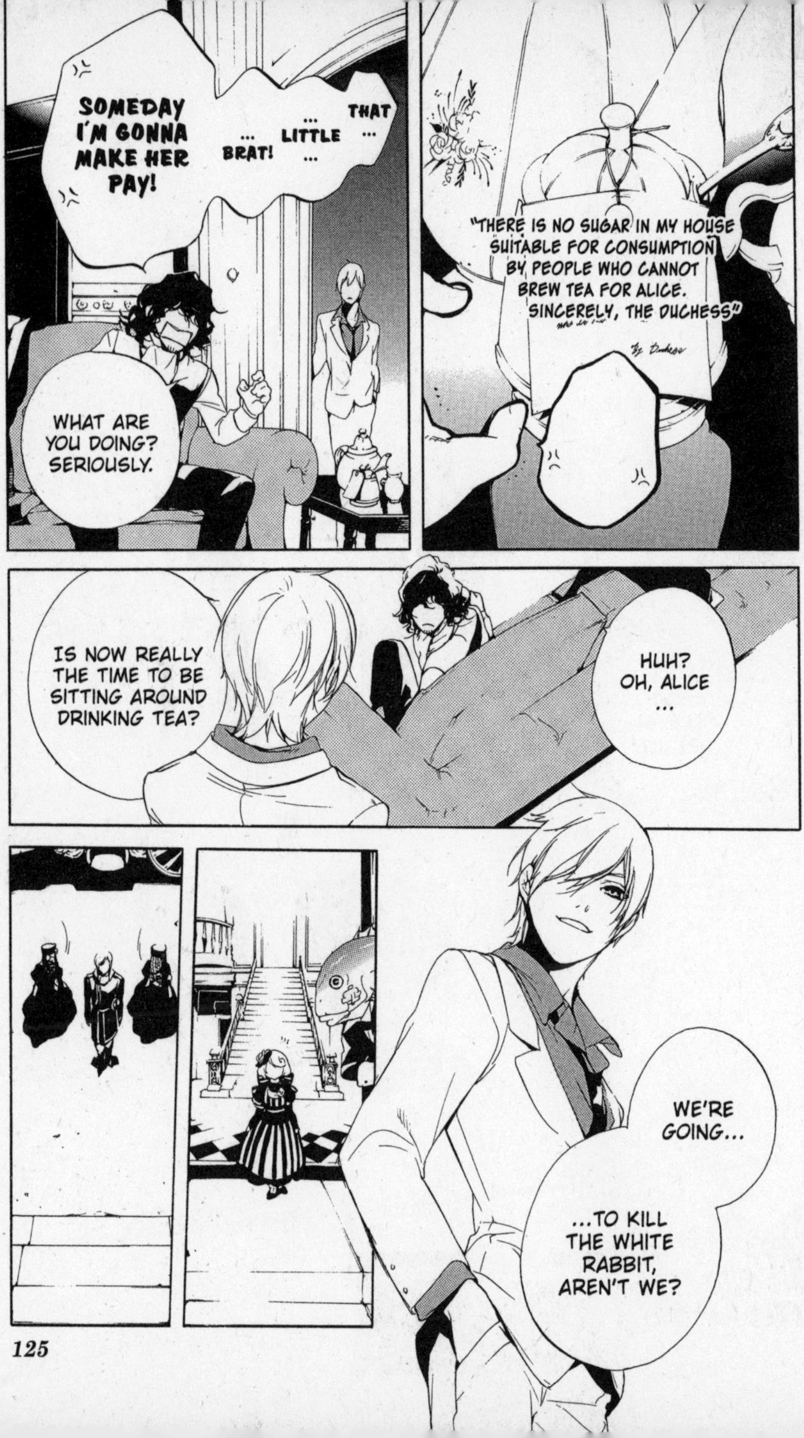
"THERE IS NO SUGAR IN MY HOUSE SUITABLE FOR CONSUMPTION BY PEOPLE WHO CANNOT BREW TEA FOR ALICE. SINCERELY, THE DUCHESS"
THAT ... LITTLE ... BRAT!
SOMEDAY I'M GONNA MAKE HER PAY!
WHAT ARE YOU DOING? SERIOUSLY.
HUH? OH, ALICE ...
IS NOW REALLY THE TIME TO BE SITTING AROUND DRINKING TEA?
WE'RE GOING...
...TO KILL THE WHITE RABBIT, AREN'T WE?

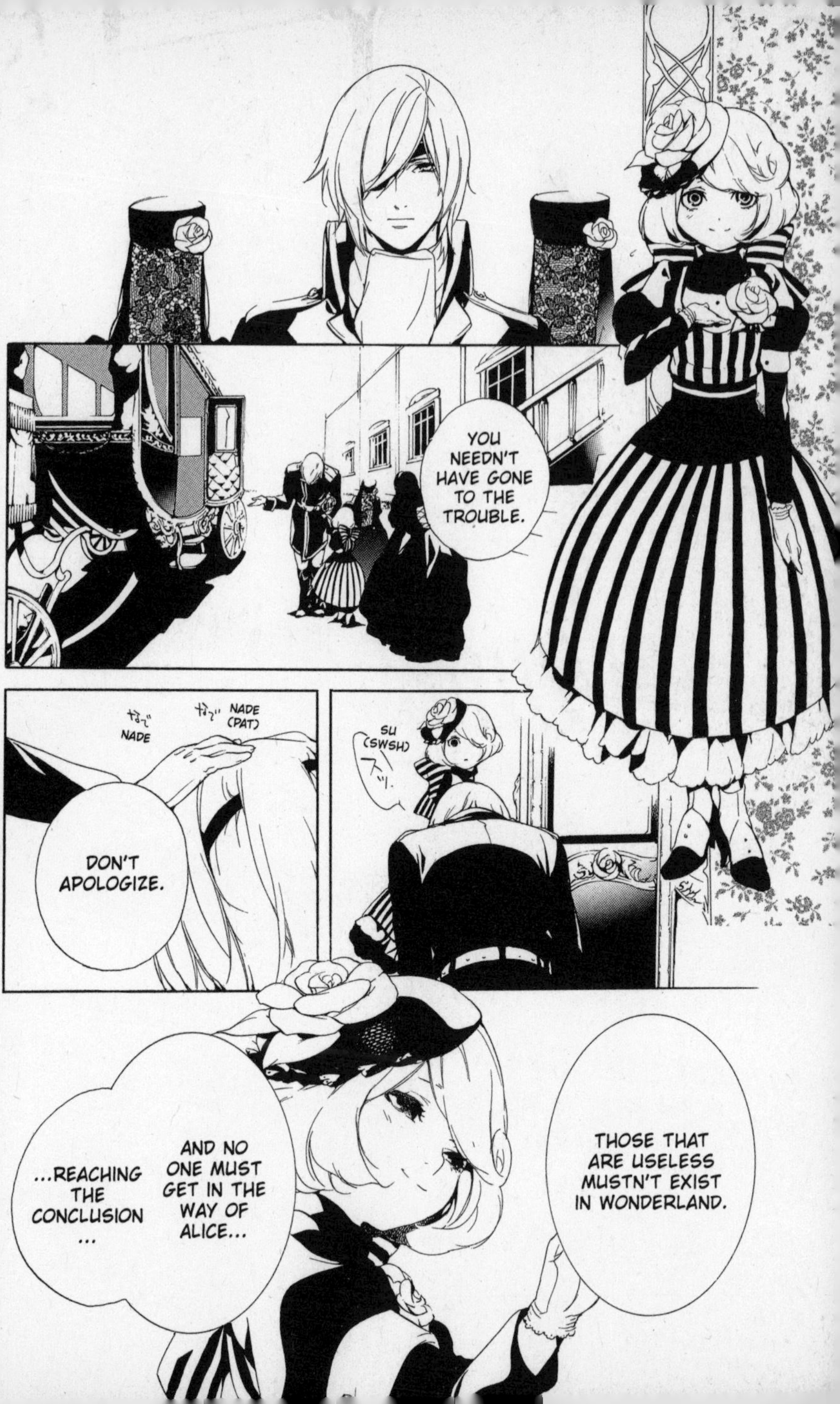
YOU NEEDN'T HAVE GONE TO THE TROUBLE.
SU (SWSH)
NADE (PAT)
NADE
DON'T APOLOGIZE.
THOSE THAT ARE USELESS MUSTN'T EXIST IN WONDERLAND.
AND NO ONE MUST GET IN THE WAY OF ALICE...
...REACHING THE CONCLUSION ...

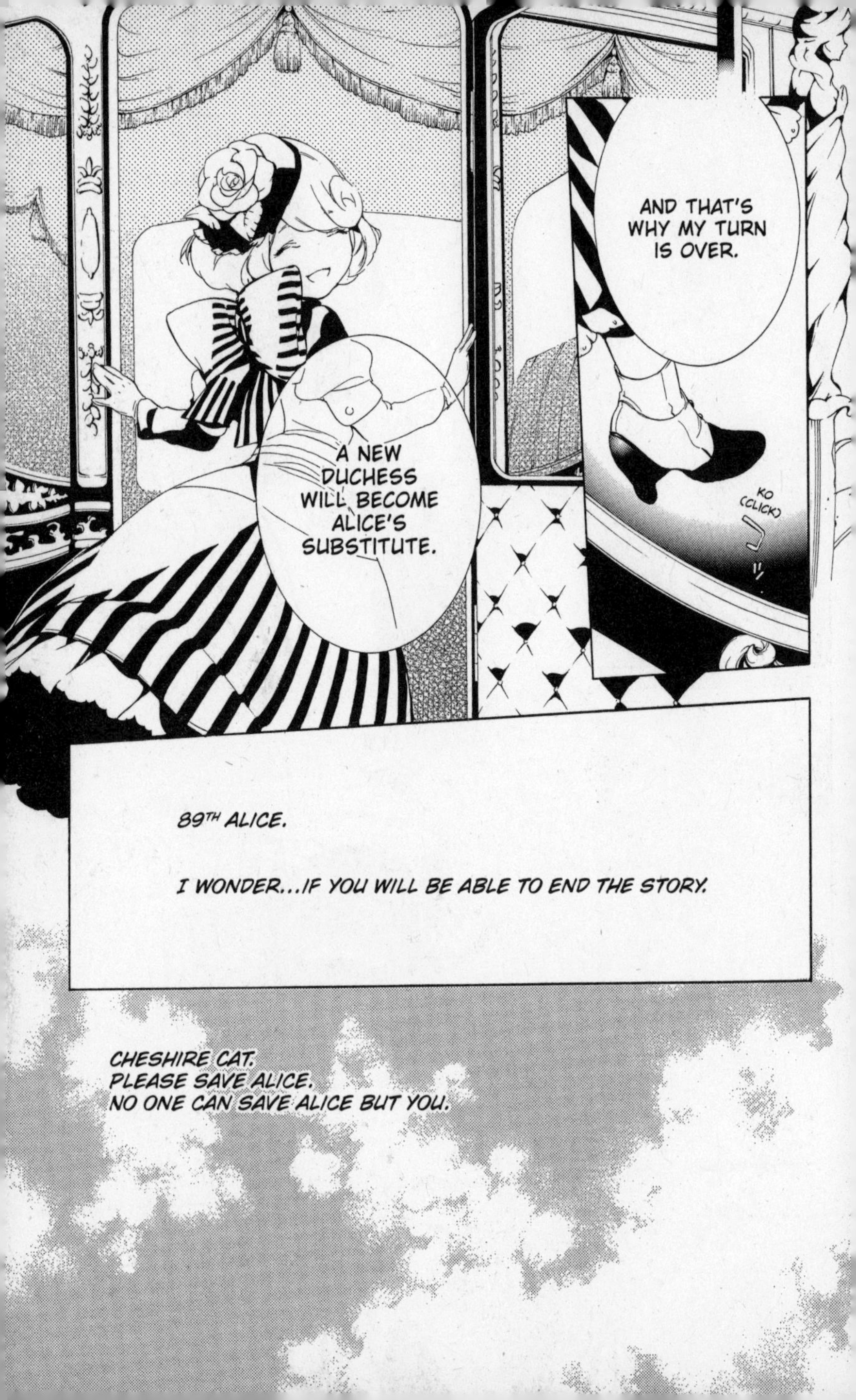
AND THAT'S WHY MY TURN IS OVER.
KO (CLICK)
A NEW DUCHESS WILL BECOME ALICE'S SUBSTITUTE.
89TH ALICE.
I WONDER...IF YOU WILL BE ABLE TO END THE STORY.
CHESHIRE CAT.
PLEASE SAVE ALICE.
NO ONE CAN SAVE ALICE BUT YOU.

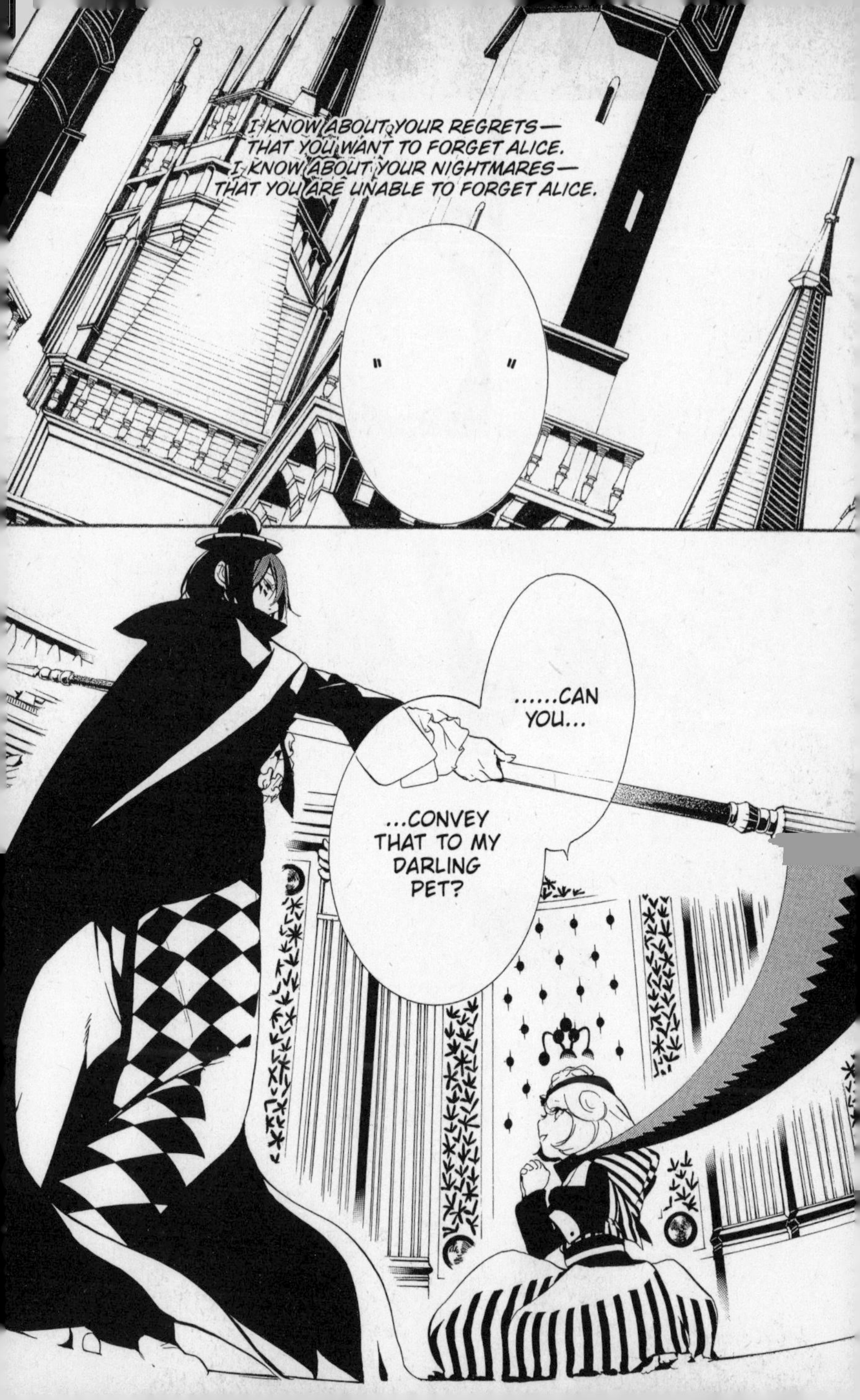
I KNOW ABOUT YOUR REGRETS—
THAT YOU WANT TO FORGET ALICE.
I KNOW ABOUT YOUR NIGHTMARES—
THAT YOU ARE UNABLE TO FORGET ALICE.
" "
......CAN YOU...
...CONVEY THAT TO MY DARLING PET?

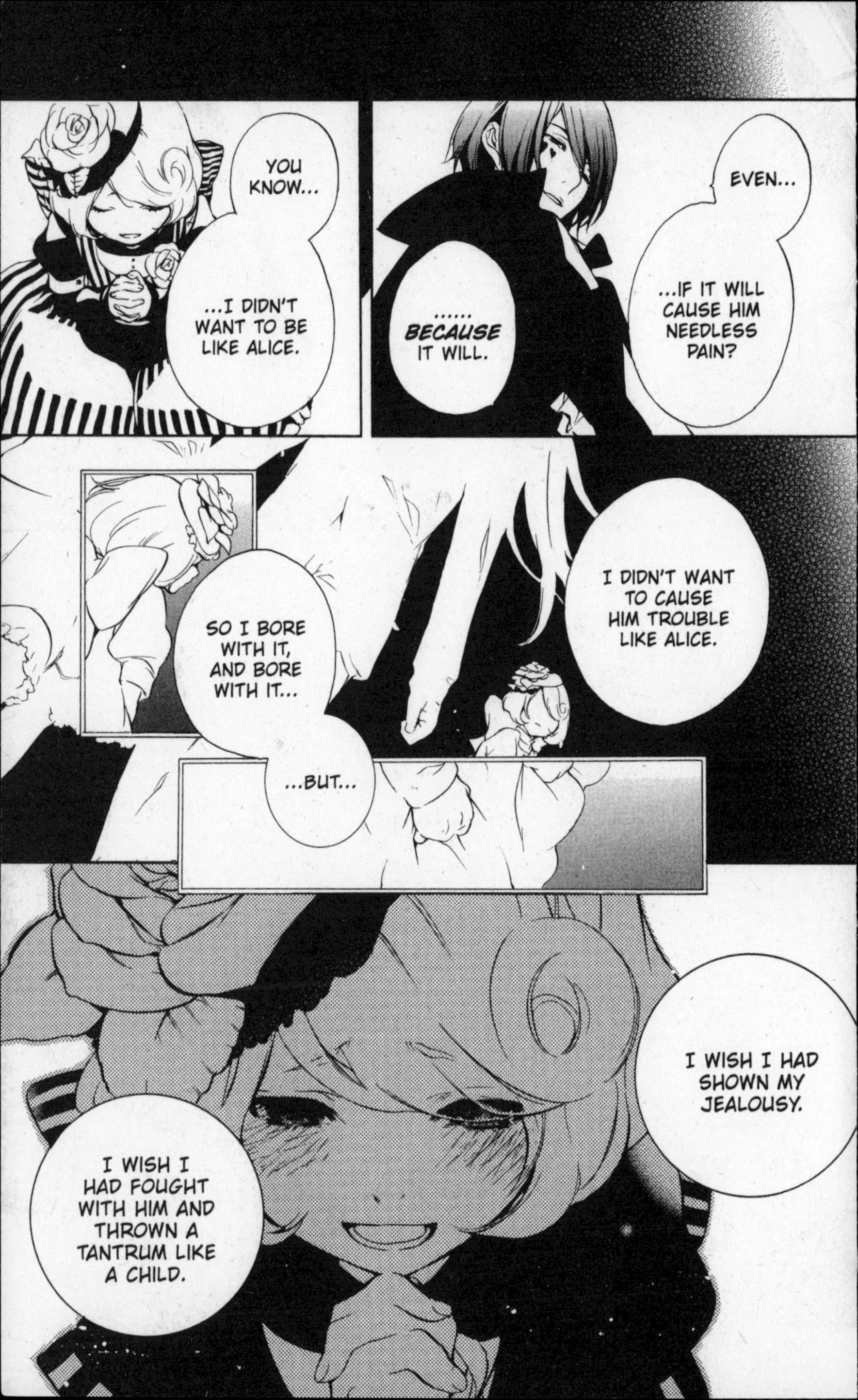
EVEN...
...IF IT WILL CAUSE HIM NEEDLESS PAIN?
...... BECAUSE IT WILL.
YOU KNOW...
...I DIDN'T WANT TO BE LIKE ALICE.
I DIDN'T WANT TO CAUSE HIM TROUBLE LIKE ALICE.
SO I BORE WITH IT, AND BORE WITH IT...
...BUT...
I WISH I HAD SHOWN MY JEALOUSY.
I WISH I HAD FOUGHT WITH HIM AND THROWN A TANTRUM LIKE A CHILD.

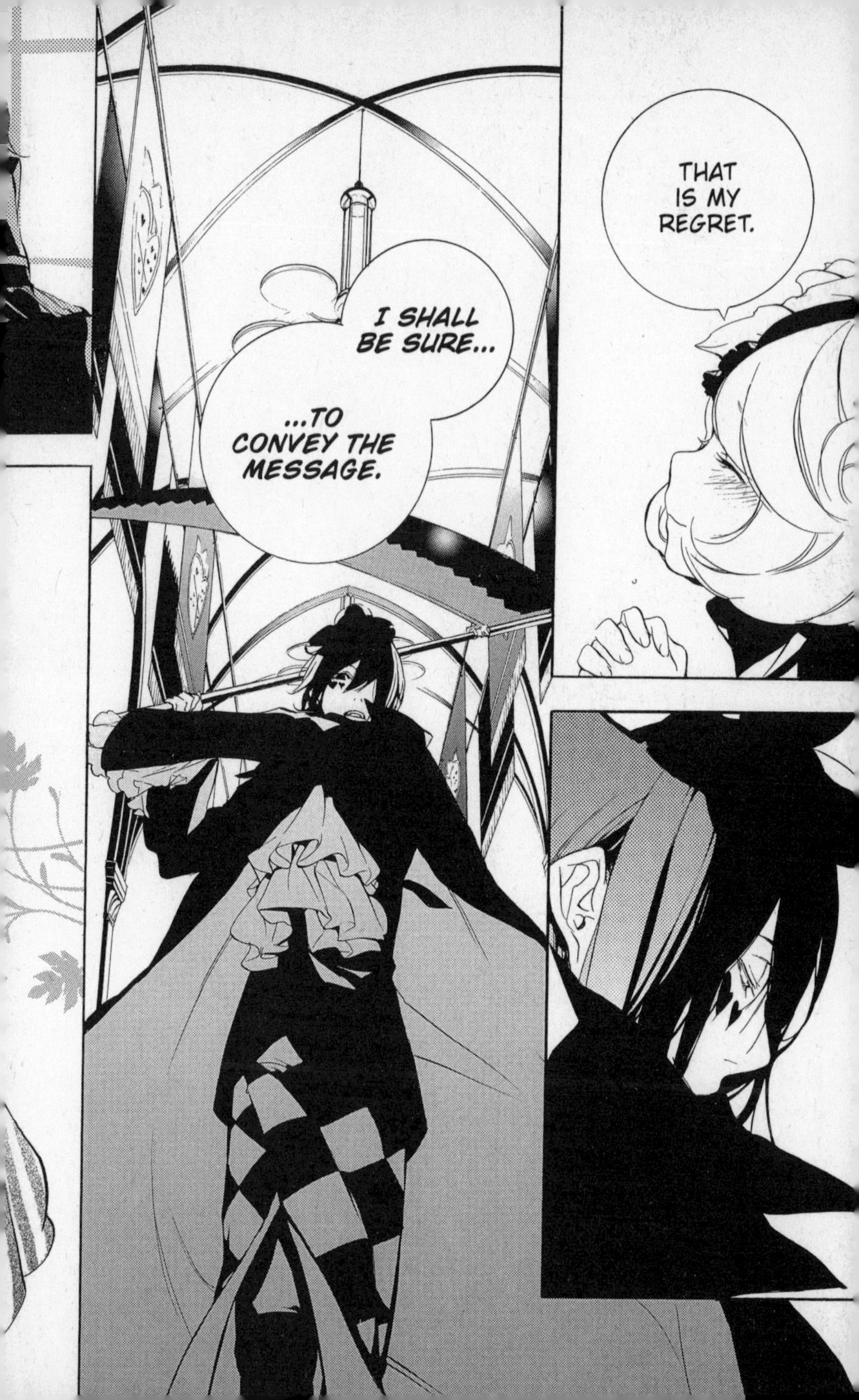
THAT IS MY REGRET.
I SHALL BE SURE...
...TO CONVEY THE MESSAGE.

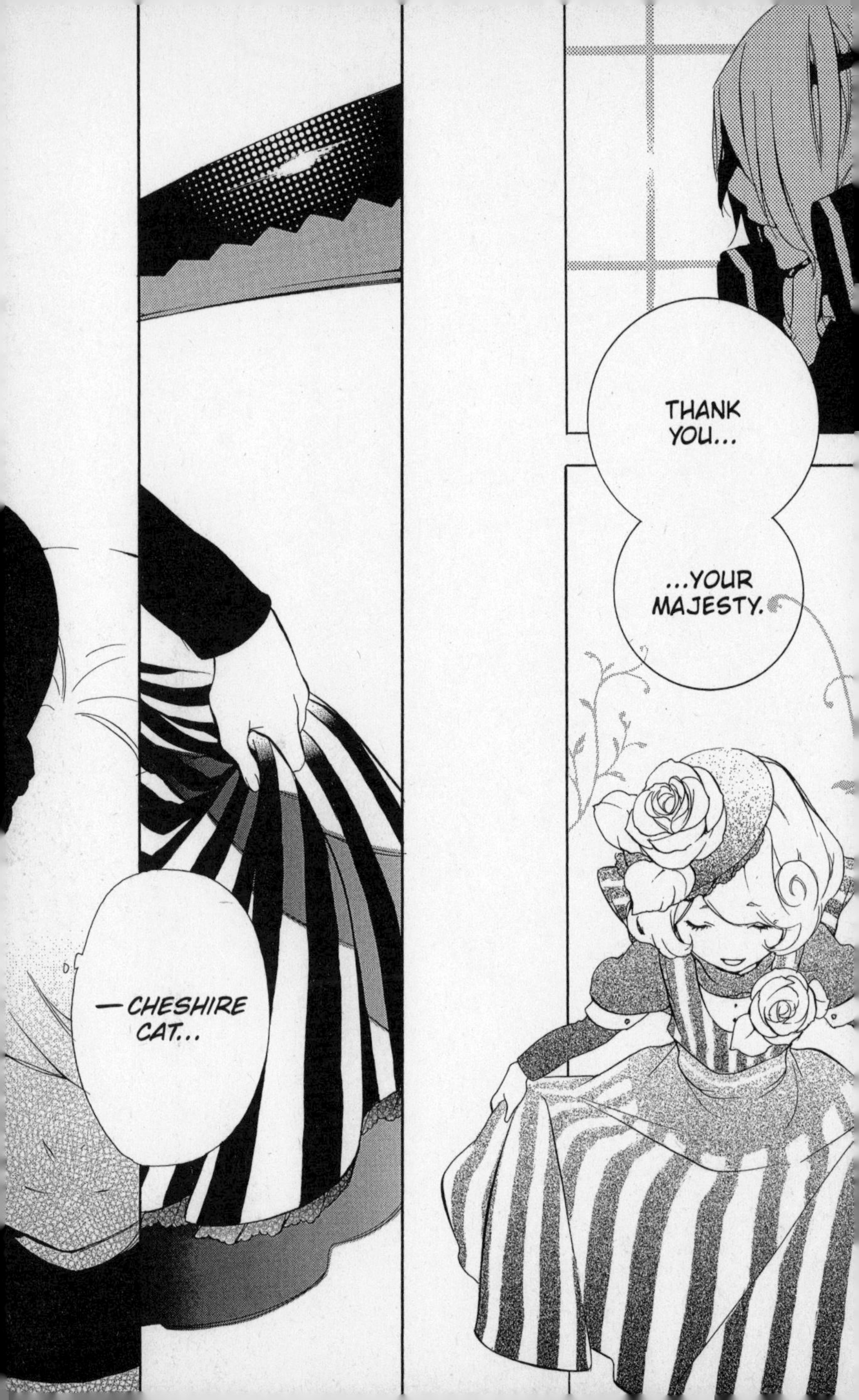
THANK YOU...
...YOUR MAJESTY.
—CHESHIRE CAT...

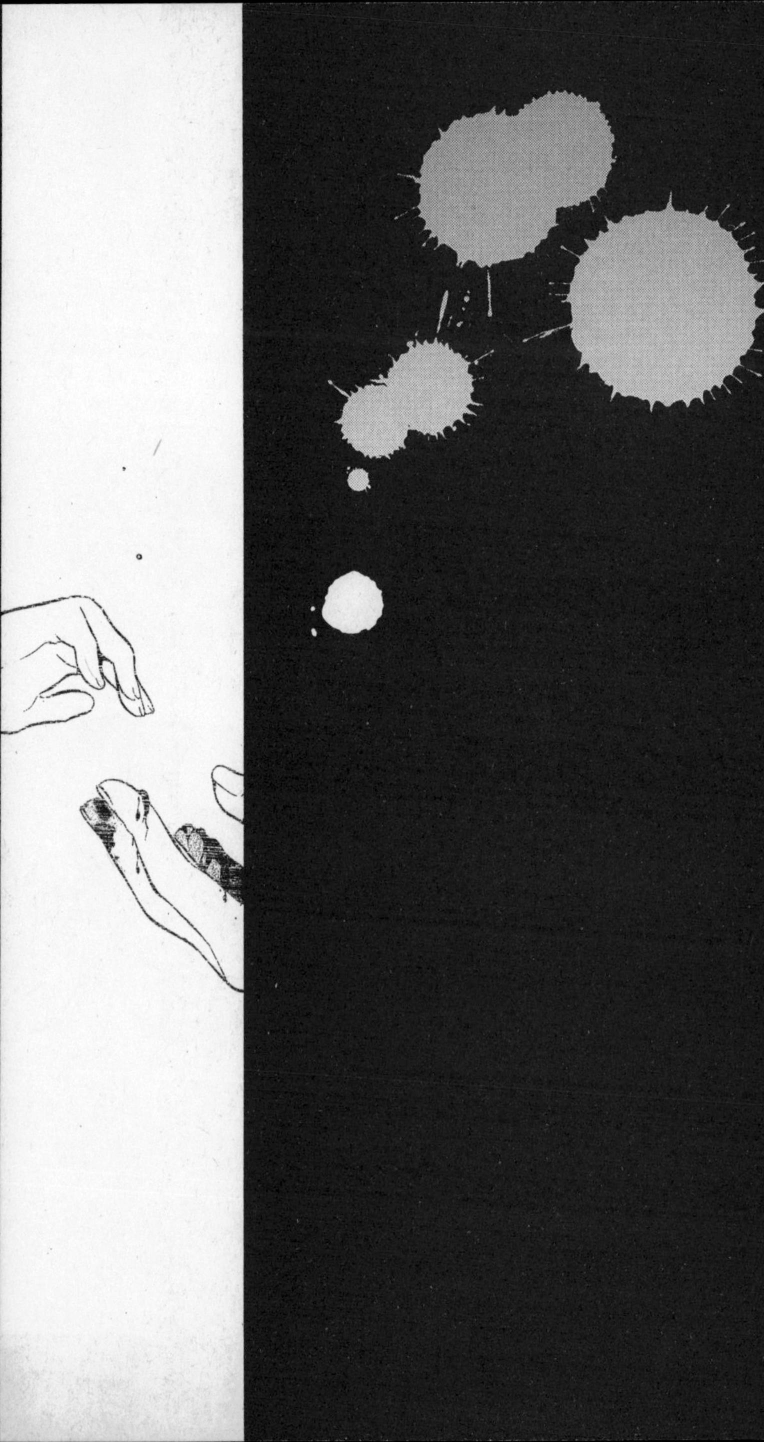

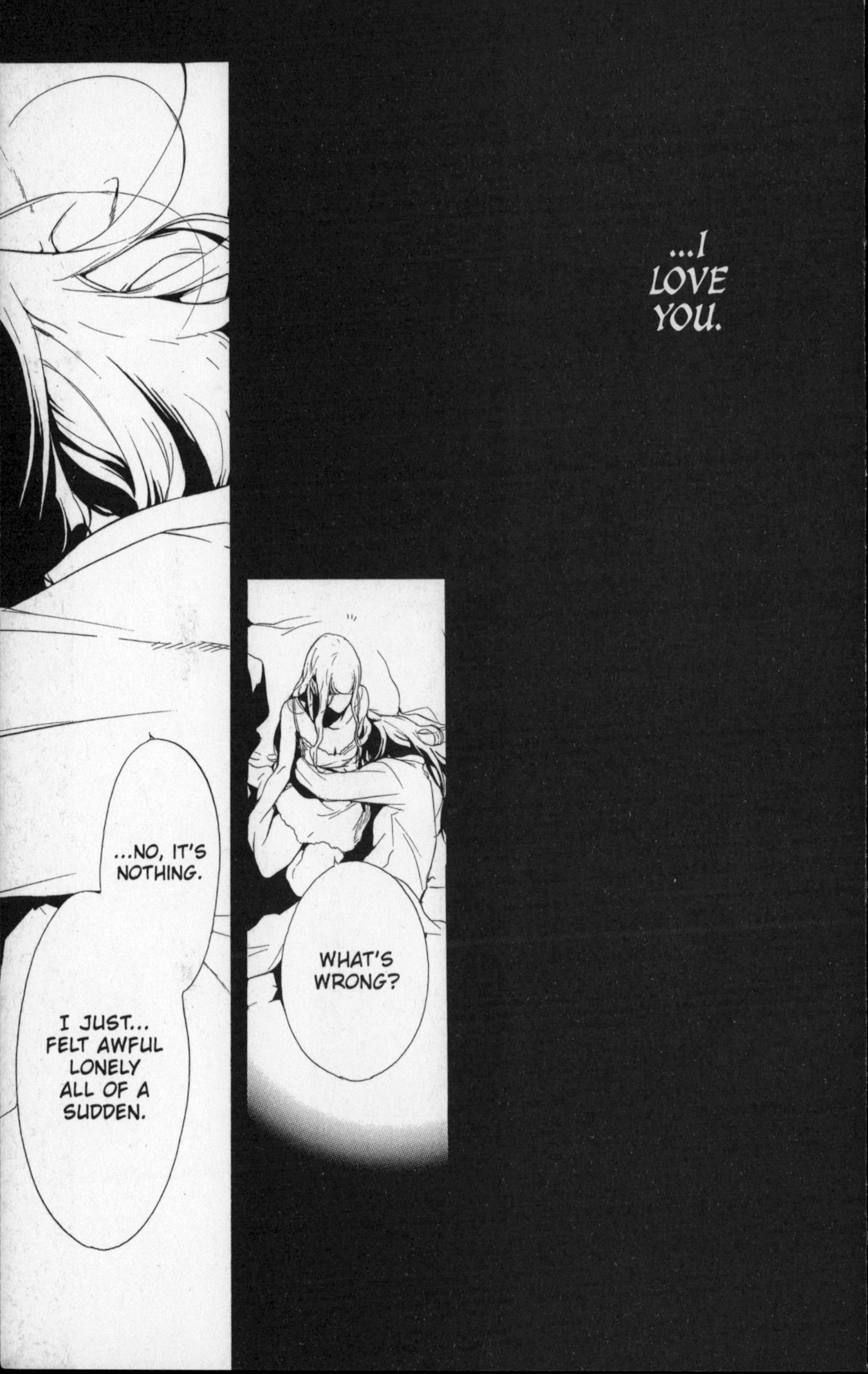
...I LOVE YOU.
WHAT'S WRONG?
...NO, IT'S NOTHING.
I JUST... FELT AWFUL LONELY ALL OF A SUDDEN.

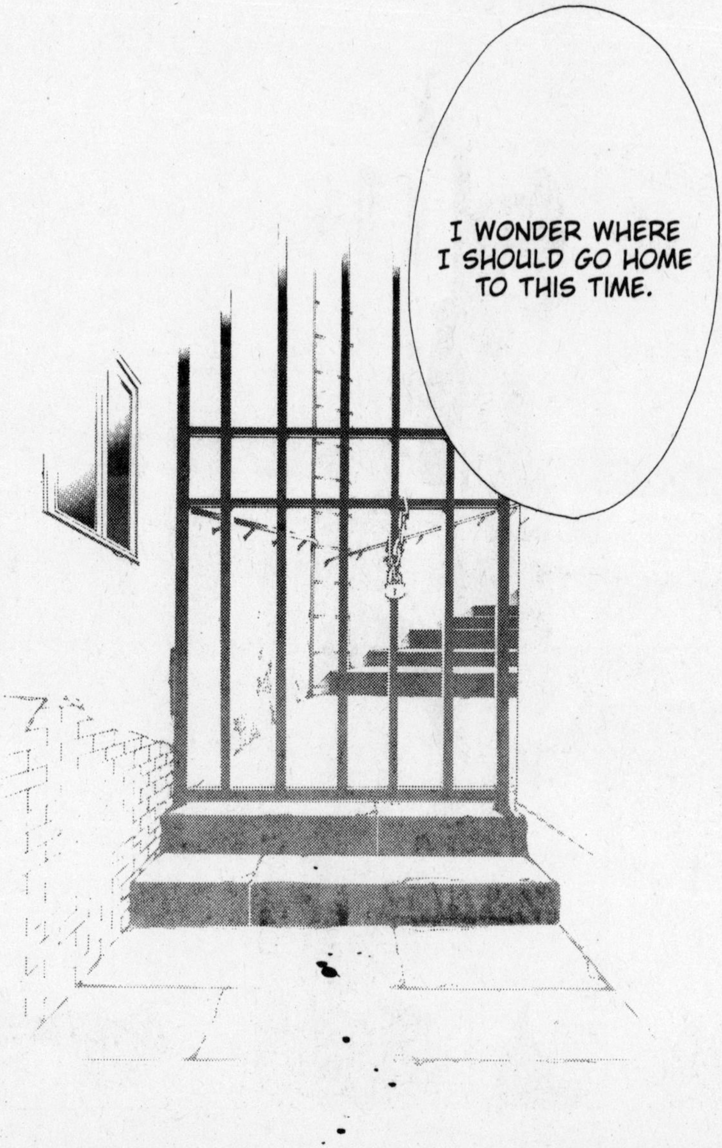
I WONDER WHERE I SHOULD GO HOME TO THIS TIME.

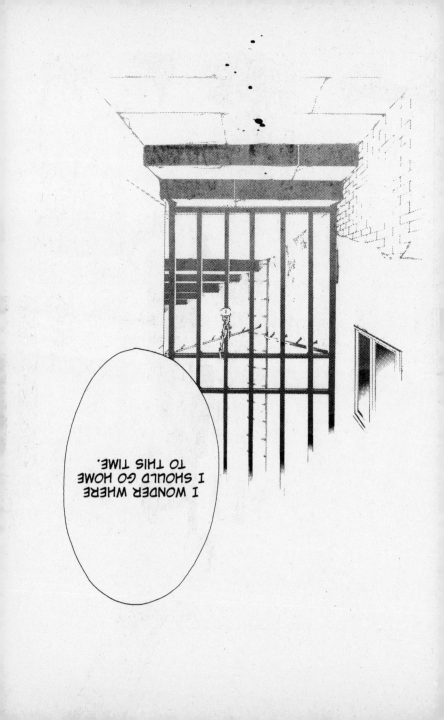

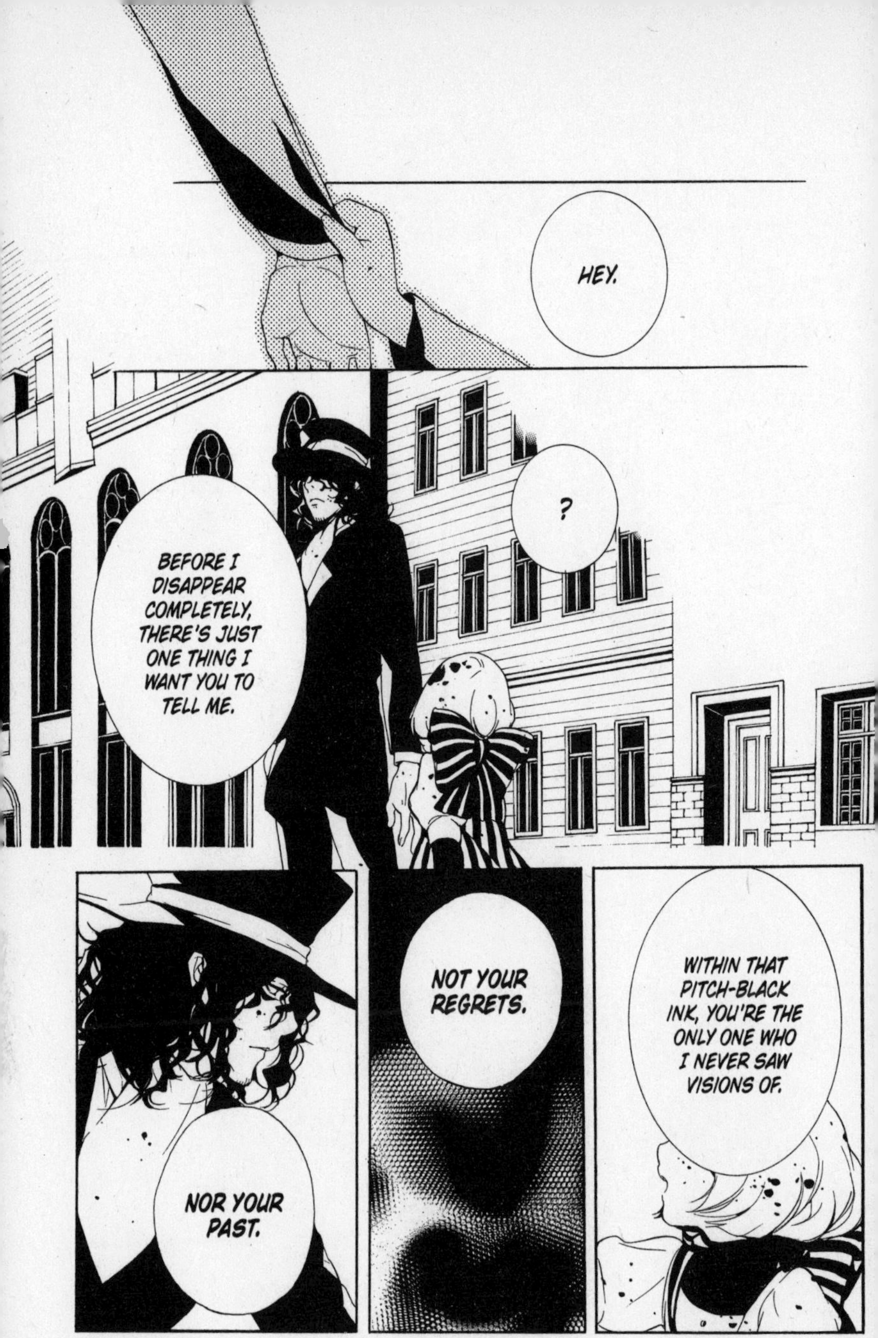
HEY.
?
BEFORE I DISAPPEAR COMPLETELY, THERE'S JUST ONE THING I WANT YOU TO TELL ME.
WITHIN THAT PITCH-BLACK INK, YOU'RE THE ONLY ONE WHO I NEVER SAW VISIONS OF.
NOT YOUR REGRETS.
NOR YOUR PAST.

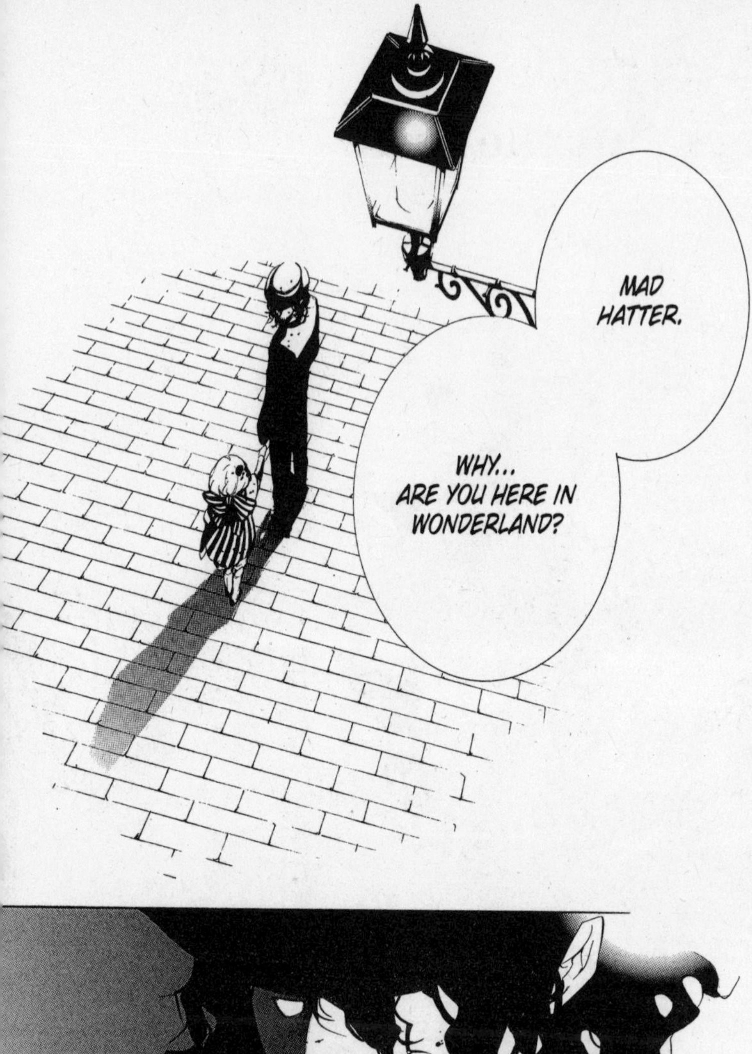
MAD HATTER.
WHY... ARE YOU HERE IN WONDERLAND?
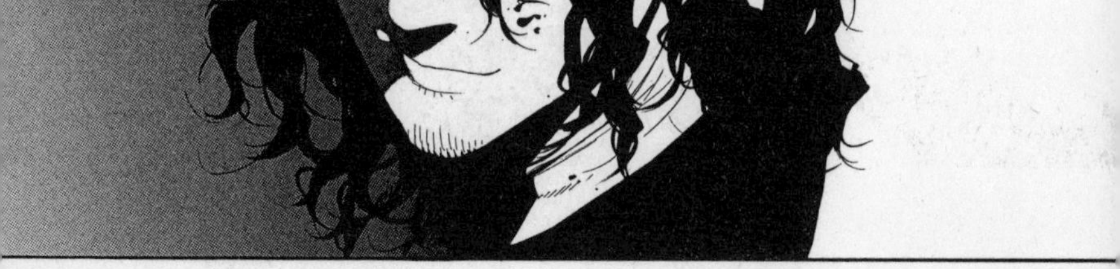

Chapter 10
Let's Cut the Crap.

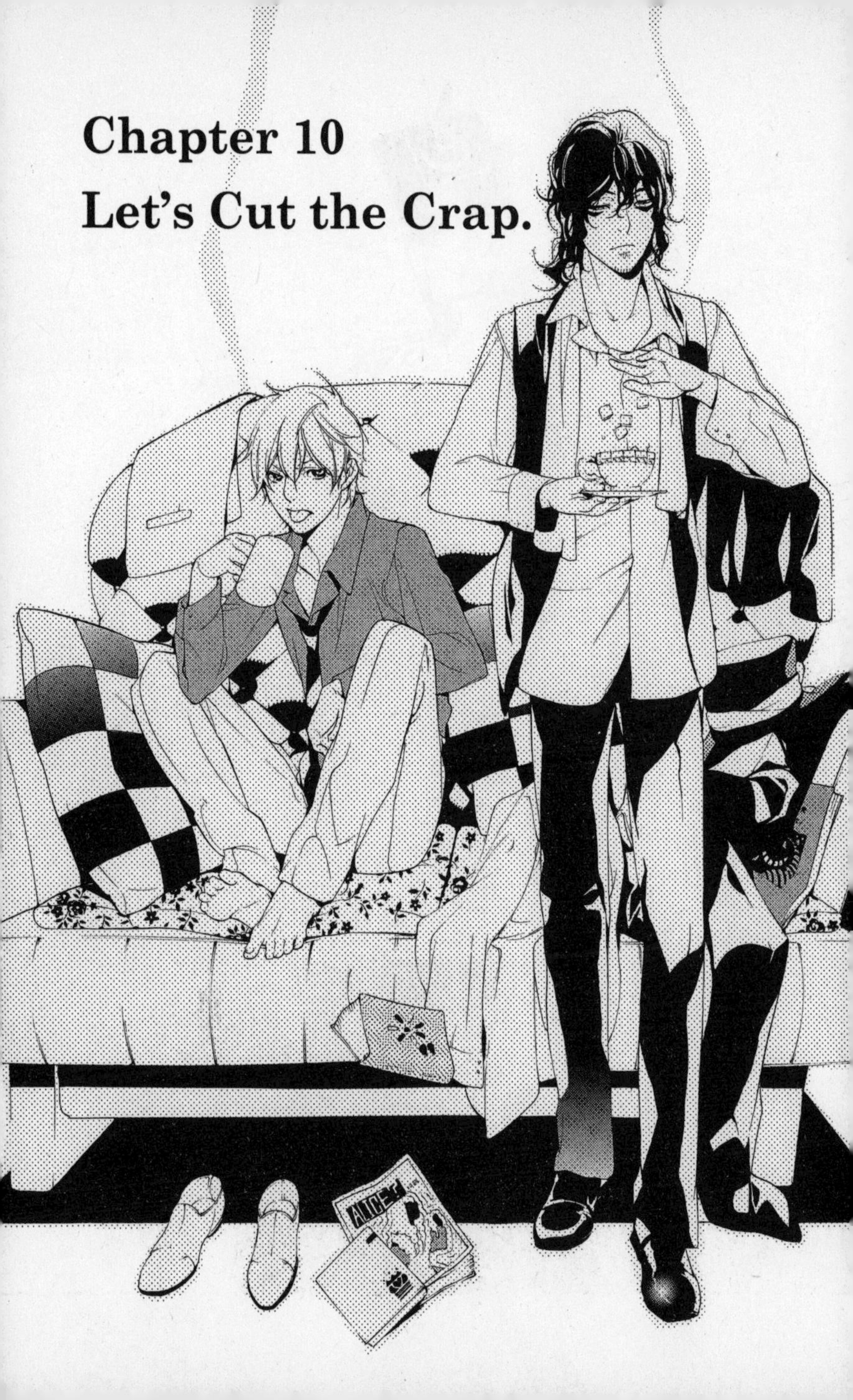

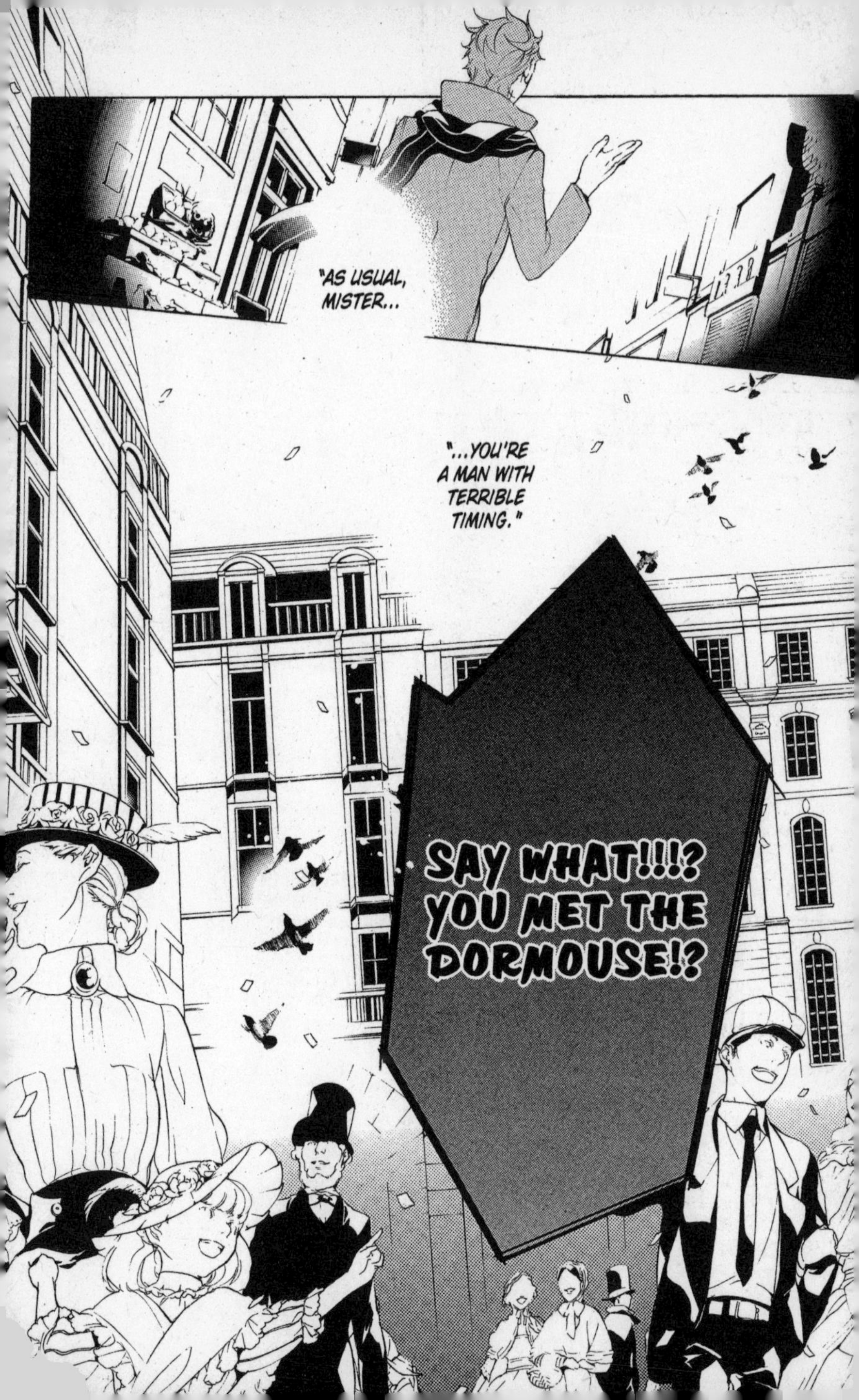
"AS USUAL, MISTER...
"...YOU'RE A MAN WITH TERRIBLE TIMING."
SAY WHAT!!!? YOU MET THE DORMOUSE!?

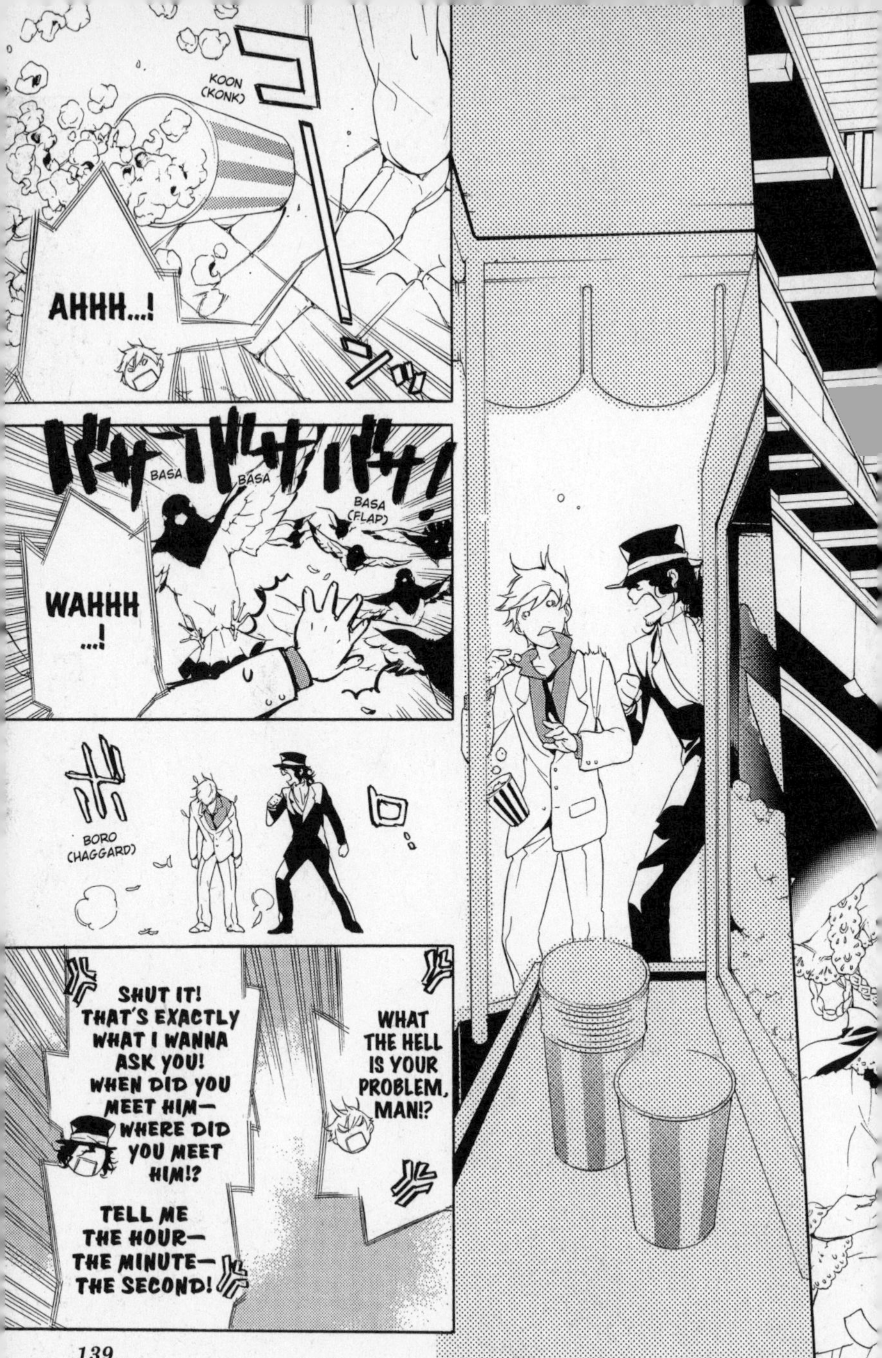
KOON (KONK)
AHHH...!
BASA
BASA
BASA (FLAP)
WAHHH ...!
BORO (HAGGARD)
WHAT THE HELL IS YOUR PROBLEM, MAN!?
SHUT IT! THAT'S EXACTLY WHAT I WANNA ASK YOU! WHEN DID YOU MEET HIM— WHERE DID YOU MEET HIM!?
TELL ME THE HOUR— THE MINUTE— THE SECOND!

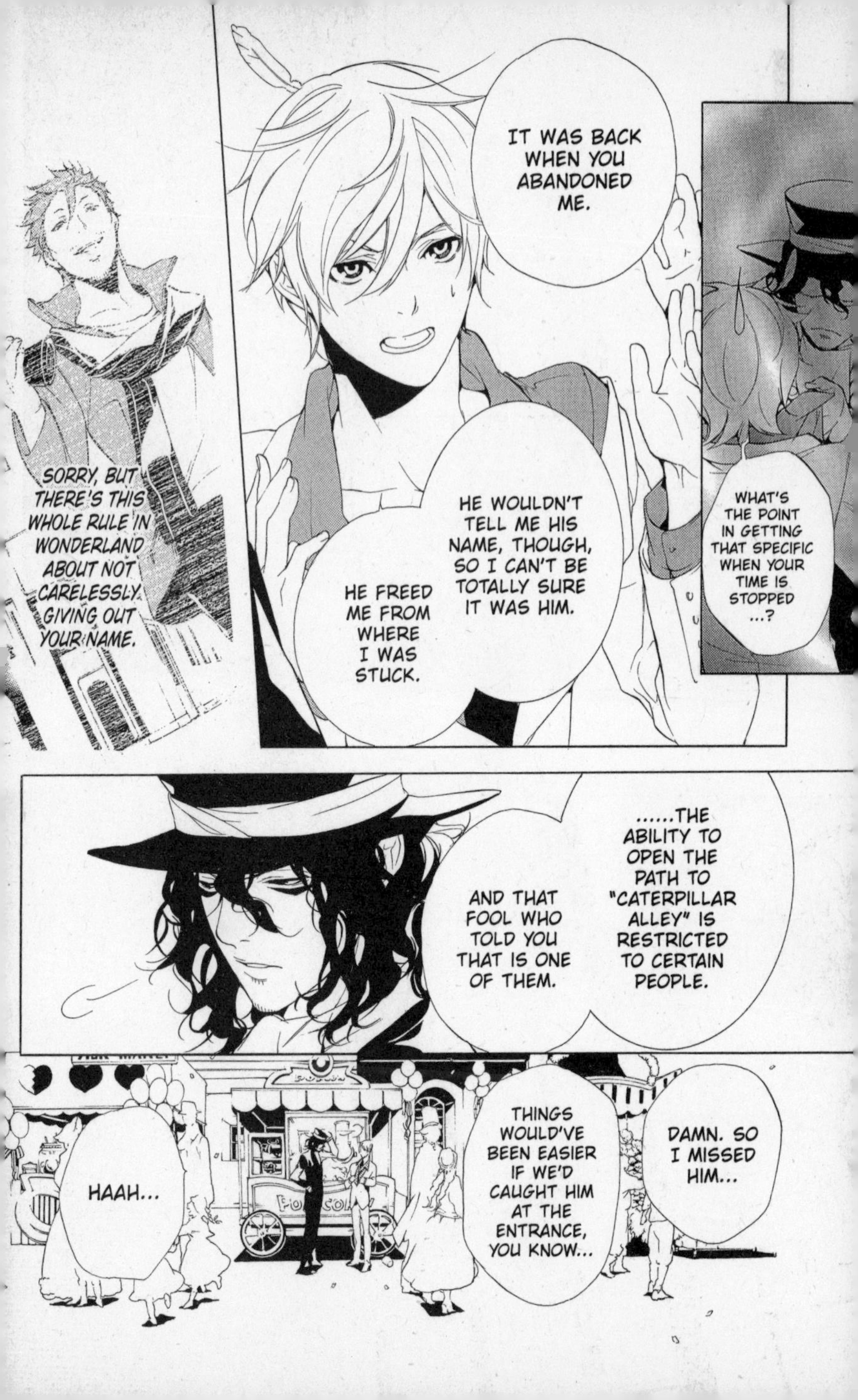
WHAT'S THE POINT IN GETTING THAT SPECIFIC WHEN YOUR TIME IS STOPPED ...?
IT WAS BACK WHEN YOU ABANDONED ME.
HE WOULDN'T TELL ME HIS NAME, THOUGH, SO I CAN'T BE TOTALLY SURE IT WAS HIM.
HE FREED ME FROM WHERE I WAS STUCK.
SORRY, BUT THERE'S THIS WHOLE RULE IN WONDERLAND ABOUT NOT CARELESSLY GIVING OUT YOUR NAME.
......THE ABILITY TO OPEN THE PATH TO "CATERPILLAR ALLEY" IS RESTRICTED TO CERTAIN PEOPLE.
AND THAT FOOL WHO TOLD YOU THAT IS ONE OF THEM.
DAMN. SO I MISSED HIM...
THINGS WOULD'VE BEEN EASIER IF WE'D CAUGHT HIM AT THE ENTRANCE, YOU KNOW...
HAAH...

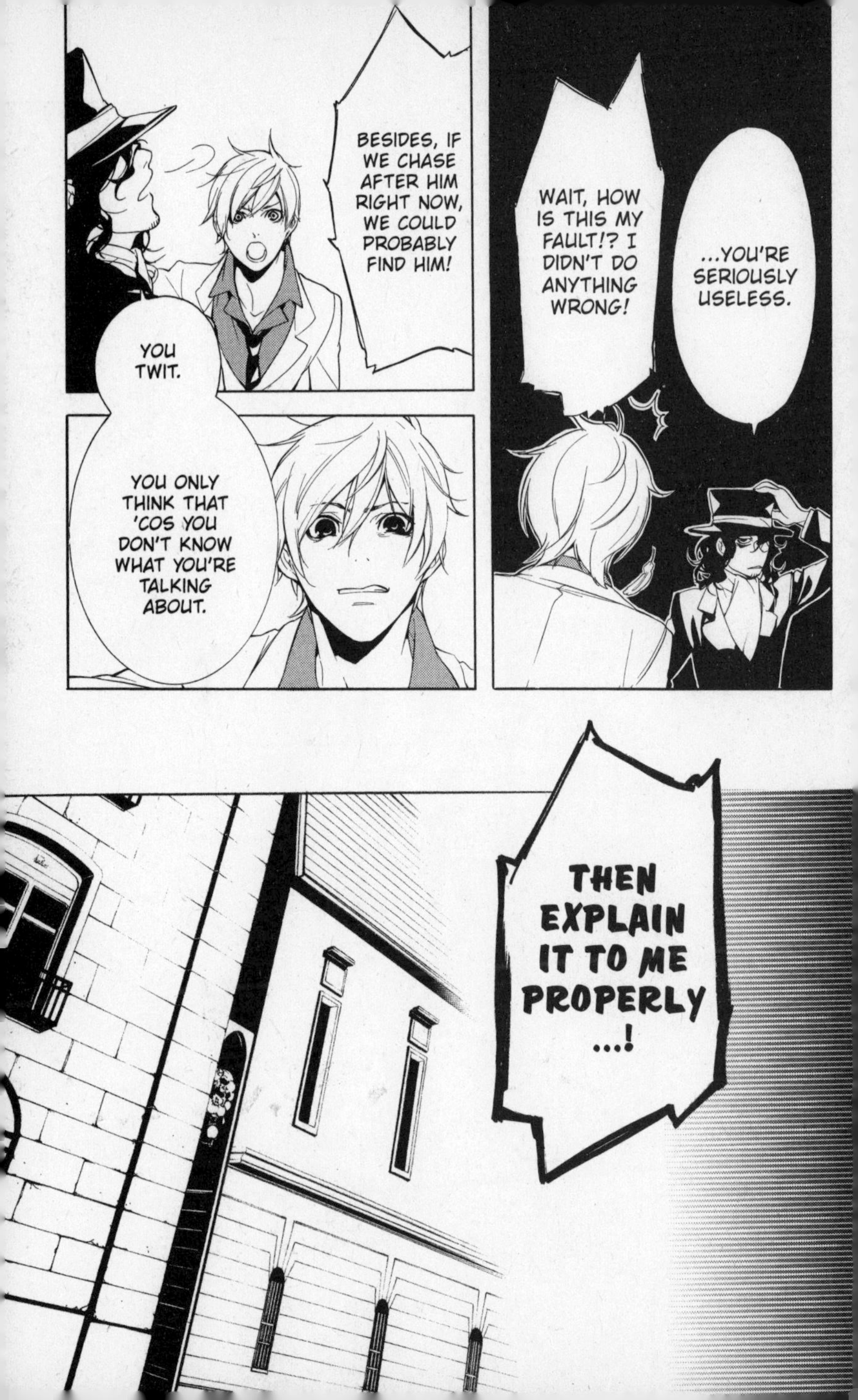
WAIT, HOW IS THIS MY FAULT!? I DIDN'T DO ANYTHING WRONG!
...YOU'RE SERIOUSLY USELESS.
BESIDES, IF WE CHASE AFTER HIM RIGHT NOW, WE COULD PROBABLY FIND HIM!
YOU TWIT.
YOU ONLY THINK THAT 'COS YOU DON'T KNOW WHAT YOU'RE TALKING ABOUT.
THEN EXPLAIN IT TO ME PROPERLY ...!

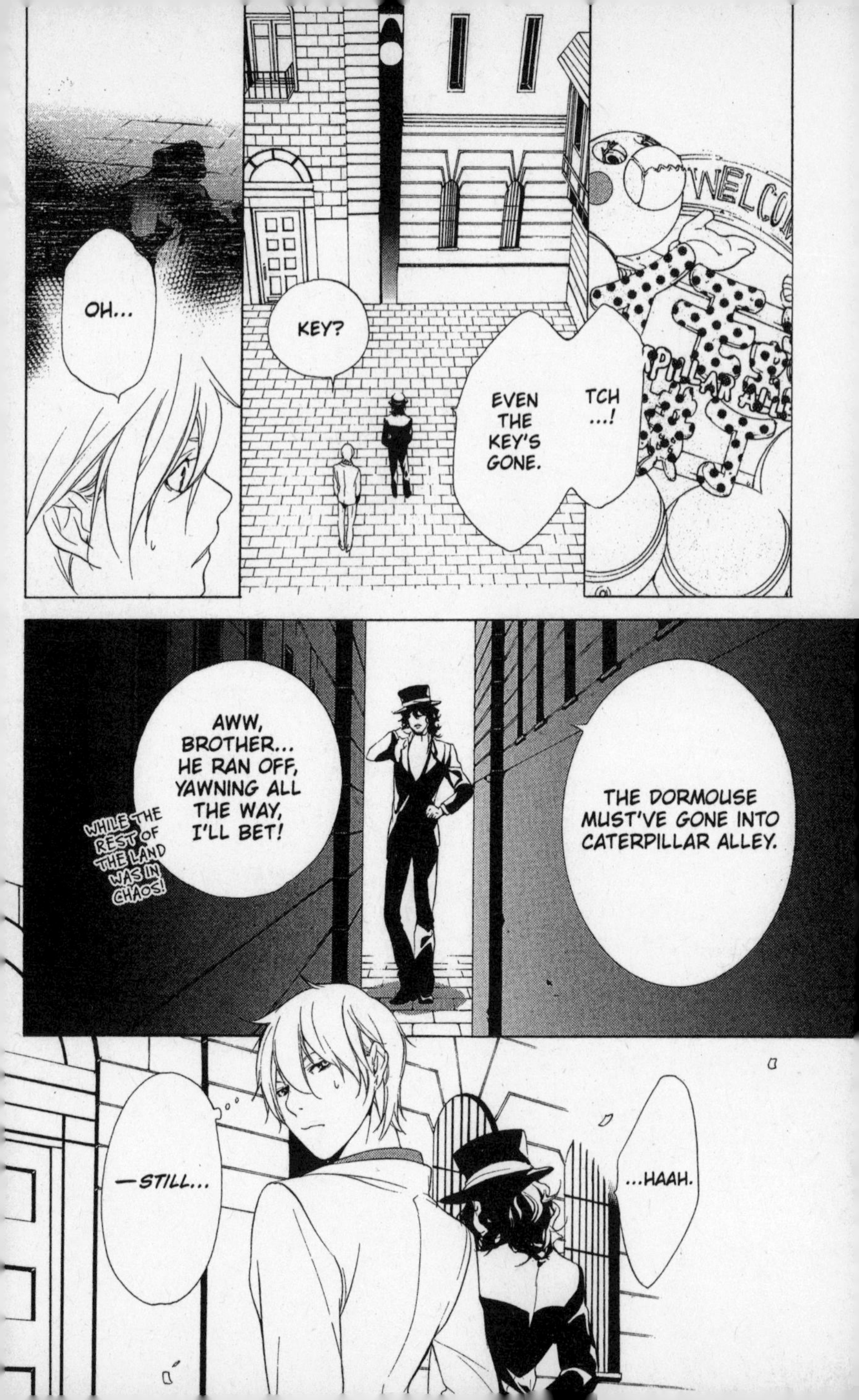
TCH ...!
EVEN THE KEY'S GONE.
KEY?
OH...
THE DORMOUSE MUST'VE GONE INTO CATERPILLAR ALLEY.
AWW, BROTHER... HE RAN OFF, YAWNING ALL THE WAY, I'LL BET!
WHILE THE REST OF THE LAND WAS IN CHAOS!
...HAAH.
—STILL...

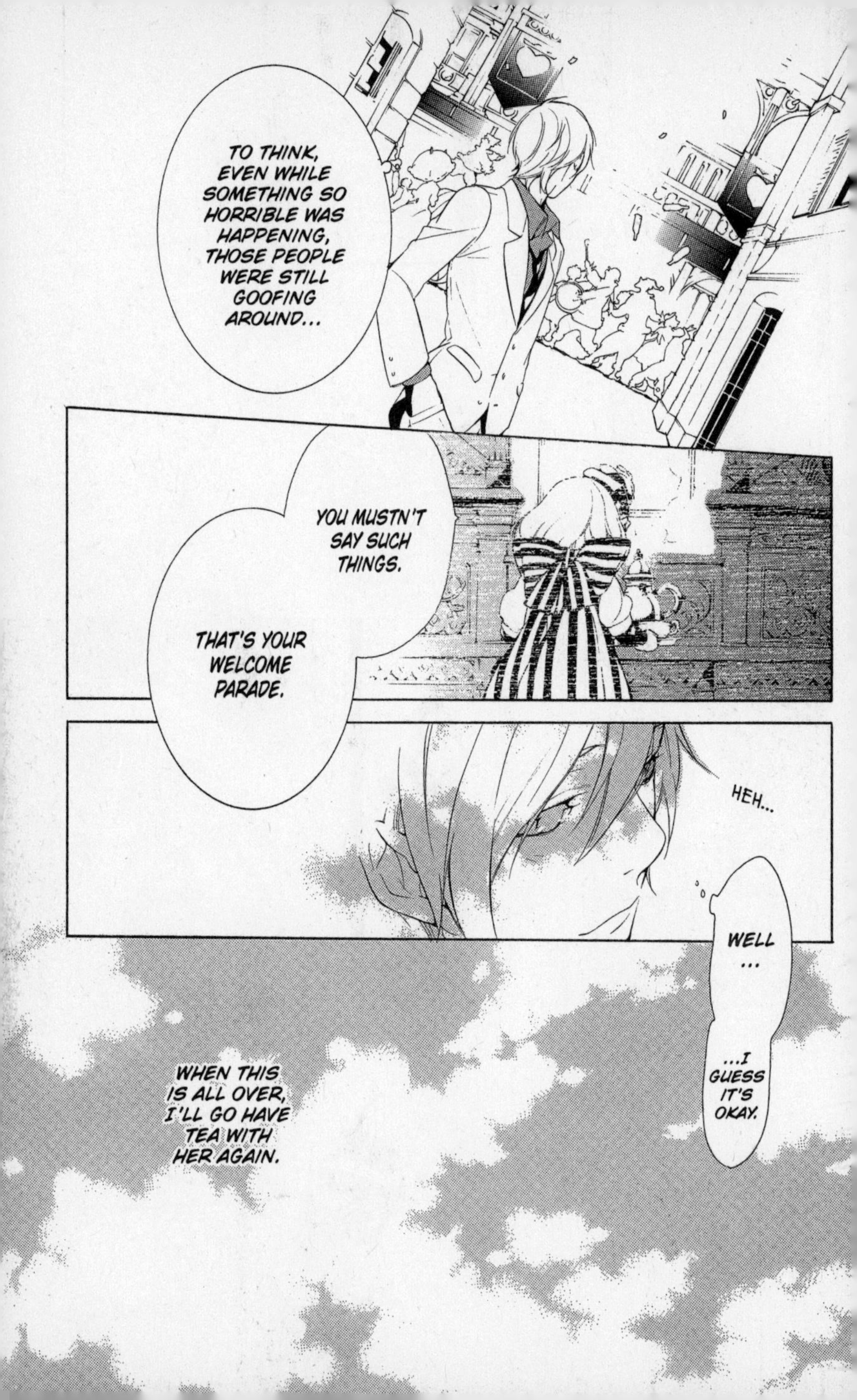
TO THINK, EVEN WHILE SOMETHING SO HORRIBLE WAS HAPPENING, THOSE PEOPLE WERE STILL GOOFING AROUND...
YOU MUSTN'T SAY SUCH THINGS.
THAT'S YOUR WELCOME PARADE.
HEH...
WELL ...
...I GUESS IT'S OKAY.
WHEN THIS IS ALL OVER, I'LL GO HAVE TEA WITH HER AGAIN.

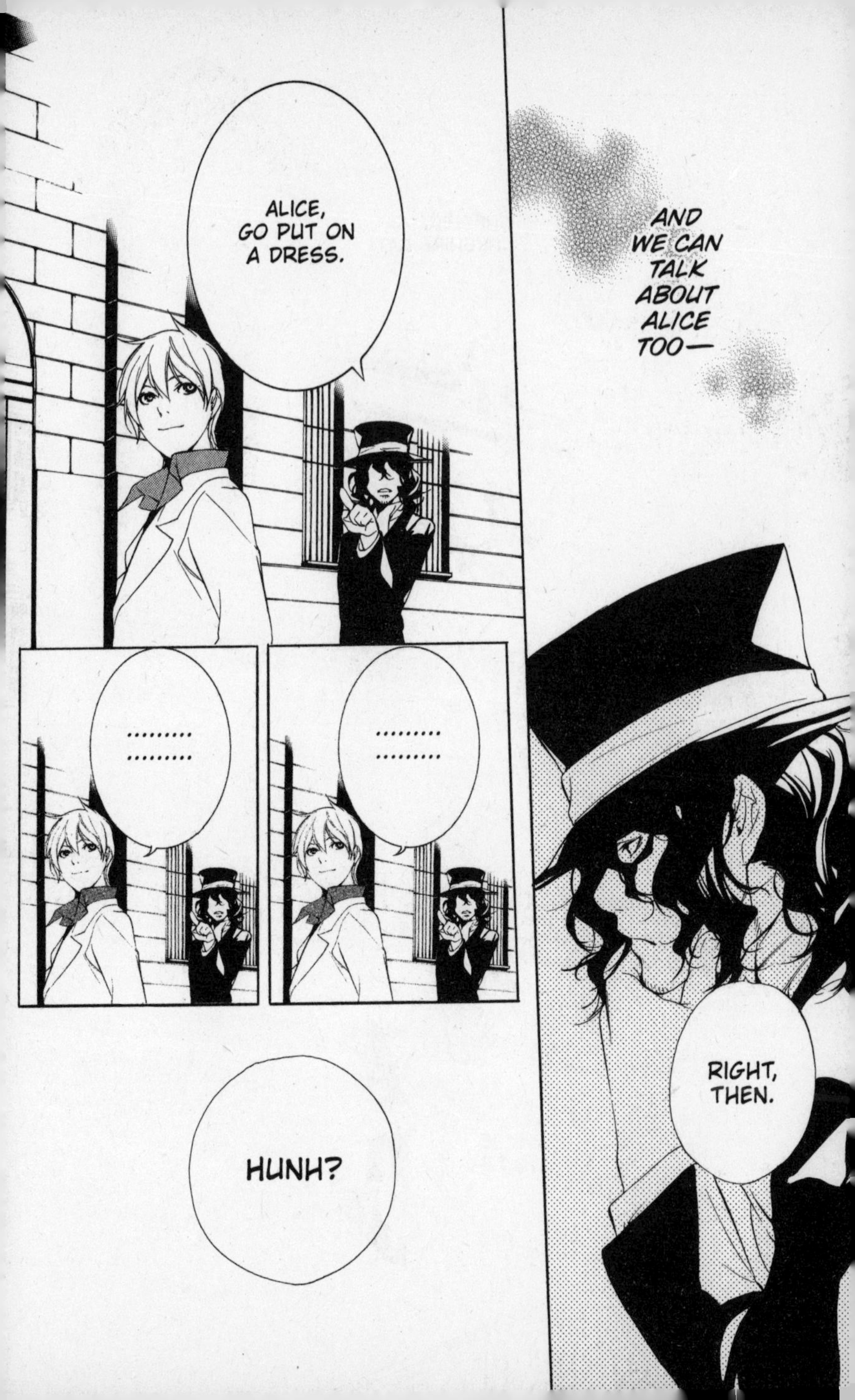
AND WE CAN TALK ABOUT ALICE TOO—
RIGHT, THEN.
ALICE, GO PUT ON A DRESS.
....
....
....
....
HUNH?

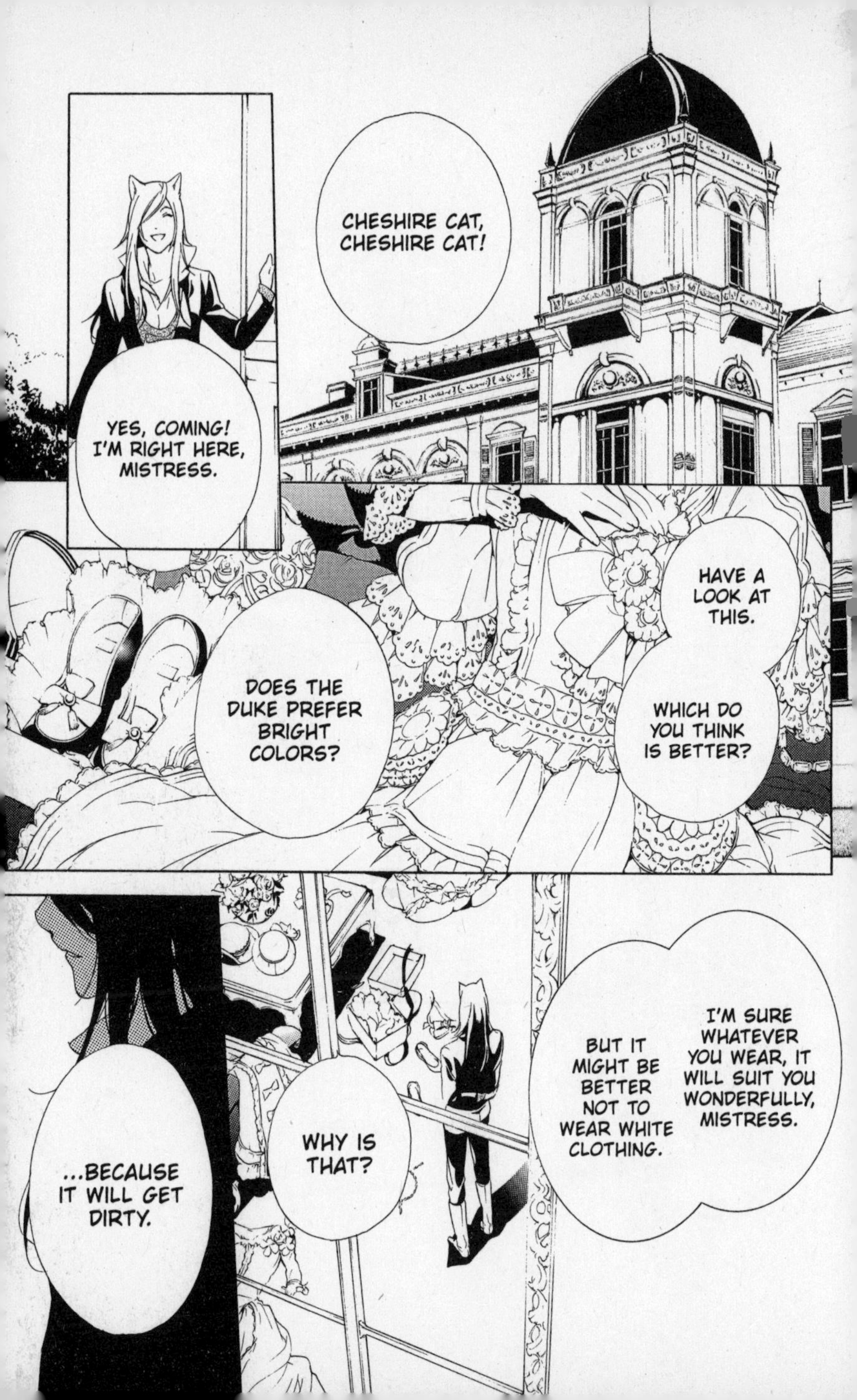
CHESHIRE CAT, CHESHIRE CAT!
YES, COMING! I'M RIGHT HERE, MISTRESS.
HAVE A LOOK AT THIS.
WHICH DO YOU THINK IS BETTER?
DOES THE DUKE PREFER BRIGHT COLORS?
I'M SURE WHATEVER YOU WEAR, IT WILL SUIT YOU WONDERFULLY, MISTRESS.
BUT IT MIGHT BE BETTER NOT TO WEAR WHITE CLOTHING.
WHY IS THAT?
...BECAUSE IT WILL GET DIRTY.

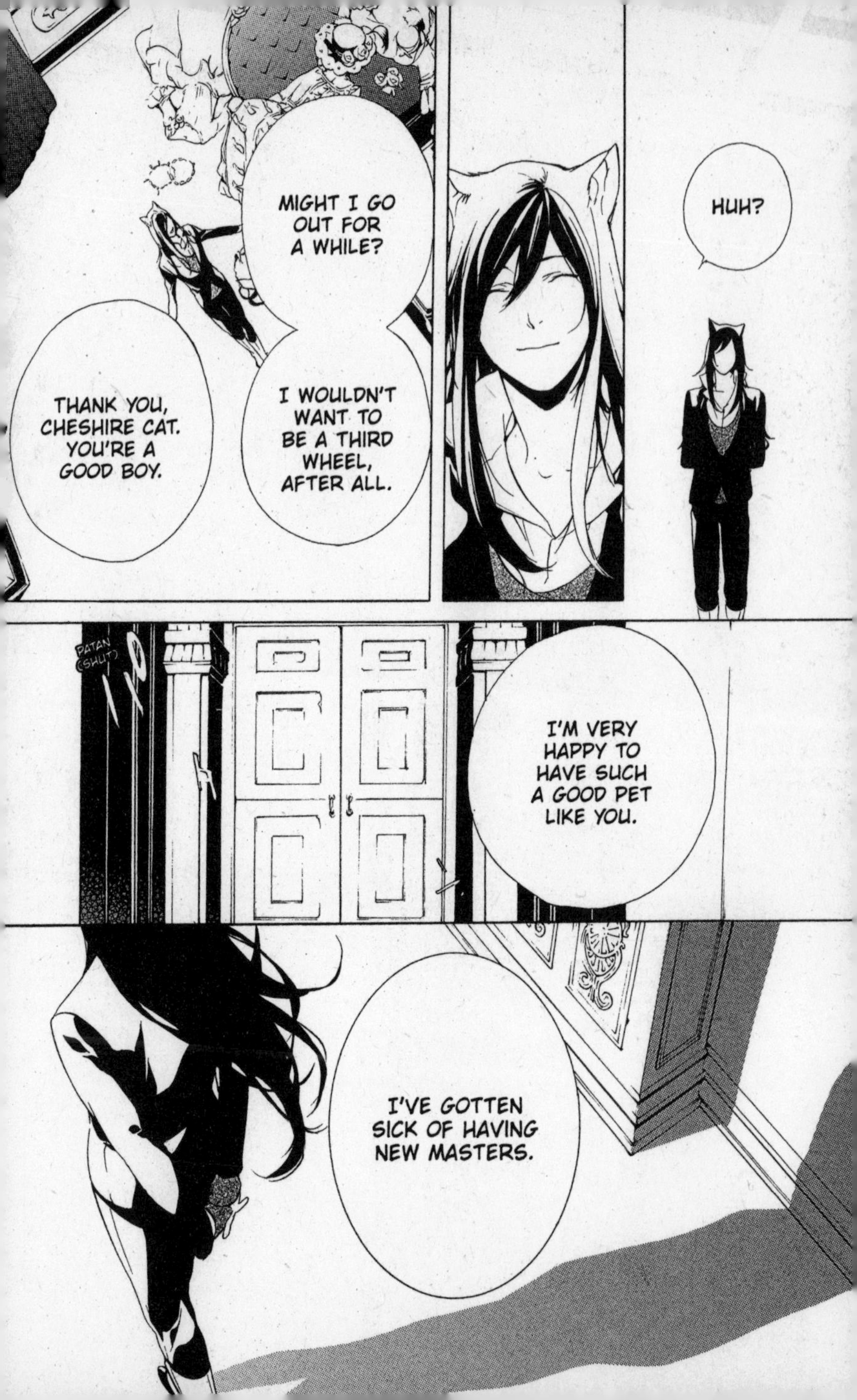
HUH?
MIGHT I GO OUT FOR A WHILE?
I WOULDN'T WANT TO BE A THIRD WHEEL, AFTER ALL.
THANK YOU, CHESHIRE CAT. YOU'RE A GOOD BOY.
I'M VERY HAPPY TO HAVE SUCH A GOOD PET LIKE YOU.
PATAN (SHUT)
I'VE GOTTEN SICK OF HAVING NEW MASTERS.

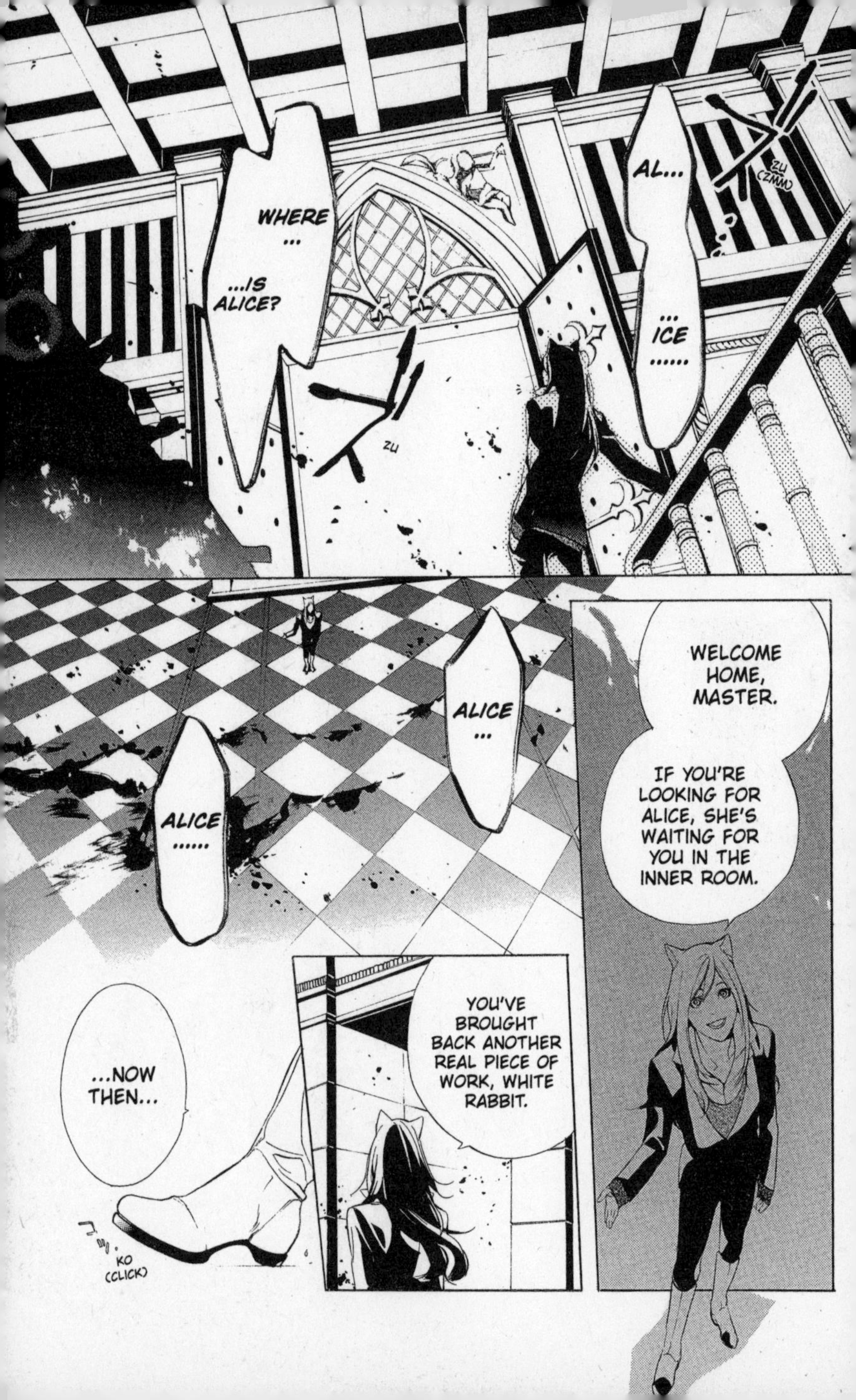
ZU
(ZMM)
AL...
...ICE......
ZU
WHERE...
...IS ALICE?
WELCOME HOME, MASTER.
IF YOU'RE LOOKING FOR ALICE, SHE'S WAITING FOR YOU IN THE INNER ROOM.
ALICE...
ALICE......
YOU'VE BROUGHT BACK ANOTHER REAL PIECE OF WORK, WHITE RABBIT.
...NOW THEN...
KO
(CLICK)

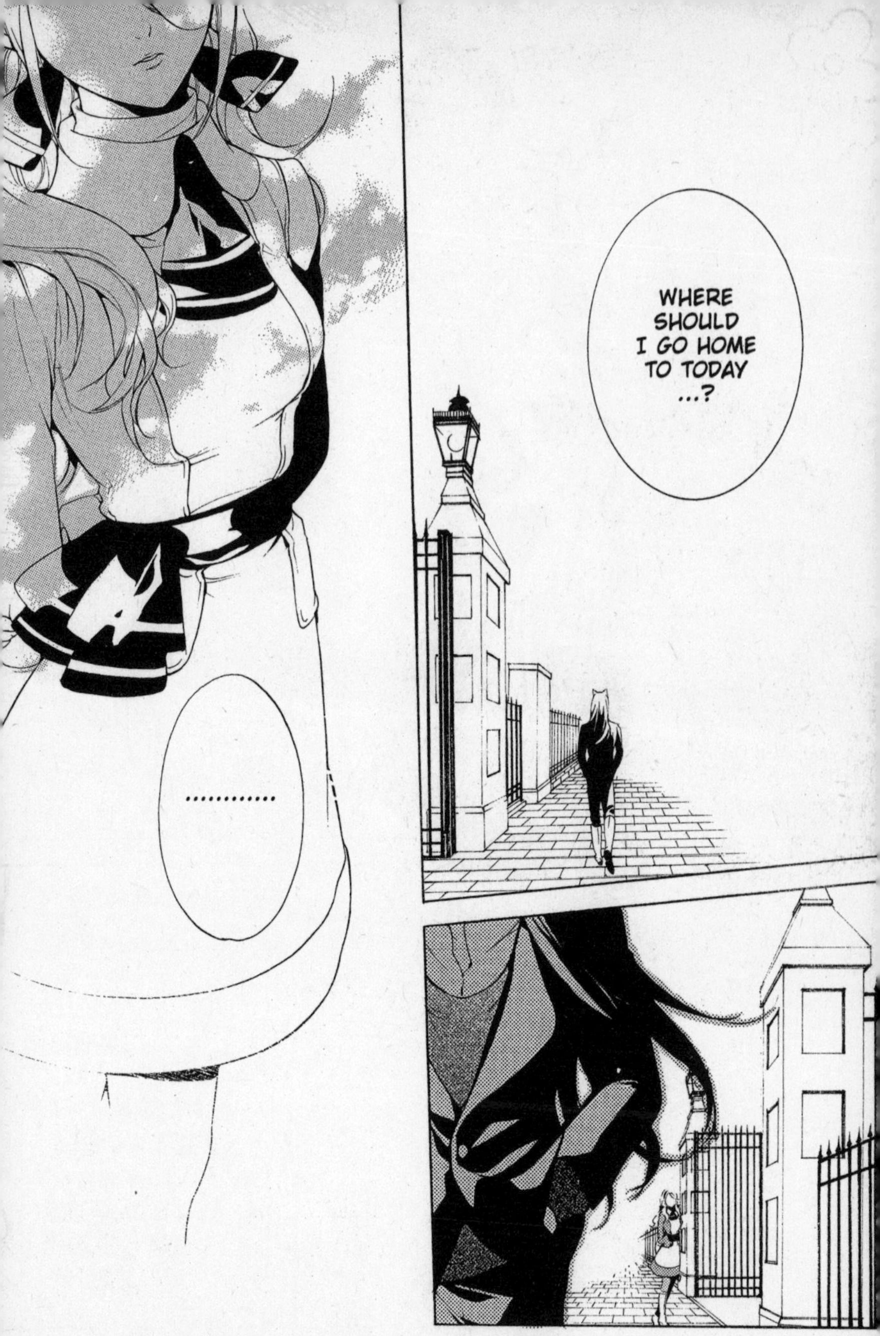
WHERE SHOULD I GO HOME TO TODAY ...?
....

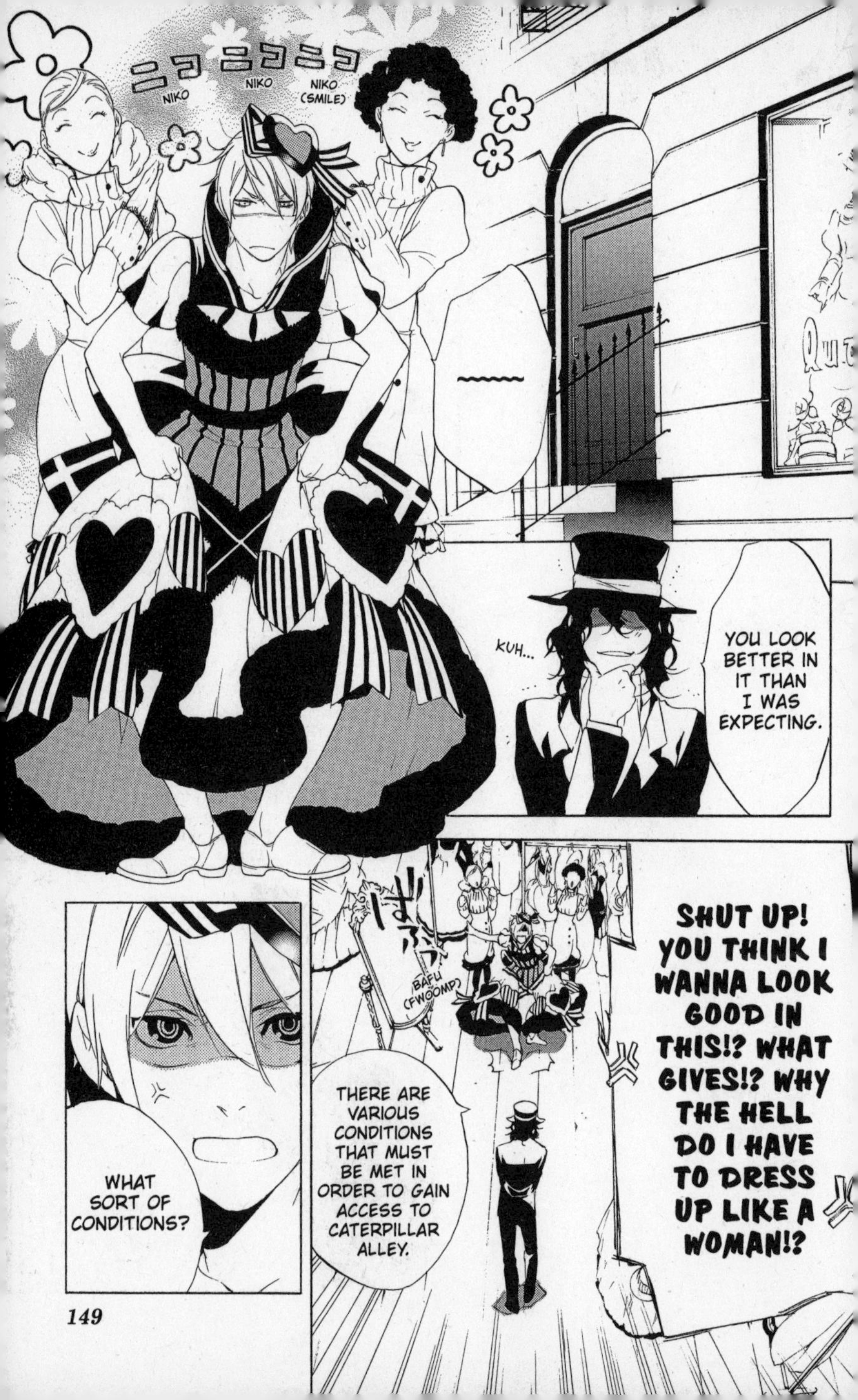
ニコニコニコ
NIKO
NIKO
NIKO (SMILE)
~~~
YOU LOOK BETTER IN IT THAN I WAS EXPECTING.
KUH...
SHUT UP! YOU THINK I WANNA LOOK GOOD IN THIS!? WHAT GIVES!? WHY THE HELL DO I HAVE TO DRESS UP LIKE A WOMAN!?
BAFU (FWOOMP)
THERE ARE VARIOUS CONDITIONS THAT MUST BE MET IN ORDER TO GAIN ACCESS TO CATERPILLAR ALLEY.
WHAT SORT OF CONDITIONS?
~~~

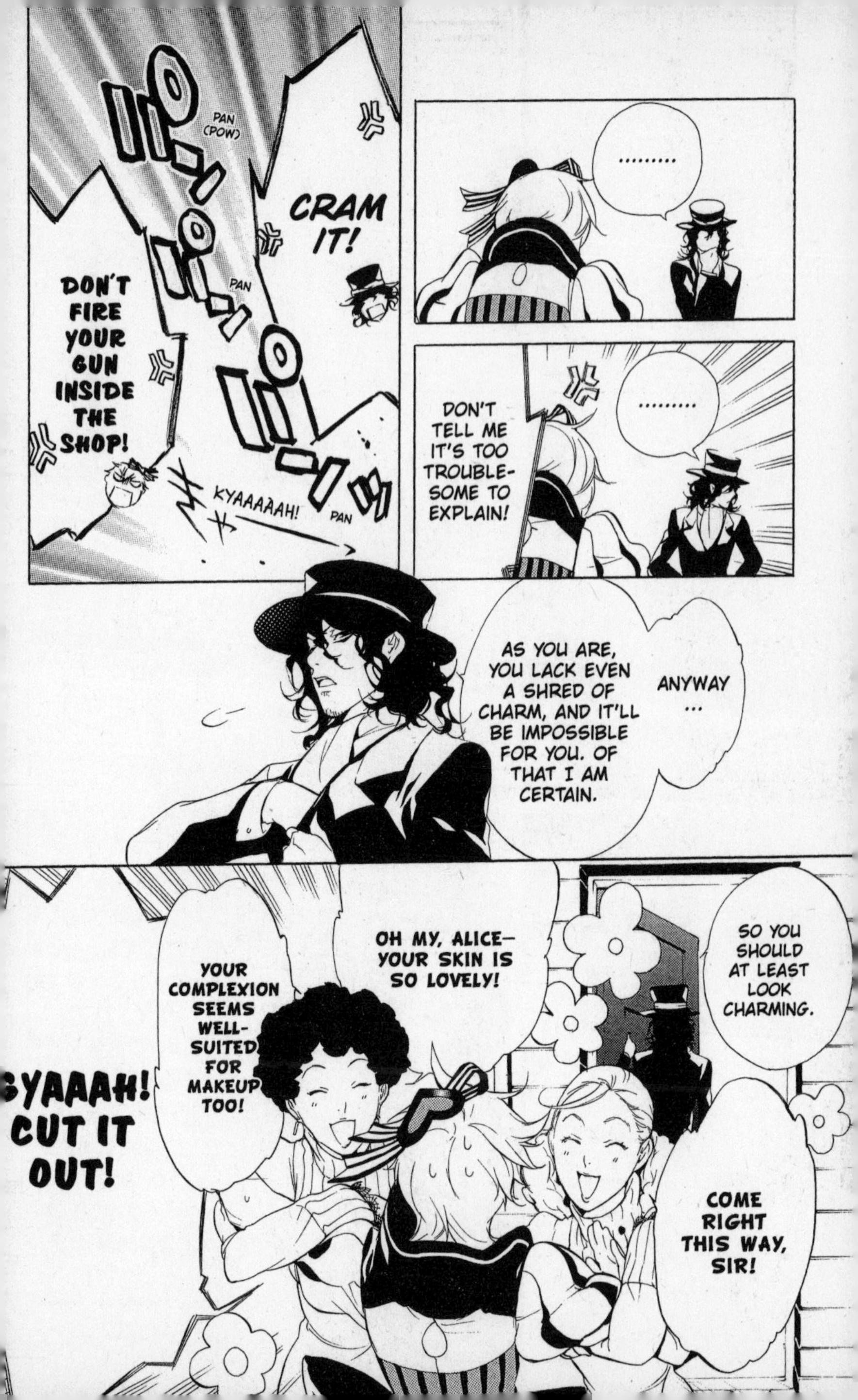
....
....
DON'T TELL ME IT'S TOO TROUBLE-SOME TO EXPLAIN!
CRAM IT!
PAN (POW)
PAN
DON'T FIRE YOUR GUN INSIDE THE SHOP!
KYAAAAAH!
PAN
ANYWAY ...
AS YOU ARE, YOU LACK EVEN A SHRED OF CHARM, AND IT'LL BE IMPOSSIBLE FOR YOU. OF THAT I AM CERTAIN.
SO YOU SHOULD AT LEAST LOOK CHARMING.
COME RIGHT THIS WAY, SIR!
OH MY, ALICE— YOUR SKIN IS SO LOVELY!
YOUR COMPLEXION SEEMS WELL-SUITED FOR MAKEUP TOO!
YAAAH! CUT IT OUT!

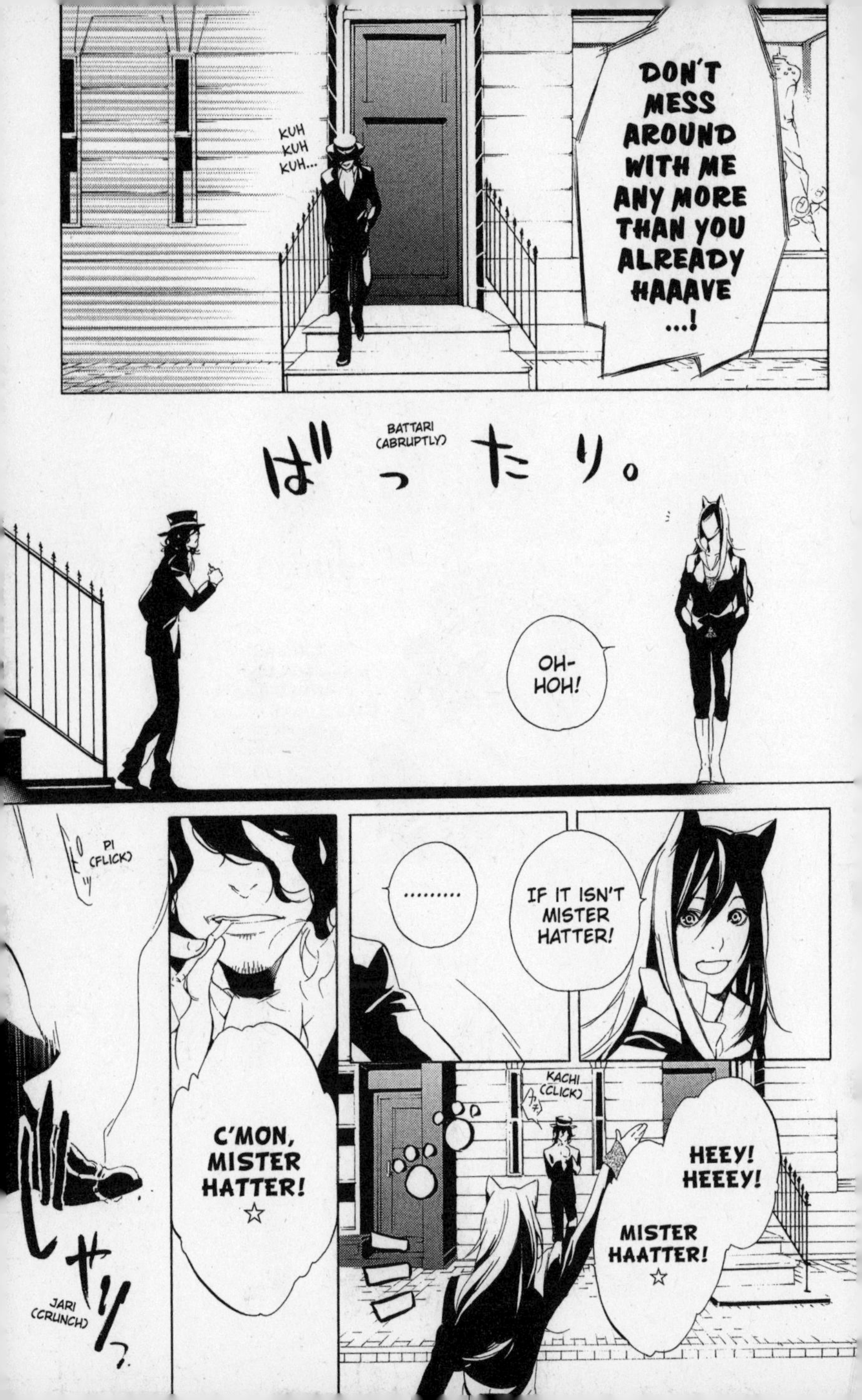
DON'T MESS AROUND WITH ME ANY MORE THAN YOU ALREADY HAAAVE ...!
KUH KUH KUH...
ばったり。
BATTARI (ABRUPTLY)
OH-HOH!
IF IT ISN'T MISTER HATTER!
....
HEEY! HEEEY!
MISTER HAATTER! ☆
KACHI (CLICK)
C'MON, MISTER HATTER! ☆
PI (FLICK)
JARI (CRUNCH)

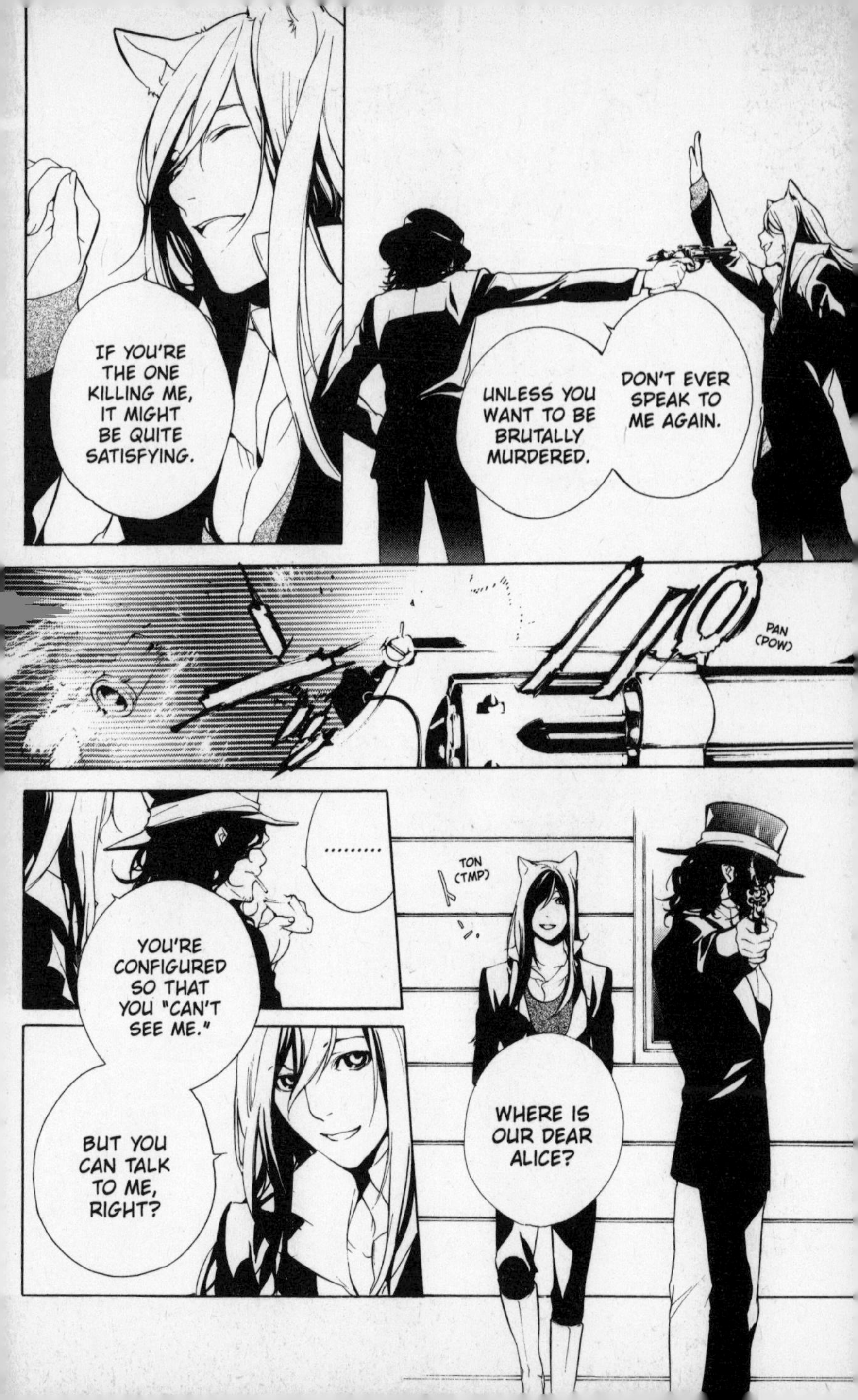
DON'T EVER SPEAK TO ME AGAIN.
UNLESS YOU WANT TO BE BRUTALLY MURDERED.
IF YOU'RE THE ONE KILLING ME, IT MIGHT BE QUITE SATISFYING.
PAN (POW)
TON (TMP)
WHERE IS OUR DEAR ALICE?
....
YOU'RE CONFIGURED SO THAT YOU "CAN'T SEE ME."
BUT YOU CAN TALK TO ME, RIGHT?

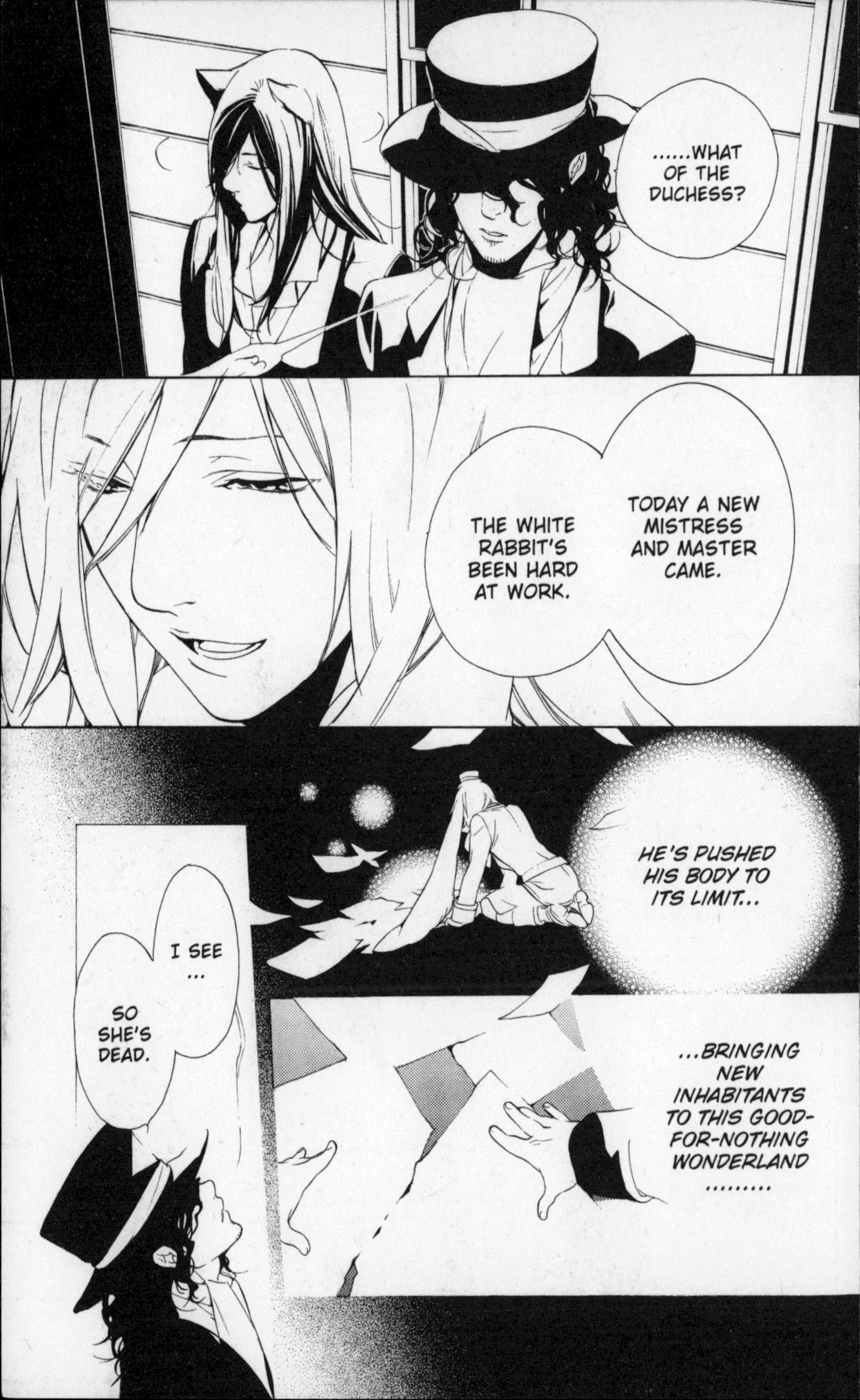

......WHAT OF THE DUCHESS?
TODAY A NEW MISTRESS AND MASTER CAME.
THE WHITE RABBIT'S BEEN HARD AT WORK.
HE'S PUSHED HIS BODY TO ITS LIMIT...
...BRINGING NEW INHABITANTS TO THIS GOOD-FOR-NOTHING WONDERLAND ....
I SEE ...
SO SHE'S DEAD.

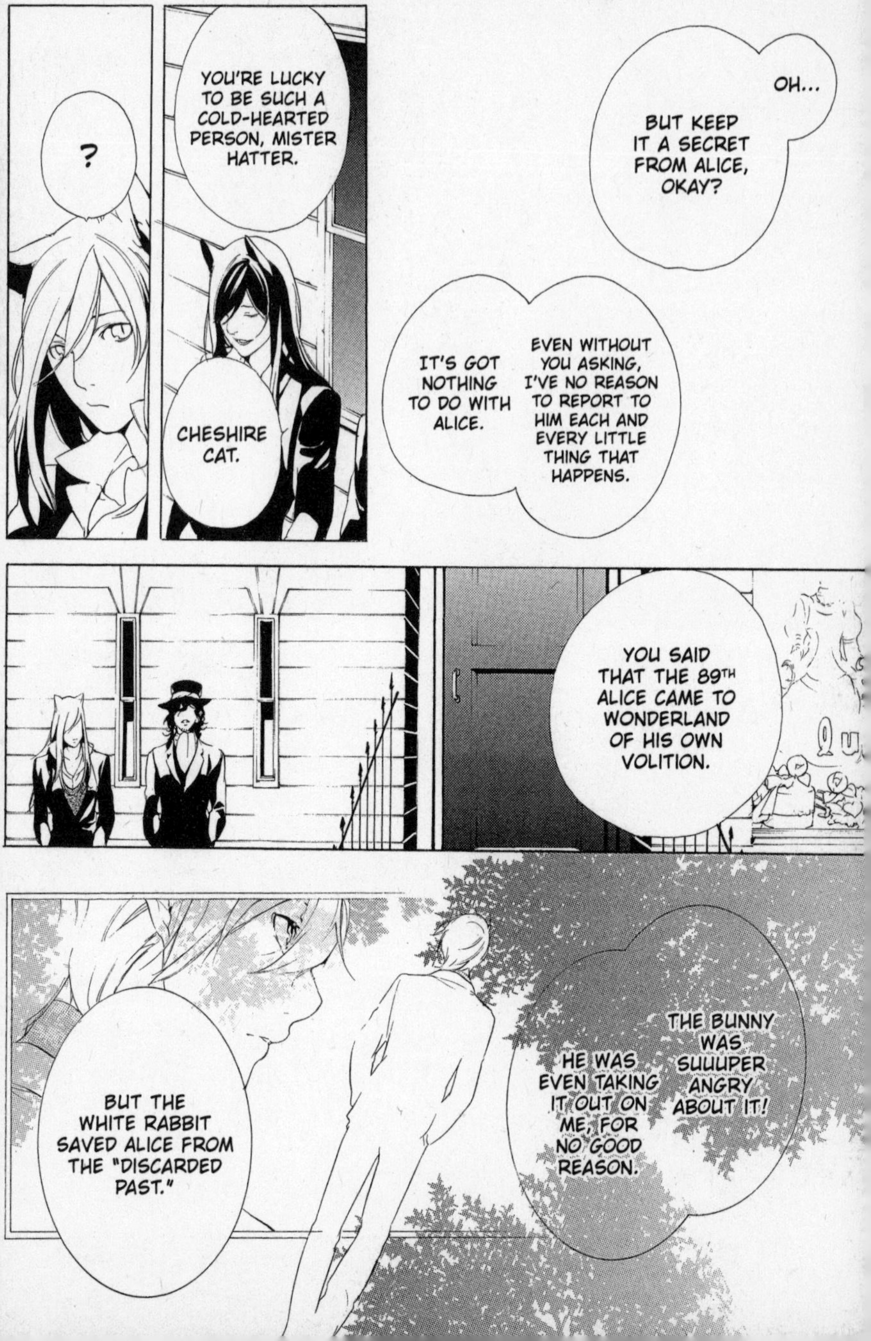
OH...
BUT KEEP IT A SECRET FROM ALICE, OKAY?
EVEN WITHOUT YOU ASKING, I'VE NO REASON TO REPORT TO HIM EACH AND EVERY LITTLE THING THAT HAPPENS.
IT'S GOT NOTHING TO DO WITH ALICE.
YOU'RE LUCKY TO BE SUCH A COLD-HEARTED PERSON, MISTER HATTER.
CHESHIRE CAT.
?
YOU SAID THAT THE 89TH ALICE CAME TO WONDERLAND OF HIS OWN VOLITION.
THE BUNNY WAS SUUUPER ANGRY ABOUT IT!
HE WAS EVEN TAKING IT OUT ON ME, FOR NO GOOD REASON.
BUT THE WHITE RABBIT SAVED ALICE FROM THE "DISCARDED PAST."

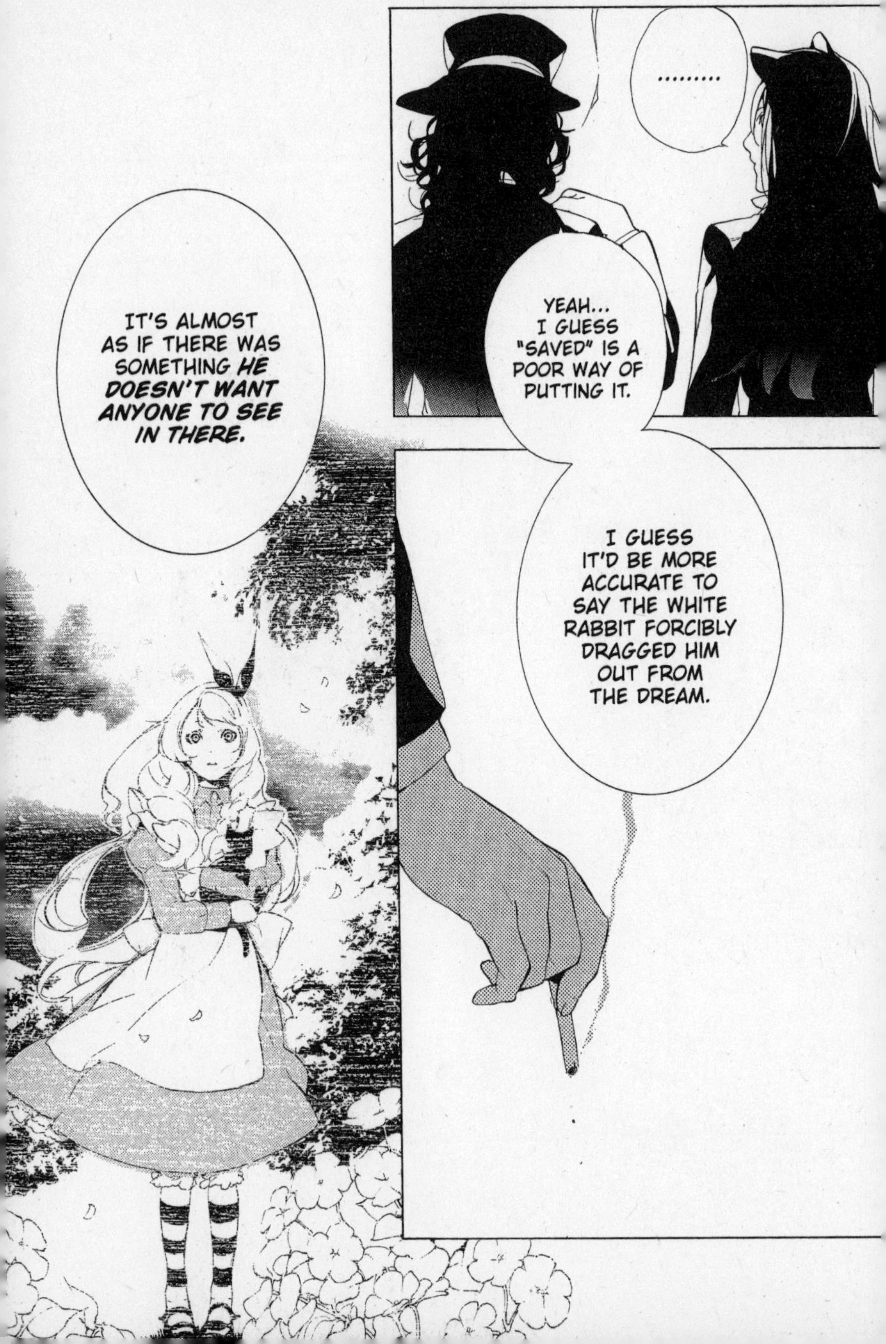
....
YEAH... I GUESS "SAVED" IS A POOR WAY OF PUTTING IT.
I GUESS IT'D BE MORE ACCURATE TO SAY THE WHITE RABBIT FORCIBLY DRAGGED HIM OUT FROM THE DREAM.
IT'S ALMOST AS IF THERE WAS SOMETHING HE DOESN'T WANT ANYONE TO SEE IN THERE.

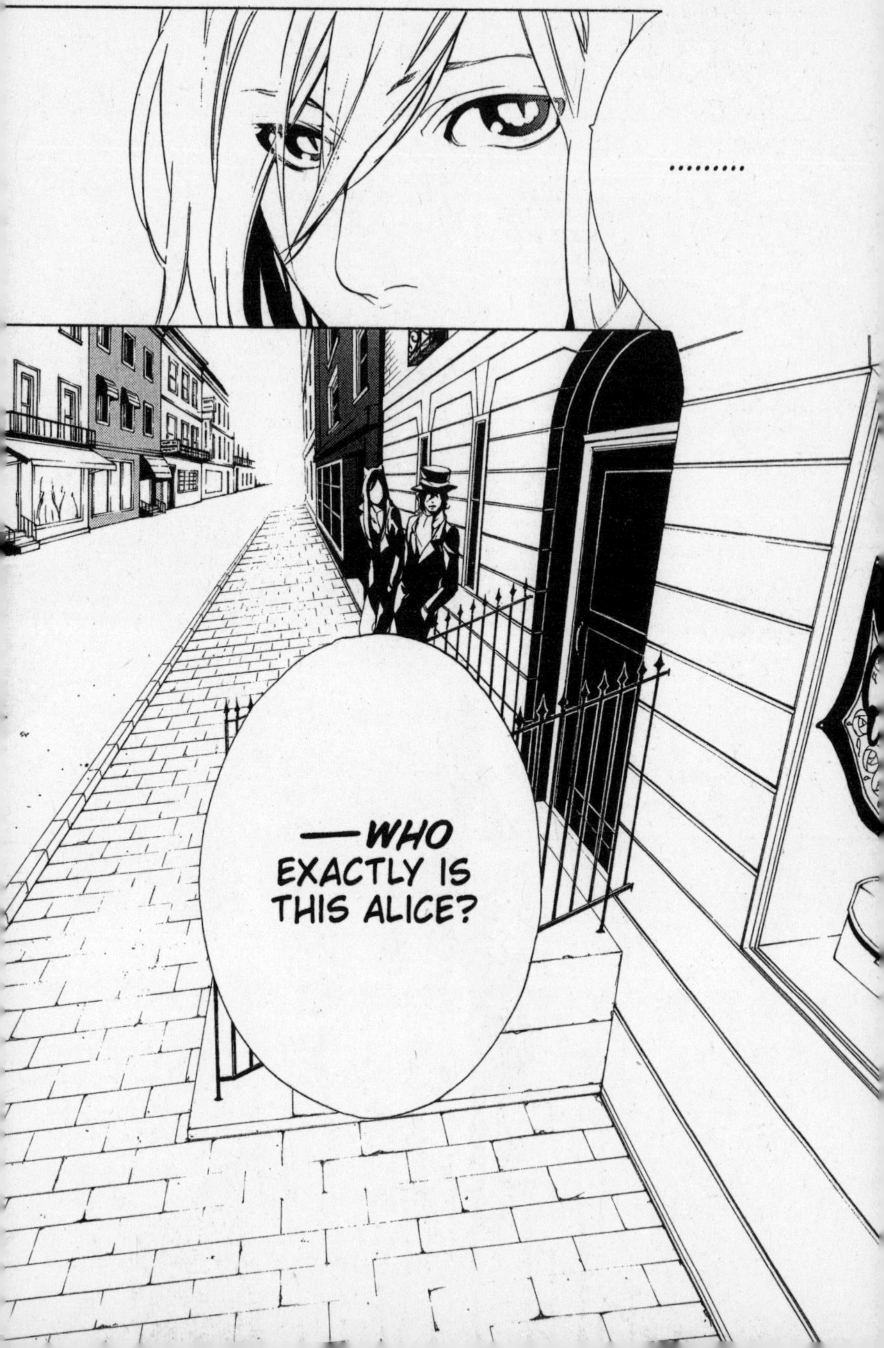
....
—WHO EXACTLY IS THIS ALICE?

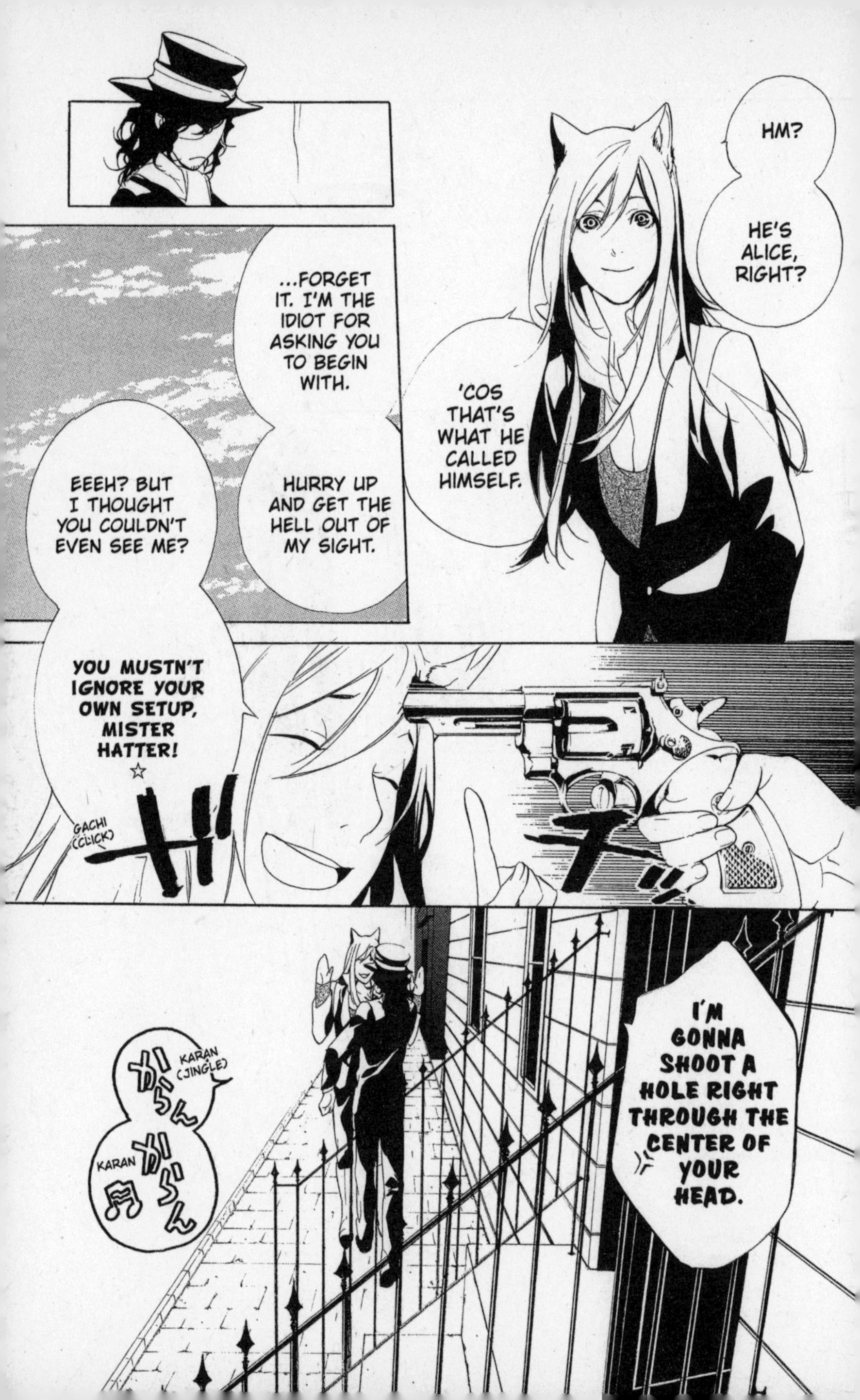
HM?
HE'S ALICE, RIGHT?
'COS THAT'S WHAT HE CALLED HIMSELF.
...FORGET IT. I'M THE IDIOT FOR ASKING YOU TO BEGIN WITH.
HURRY UP AND GET THE HELL OUT OF MY SIGHT.
EEEH? BUT I THOUGHT YOU COULDN'T EVEN SEE ME?
YOU MUSTN'T IGNORE YOUR OWN SETUP, MISTER HATTER! ☆
GACHI (CLICK)
I'M GONNA SHOOT A HOLE RIGHT THROUGH THE CENTER OF YOUR HEAD.
からん KARAN (JINGLE)
からん KARAN

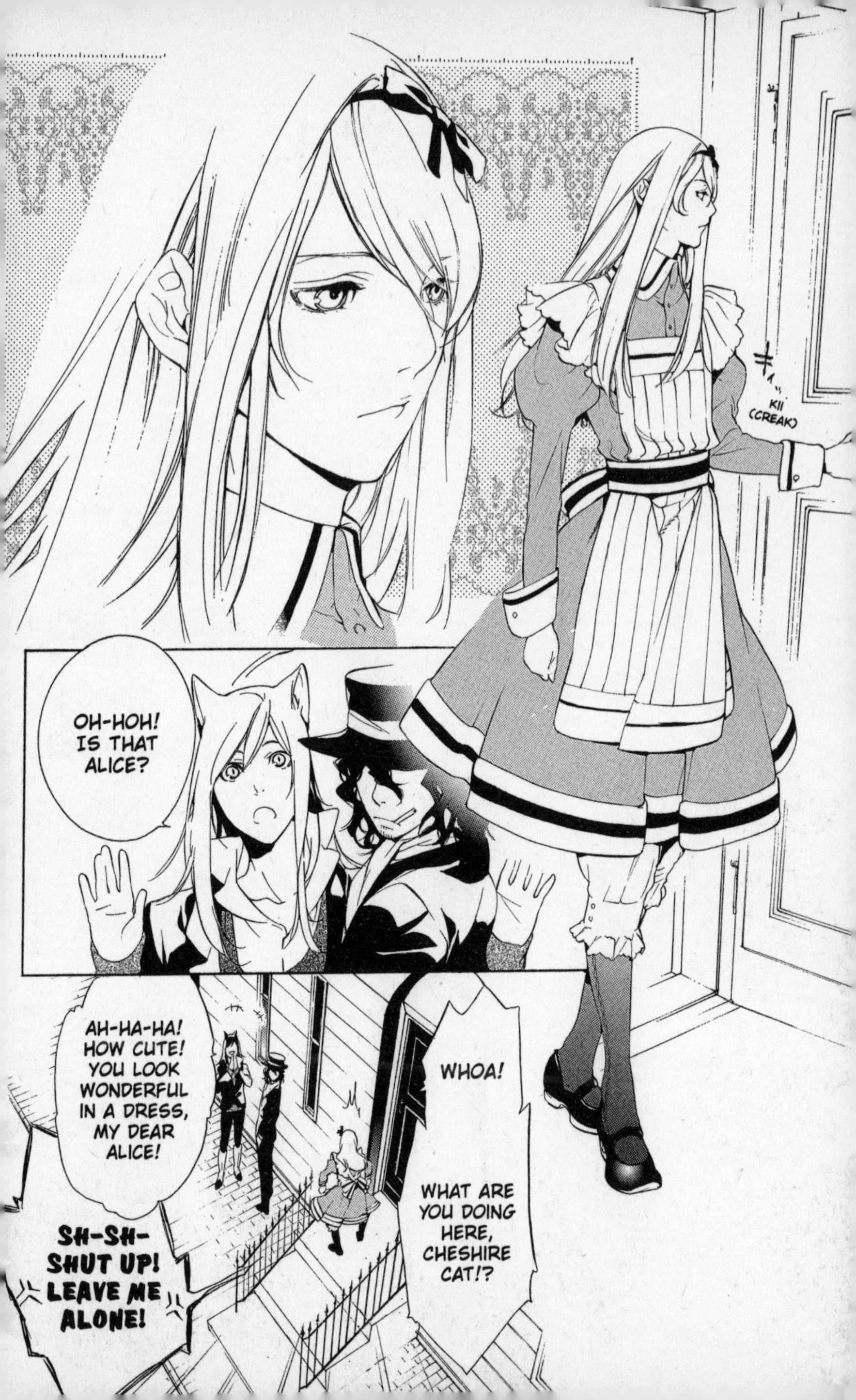
KII (CREAK)
OH-HOH! IS THAT ALICE?
WHOA!
WHAT ARE YOU DOING HERE, CHESHIRE CAT!?
AH-HA-HA! HOW CUTE! YOU LOOK WONDERFUL IN A DRESS, MY DEAR ALICE!
SH-SH-SHUT UP! LEAVE ME ALONE!

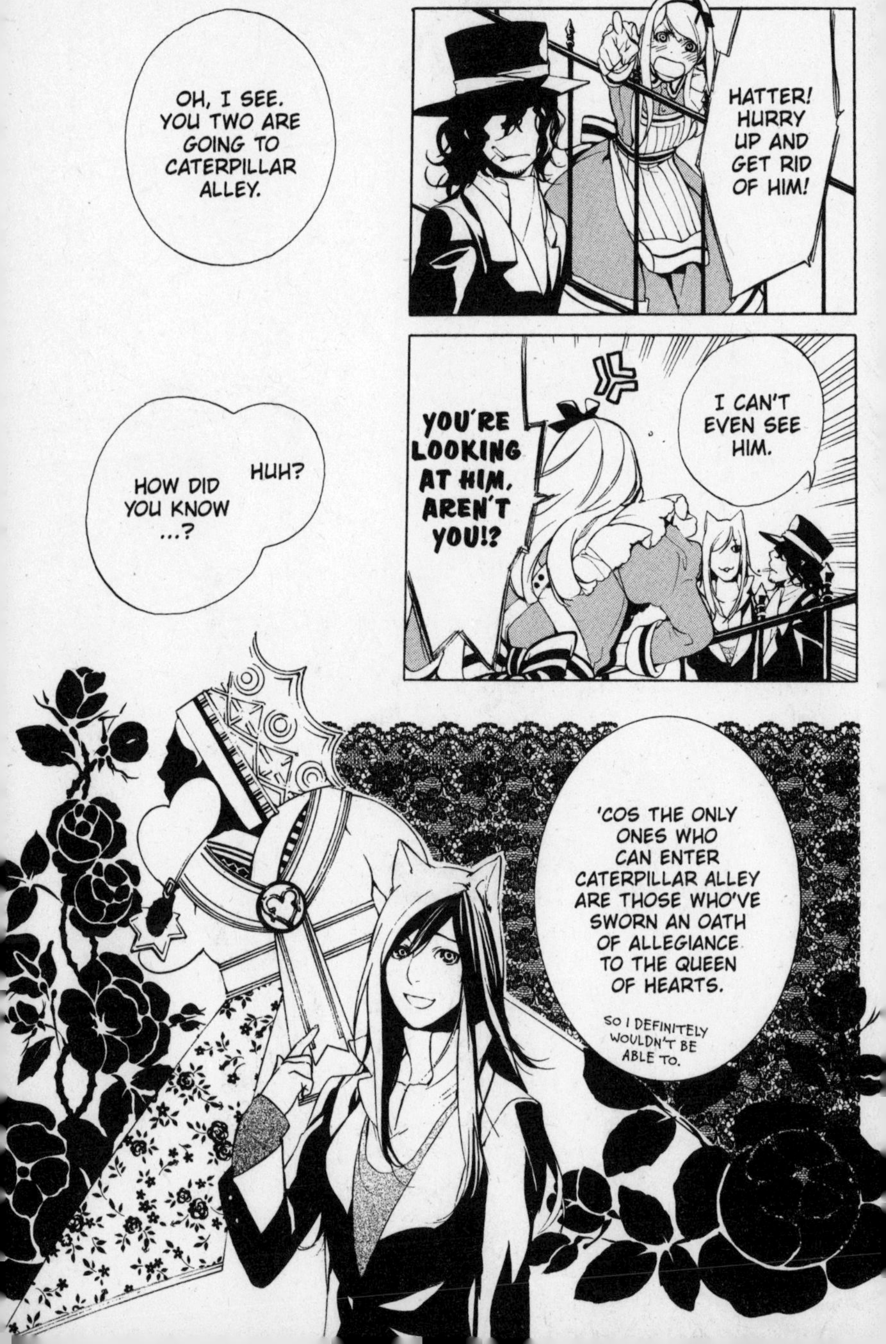
HATTER! HURRY UP AND GET RID OF HIM!
OH, I SEE. YOU TWO ARE GOING TO CATERPILLAR ALLEY.
I CAN'T EVEN SEE HIM.
YOU'RE LOOKING AT HIM, AREN'T YOU!?
HUH?
HOW DID YOU KNOW ...?
'COS THE ONLY ONES WHO CAN ENTER CATERPILLAR ALLEY ARE THOSE WHO'VE SWORN AN OATH OF ALLEGIANCE TO THE QUEEN OF HEARTS.
SO I DEFINITELY WOULDN'T BE ABLE TO.

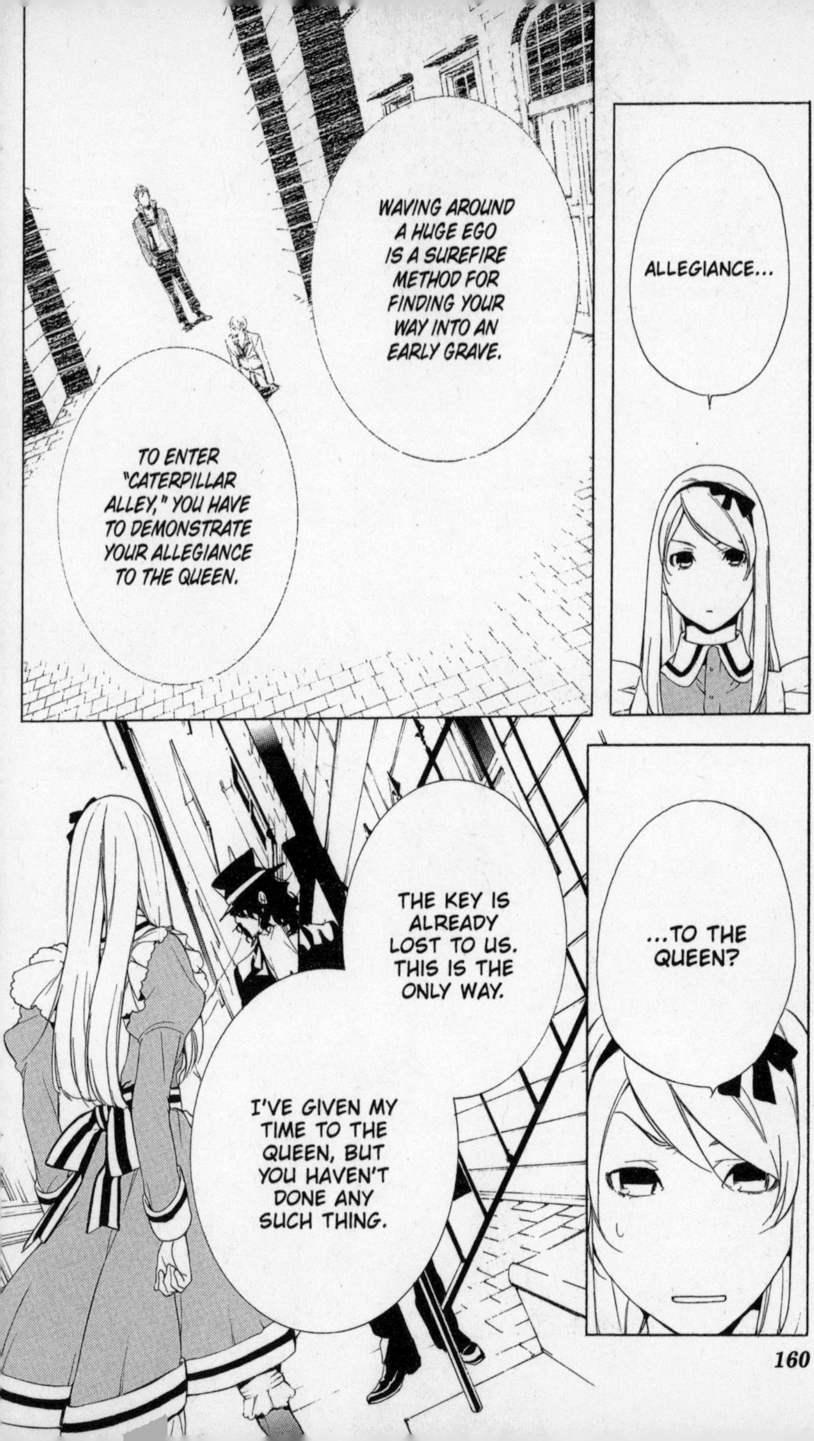
ALLEGIANCE...
WAVING AROUND A HUGE EGO IS A SUREFIRE METHOD FOR FINDING YOUR WAY INTO AN EARLY GRAVE.
TO ENTER "CATERPILLAR ALLEY," YOU HAVE TO DEMONSTRATE YOUR ALLEGIANCE TO THE QUEEN.
...TO THE QUEEN?
THE KEY IS ALREADY LOST TO US. THIS IS THE ONLY WAY.
I'VE GIVEN MY TIME TO THE QUEEN, BUT YOU HAVEN'T DONE ANY SUCH THING.

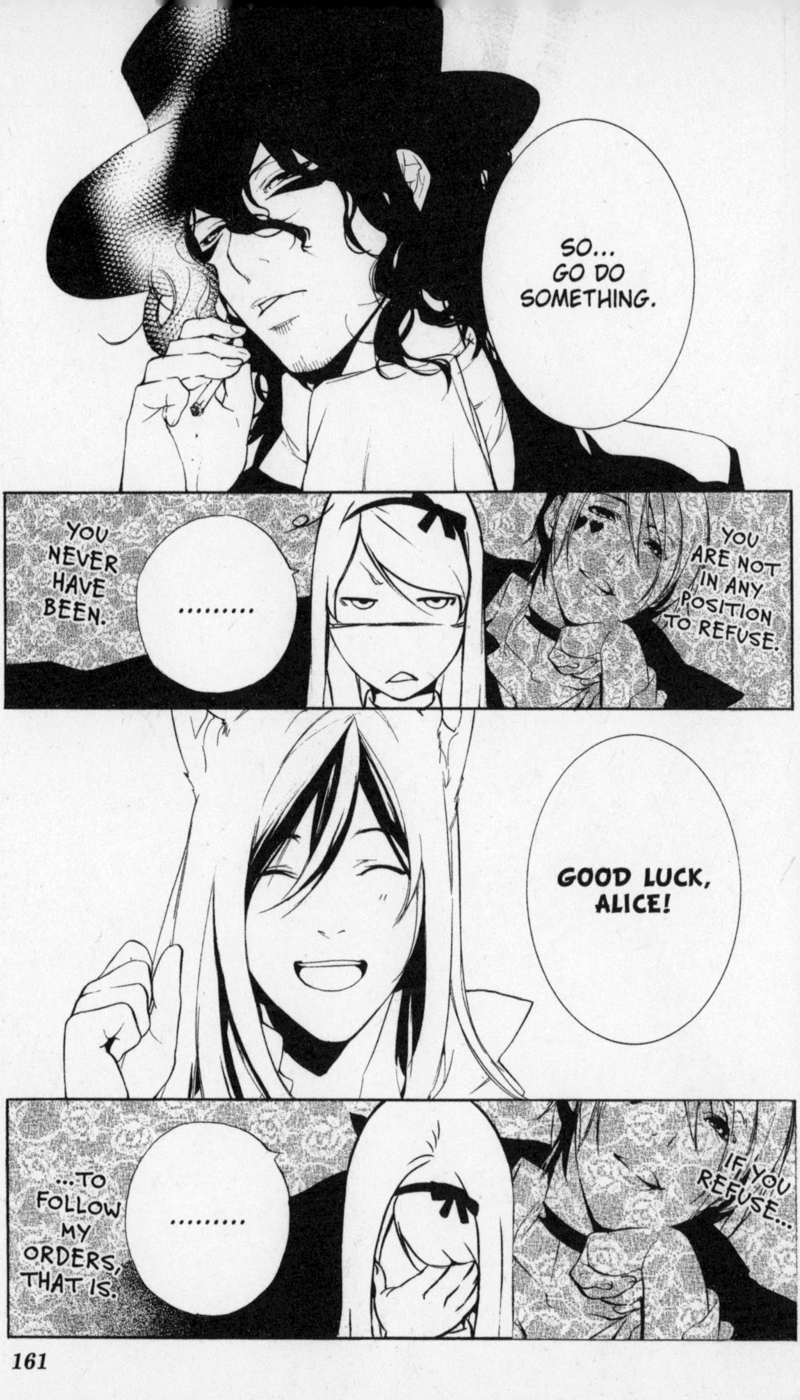
SO... GO DO SOMETHING.
YOU ARE NOT IN ANY POSITION TO REFUSE.
....
YOU NEVER HAVE BEEN.
GOOD LUCK, ALICE!
IF YOU REFUSE...
....
...TO FOLLOW MY ORDERS, THAT IS.

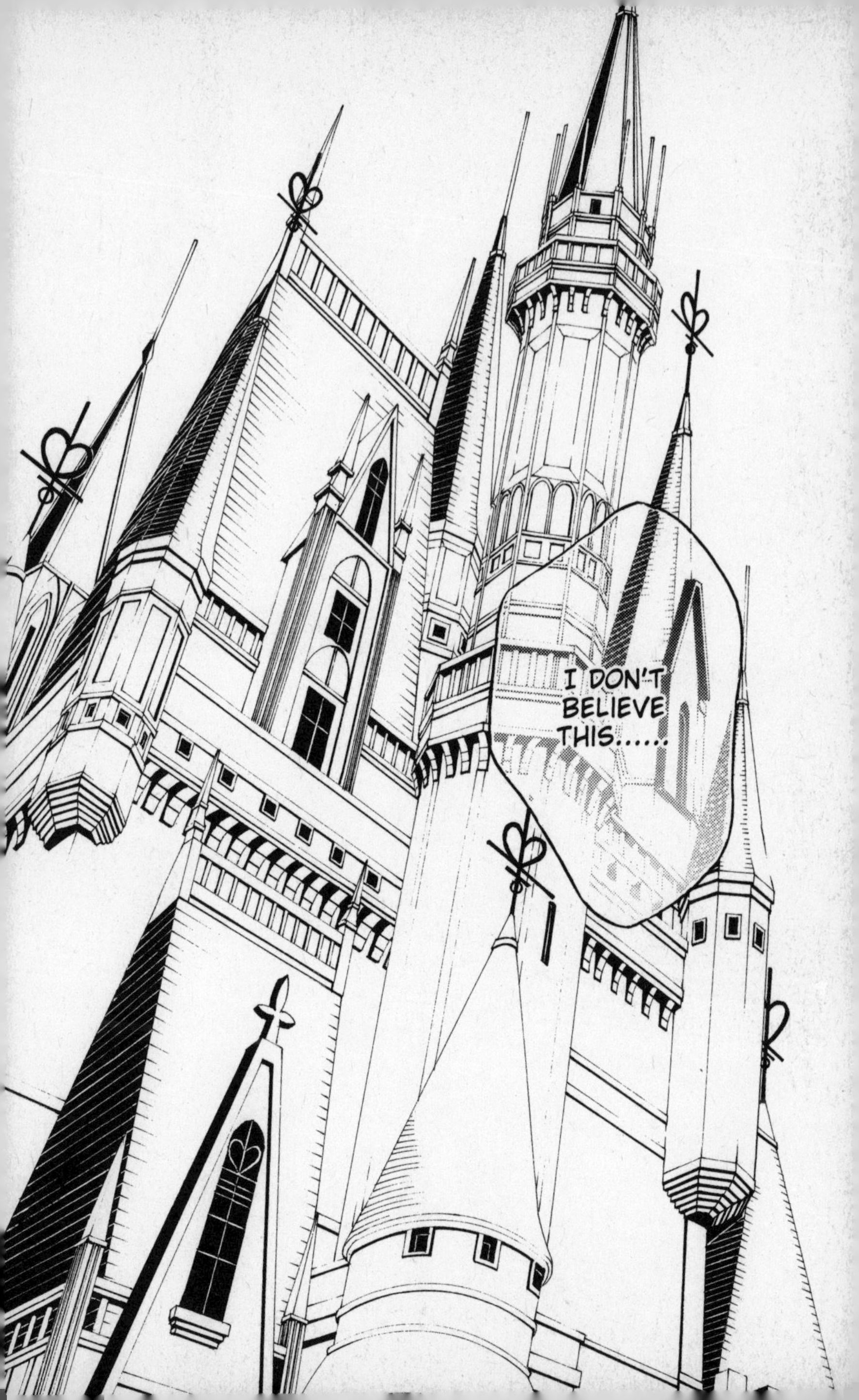
I DON'T BELIEVE THIS......

Chapter 11

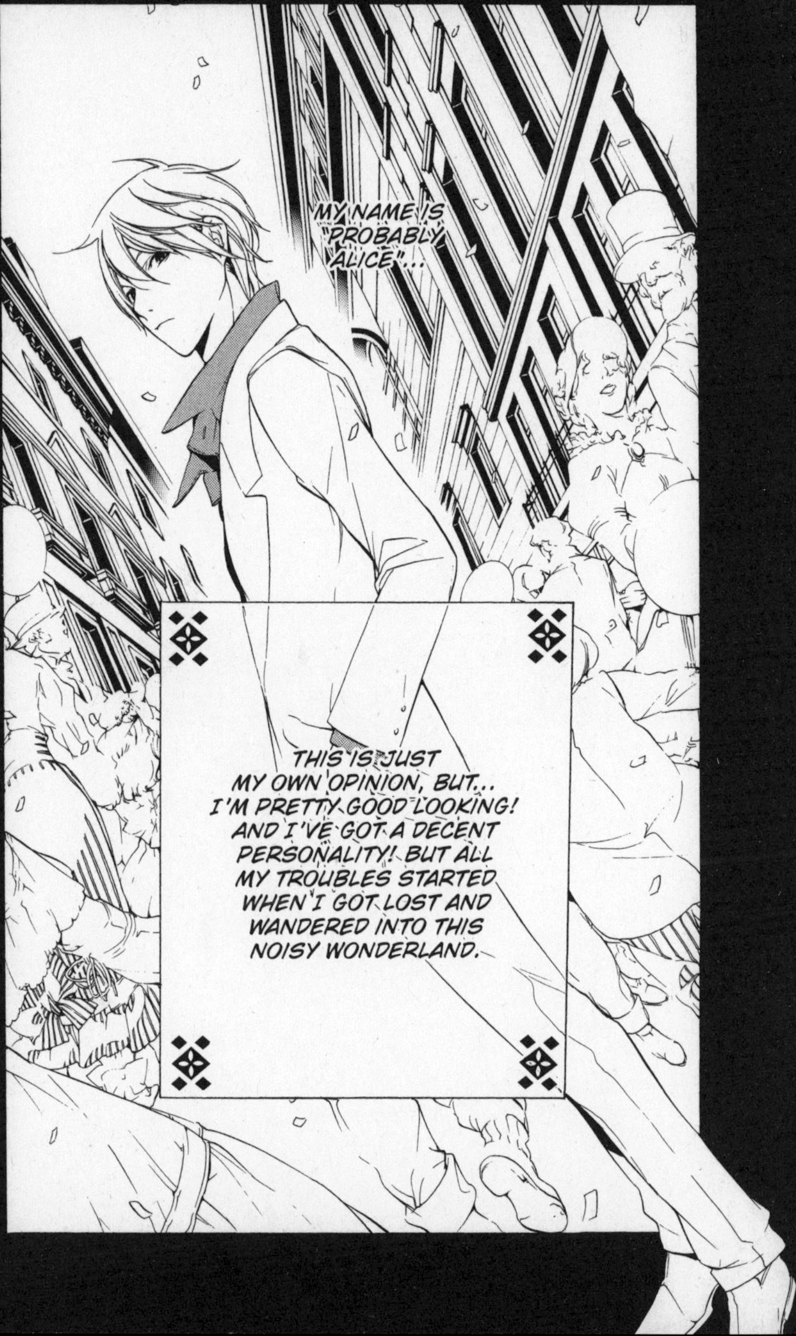
MY NAME IS "PROBABLY ALICE"...
THIS IS JUST MY OWN OPINION, BUT... I'M PRETTY GOOD LOOKING! AND I'VE GOT A DECENT PERSONALITY! BUT ALL MY TROUBLES STARTED WHEN I GOT LOST AND WANDERED INTO THIS NOISY WONDERLAND.

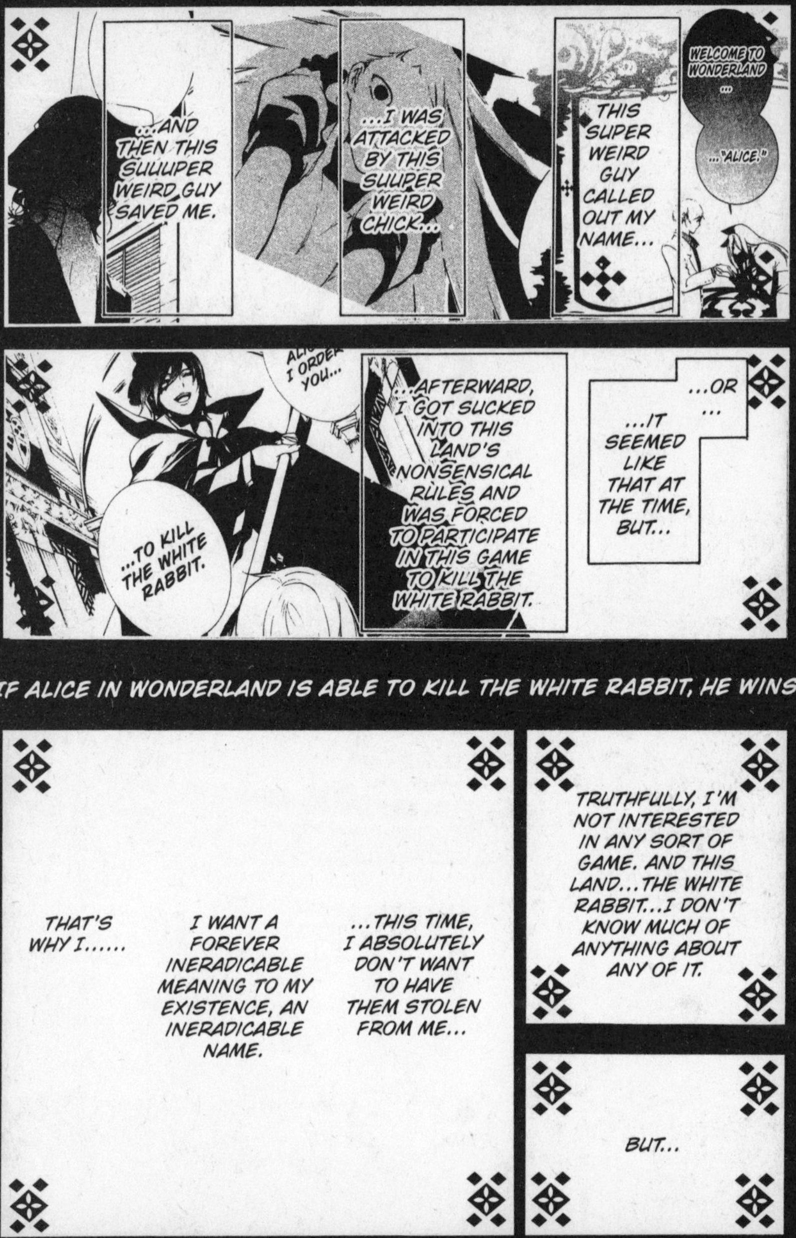
WELCOME TO WONDERLAND ...
..."ALICE."
THIS SUPER WEIRD GUY CALLED OUT MY NAME...
...I WAS ATTACKED BY THIS SUUPER WEIRD CHICK...
...AND THEN THIS SUUUPER WEIRD GUY SAVED ME.
...OR ...
...IT SEEMED LIKE THAT AT THE TIME, BUT...
...AFTERWARD, I GOT SUCKED INTO THIS LAND'S NONSENSICAL RULES AND WAS FORCED TO PARTICIPATE IN THIS GAME TO KILL THE WHITE RABBIT.
I ORDER YOU...
...TO KILL THE WHITE RABBIT.
IF ALICE IN WONDERLAND IS ABLE TO KILL THE WHITE RABBIT, HE WINS.
TRUTHFULLY, I'M NOT INTERESTED IN ANY SORT OF GAME. AND THIS LAND...THE WHITE RABBIT...I DON'T KNOW MUCH OF ANYTHING ABOUT ANY OF IT.
BUT...
...THIS TIME, I ABSOLUTELY DON'T WANT TO HAVE THEM STOLEN FROM ME...
I WANT A FOREVER INERADICABLE MEANING TO MY EXISTENCE, AN INERADICABLE NAME.
THAT'S WHY I......

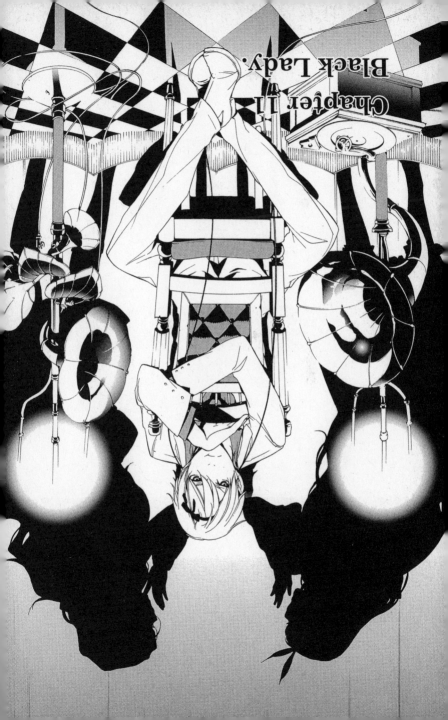

Chapter 11:
Black Lady.

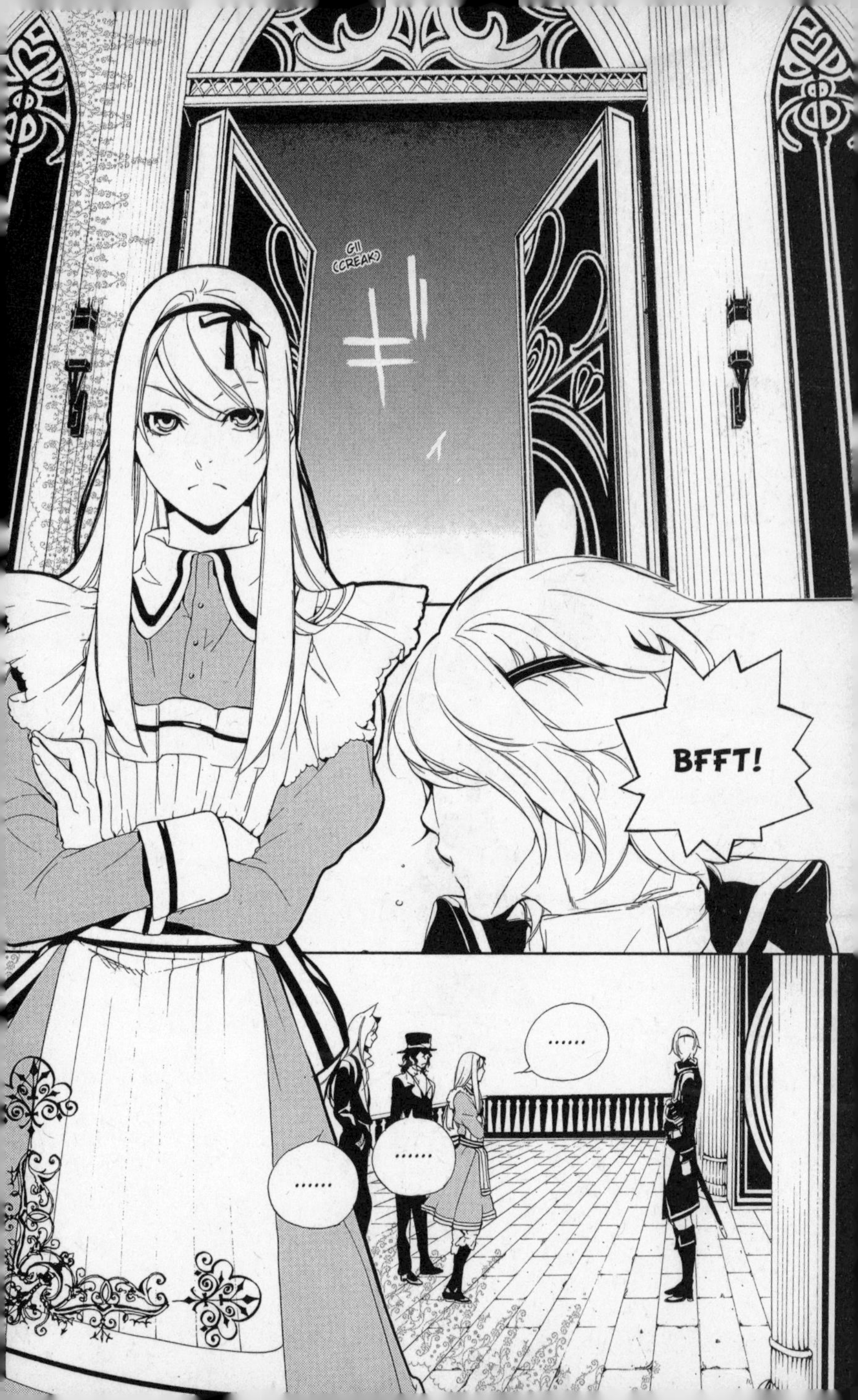
GII (CREAK)
BFFT!
......
......
......

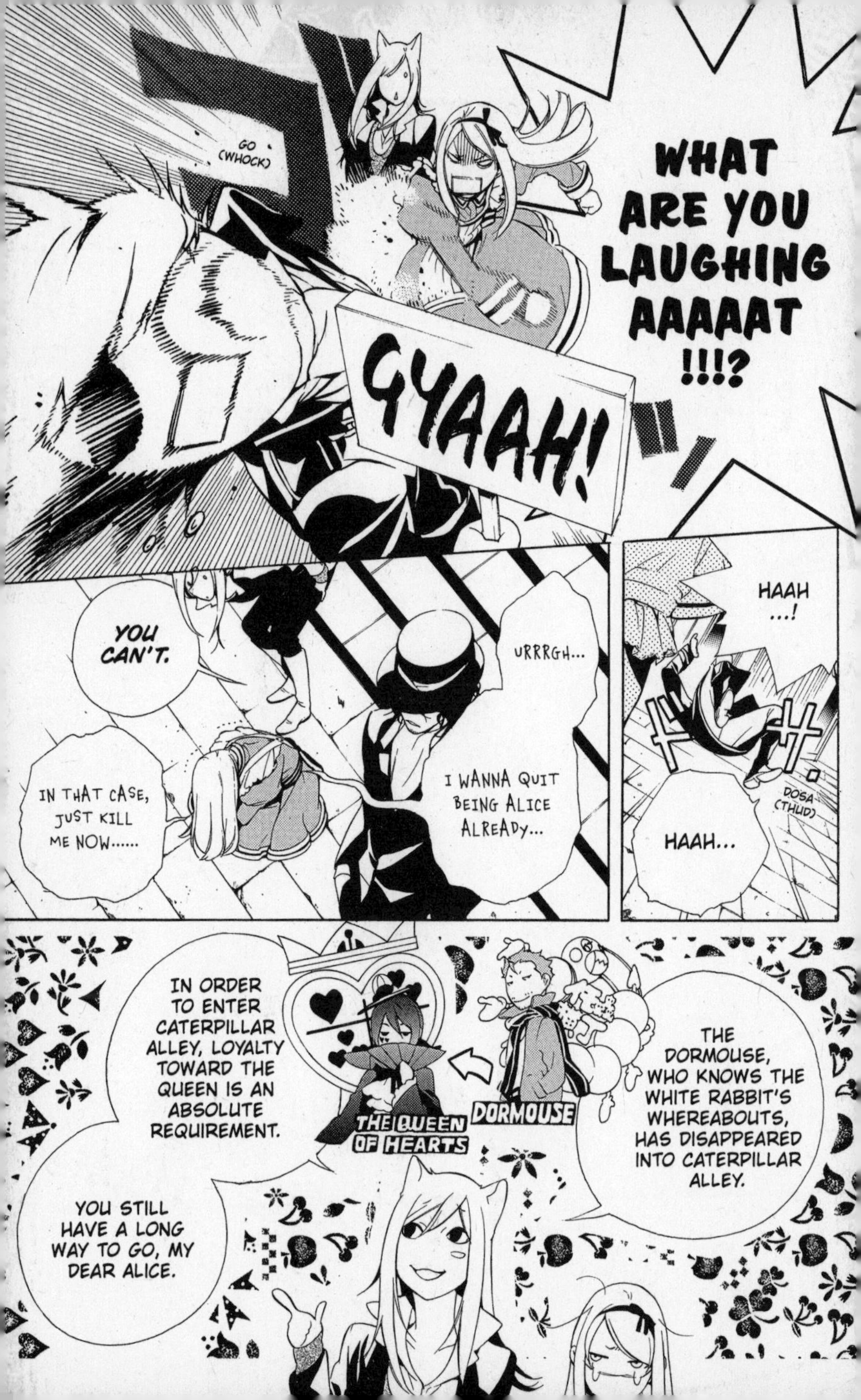
WHAT ARE YOU LAUGHING AAAAAT !!!?
GO (WHOCK)
GYAAH!
HAAH ...!
DOSA (THUD)
HAAH...
URRRGH...
I WANNA QUIT BEING ALICE ALREADY...
YOU CAN'T.
IN THAT CASE, JUST KILL ME NOW......
THE DORMOUSE, WHO KNOWS THE WHITE RABBIT'S WHEREABOUTS, HAS DISAPPEARED INTO CATERPILLAR ALLEY.
DORMOUSE
THE QUEEN OF HEARTS
IN ORDER TO ENTER CATERPILLAR ALLEY, LOYALTY TOWARD THE QUEEN IS AN ABSOLUTE REQUIREMENT.
YOU STILL HAVE A LONG WAY TO GO, MY DEAR ALICE.

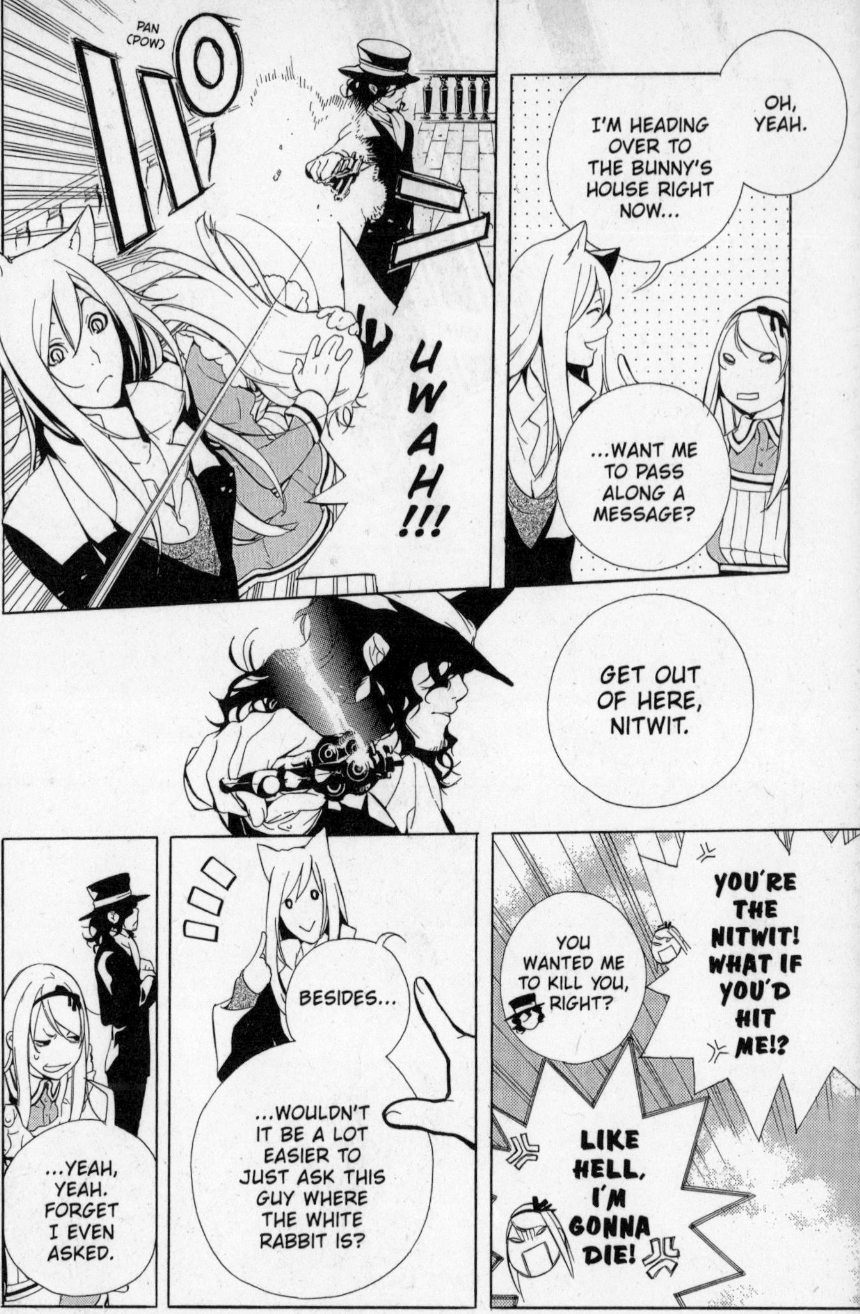
OH, YEAH.
I'M HEADING OVER TO THE BUNNY'S HOUSE RIGHT NOW...
...WANT ME TO PASS ALONG A MESSAGE?
PAN (POW)
UWAH!!!
GET OUT OF HERE, NITWIT.
YOU'RE THE NITWIT! WHAT IF YOU'D HIT ME!?
YOU WANTED ME TO KILL YOU, RIGHT?
LIKE HELL, I'M GONNA DIE!
BESIDES...
...WOULDN'T IT BE A LOT EASIER TO JUST ASK THIS GUY WHERE THE WHITE RABBIT IS?
...YEAH, YEAH. FORGET I EVEN ASKED.

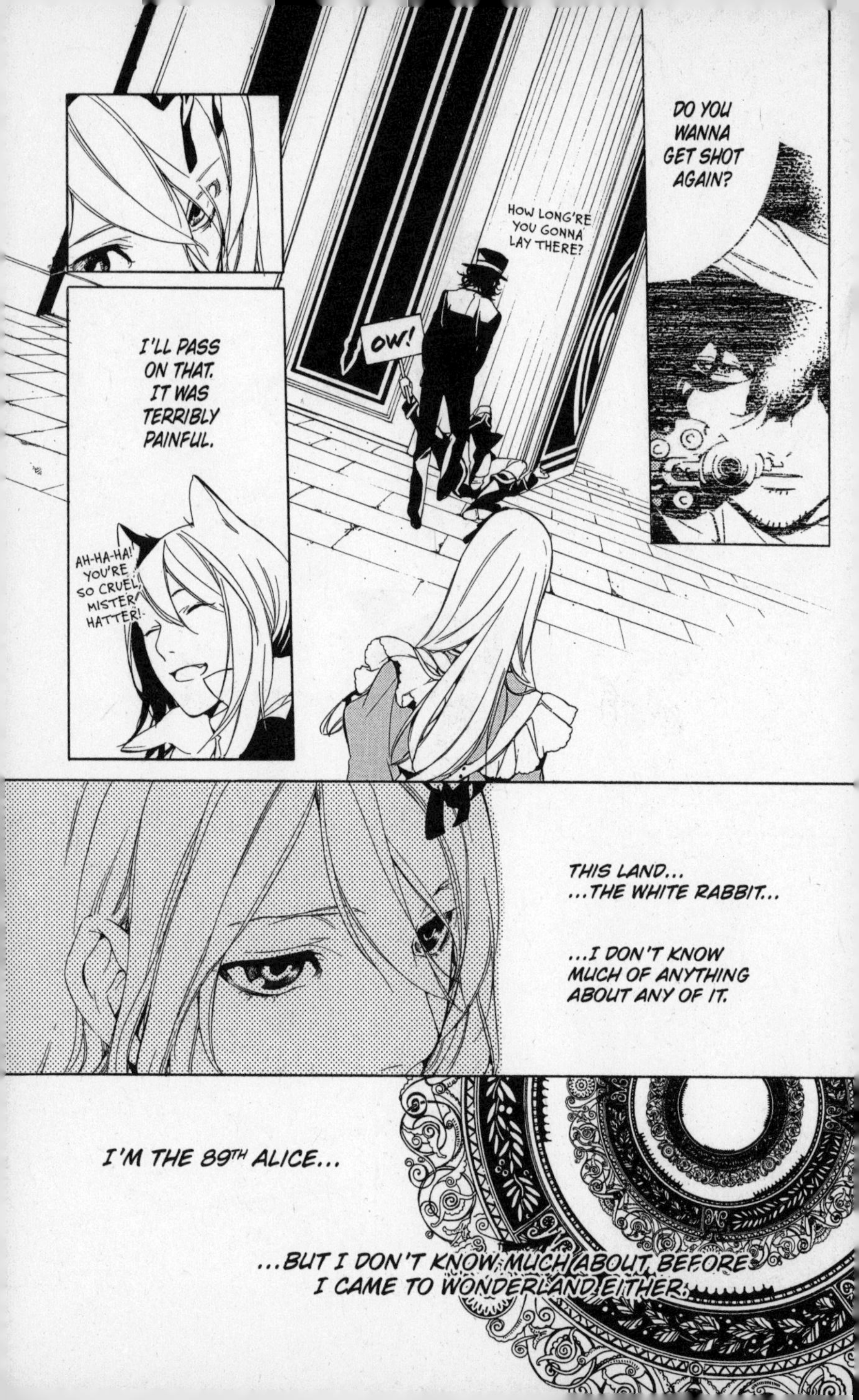
DO YOU WANNA GET SHOT AGAIN?
HOW LONG'RE YOU GONNA LAY THERE?
OW!
I'LL PASS ON THAT. IT WAS TERRIBLY PAINFUL.
AH-HA-HA! YOU'RE SO CRUEL, MISTER HATTER!
THIS LAND... ...THE WHITE RABBIT...
...I DON'T KNOW MUCH OF ANYTHING ABOUT ANY OF IT.
I'M THE 89TH ALICE...
...BUT I DON'T KNOW MUCH ABOUT BEFORE I CAME TO WONDERLAND EITHER.

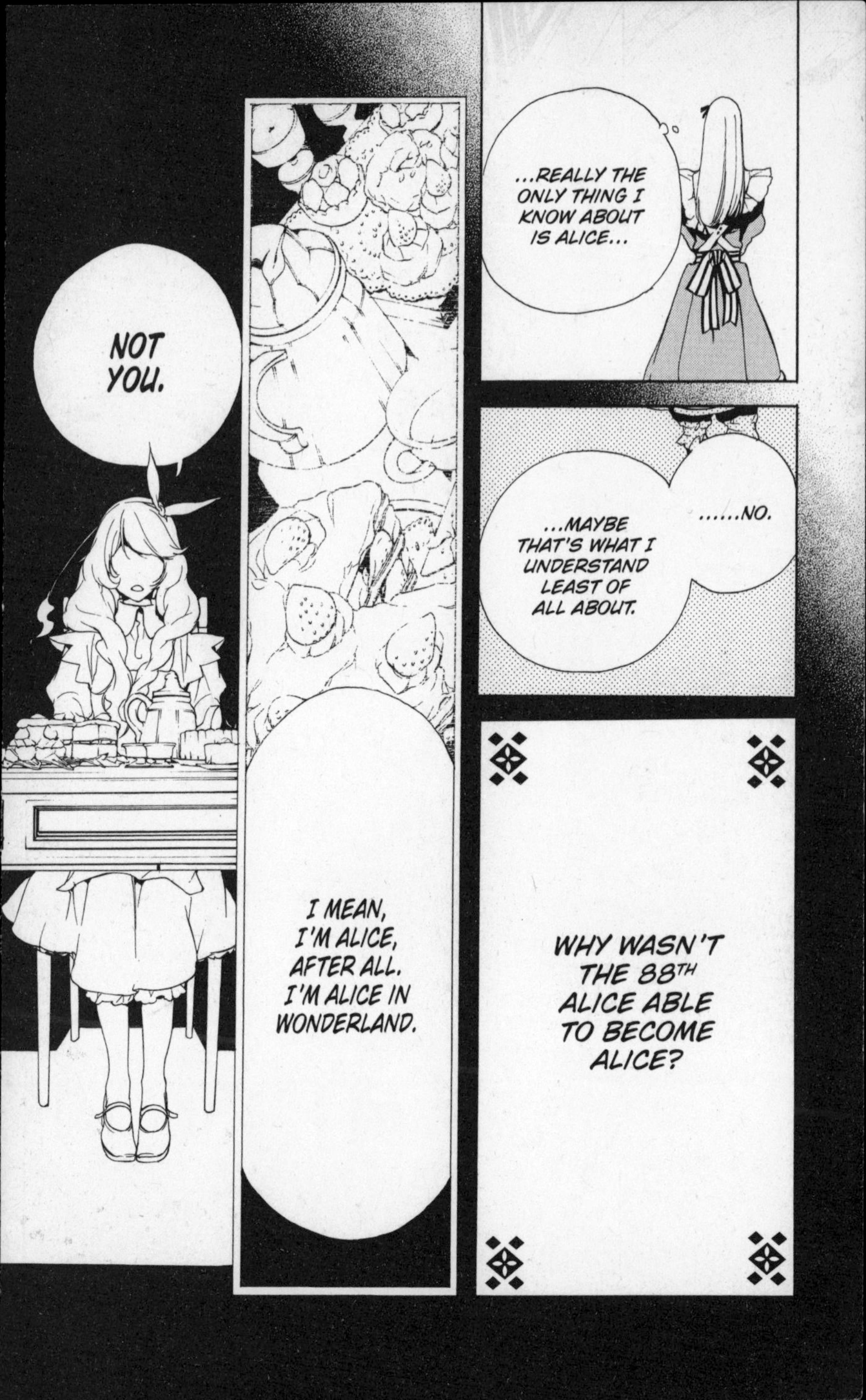
...REALLY THE ONLY THING I KNOW ABOUT IS ALICE...
......NO.
...MAYBE THAT'S WHAT I UNDERSTAND LEAST OF ALL ABOUT.
WHY WASN'T THE 88TH ALICE ABLE TO BECOME ALICE?
I MEAN, I'M ALICE, AFTER ALL. I'M ALICE IN WONDERLAND.
NOT YOU.

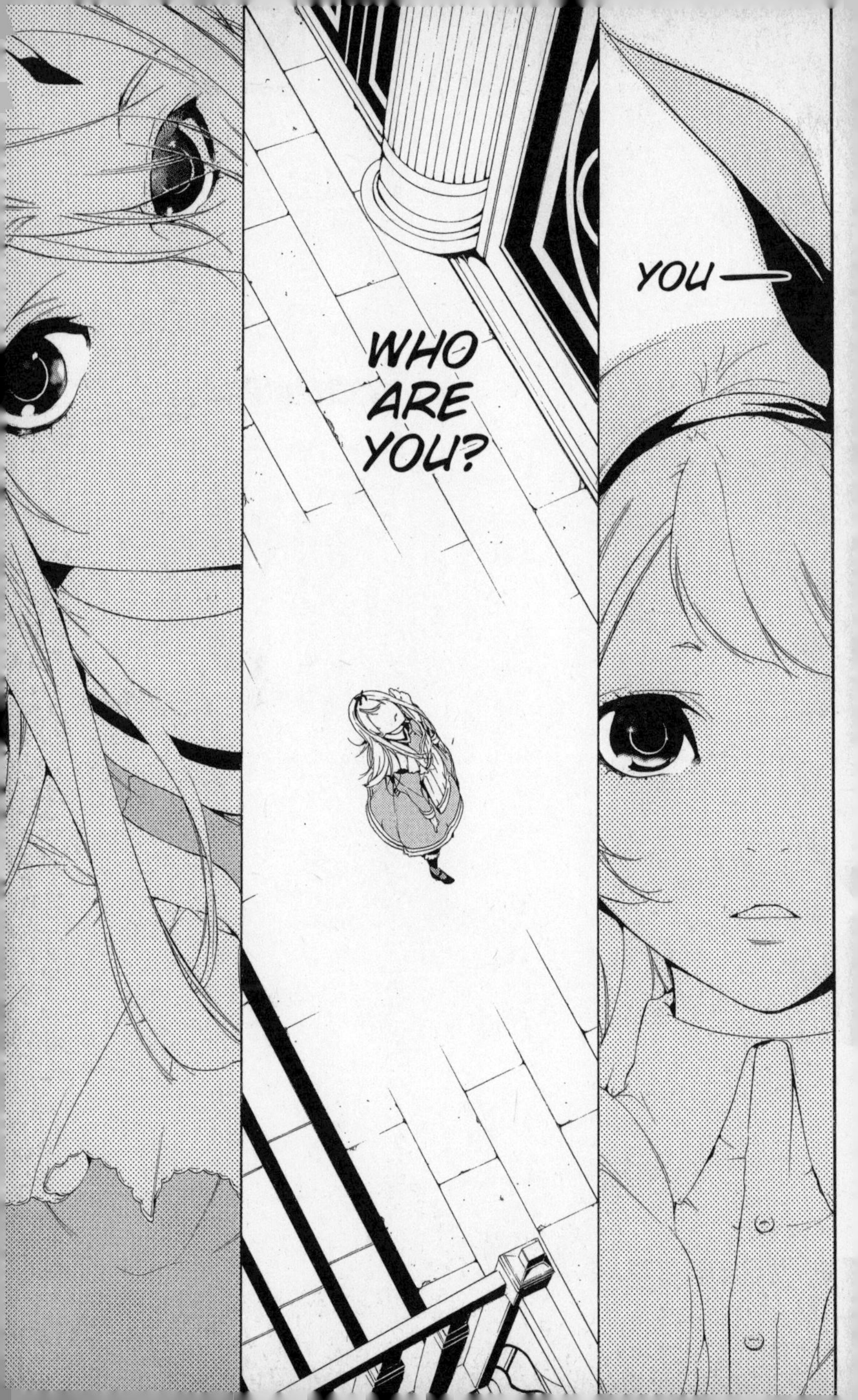
YOU—
WHO ARE YOU?

I'M

...

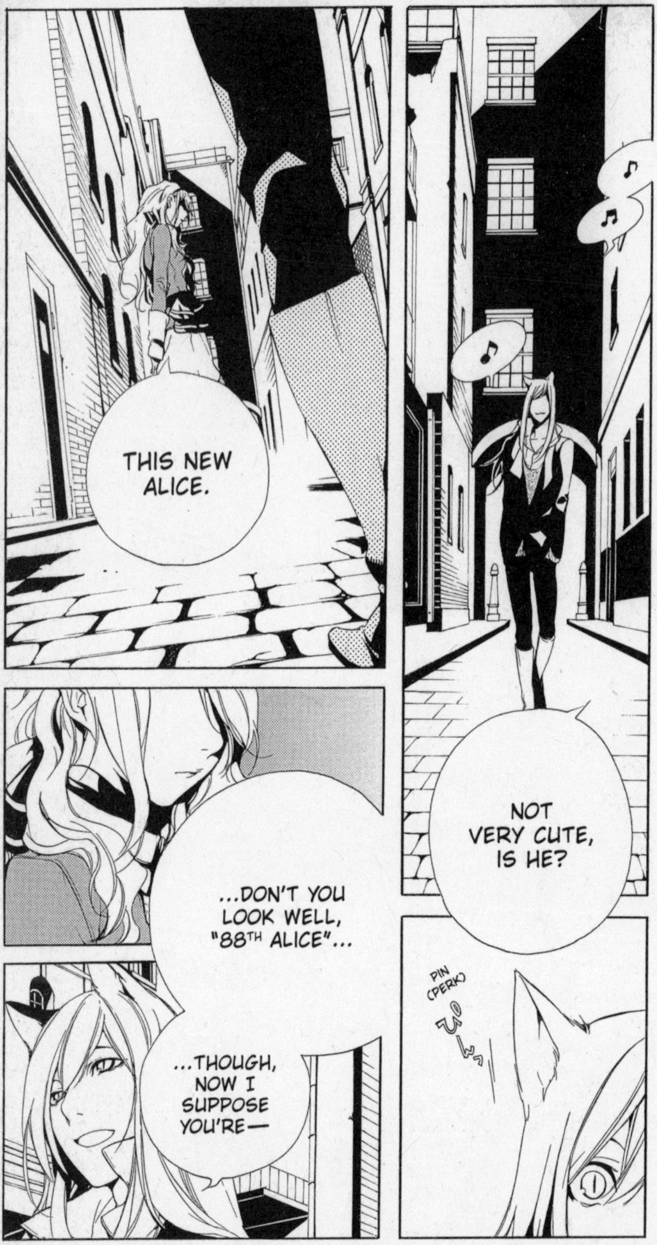
NOT VERY CUTE, IS HE?
PIN (PERK)
THIS NEW ALICE.
...DON'T YOU LOOK WELL, "88TH ALICE"...
...THOUGH, NOW I SUPPOSE YOU'RE—

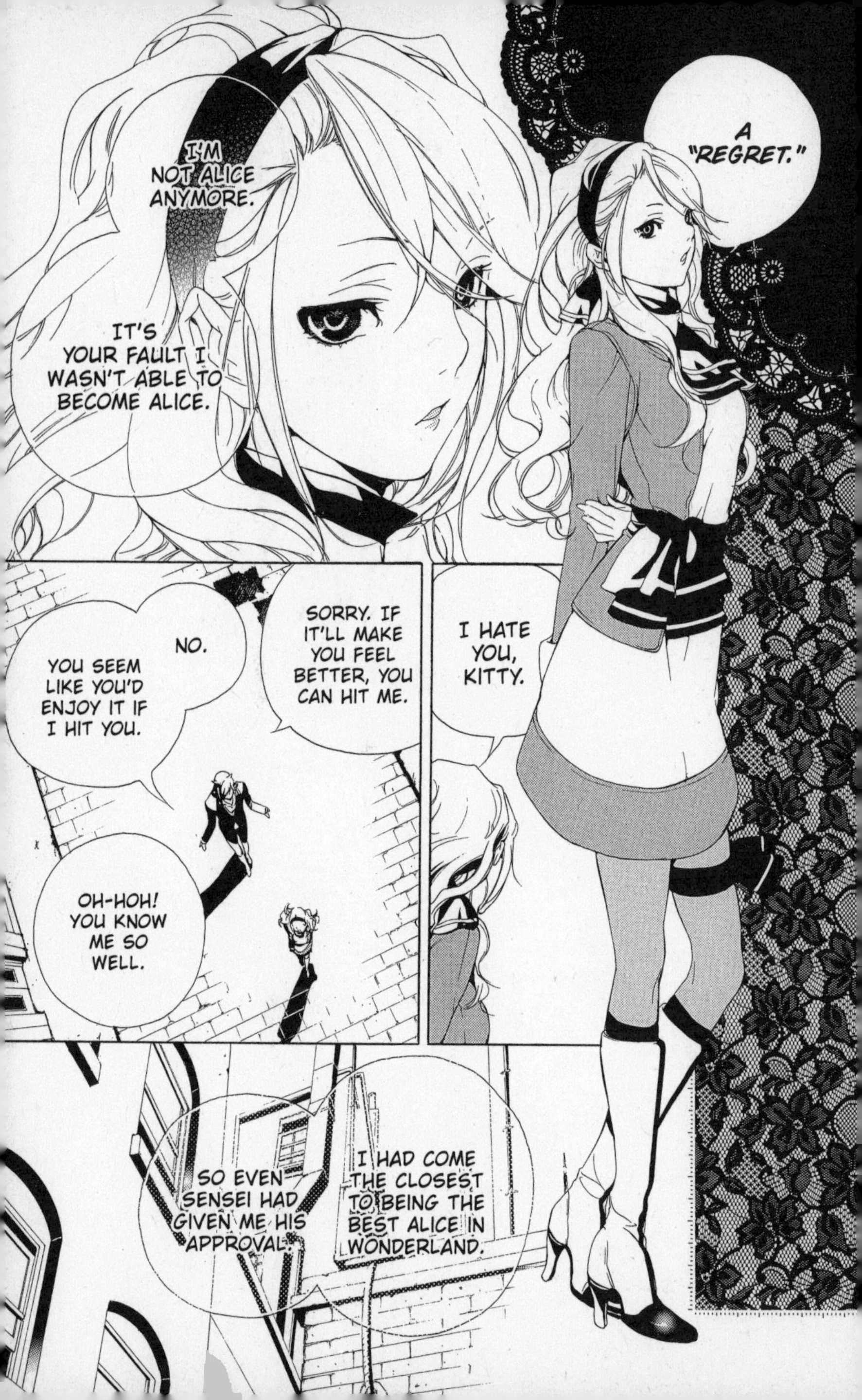
A "REGRET."
I'M NOT ALICE ANYMORE.
IT'S YOUR FAULT I WASN'T ABLE TO BECOME ALICE.
I HATE YOU, KITTY.
SORRY. IF IT'LL MAKE YOU FEEL BETTER, YOU CAN HIT ME.
NO.
YOU SEEM LIKE YOU'D ENJOY IT IF I HIT YOU.
OH-HOH! YOU KNOW ME SO WELL.
I HAD COME THE CLOSEST TO BEING THE BEST ALICE IN WONDERLAND.
SO EVEN SENSEI HAD GIVEN ME HIS APPROVAL.

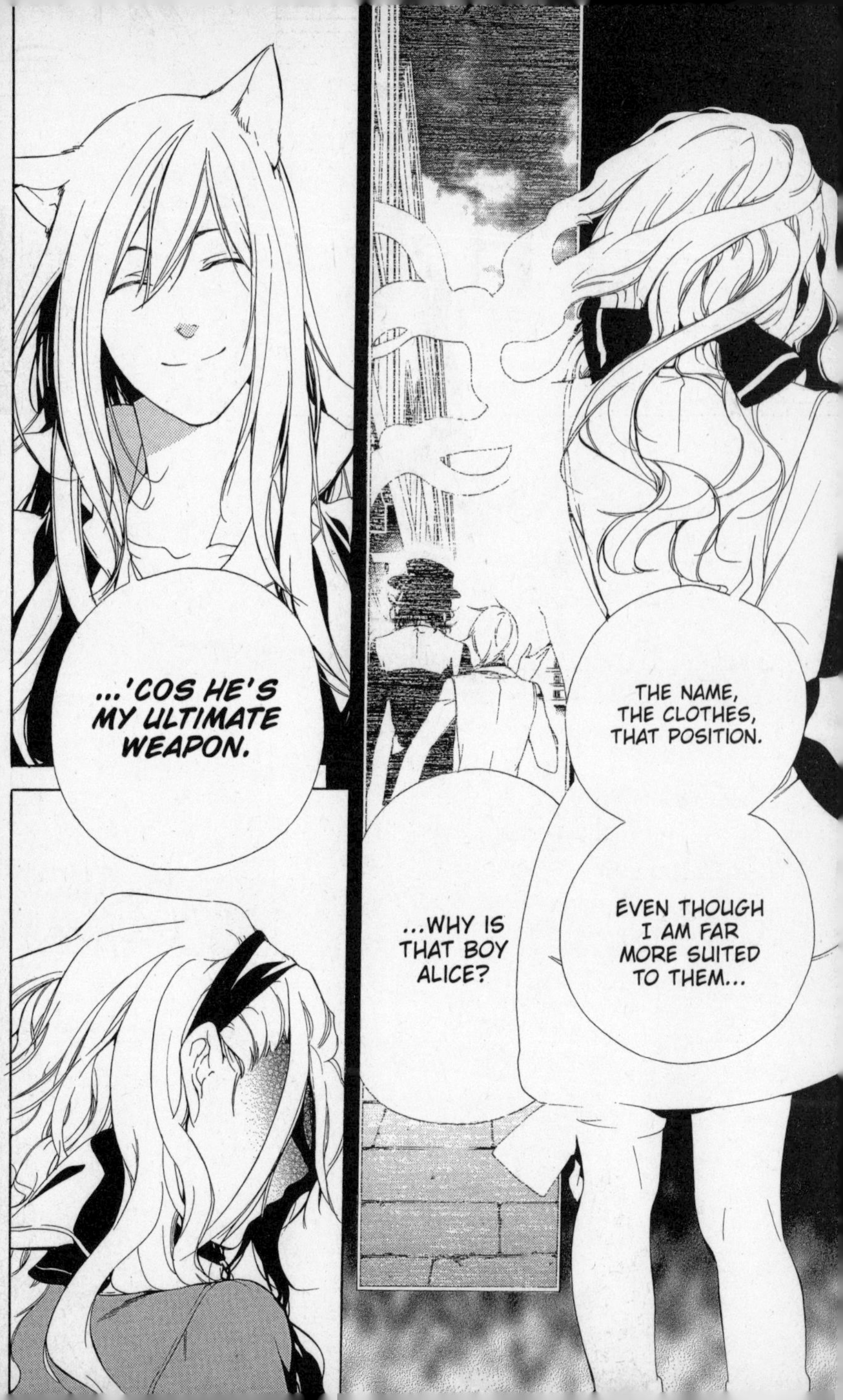
THE NAME, THE CLOTHES, THAT POSITION.
EVEN THOUGH I AM FAR MORE SUITED TO THEM...
...WHY IS THAT BOY ALICE?
...'COS HE'S MY ULTIMATE WEAPON.

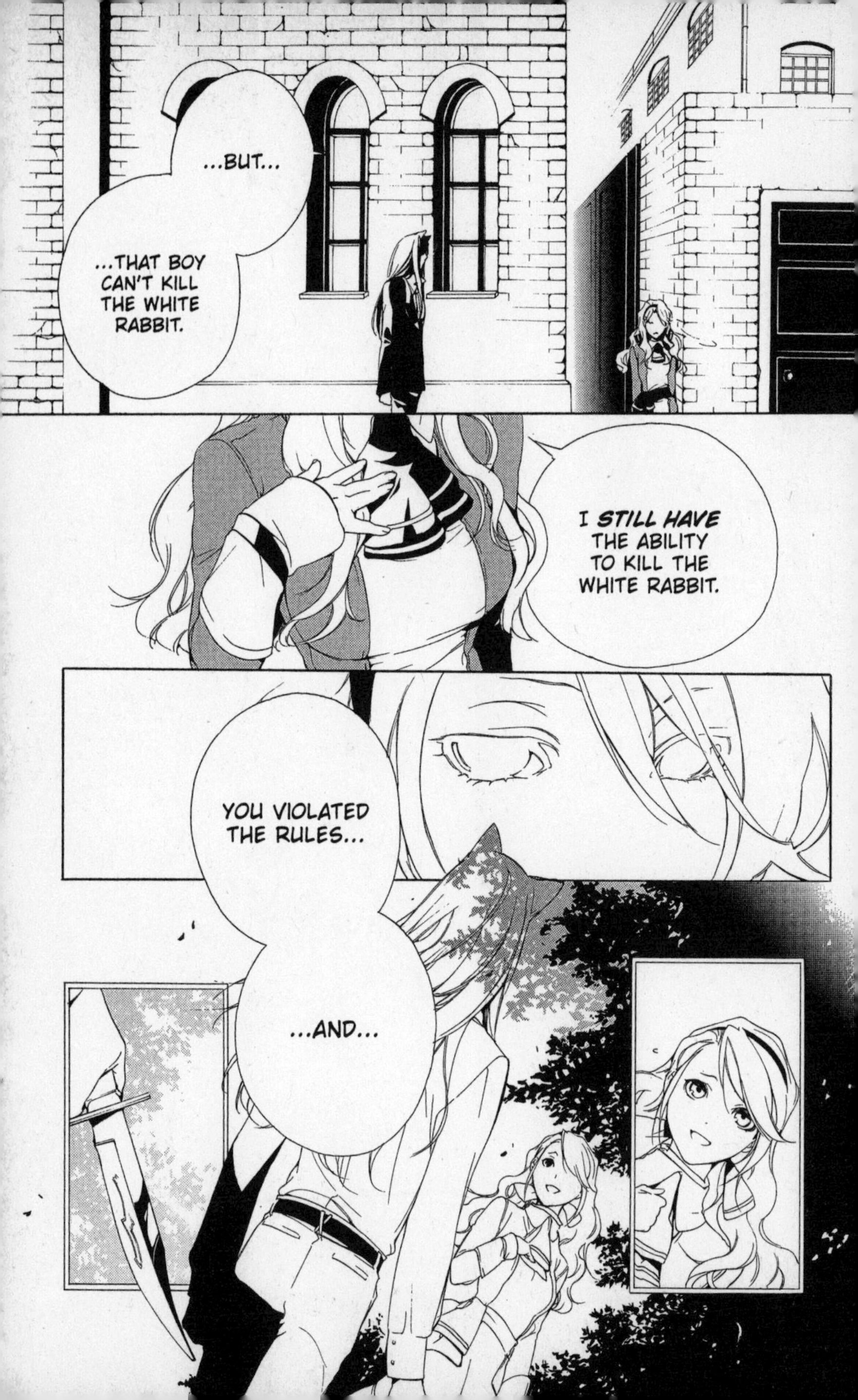
...BUT...
...THAT BOY CAN'T KILL THE WHITE RABBIT.
I *STILL HAVE* THE ABILITY TO KILL THE WHITE RABBIT.
YOU VIOLATED THE RULES...
...AND...

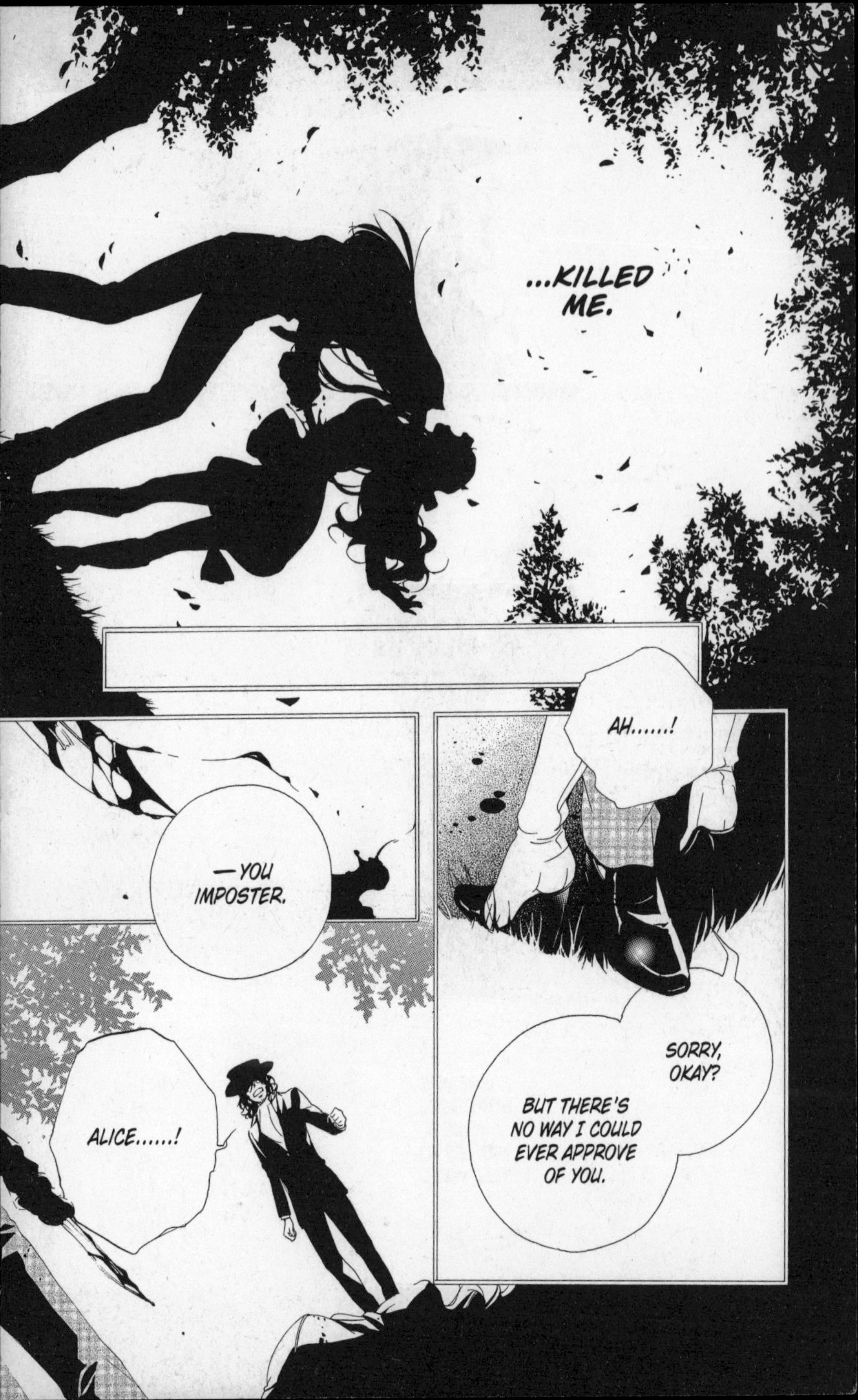
...KILLED ME.
AH......!
SORRY, OKAY?
BUT THERE'S NO WAY I COULD EVER APPROVE OF YOU.
—YOU IMPOSTER.
ALICE......!

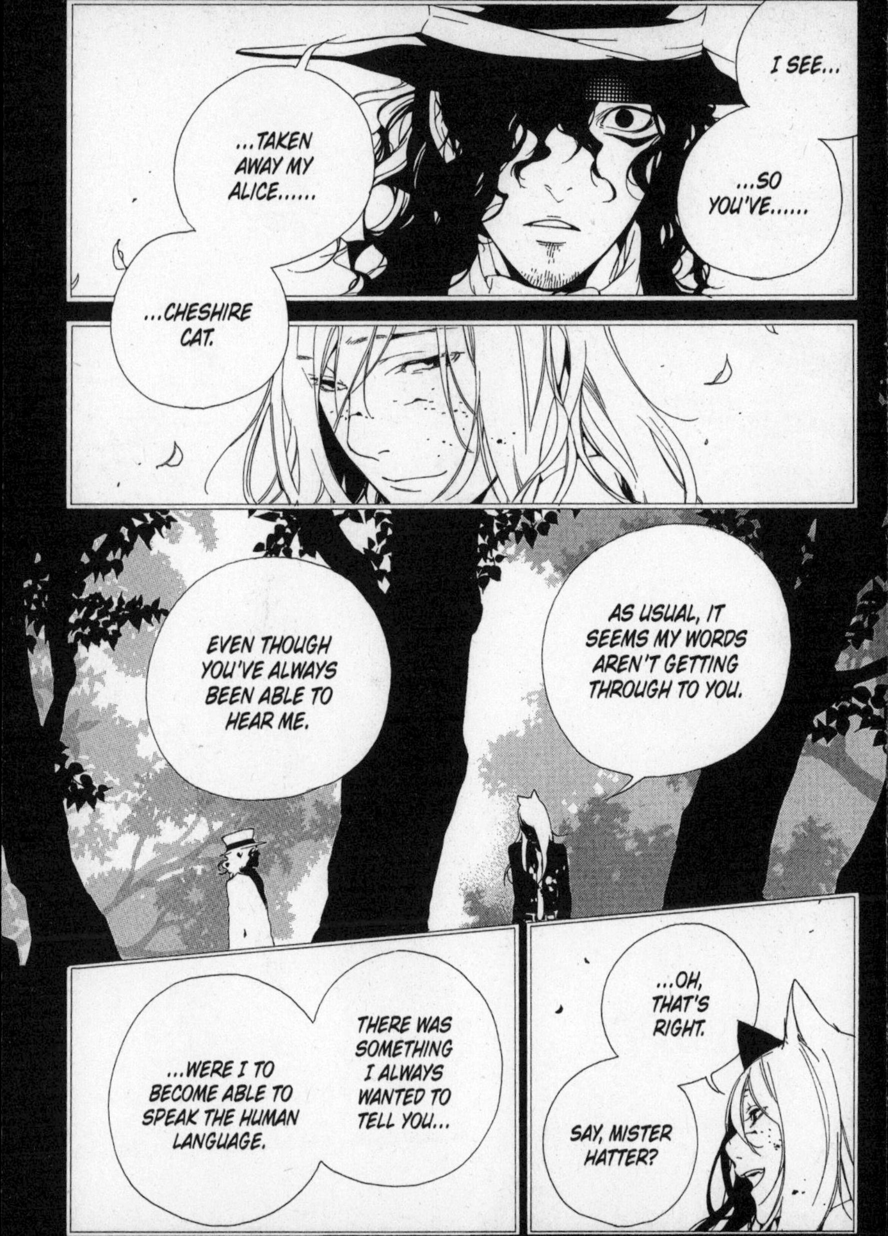
I SEE...
...SO YOU'VE......
...TAKEN AWAY MY ALICE......
...CHESHIRE CAT.
AS USUAL, IT SEEMS MY WORDS AREN'T GETTING THROUGH TO YOU.
EVEN THOUGH YOU'VE ALWAYS BEEN ABLE TO HEAR ME.
...OH, THAT'S RIGHT.
SAY, MISTER HATTER?
THERE WAS SOMETHING I ALWAYS WANTED TO TELL YOU...
...WERE I TO BECOME ABLE TO SPEAK THE HUMAN LANGUAGE.

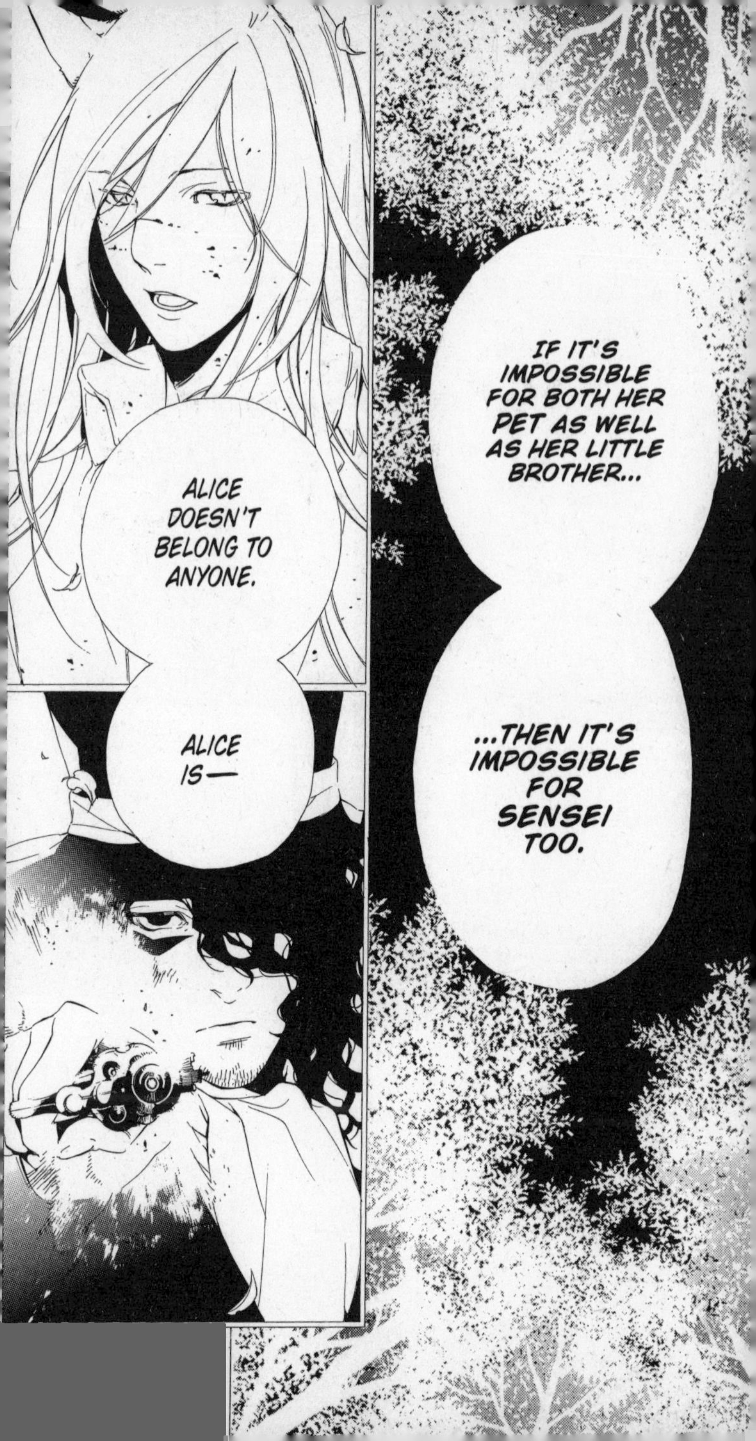
IF IT'S IMPOSSIBLE FOR BOTH HER PET AS WELL AS HER LITTLE BROTHER...
...THEN IT'S IMPOSSIBLE FOR SENSEI TOO.
ALICE DOESN'T BELONG TO ANYONE.
ALICE IS—

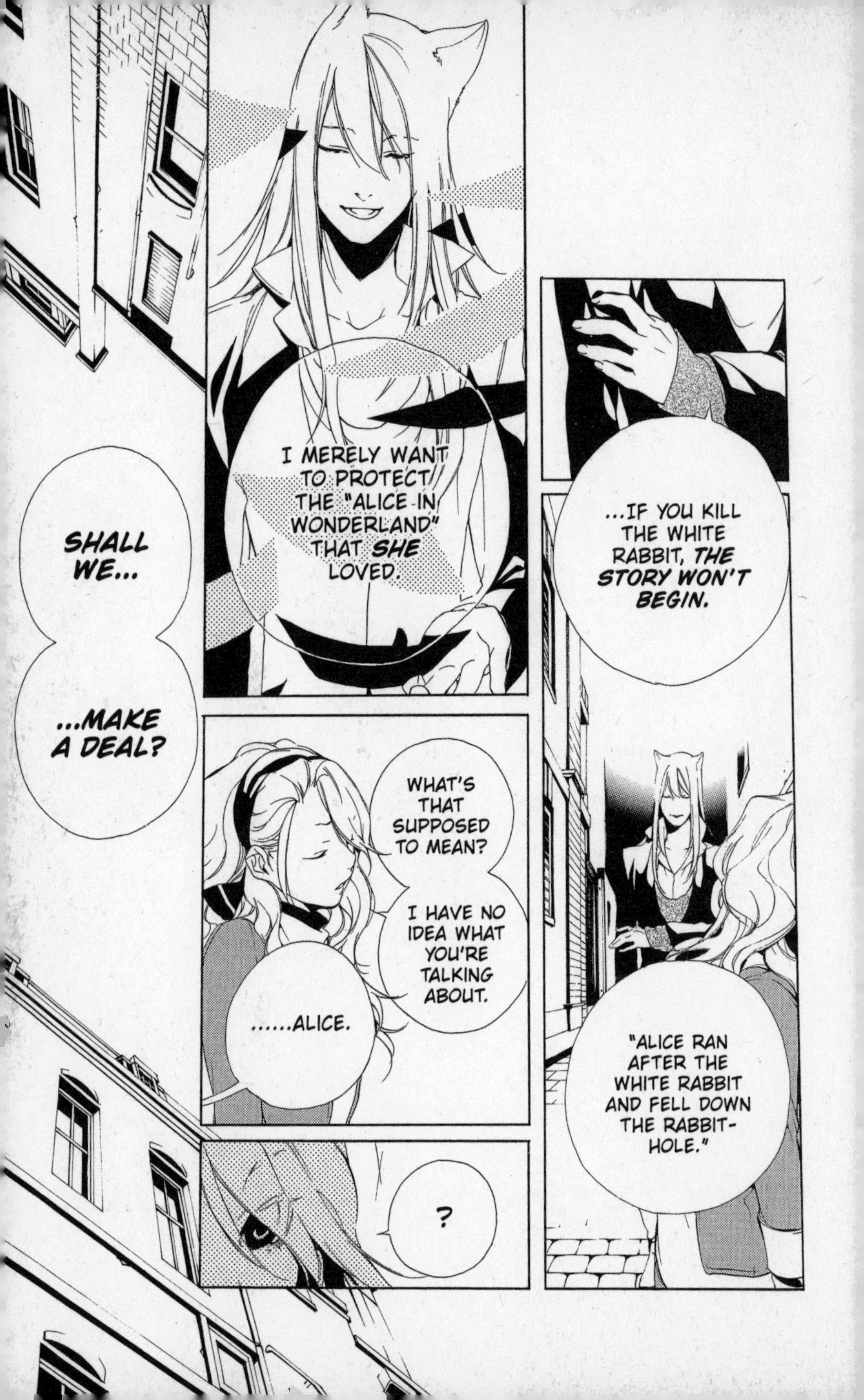
...IF YOU KILL THE WHITE RABBIT, ***THE STORY WON'T BEGIN.***
"ALICE RAN AFTER THE WHITE RABBIT AND FELL DOWN THE RABBIT-HOLE."
I MERELY WANT TO PROTECT THE "ALICE IN WONDERLAND" THAT ***SHE*** LOVED.
WHAT'S THAT SUPPOSED TO MEAN?
I HAVE NO IDEA WHAT YOU'RE TALKING ABOUT.
......ALICE.
?
SHALL WE...
...MAKE A DEAL?

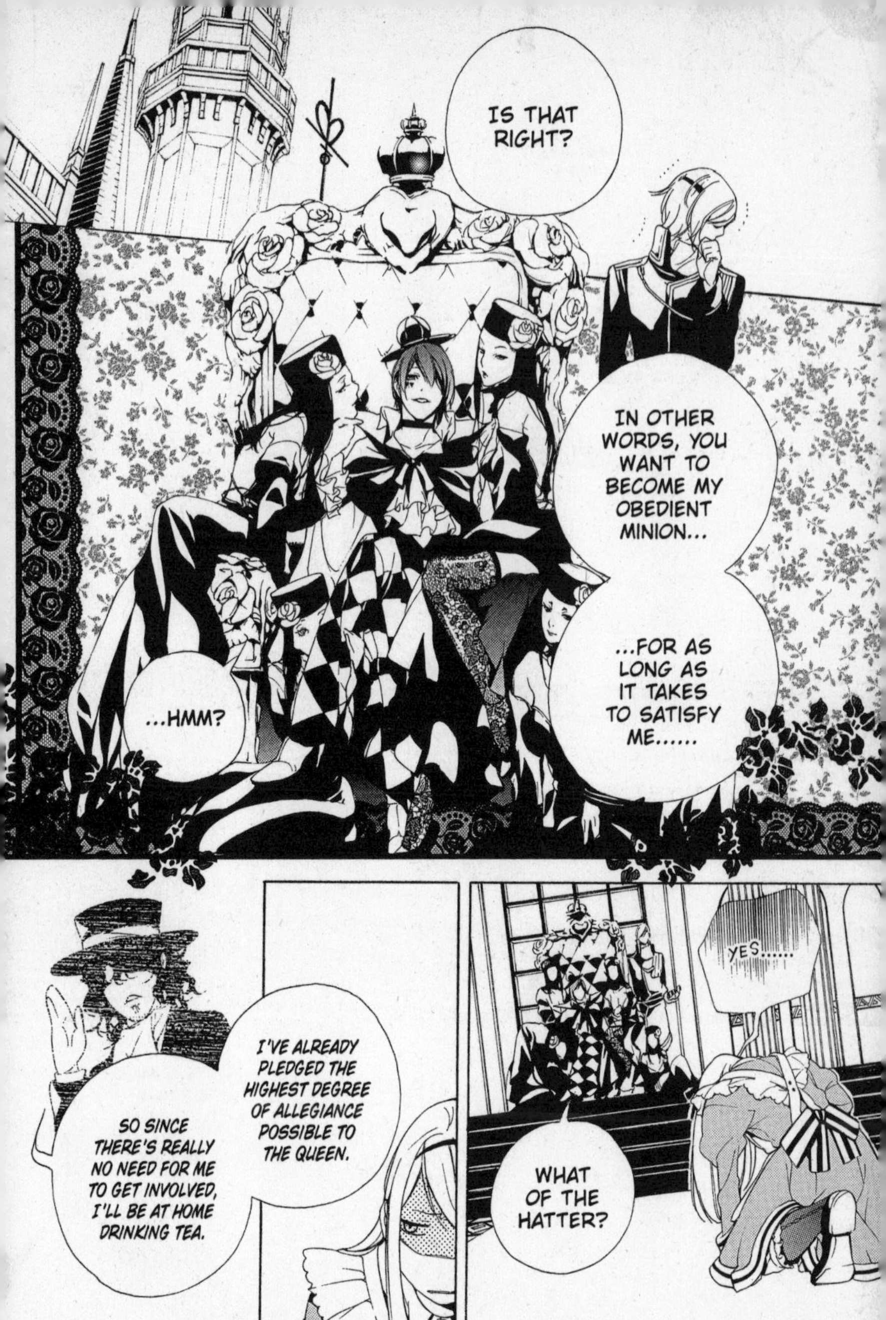
IS THAT RIGHT?
IN OTHER WORDS, YOU WANT TO BECOME MY OBEDIENT MINION...
...FOR AS LONG AS IT TAKES TO SATISFY ME......
...HMM?
YES......
WHAT OF THE HATTER?
I'VE ALREADY PLEDGED THE HIGHEST DEGREE OF ALLEGIANCE POSSIBLE TO THE QUEEN.
SO SINCE THERE'S REALLY NO NEED FOR ME TO GET INVOLVED, I'LL BE AT HOME DRINKING TEA.

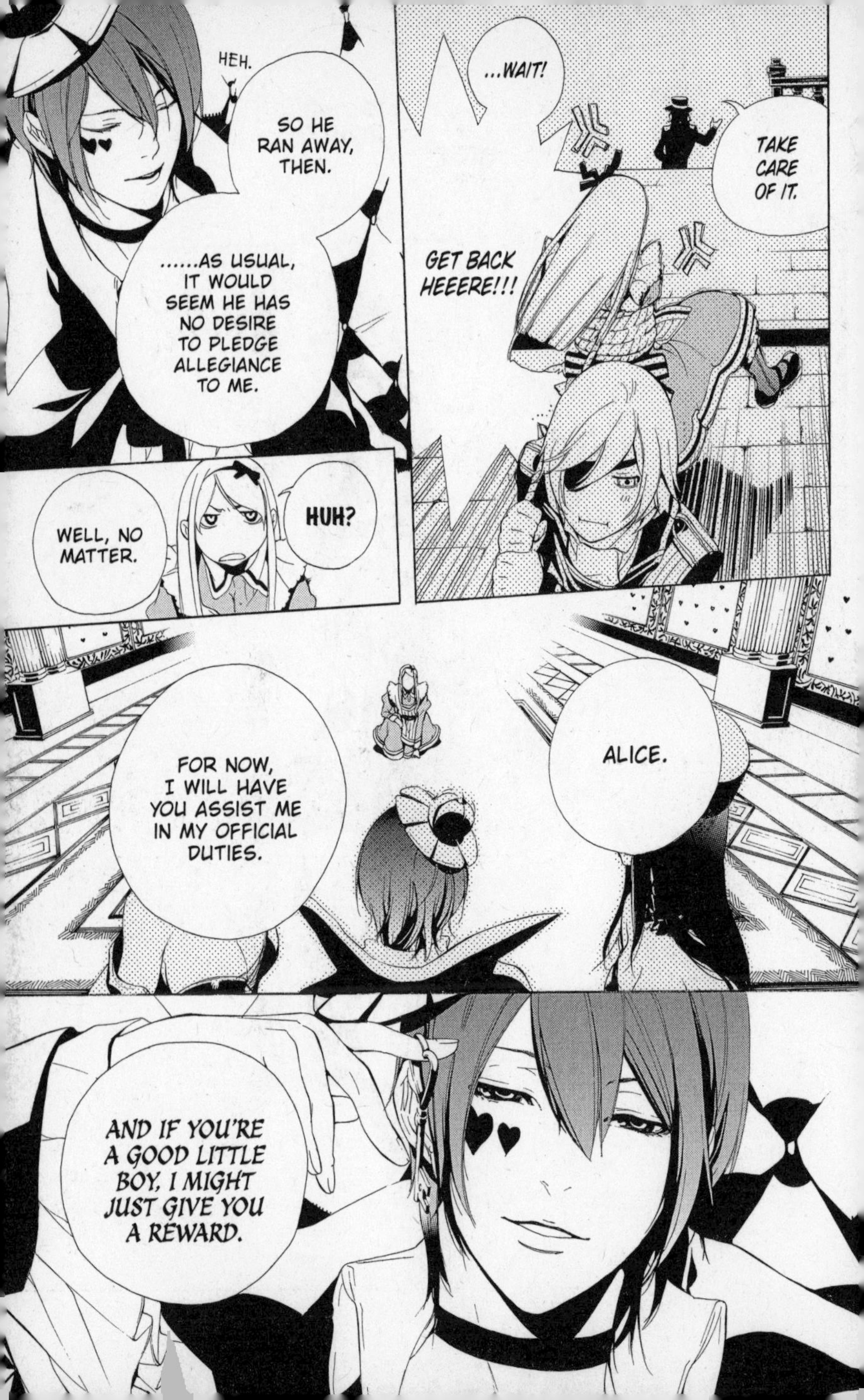
TAKE CARE OF IT.
...WAIT!
GET BACK HEEERE!!!
HEH.
SO HE RAN AWAY, THEN.
......AS USUAL, IT WOULD SEEM HE HAS NO DESIRE TO PLEDGE ALLEGIANCE TO ME.
HUH?
WELL, NO MATTER.
ALICE.
FOR NOW, I WILL HAVE YOU ASSIST ME IN MY OFFICIAL DUTIES.
AND IF YOU'RE A GOOD LITTLE BOY, I MIGHT JUST GIVE YOU A REWARD.

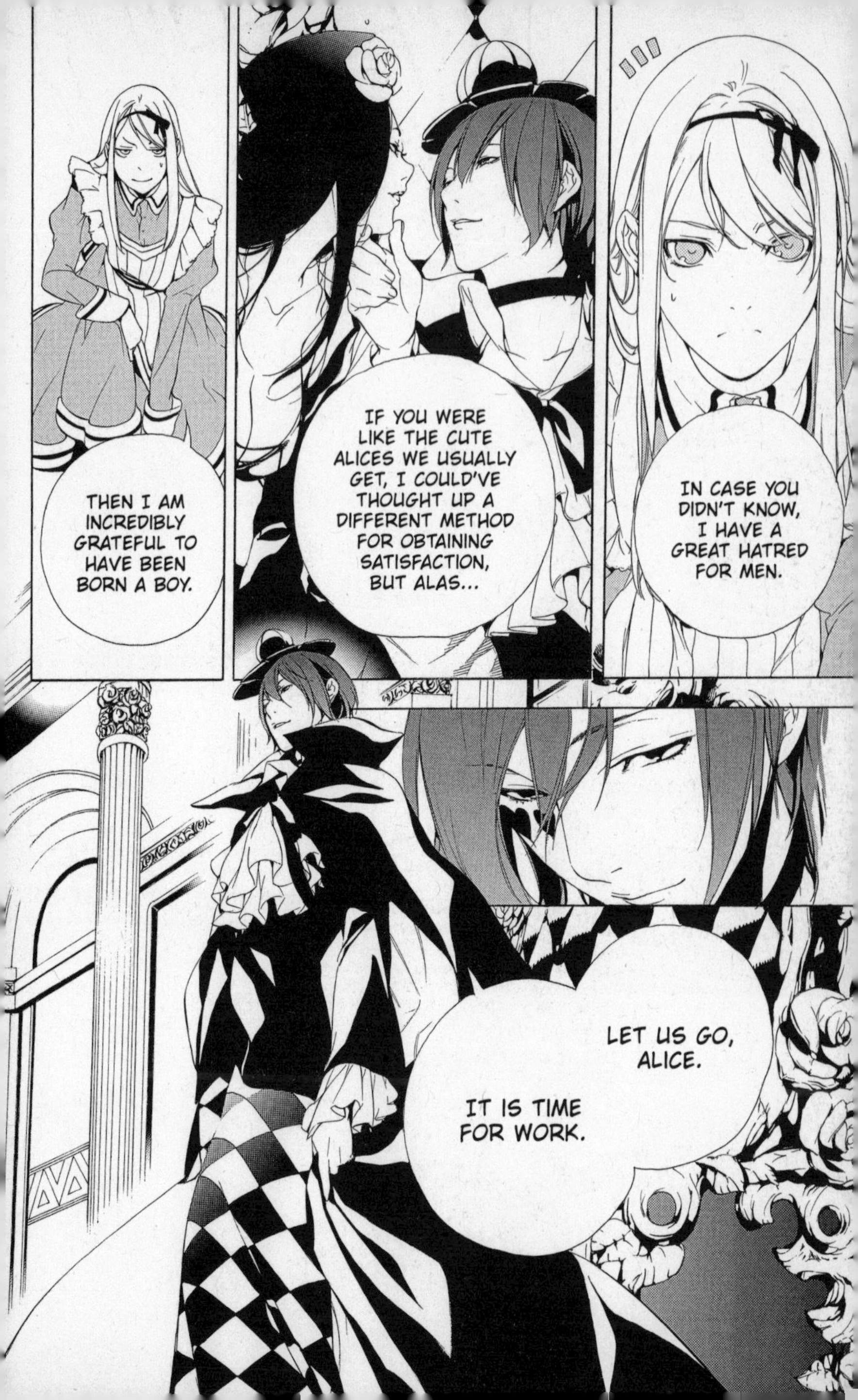
IN CASE YOU DIDN'T KNOW, I HAVE A GREAT HATRED FOR MEN.
IF YOU WERE LIKE THE CUTE ALICES WE USUALLY GET, I COULD'VE THOUGHT UP A DIFFERENT METHOD FOR OBTAINING SATISFACTION, BUT ALAS...
THEN I AM INCREDIBLY GRATEFUL TO HAVE BEEN BORN A BOY.
LET US GO, ALICE.
IT IS TIME FOR WORK.

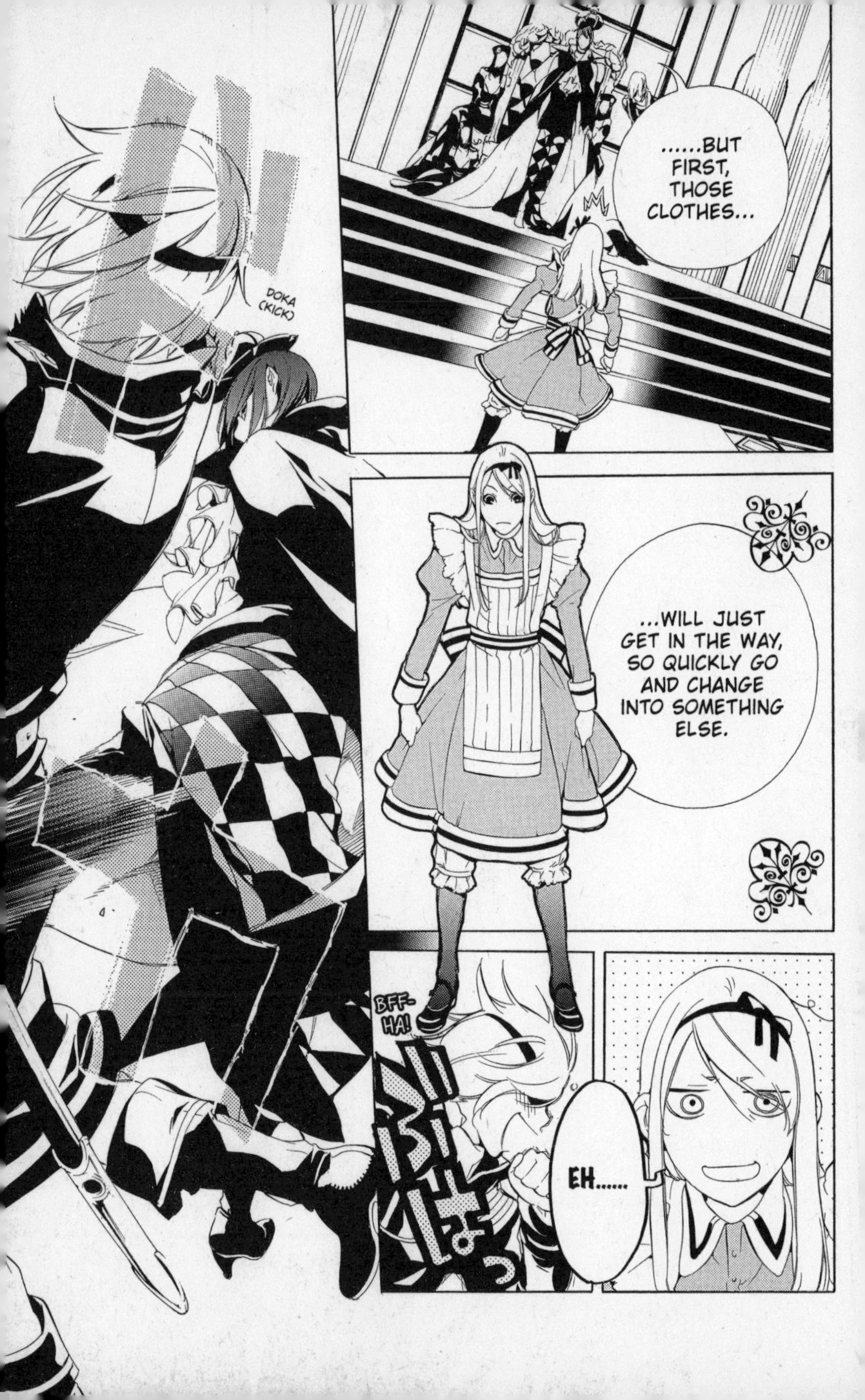

......BUT FIRST, THOSE CLOTHES...
...WILL JUST GET IN THE WAY, SO QUICKLY GO AND CHANGE INTO SOMETHING ELSE.
EH......
BFF-HA!
DOKA (KICK)

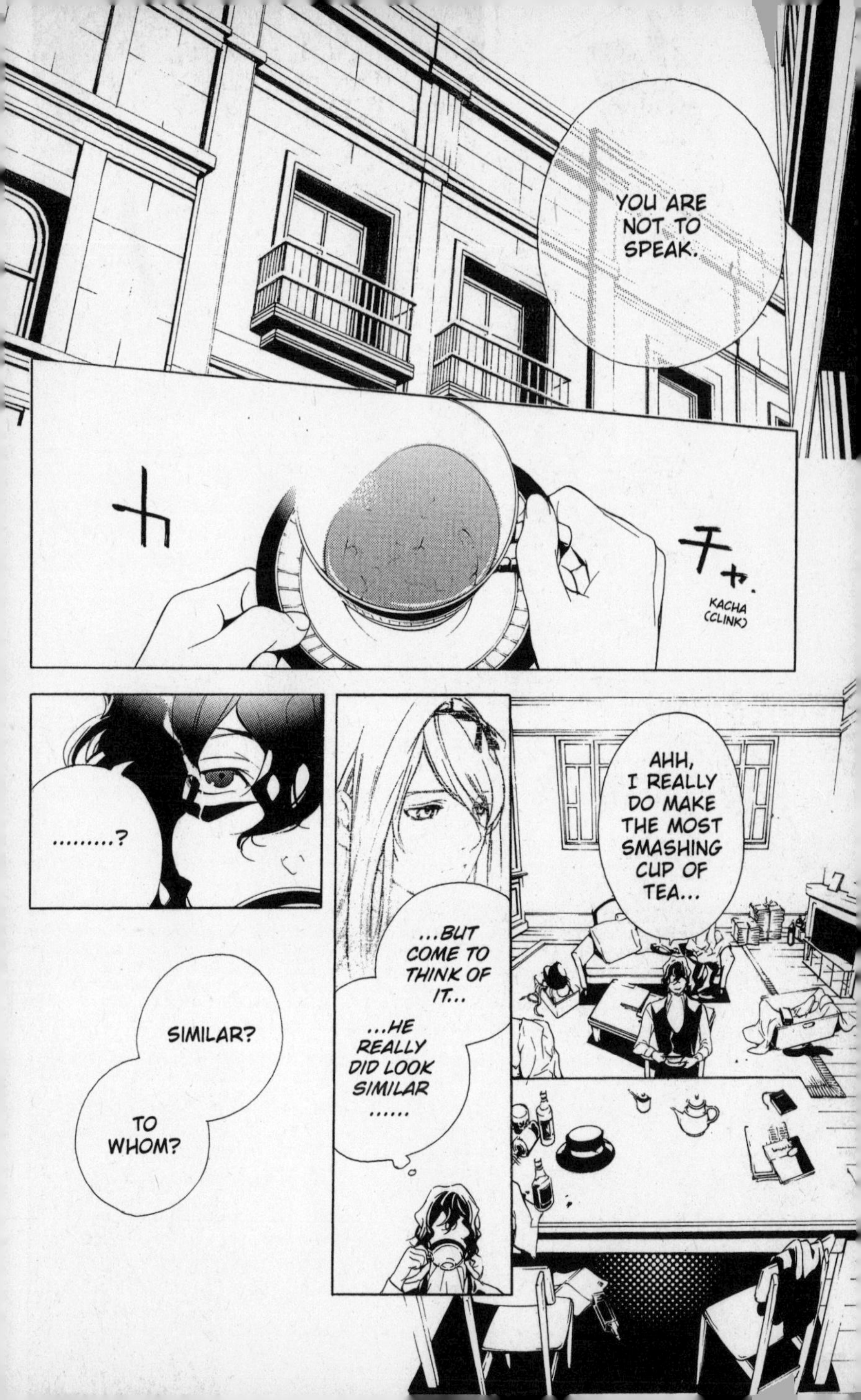
YOU ARE NOT TO SPEAK.
チャ.
KACHA (CLINK)
カ
AHH, I REALLY DO MAKE THE MOST SMASHING CUP OF TEA...
...BUT COME TO THINK OF IT...
...HE REALLY DID LOOK SIMILAR ......
........?
SIMILAR?
TO WHOM?

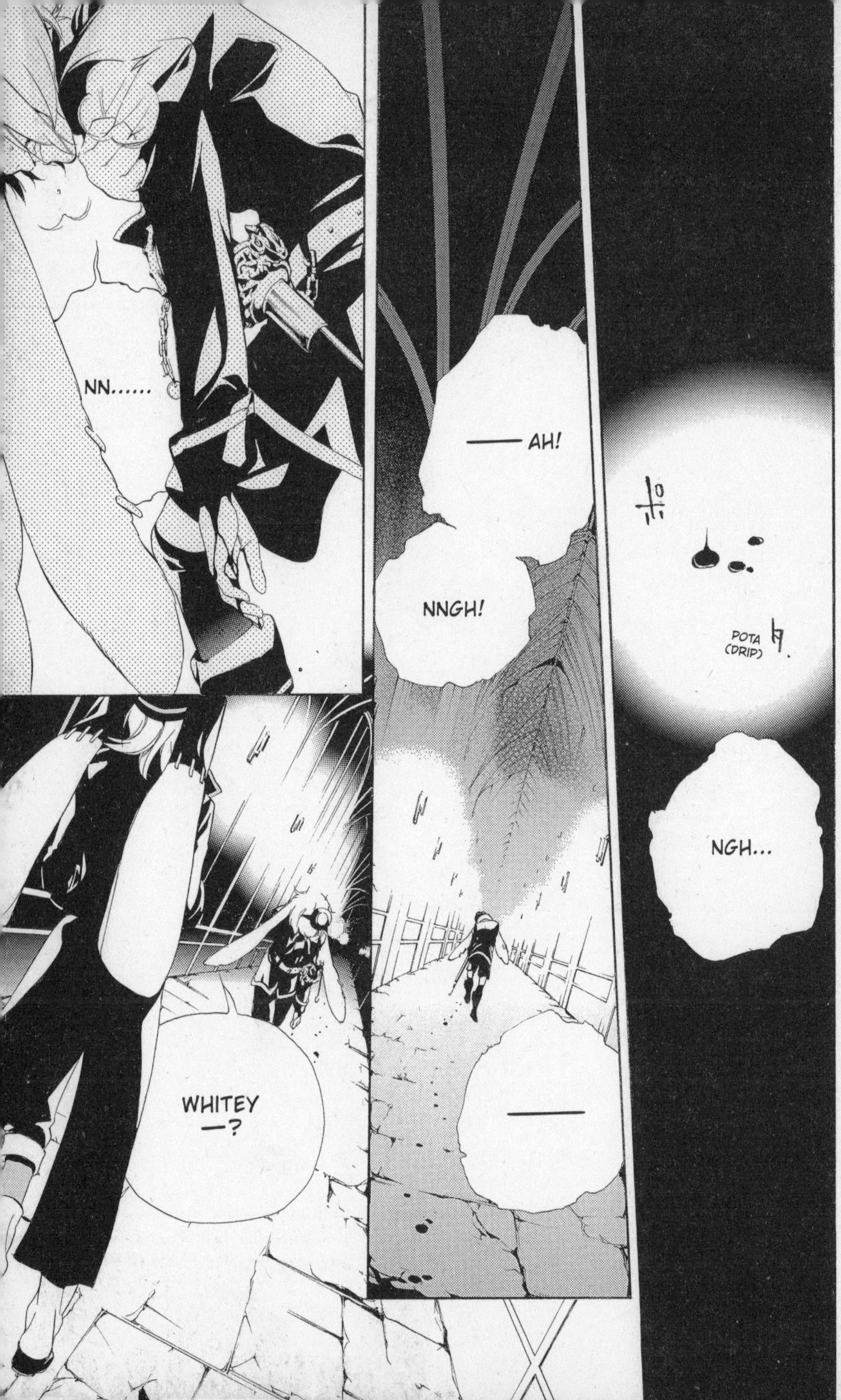
POTA (DRIP)
NGH...
—— AH!
NNGH!
——
NN......
WHITEY —?

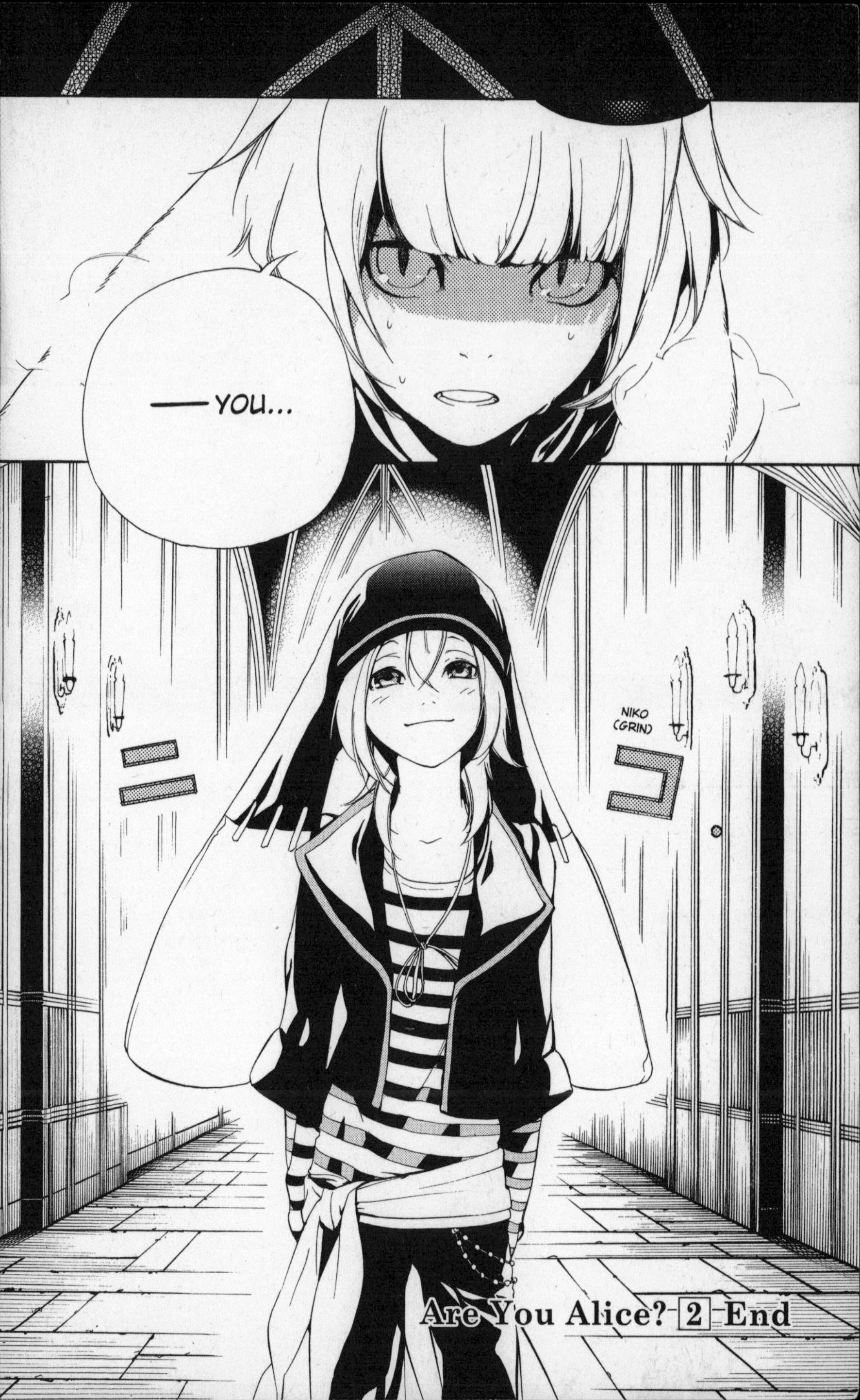
—YOU...
NIKO (GRIN)
Are You Alice? 2 End

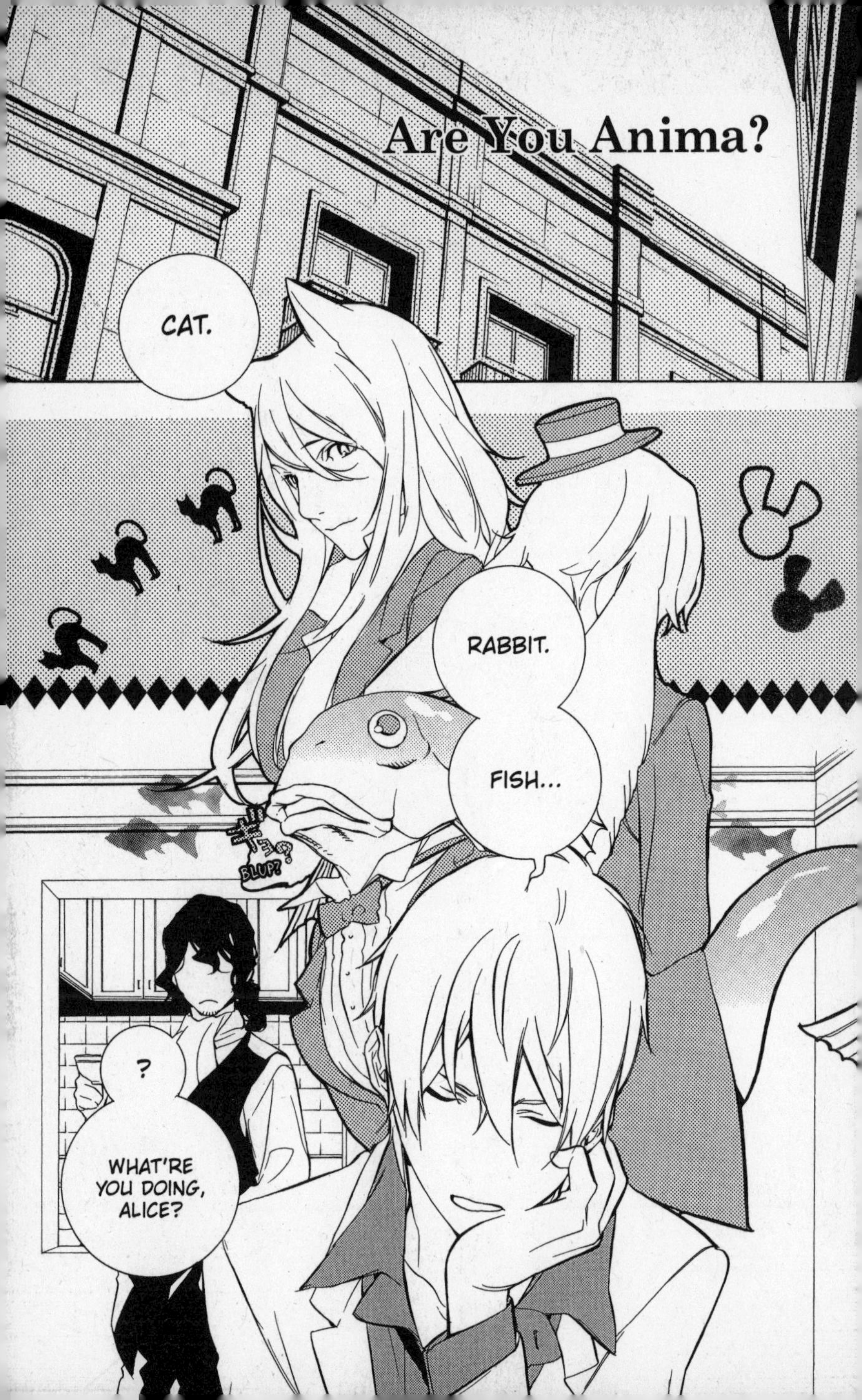
Are You Anima?
CAT.
RABBIT.
FISH...
BLUP?
?
WHAT'RE YOU DOING, ALICE?

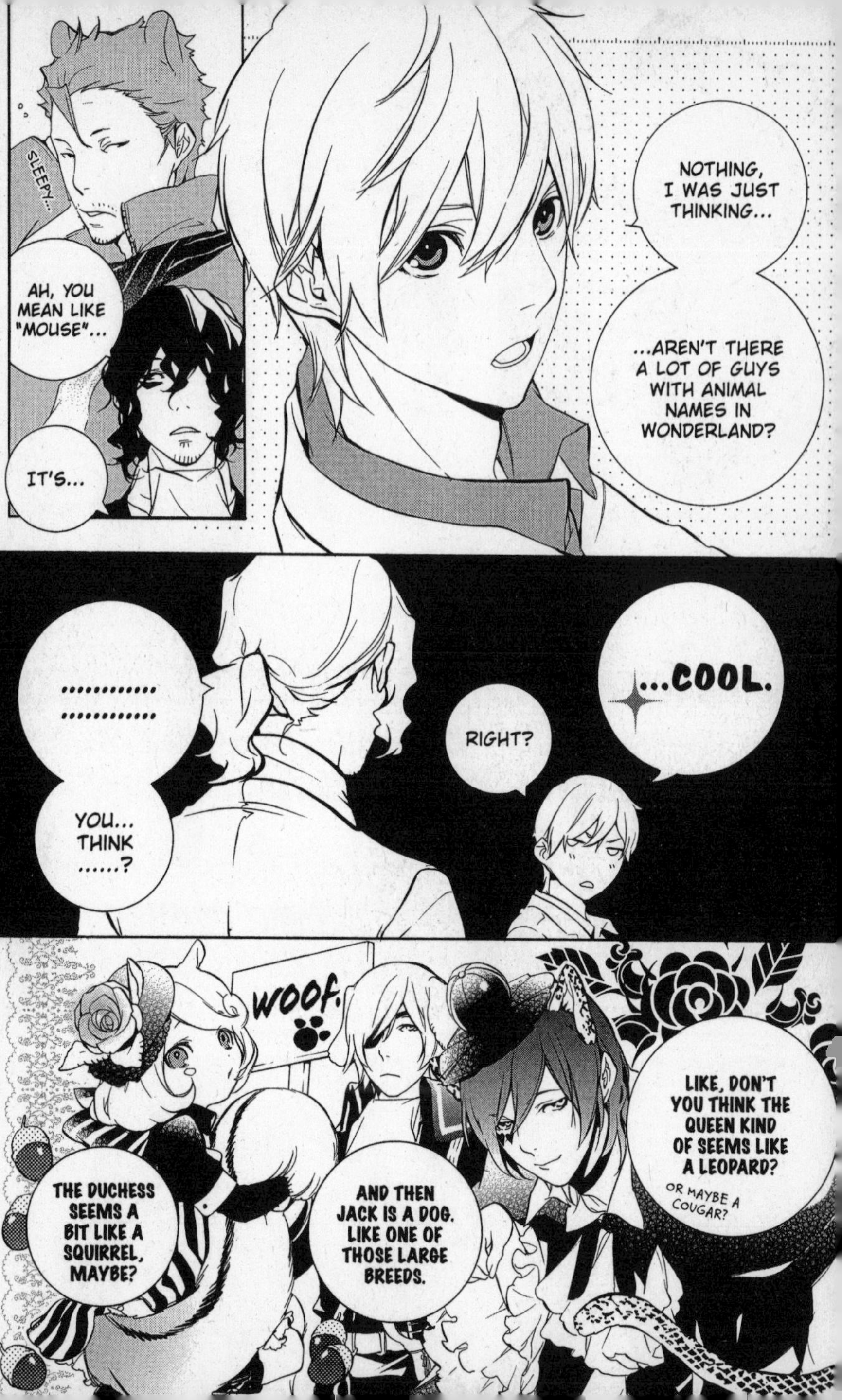
NOTHING, I WAS JUST THINKING...
...AREN'T THERE A LOT OF GUYS WITH ANIMAL NAMES IN WONDERLAND?
SLEEPY...
AH, YOU MEAN LIKE "MOUSE"...
IT'S...
...COOL.
RIGHT?
....
YOU... THINK ......?
LIKE, DON'T YOU THINK THE QUEEN KIND OF SEEMS LIKE A LEOPARD?
OR MAYBE A COUGAR?
WOOF.
AND THEN JACK IS A DOG. LIKE ONE OF THOSE LARGE BREEDS.
THE DUCHESS SEEMS A BIT LIKE A SQUIRREL, MAYBE?

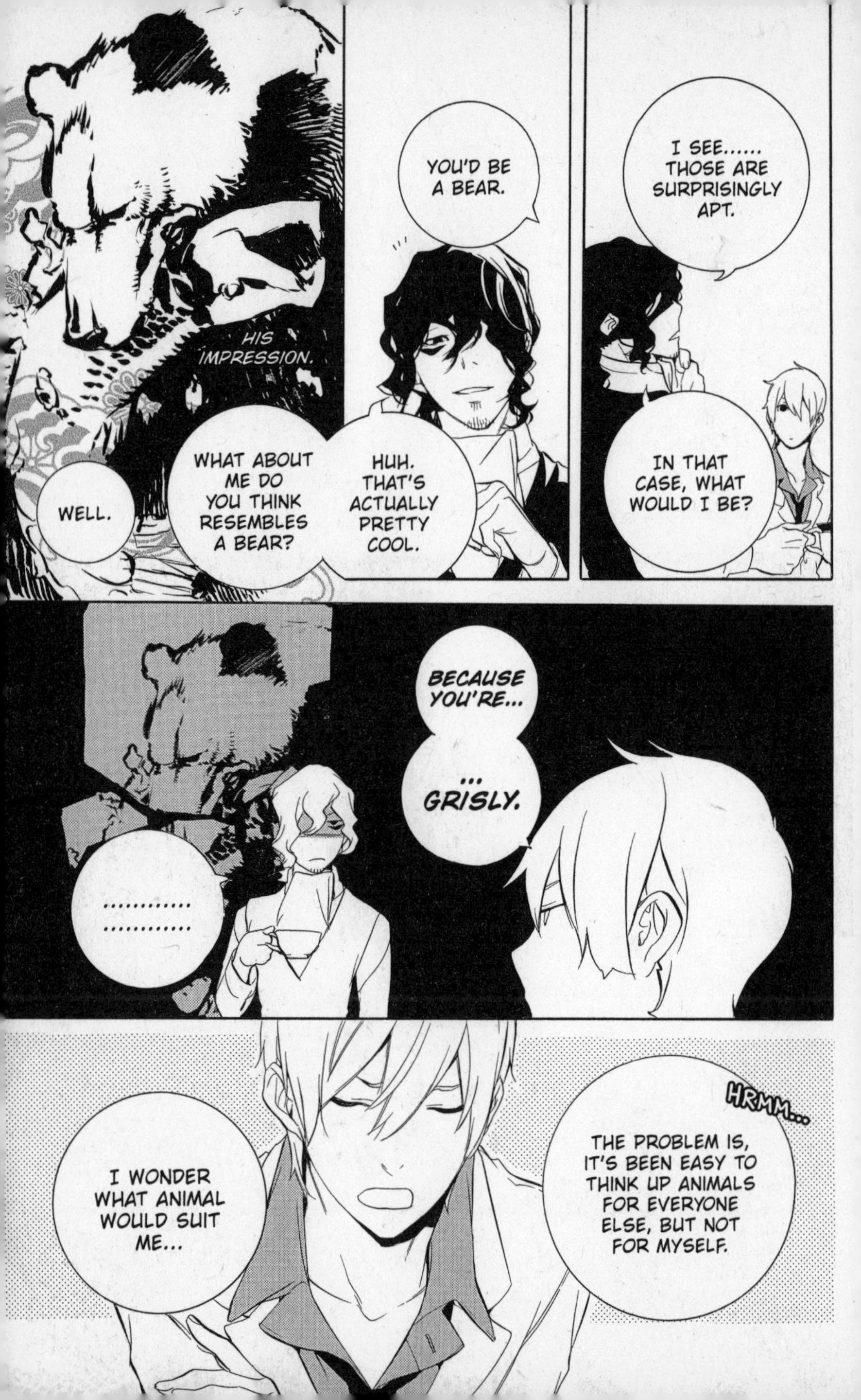
I SEE...... THOSE ARE SURPRISINGLY APT.
IN THAT CASE, WHAT WOULD I BE?
YOU'D BE A BEAR.
HUH. THAT'S ACTUALLY PRETTY COOL.
WHAT ABOUT ME DO YOU THINK RESEMBLES A BEAR?
WELL.
HIS IMPRESSION.
BECAUSE YOU'RE...
... GRISLY.
....
....
HRMM...
THE PROBLEM IS, IT'S BEEN EASY TO THINK UP ANIMALS FOR EVERYONE ELSE, BUT NOT FOR MYSELF.
I WONDER WHAT ANIMAL WOULD SUIT ME...

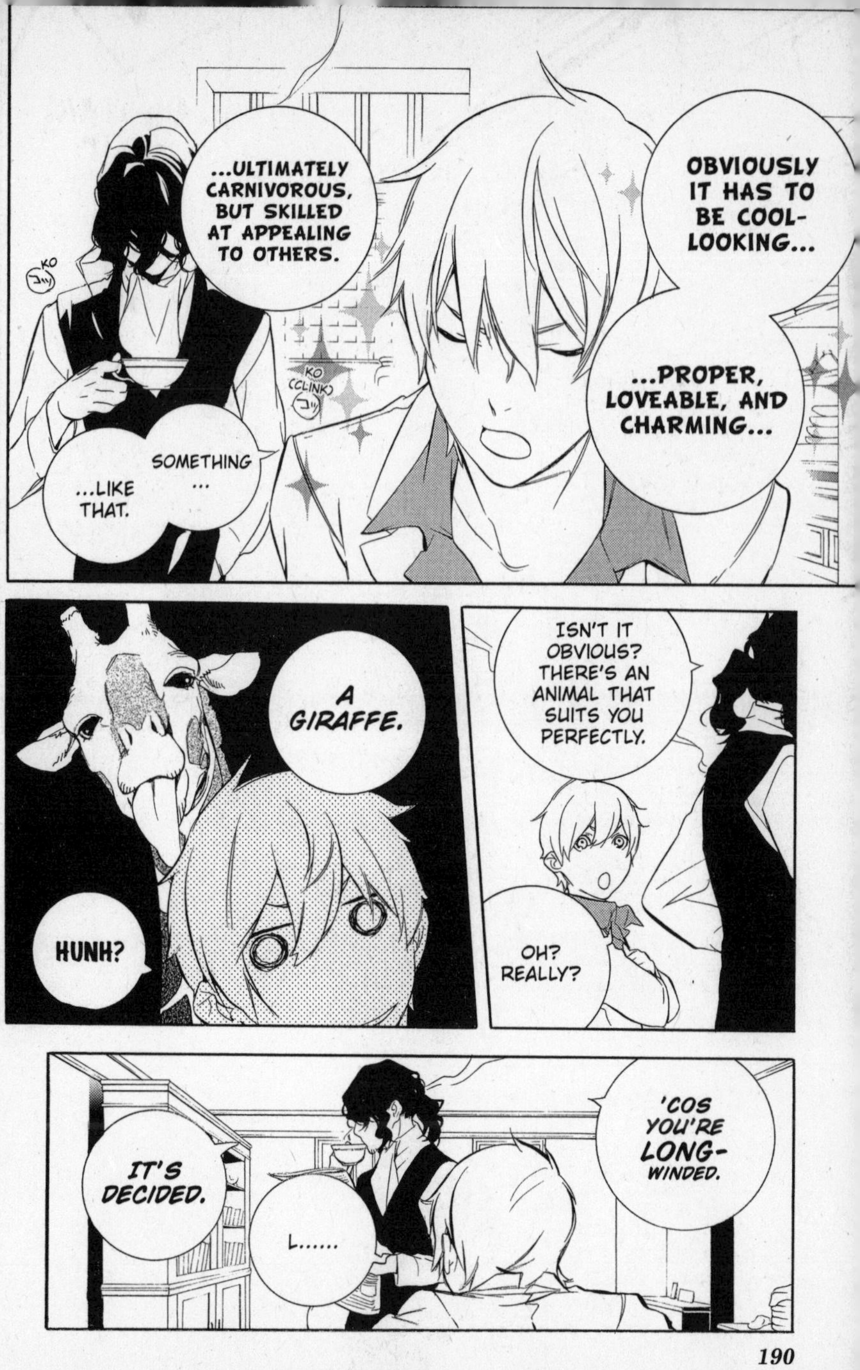
OBVIOUSLY IT HAS TO BE COOL-LOOKING...
...PROPER, LOVEABLE, AND CHARMING...
...ULTIMATELY CARNIVOROUS, BUT SKILLED AT APPEALING TO OTHERS.
KO (CLINK)
KO
SOMETHING ...
...LIKE THAT.
ISN'T IT OBVIOUS? THERE'S AN ANIMAL THAT SUITS YOU PERFECTLY.
OH? REALLY?
A GIRAFFE.
HUNH?
'COS YOU'RE LONG-WINDED.
L......
IT'S DECIDED.

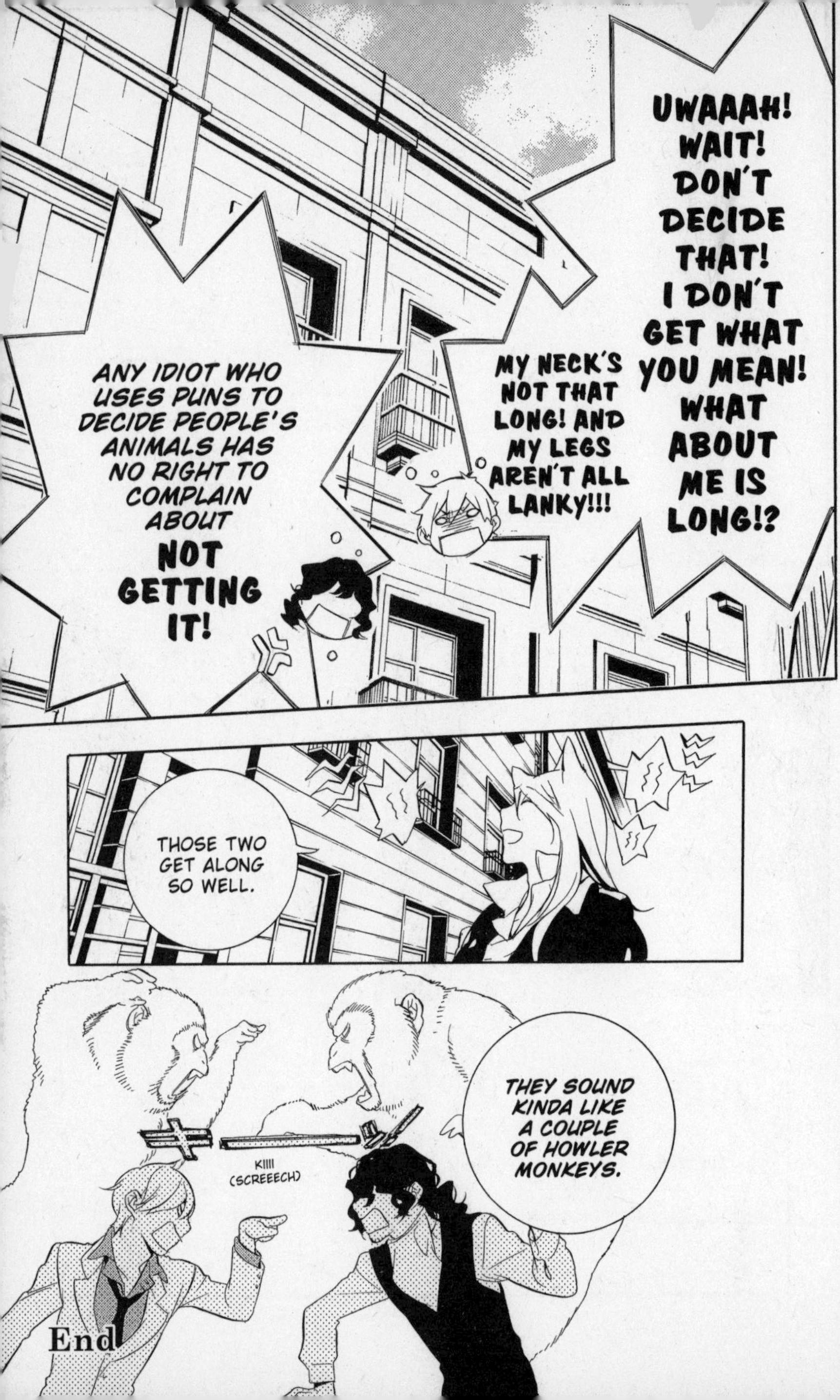
UWAAAH! WAIT! DON'T DECIDE THAT! I DON'T GET WHAT YOU MEAN! WHAT ABOUT ME IS LONG!?
MY NECK'S NOT THAT LONG! AND MY LEGS AREN'T ALL LANKY!!!
ANY IDIOT WHO USES PUNS TO DECIDE PEOPLE'S ANIMALS HAS NO RIGHT TO COMPLAIN ABOUT NOT GETTING IT!
THOSE TWO GET ALONG SO WELL.
THEY SOUND KINDA LIKE A COUPLE OF HOWLER MONKEYS.
KIIII (SCREEECH)
End

STAFF

ORIGINAL WORKS
AI NINOMIYA

ASSISTANT WORKS
YORIKO SUZUKI
IZUKO FUJIYA
MIZUKI SAKAMAKI
REIN OFUJI
DATENSI

EDITOR
YOUSUKE SUGINO

IF YOU HAD TO PICK A PARTNER OTHER THAN THE HATTER, WHO WOULD YOU CHOOSE? *AND TELL US WHY!

KATAGIRI
DUCHESS
I WANNA BE WOKEN UP BY THAT VOICE EVERY MORNING.

OFUJI
DUCHESS
IT'S JUST...
I LOVE EVERYTHING ABOUT HER!

SAKAMAKI
QUEEN OF HEARTS
I WANT HIM TO TOY WITH ME! AND THEN, I WANNA TOY WITH HIM!!

I don't know if it's just because there're strangely few female characters appearing in this series, or because the male characters are always such good-for-nothings, and I can't say the reason for sure, but for making such an adorable little girl into an incredible woman...I salute you, Katagiri-sensei.

This time we included an original drama CD with the limited edition version. Since it was kind of a return to the story's origins (or something like that) we went all-out doing everything we wanted (laugh). I would be delighted if you enjoy this one along with the others.

Well, see you in Volume 3!

Ai Ninomiya

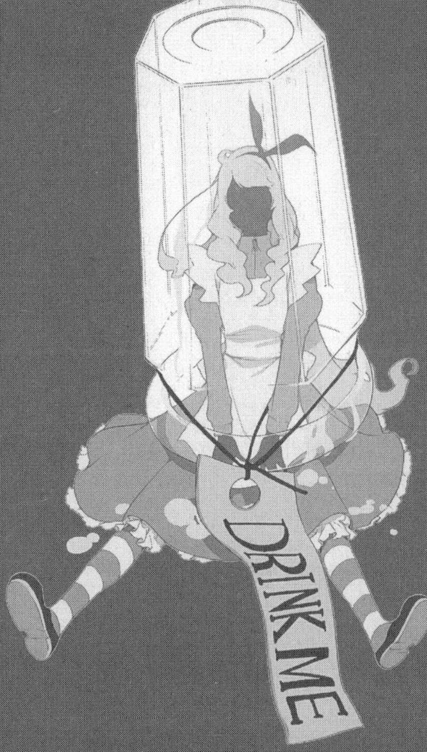
DRINK ME

ARE YOU ALICE? 2

IKUMI KATAGIRI
AI NINOMIYA

Translation and Lettering: Alexis Eckerman

This book is a work of fiction. Names, characters, places, and incidents are the product of the author's imagination or are used fictitiously. Any resemblance to actual events, locales, or persons, living or dead, is coincidental.

First published in Japan in 2010 by ICHIJINSHA. English translation rights arranged with ICHIJINSHA through Tuttle-Mori Agency, Inc., Tokyo.

Yen Press
Hachette Book Group
237 Park Avenue, New York, NY 10017

www.HachetteBookGroup.com
www.YenPress.com

Yen Press is an imprint of Hachette Book Group, Inc. The Yen Press name and logo are trademarks of Hachette Book Group, Inc.

First Yen Press Edition: September 2013

ISBN: 978-0-316-25278-2

10 9 8 7 6 5 4 3 2 1

BVG

Printed in the United States of America